Breakfast with Jesus:

365 days

Published by Crossbridge Books
Worcester WR6 6PL
www.crossbridgeeducational.com

©Crossbridge Books 2025

All rights reserved. No part of this publication
may be reproduced, stored in a retrieval system,
or transmitted in any form or by any means –
electronic, mechanical, photocopying, recording
or otherwise – without prior permission of the
Copyright owner.

ISBN 978 1 916945 32 6

British Library Cataloguing in Publication Data
A catalogue record for this book is available from the British Library

Scripture quotations taken from The Holy Bible, New International Version®, NIV®.
Copyright © 1973, 1978, 1984, 2011 by Biblica, Inc. Used with permission of Zondervan.
All rights reserved worldwide. www.zondervan.com

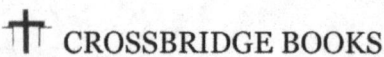 CROSSBRIDGE BOOKS

Breakfast with Jesus:

365 days

Leslene Peat-Brown

About the Author

Leslene Peat-Brown has served in various leadership and administrative roles in her church. She has led in Adult, Children's, Teens, Youth, and Prayer Ministries. She has also led the Training and Strategic Planning Team for a number of years. Her areas of interest are: Church Governance, Training and Strategic Planning, and Evangelism.

Leslene Peat- Brown holds an MA in Education and a BA (Honours) degree in Psychology. She is also a teacher, registered nurse, midwife, a nutrition adviser, and author of the book, Ordinary People; Extraordinary Stories.

FOREWARD

"In the morning, Lord, you hear my voice; in the morning I lay my requests before you and wait expectantly". (Psalm 5:3)

Breakfast with Jesus: 365 Days invites you into a devotional time with Jesus, which aims to help you form a deep, intimate, and lasting relationship with Him. It is your opportunity to commune with Him through Scripture and prayer. Prayer was a vital part of Christ's ministry. It was natural for Him to wake up in the early hours of the morning to commune with His Father before starting the day. One writer says that, "prayer is unnatural for us because we are more connected with sin than with God, and therefore we tend to reject the heavenly atmosphere that prayer brings." These daily readings will help you to follow in His footsteps as you pray and meditate on His word.

"It would be well for us to spend a thoughtful hour each day in contemplation of the life of Christ. We should take it point by point, and let the imagination grasp each scene, especially the closing ones. As we dwell upon His great sacrifice for us, our confidence in Him will be more constant, our love will be quickened, and we shall be more deeply imbued with His Spirit". (The Desire of Ages, Ellen G White, p. 83)

As you start your day each morning with Jesus, consider it a sacred act of meeting with the Creator of the universe before you face the outside world. Start your day with God and meditate on His word as you go through the day. May Angelou says, when you begin your day with God, it is about "putting on the whole armour to meet the foe; your day will collapse when you don't begin your day with Him. As you rise from sleep each morning, listen to the 'still small voice' in the stillness of the morning; as you meditate on the Scriptures, and open your heart to Him. Give Him thanks for waking you up, and for giving you another chance to get to know Him better. Let each morning spent in communion with Him become a mountain-top experience." - An experience that will keep you on a high throughout the day.

"Give thanks for mercy, you did not earn, and grace you cannot repay...Before rushing out, listen to the still small voice of God...this is the highest form of self-care." (Maya Angelou)

My prayer is not only that you read this devotional, but that each morning's message will bring you closer to God. Be encouraged, and be blessed and inspired by His word as you experience His presence in your life. As you converse with Him, ensure that it is a two-way conversation as you learn to listen.

You will find that there is a short prayer after each reading.

*Unless otherwise stated, all Scriptural references are from the New International Version (NIV).

January 1

BREAKFAST WITH JESUS

'When they landed, they saw a fire of burning coals there with fish on it and some bread. Jesus said to them, "Come and have breakfast."' (John 21:9 & 12)

Can you imagine being invited to have breakfast with Jesus? He was now risen from the dead and was about to show himself again to His disciples as He walked along the beach by the Sea of Tiberius.

They had been fishing all night but caught nothing. Jesus appeared on the beach. However, they did not recognise Him. He told them to cast their nets on the right side of the ship. In the story, we are told that Peter, Thomas, Nathaniel and two other disciples did so, and the catch was so large that they were unable to haul the net in.

According to John 21:9, when they reached the shore, there was a fire on which fish and bread was being cooked. Jesus invited them to breakfast, saying, "Come and have some breakfast". Jesus came, took the bread, broke it and gave it to them.
What can we learn from this breakfast scene?

- The miraculous haul of fish reminds us that we have no power in ourselves to accomplish anything; we are totally dependent on Jesus.

- Jesus provides. He helped His disciples to catch fish, thereby supplying their daily bread and a source of income; they were fishermen by trade. However, one day they would become 'fishers of men' and would leave their families to follow Jesus. The huge number, importantly, as fishers of men, was a foretaste of the many they would bring to Christ.

- Jesus showed humility. As the Son of God, He was humble enough to serve the disciples breakfast; we, too, are called to serve others.

- The huge catch of fish signified that the gospel would be preached to all nations, not just to the Jews.

- It was God who gave the disciples the skills and resources to fish for their living; they would one day be equipped to fish for men. In the same way, He equips everyone who accepts Him to win souls to Him.

Today's Prayer: Father, help me to follow you so that I can become a fisher of men. Amen.

January 2

SEEK GOD FIRST (1)

"But seek first His kingdom and His righteousness, and all these things will be given to you as well". (Matthew 6:33)

It is important that you put God first in your life. When you wake up each morning, you might sometimes feel uncertain about what the day will bring. You might be anxious about your job or your family. You may even be feeling discouraged, but you don't have to worry about anything, just put God first and remind yourself that this is the day the Lord has made and nothing is going to happen that together He and you cannot handle.

As you begin your day, find out from Him what plans He has for you, and He will outline His plan to you. In Jeremiah 29:11 He says, "For I know the plans that I think toward you," says the Lord, "thoughts of peace, and not of evil", to give you an expected end. God has a plan for your life, regardless of the situation you might be in at the moment. He plans to give you hope and to prosper you in whatever you do. If you are going to make it through the day, you must tap into the Source of all power, God himself. It is by making Him first in your life that you will find yourself.

Today, instead of asking God to bless your agenda, ask Him to give you an agenda. You might sometimes wonder what has gone wrong with your plans; nothing seems to be working. Could it be that you have gone ahead of God, thinking you can manage without Him, only to find you have fallen flat on your face because you have not given Him first priority? God wants to be first in your life; He says, "Seek first His kingdom and His righteousness, and all these things will be given to you as well". (Matthew 6:33). When King Jehoshaphat was told that a vast army was coming against him and his people, his first response was to 'enquire of the Lord'. When you become overwhelmed by situations in your life, put God first and He will fight your battles for you. Jehoshaphat did this when the nation faced disaster, and God fought the battle for them.

If you find that often things have come crashing down, and you have to start over again, if you have been doing it on your own and failed, turn to God now. Are you willing to put him first in your life?

Today's Prayer: Dear God, I have decided to put you first in my life so I can be guided by you and be successful in all I do. Amen.

January 3

SEEK GOD FIRST (2)

'In the morning, Lord, you hear my voice; in the morning I lay my requests before you and wait expectantly.' (Psalm 5:3)

I once knew a man who had a beautiful and expensive car, which was perhaps his most treasured possession. It was so precious to him that he would not drive it if it rained; it was never allowed to get wet, or even get cold in the winter. It was kept in his garage with a heater nearby, so it did not 'feel the cold'. You might laugh at this man and dismiss his behaviour as being insane; however, there are people in this world who would rather worship their worldly goods than worship God. In Matthew 6:33, Jesus is saying that we are to put Him first in our lives and not focus on the things of this world that will perish. He wants you to make Him the most important person in your life. By doing so, you will be developing a lasting relationship with Him.

If your focus is on the material things of this world, they can soon become your god. They can quickly become the most important things in your life; therefore, you should purposely and actively choose to make God first place in your life. Making Him first place in your life might mean going against the odds. You are being asked to prioritise your relationship with God, and when you do, He will take care of everything else. He will meet all your needs.

Rather than rushing out each morning to be at work on time and not spending time praying and studying God's word, it would suggest that work is your priority. You might say you have to work to earn a living, and that is true; however, is it not God who has provided the job for you and the skills with which to do it? When He is not a priority in your life, you will find that you will become anxious and fretful, because you will not have confidence in Him. However, when you make Him first in your life, you will learn to depend on Him and refuse to worry about your needs because you know that you can trust Him.

When you awake in the morning, let your voice be heard saying, "O Jesus, my Saviour, my all: while nature its music is waking, on thee from my heart will I call. My voice shall thou hear in the morning, O Jesus my Shepherd and King; refreshed with the dews of thy mercy, thy wonderful love will I sing". When Lewis Hartsough wrote this hymn, he was expressing the very sentiment of David that the secret of a close relationship with God is to seek Him first, to pray to Him earnestly each morning. In the morning, we are more alert, our minds are not focused on our problems, and we can then commit ourselves to God for His guidance throughout the day.

Today's Prayer: Father, I commit myself to you and will make you first in my life today. Amen.

January 4

RICHES

Jesus answered, "If you want to be perfect, go, sell your possessions and give to the poor, and you will have treasure in heaven. Then come, follow me". (Matthew 19:21)

Living in a world of materialism, where people are becoming more and more preoccupied with gaining earthly possessions and wealth, you can be in danger of being caught up in wanting to amass more. There is nothing wrong with being rich. Abraham was a rich man; God blessed him with much. Job was also a very rich man. In the Bible, he is portrayed as a very wealthy man of upright character and one who loved God.

Is it possible to love God and not your wealth? If you are not content with what you have, and are always seeking material things, you might, in your pursuit to become rich, forget about the One who has blessed you with much. "No one can serve two masters. Either you will hate the one and love the other, or you will be devoted to the one and despise the other. You cannot serve both God and Money". (Matthew 6:24).

Are you content with what you have? But when do you have enough? Do you always want more? There is a difference between what we need and what we want. You may have all you need to live on (that's when you have enough). However, when you are rich, it might be difficult not to want more or even share it with others. When the rich young man came to Jesus wanting to find out how he could have eternal life, Jesus told him that he should sell his possessions and give to the poor. Sadly, he was not prepared to part with his riches, and when he heard this, 'he went away sad, because he had great wealth'. (Matthew 19:22). You cannot say you love God and keep your money to yourself. If you love God, you will try to please Him in every way, even if it means giving away some of your wealth to others.

When Jesus saw the rich man's response, His comments astounded His disciples. Jesus said, "Truly I tell you, it is hard for someone rich to enter the kingdom of heaven" (Verse 24). Because a camel can't go through the eye of a needle, it would almost appear as if Jesus is saying that a rich person can't be saved in His kingdom. However, even the rich can be saved in God's kingdom if they accept Him and exercise faith in Him and not their riches. Jesus reminds us that we should "store up for yourselves riches in heaven, where neither moth nor vermin destroy, and where thieves do not break through and steal. For where your treasure is, there will your heart be also". (Matthew 6:19-20). Jesus is making it clear that we should not focus on earthly riches, for what you treasure most will control you, and they have no eternal value. Are you willing to give up everything if God asks you to? Do you want to be rich? Seek Jesus; seek eternal values, for earthly values will soon vanish away.

Today's Prayer: Lord, I desire you more than anything in life. Help me to store up treasures in heaven and not on earth. Amen.

January 5.

WHAT IS YOUR RESPONSE TO BAD NEWS?

'Hezekiah received the letter from the messenger and read it. Then he went up to the temple of the Lord and spread it out before the Lord. And Hezekiah prayed to the Lord…' (2 Kings 19:14 &15)

At forty-six years old, Jim was diagnosed with type 2 diabetes. This was not the diagnosis he expected, and he found it difficult to come to terms with it. What do you do when you receive bad news? The Bible tells us that Hezekiah spread the letter before God and prayed. In 2 Kings 19:1-7, we read where Sennacherib, whose armies had captured the fortified cities of Judah, sent a message to Hezekiah to surrender. Realising that he was no match for Sennacherib and his army, Hezekiah went to the temple, spread the letter before God and prayed. God answered his prayer and delivered the people of Judah.

What is your first response when faced with difficult or impossible situations? It might be news of a terminal illness, loss of a loved one, or an accident that has left you disabled for the rest of your life, or loss of your job. Was God your first response? When Hezekiah received the news of impending disaster, his first response was to turn to God. It would appear that this was what he normally did, that is, calling on God first, praying and seeking his help. You, too, must do the same when faced with distressing and bad news. (However, we should of course always seek God first in all things, not just when a crisis occurs.)

You should bring your challenges to God. He says you are to cast all your cares upon Him (1 Peter 5:7), just as Hezekiah acknowledged God's might and power to change our situation. In his prayer, he says, "You alone are God over the kingdoms of the earth. You made the heavens and the earth." Hezekiah acknowledged God's sovereignty and Judah's total dependence on Him. You, too, must acknowledge that God is almighty and all powerful, and nothing is too hard for Him. "I am the Lord, the God of all mankind. Is anything too hard for me?" (Jeremiah 32:27).

If you are going through difficult times in your life, come to Jesus today; make Him your first response. 'Spread' out your difficulties before Him and see what He will do for you.

Today's Prayer: Dear God, you alone are God, let me not fail to respond as Hezekiah did, and bring all my concerns and problems to you. Amen.

January 6

COVETEOUSNESS

'You shall not covet your neighbour's house. You shall not covet your neighbour's wife, or his male nor female servant, his ox or donkey, or anything that belongs to your neighbour' (Exodus 20:17).

Covetousness is a sin against God, and that's why it is included in the Ten Commandments. To covet is to want what someone else has. It goes beyond admiring what the other person possesses; it includes envy, not being satisfied with what one has, and it is about resenting another person for having what they have instead of you. According to the Tyndale Bible Dictionary, it is the desire to have something for yourself that belongs to another - a craving or passionate desire.

It is actually saying, God, why did you give him/her that talent or ability/success and not me, and making God look unfair and selective. It is being envious. Envy is defined as 'an emotion which occurs when a person lacks another's quality, skill, achievement, or possession, and they would like to have it.'

Covetousness is insidious and dangerous, and because it is invisible and concerns the deep desires of the heart, it can silently destroy soul and body; others can also be affected by it. In the book of Joshua, chapter 7, the story of Achan, shows the effect of covetousness and its consequences. God had instructed the Israelites to conquer the Canaanite city of Ai; they were an easy target. However, the Israelites were 'routed by the men of Ai, who killed thirty-six of them'. Why did this happen? The Bible tells us that there was sin in the camp. Achan, son of Karmi, took the 'devoted things' (verse 1), clothing, cattle and other plunder that God said Israel should destroy when they conquered Jericho.

When confronted by Joshua, Achan confessed that he had taken a beautiful robe from Babylonia, two hundred shekels of silver and a bar of gold. Achan had coveted and stolen the goods and committed a serious offence, which was in defiance of an explicit command given by God. (Deuteronomy 20:16-18). As a result of Achan's sin God threatened to withdraw His presence from the people, and Achan and his entire family were stoned to death.

This story shows very clearly the consequences of covetousness. We should therefore 'be on our guard against all covetousness'. When you covet, it means you are not satisfied with what God has given you. You might ask Him for something which He knows is not good for you. He knows what is best for you, so don't covet someone else who has what you would like to have. "...No good thing does He withhold from those whose way of life is blameless" (Psalm 84:11). God does not promise to give us everything we think is good, but He will not withhold anything that He knows is good for us as long as we obey and serve Him.

Today's Prayer: Father, help me to be content with what I have. Amen.

January 7

WHO TOUCHED ME?

'At once, Jesus realised that power had gone out from Him. He turned round in the crowd and asked, "Who touched me?"' (Mark 5:30)

A crowd of people had surrounded Jesus, wanting to see Him. However, the woman in this story wanted to be healed by Him. She had been ill, haemorrhaging for twelve years and had spent all her money going to doctors, but instead of getting better, she only got worse. Because of her condition, she was considered ritually unclean, which obviously compounded her situation.

Hearing that Jesus had come into the area, she thought, 'if only I could get through the crowd to Him', so with determined effort she pressed through the throng, thinking, 'If I just touch His clothes, I will be healed' (Verse 27). She now managed to touch His clothes, 'Immediately her bleeding stopped and she felt in her body that she was freed from her suffering' (Verse 29). After having suffered ill health for twelve years, she was suddenly healed!

However, she did not anticipate Jesus' reaction when He asked, "Who touched me?" Knowing what she had done, falling down before Him, trembling, she confessed that she had touched Him. To her utter amazement, Jesus responded, "Daughter, thy faith hath made thee whole, go in peace, and be whole of thy plague."

What about you? Do you have a condition that has been afflicting you for years? Are you feeling hopeless and helpless? Do you long to touch the Master? You may touch Him for He is not far away. You, too, like the woman, can be restored, but like her, you must reach out to Him in faith.

However, it was not the touch of the woman herself that brought her restoration; it was her faith. You must exercise faith in Jesus if you are seeking healing and restoration.

If the woman had given up after many attempts, she would not have been healed. Had she not exercised faith, she would have remained ostracised and remained on the fringes of society and would have missed out on the blessings of God. Jesus healed not just her body but also her soul.

**Today's Prayer: Dear Jesus, I need to be restored and made well. I refuse to be restricted by circumstances in my life. Help me to learn to exercise faith in you.
Amen.**

January 8

THE NEED TO PRAY

'Very early in the morning, while it was still dark, Jesus got up, left the house and went off to a solitary place, where He prayed.' (Mark 1:34)

It was early morning, while it was still dark, when Jesus left the house to pray. According to verse 36, his disciples were also in the house, 'Simon and his companions went to look for Him'. We don't know what time they awoke; however, it is clear that when they woke up, they realised that Jesus was missing, so they went to find Him, and found Him praying. What a beautiful sight that must have been, the Son communing with His Father!

Jesus felt the need to connect with His Father. How about you? If prayer was so important to Him, it should be important to His followers, too. Because the enemy was always on His heels, Jesus knew that it was vital that He was in constant connection with His Father.

Think of astronauts; to complete their mission, communication with Mission Control on Earth is crucial. Apparently, communication relies on a complex network of satellites, ground stations, and on-board communication systems. However, Jesus did not need any complicated man-made systems; all He needed to do was to connect with His Father through prayer.

Prayer is not so much about bringing our requests to God; it is about forming and maintaining a relationship with Him. Jesus knew that He needed to strengthen and enrich His relationship with His Father if He were to live victoriously.

It was Jesus' habit in those quiet hours when there were no distractions, to withdraw and spend precious and intimate times with His Father. In the same way, we should emulate Christ and see it as an honour and privilege to come into His presence and seek an audience with Him. Coming to Jesus in prayer, especially in the stillness of the early morning, we can draw closer to Him and receive direction, guidance, and strength to meet our daily challenges.

Will you choose today to rise early while it is still dark to spend quality time with the One who wants to bless you and align your heart with His?

Today's Prayer: Heavenly Father, I thank you for showing me how to live victoriously in you. Help me to follow your leading today and learn to listen to your 'still small voice' amidst the din and clamour around me. Amen.

January 9

DIVINE ENCOUNTER (1)

'Now he had to go through Samaria, so He came to a town in Samaria called Sychar...' (John 4:4-5)

In this familiar story, we find Jesus, conversing with a Samaritan woman at Jacob's well. She had come at noon to draw water, possibly to avoid meeting others because she was a woman of poor repute. Superficially, this appears to be a chance encounter, perhaps from the woman's standpoint it might have been, but Jesus 'had to go through Samaria'. Because of the animosity between the Jews and the Samaritans, most Jews did everything possible to avoid travelling to Samaria. However, Jesus deliberately went to Samaria because He knew there was someone there who needed to have an encounter with Him. The woman left home that day, not even knowing that she would have a divine encounter that would forever change her life.

In engaging the woman in conversation, Jesus went against the grain of society in His effort to bring the gospel of salvation to her. He, being a Jew, under no circumstances should be speaking to a woman, let alone a Samaritan one!

The Samaritans were a mixed-race people of Jewish descent. The pure Jews hated them and so there was long-standing prejudice and hatred between them.

However, in order to offer this woman the Water of Life, Jesus broke down all barriers because He did not live by societal restrictions of any kind. Yes, the woman was a member of the much-hated mixed-race Samaritans; she was known to be living in sin, so why would a respectable Jewish man allow himself to be seen speaking with her in public? However, His mission was to seek the lost (Luke19:10), and bring them into a saving relationship with Him, so it didn't really matter, for He was also breaking down the walls of prejudice, discrimination, and religious hatred as He spoke to the woman. In sharing the gospel with her, Jesus was willing to break down all barriers.

Are you willing to share the gospel with everyone you meet, regardless of their race, ethnicity, gender, or social standing?

Today's Prayer: Father, you have commissioned me to disciple others regardless of who they are. Please give me the courage to do so. Amen.

January 10

DIVINE ENCOUNTER (2)

Then Jesus declared, "I, the one speaking to you – I am He." (John 4:26)

As the woman arrived at the well, Jesus engaged her in conversation by asking a simple and direct question, "Will you give me a drink?" (John 4:7).
The woman then gave valid reasons why she was unable to give Him a drink, citing quite truthfully that Jews and Samaritans did not associate with each other. In verse 11, Jesus offered her living water. She very clearly had no understanding of what He meant. So, what did He mean? He was offering her the gift of salvation, as only He could. The woman was hungering for spiritual water and food, but did not realise it.

The full impact of this encounter came when, in verses 16-26, the woman recognised that Jesus must be a prophet, otherwise He would not have known about her private life. This was a 'no-go' area of her life, which she did not wish to discuss because it would cause her much discomfort, so she quickly changed the subject. She then proceeded by bringing up a theological issue – the correct place of worship, but Jesus told her that the place of worship is not as important as the attitude of the worshipper: "God is Spirit, and His worshippers must worship in the Spirit and in truth," He declared (v.24).

How about you? How do you worship? Do you just go through the motions? Is your worship from the heart, genuine, and true?

The woman continued, "I know that Messiah (called Christ) is coming; when He comes, He will explain all things to us."
Jesus declared, "I, the one speaking to you – I am he." What a revelation! Here, Jesus revealed that He is not just a prophet or one of the religious teachers of His day, but the long-awaited Messiah, the one who would bring salvation to humanity, even to Gentiles and not just to the Jews.

Jesus desires to reveal Himself to you. Do you wish to have Him reveal Himself to you today so that you, too, can accept His gift of salvation?

Today's Prayer: Jesus, it is my desire to serve and do your will, reveal yourself to me as you did to this woman, so I can model your love to others and spread the good news of salvation. Amen.

January 11

WHAT IS TRUTH?

'Jesus answered, "I am the way and the truth and the life."' (John 14:6)

When Jesus stood in Pilate's judgment hall, Pilate asked "What is truth?" Blinded by arrogance, bigotry, and falsehood, he failed to see that 'Truth' was standing there in front of Him. He did not understand that truth is not a concept, or ideology, but a person, Jesus himself! In John 14:6, Jesus says, "I am the way and the truth and the life..." In today's world, some say that truth is relative, that 'truth is always relative to the person and their situation'.

In two national surveys conducted by Barna Research, one among adults and one among teenagers, people were asked if they believe that there are moral absolutes that are unchanging or that moral truth is relative to the circumstances. By a 3-to-1 margin (64% vs. 22%) adults said that truth is always relative to the person and their situation. The perspective was even more lopsided among teenagers; 83% said moral truth depends on the circumstances, and only 6% said moral truth is absolute.

These results are startling. If truth is relative, it then begs the question, what is truth? This perspective would seemingly deny the fact that Jesus is the embodiment of truth; that He is the truth and life, the only living way to the Father. It would seem that the perspective of truth as being relative aligns with Pilate's refusal to accept Jesus as truth. If Jesus is the way, the truth and the life, then truth must be absolute. It was Martin Luther, the great reformer, who said, "If truth is not absolute, it is not truth at all." To know the truth is to know Jesus. 'He is the Truth because He is the self-revelation of God which has been manifested'. (John 14:7) If you are searching for truth today, you will surely find Him, for Jesus is the truth.

Today's prayer: Jesus, I accept that you are the way and the truth and the life. May truth reign in my heart. Amen.

January 12

PATIENCE

'I waited patiently for the Lord; He turned to me and heard my cry.' (Psalm 40:1)

You have only gone a few miles when the children travelling with you, in chorus, ask, "Are we there yet?" This question will be asked many times before you finally arrive at your destination. Children are naturally impatient. Are we sometimes like children, who want God to answer us immediately?

In the above text, David seems to be indicating that waiting for God is not easy. Have you been praying to God for a long time, and you've had no answers? Are there times when you question whether He has heard you or whether He cares about your situation?

It is easy to think God is taking too long when your situation appears to be getting worse; however, Psalm 27:14 tells us: 'Wait on the Lord: be of good courage, and He will strengthen thine heart, wait I say on the Lord.' David waited on the Lord and received many benefits. (v1) God lifted him out of the despair that he had been experiencing. (v2) God set his feet on a rock and gave him a firm place to stand and put a new song of praise in his mouth (v.3).

We live in a fast-paced world today where people find it hard to wait. Waiting for the bus or for a train can be a stressful experience for some. How quickly they become irritated and frustrated if they have to wait. Motorists can barely wait for the lights to change; they become so impatient that today, incidents of road rage are becoming alarmingly high.

However, for us as children of God, we are to possess the fruit of the Spirit, which consists of love, joy, peace, long-suffering (*patience*), gentleness, goodness, faith, meekness, and temperance. As we grow in

22

Christ, the fruit of the Spirit will be exhibited in our lives, a physical manifestation that the Holy Spirit is working in our lives.

As the fruit of the Spirit is exhibited in our lives, we will exercise patience and all the other attributes, which will be an outward manifestation that the very nature of Christ is being developed in us.

Today's prayer: Father, you know that I am easily frustrated and find it hard to wait. I pray for your Holy Spirit to give me patience so that your character will be reproduced in me. Amen.

January 13

GOD'S GIFT OF PEACE

"Peace, I leave with you; my peace I give you. I do not give to you as the world gives. Do not let your hearts be troubled and do not be afraid." (John 14:27)

The Treaty of Versailles was a peace agreement that marked the end of World War 1; peace it was hoped that would end all wars. However, many treaties have been signed since this, and yet there are still more wars than ever before. The world has only been free of war for over 200 years out of approximately three thousand years. Peace on earth appears to be elusive.

Everyone indeed wants peace; isn't it what we all long for? Are peace treaties broken because we do not understand what peace is? Can it be that peace is much more than the absence of conflict?

To find answers to these questions, let us see what the Bible has to say about peace. From what Jesus says, it would appear that peace does not mean the absence of noise or turmoil. In John 16:33, He says, "I have told you these things that in Me you may have peace. In this world you will have trouble. But take heart! I have overcome the world". Is Jesus saying that even in troublesome times, we can still experience peace? He is saying that as long as we have Him in our hearts, we can experience peace in a noisy and chaotic world; it is about peace with God. Once we have peace with God, we won't allow the chaos around us to define how we live our lives.

Jesus knew it would be hard to experience peace in a sinful world, and this is why He said He would supply the peace we need. In John 14:27, He says, "Peace I leave with you; my peace I give to you. Not as the world gives do I give to you. Let not your hearts be troubled, neither let them be afraid."

It is reassuring to know that Jesus gives us true peace, peace that the world cannot give, peace that emanates from a heart from where the spirit of God dwells. Peace that is found by accepting the One whose name is the 'Prince of Peace'. It is only He who can give us lasting peace. It is His gift to us; therefore, we do not need to worry or be fearful as long as the peace of God is in our hearts and our lives. If you are worried or anxious about your life, allow the Holy Spirit to fill you with peace, the gift that God has given to all who will accept it. Why worry when we have a great future ahead of us, 'a future awaits those who seek peace' (Psalm 37:37).

Today's Prayer: Father, I thank you for your peace that passes all understanding. You have promised that you will give me strength and bless me with peace. May I find this peace today in this restless world in which I live. Amen.

January 14

PRIDE COMES BEFORE A FALL

'Pride goes before destruction, a haughty spirit before a fall.' (Proverbs 16:18)

The story is told of an oak tree that lived near the banks of the river. Some reeds also lived near the river. It was a beautiful tree to look at, and everyone who passed by admired it. However, the oak tree had a problem; it was extremely proud of itself, so proud that it boasted about how strong it was. It told the reeds and everyone that nothing could break or uproot it, because it was mighty and strong.

The reeds warned the oak tree not to be so proud and that it was better to be modest and humble. Of course, the oak tree just laughed at them and mocked them for being weak and feeble. It even boasted that it was the strongest tree in the woods.

One day, after boasting and laughing at the reeds, the wind began to blow, at which point the reeds kept their heads bowed, but the oak tree stood tall. However, the wind got stronger and stronger and before long, the wind became a full-blown hurricane, and the oak tree began to sway. By now, the reeds had bowed their heads low to the ground. The oak tree was struggling to stand straight. Suddenly, and almost without warning, there came a crashing sound, and the proud oak tree crashed and fell into the river; the reeds, however, were still standing.

We should never be proud and think ourselves better than others. The Bible says, pride comes before a fall. The pride in us wants to be praised, worshipped, and given all the glory and be highly talked about.

There is a danger in being proud; it causes us to evaluate ourselves by worldly standards and achievements, thus causing us to think too much about our worth in the eyes of others rather than our true value in God's eyes. God 'detests all the proud of heart, and they will not go unpunished.' (Proverbs 16:5)

Like the oak tree, pride will bring you down. 'Pride brings a person low, but the lowly in spirit gain honour.' (Proverbs 29:30) It is so easy to be lifted in pride and boast of one's greatness, but in an instant, God can bring the individual down to nothingness.

Think about it, Jesus - who is equal to God, to be our Saviour, to redeem us, stepped all the way down, humbled Himself to the point of dying for us. What condescension, what humility!

Today's Prayer: Dear God, if pride dwells in my heart, please remove it and let my entire being be clad with your pure, humble, and righteous spirit. Amen.

January 15

THE PAIN OF REJECTION

'He came to that which was His own, but the world did not receive Him.' (John 1:11)

This is probably one of the saddest verses in the Bible. Just to think that Jesus, the only Son of God, whom He sacrificed to save mankind from eternal death, that mankind did not acknowledge Him as the Messiah, but rejected Him and put Him to death. This is difficult to contemplate, let alone to understand.

Yet in Isaiah 53:3-4 the prophet expresses this fact so poignantly when he says, 'He was despised and rejected by mankind, a man of suffering, and familiar with pain. Like one from who people hide their faces, He was despised, and we held Him in low esteem.'

Rejection is painful; it really hurts. Why is it so painful? MRI studies of the brain show that the same areas of the brain where we experience pain are also activated when we experience rejection. This means that the way that the brain reacts to physical pain; it also reacts in the same way to rejection. Rejection actually mimics physical pain. Research also shows that we can relive and re-experience the pain of rejection more vividly than we can physical pain.

If you are feeling vulnerable because you have experienced the pain of rejection, remember Jesus bore it all for you, and because of what He accomplished on the cross, even if you feel rejected by others, He has not rejected you. He loves you and wants you to experience His love and acceptance. You are of value and worth to Him, so rejoice and embrace Him as your own.

When feeling rejected, remember that you were created in the image and likeness of God. Know and accept that you are special in His sight. God did not create you to be a second-class citizen, but a citizen of heaven.

Today's Prayer: Father, you know there are times when I have felt the pain of rejection. Help me not to relive it, but to accept that my worth is found in you and no one can cause me pain anymore. Amen.

January 16

EXPERIENCING JOY THROUGH TRIALS

'Consider it pure joy, my brothers and sisters, whenever you face trials of many kinds, because you know that the testing of your faith produces perseverance.' (James 1:2-3)

What is James saying in this text? He makes it clear that we will face trials; he is not saying 'if' we will, but 'when' we do. In other words, we will inevitably experience trials in our lives, but how can we be joyful during these times? Can James be saying that we should remain positive even during painful experiences? It is clear that what he is saying is that when we face trials, we must remain positive because of what trials can produce in our lives, 'pure joy'.

Rather than doubt whether God will carry you through your trials, and give up in despair, trust Him. Think about the lessons He wants you to learn and be joyful.

I am reminded of the story of Job, who knew what suffering was about. However, throughout his period of testing, he was still able to think positively. As a result of his trials, Job was able to experience God powerfully. Although his suffering did not make sense, he learnt how to trust God and was able to experience joy in the midst of his suffering.

Job learnt how to persevere during his suffering and as a result was able to confidently say, "But He knows the way that I take, when He has tested me, I shall come forth as gold." (Job 23:10)

To 'consider it pure joy' when we are tested is to understand that we are privileged to be participating in Christ's sufferings. Peter says, "Dear friends, do not be surprised at the fiery ordeal that has come on you to test you, as though something strange were happening to you. But rejoice inasmuch as you participate in the sufferings of Christ, so that you may be overjoyed when His glory is revealed." (1Peter4:12-13)

If you are going through trials today, be assured that God will be with you all the way, and for this reason, you can be joyful because the outcome will indeed be a joyous one. David puts it succinctly, 'Weeping may stay for a night, but rejoicing comes in the morning'. (Psalm 30:5)

Today's Prayer: Lord, you know how I respond to trials in my life. Forgive me for the times I have given up in despair. Help me to be joyful knowing that I am privileged to participate in your sufferings. Amen.

January 17

WHOLENESS IN HOPELESSNESS

'When Jesus saw him lying there and learned that he had been in this condition for a long time, He asked him, "Do you want to get well?"' (John 5:6)

The paralysed man had been ill for thirty-eight years, and though he sat by the pool, he had no hope of ever being healed. He seemed to have accepted his condition that he would possibly die by the pool, because there was no one to help him.

It would appear that the city of Bethesda was a centre for healing. 'In these lay a great multitude of impotent folk, of blind, halt, withered, waiting for the moving of the water'. John 5:3 (KJV). According to tradition, it was believed that 'an angel went down at a certain season into the pool, and troubled the water', and whoever stepped in first would be healed.

The paralysed man had no one to help him into the pool. His situation was hopeless; in fact, hopelessness had become a way of life for him.

How about you? Are there situations in your life that have caused you to give up hope like this paralysed man? Do you feel helpless and hopeless? No matter how broken you might feel in your circumstances or hardships, don't lose hope, for God can minister to your greatest needs.

There were many sick and hurting people at the pool that day yet Jesus, for some reason, selected this man. He saw him lying there hopeless and dejected and approached him, and asked, "Do you want to get well?" The man did not really answer Jesus' question but explained why he hadn't been healed. Jesus then commanded him to take up his bed and walk, and the man obeyed and was healed. He experienced a wholeness that only God can give.

Today, you might be in despair and without hope, but don't let your problems cause you to lose hope. You cannot heal your brokenness, but God can. He can make you whole again, because wholeness can only come through Him.

It was Oswald Chambers who said, "Leave the broken, irreversible past in God's hands, and step out into the invincible future today."

Are you willing to say yes to Him? "I want to be healed". He did it for the paralysed man and is waiting to do the same for you if you will let Him. In Psalm 34:18, the psalmist says, 'The Lord is close to the broken-hearted and saves those who are crushed in spirit.'

Today's prayer: Thank you, Father, for your power to heal and bring wholeness into my life. Help me not to lose hope but to remember that your grace is sufficient for me, and even in my weakness, I can be strong. Amen.

January 18

LONGING FOR JESUS TO RETURN

"Do not let your heart be troubled. You believe in God; believe also in me. My Father's house has many rooms; if that were not so, would I have told you that I am going to prepare a place for you? And if I go and prepare a place for you, I will come back and take you to be with me that you also may be where I am."

I recall walking home from school with my five-year-old grandson one summer afternoon. We walked and talked as we did, and should. We were nearly home when he suddenly asked, "Grandma, when will Jesus come?" I told him that no one knows, but we know for sure that He will return one day soon, and we have to be ready to meet Him. "But I want Him to come back now," he insisted, "so I can hug Him and give Him a kiss." Such simple faith and trust!

Little wonder Jesus says that we must become like little children to enter into heaven. "Let the children come to me, and do not hinder them, for the kingdom of heaven belongs to such as these." (Matthew 19:14).

Are you longing for Jesus to return, just like this five-year-old? The times in which we are living should evoke in us a sense of urgency and expectation. The second coming of Jesus is referred to 380 times in the New Testament, which means that one verse in every twenty-five refers to His promise. We are therefore urged to look with expectation for His return. "While we wait for the blessed hope – the appearing of the glory of our great God and Saviour, Jesus Christ, who gave Himself for us to redeem us from all wickedness and to purify for Himself a people that are His very own; eager to do what is good." (Titus 2:13-14)

Today's prayer: Father, please give me childlike faith and a humble and sincere heart, so I can take hold of the truth that you are coming back soon. Help me to look forward with longing anticipation. Amen.

January 19

SIMPLE CHILD-LIKE FAITH. "JESUS DID IT AGAIN"!

"Now faith is the confidence in what we hope for and the assurance about what we do not see". (Hebrews 11:1)

My grandchildren and I sometimes encounter a major problem when football matches are being played in the vicinity of our church. When this happens, we often struggle to find a parking space. At times, we have had to return home and watch the worship service online. However, we no longer have that problem, because the children have learnt to pray and always ask Jesus to provide a parking spot for us.

On one particular day, they were to witness the power of prayer as they prayed in faith that God would provide parking for us. As we approached the road where we usually park, there were cars everywhere, and we knew that a football match was being held at the nearby stadium. The children kept praying and, as we drove down the street, my eldest grandson excitedly shouted, "Grandma, look, Jesus has provided a space for us." We prayed together and gave thanks. On the way home, I realised that I had lost my scarf, and straightaway the children began praying. When we finally arrived home, as I pulled up, there was the scarf lying at the very spot where the car had been parked earlier. My grandson, with a smile on his face, shouted excitedly, "Grandma, Jesus did it again!"

St. Paul makes it clear that faith is about confidence and assurance. When we believe that God will keep his promises, He will not fail us. Faith means living in anticipation that even though we don't see His promises materialising, we can still be assured, yet we are confident that God will do as He promises. Faith is also the confidence that, because God answered your prayer in the past, He will do it again. One writer says, "His new fresh surprises will surely be yours". After having experienced the answer to two prayers that day, I have no reason to doubt that my grandchildren will be assured that next time they pray, God will answer their prayers.

Today's Prayer: Dear Father, give me child-like faith and confidence in you. Amen

January 20

WHY WORRY WHEN YOU CAN PRAY?

'Do not be anxious about anything, but in every situation, by prayer and petition, with thanksgiving, present your requests to God. And the peace of God, which transcends all understanding, will guard your hearts and minds in Christ Jesus'. (Philippians 4:6-7)

There was once a popular song which said, 'Don't Worry, Be Happy'. The writer of that song must have known that worrying can rob you of happiness, resulting in a constant state of anxiety. Constant worrying can take its toll on your health. It can affect you physically, emotionally and spiritually.

Worrying may result in high blood pressure, increased heart rate, and breathing problems. At times of worry and stressful times, one can become anxious, thereby causing frequent feelings of doom, irritability, panic attacks, depression and a host of other emotional and physical problems. If these symptoms go unchecked, they can result in damage to the body and soul.

When we examine today's text, it would appear that Paul is asking us to do the impossible, because we all have reasons to worry, we worry about our family, our jobs and all the things that affect our lives. However, Paul is advising us to turn our worries into prayer instead. Why worry when you can pray? 'The same God who arrays the grass of the field…will He not much more clothe you?' (Matthew **6:30**)

Will you put God first in your life today? Will you fill your mind with His word instead of worrying? Worrying cripples our faith and robs us of peace with Him. Worrying causes us to become self-reliant, rather than relying on God and trusting in His promises (Matthew 6:31).

Worrying causes us to forfeit our peace in God, as it hinders us from knowing that He is in charge of every situation in our lives. It makes room for doubt and kills faith (Philippians 4:6-7). It stops us from listening to God's Word (Matthew 13:22).

Why not hand over your worries to God right now? He wants you to live in peace and happiness. Stop worrying and be happy and fulfilled in Him.

Today's Prayer: Father, I know that worrying affects my physical and emotional health, and that it can also damage my spiritual health. Please forgive me for worrying, and help me to bring everything to you in prayer. Amen.

January 21

TONGUE ON FIRE

'The tongue also is a fire, a world of evil among the parts of the body. It corrupts the whole body, sets the whole course of one's life on fire, and is itself set on fire by hell.' (James 3:6).

In this text, James tells us about the terrible damage an uncontrolled tongue can do. Individuals have been hurt by hateful words that someone has said, words that have caused division and broken relationships. Once these words are spoken, no matter how much we apologise, we cannot reverse the damage that has been done.

James compares the damage the tongue can cause to a raging fire, whose wickedness has its source in hell. Someone once described the tongue as not being steel, yet it cuts like steel. You might at some point in your life have been cut by the tongue of someone else and still bear the scar to this day. Our words are incredibly powerful and can inflict wounds that can do untold damage.

In chapter 3, James seeks to expose hypocritical practice and to teach good Christian behaviour to the Christians of his time. He shows the importance of controlling the tongue. Sadly, he concludes that mankind can, and has, tamed all kinds of creatures; however, "no human being can tame the tongue. It is a restless evil, full of deadly poison." (Verse 7)

If, according to James, no man can tame the tongue, then what can we do? We must think before we speak, for by doing so, we allow ourselves to become sensitive to the leading of the Holy Spirit as we draw upon His power.

It seems that the problem is not really the tongue, but the heart! Our words reflect what is in our hearts. 'The mouth speaks what the heart is full of'. (Matthew 12:34) In other words, what we say reveals what is in our hearts.

What kind of words will come from your lips today? Will they be words of encouragement and kindness, or will they be words that cut and hurt? Remember, you cannot solve your heart problem just by cleaning up your speech; you need to pray for the Holy Spirit's power in your life to create in you a clean heart. He is the only one who can change hearts.

Today's prayer: 'Create in me a pure heart, O God, and renew a steadfast spirit within me'. (Psalm 51:10). Amen.

January 22

PERSISTENCE IN PRAYER

'And there was a widow in the town who kept coming to him with the plea, "Grant me justice against my adversary."' (Luke 18:3)

Here, Jesus tells the parable of the persistent widow to show that we should always pray and not give up.

The widow had every reason to persist. If you were a widow in Bible times in Jewish culture, you would find yourself very vulnerable, for there would be no one to care for you. Throughout the Old and New Testaments, you will find that both the prophets and the disciples constantly emphasised the importance of taking care of widows, orphans and those in need.

In her desperation, the widow kept going back to the godless judge with her problem, but the more she pressured him, the more stubborn he became. However, he reached the breaking point one day and said to himself, "Even though I don't fear God or care what people think, yet because this widow keeps bothering me, I will see that she gets justice, so that she won't eventually come and attack me!"

How about you? Have you been praying and not received an answer yet? Or have you prayed once and given up on God because He has not answered you? Learn a lesson from the widow: keep on praying until there is a breakthrough. St. Paul tells us to pray without ceasing. This means we should present our requests continually before God our Father, who knows our needs, and He will answer at the right time.

The judge only responded because he was pressured to do so; however, God does not need to be pressured. He says, whoever comes to Him, He will in no wise turn away. He loves us and will grant our needs according to His riches in glory.

You may have been praying for many weeks, months or even years! Rest assured God will answer. Don't give up. He might delay answering your prayers, but He has good reasons for doing so; just keep praying regardless. Or could it be that He wants you to trust Him more and strengthen your faith in Him as you persist in prayer? Or, He might want to develop His glorious character in you.

As you face life's challenges today, remain constant in prayer, live in hope and expectancy that God will hear and answer your prayers. We should always pray and not give up.

Today's prayer: Lord, you know that I have been praying for a long time now and have not had an answer; however, I will wait upon you because you have my best interests at heart and will answer me in due course. Amen.

January 23

DEMOLITION OR CONSTRUCTION BUSINESS?

'With their mouths the godless destroy their neighbours, but through knowledge the righteous escape.' (Proverbs 11:9)

Have you ever seen or been to a demolition site? Any building on the site would be razed to the ground. According to the Collins dictionary, 'the demolition of a building is the act of deliberately destroying it, often to build something else in its place'.

In Proverbs 11:9, Solomon says, "With their mouths the godless destroy their neighbours, but through knowledge the righteous escape". He is saying here that words have the power to destroy or build someone up.

James amplifies this when he says, "With the tongue we praise our Lord and Father, and with it we curse human beings, who have been made in God's image." It is hard to understand this, but how often are words used to destroy or demolish another person, rather than build them up? Sadly, it seems that we find it easier to destroy than to build others up with our words. Those who do not guard their words are deliberately destroying another person.

Perhaps you can identify with this; you might have received more negative or destructive words than positive, encouraging words. It could be that as a child, you were constantly told you were no good and would not achieve much in life. Words and comments like these can destroy one's self-esteem. Therefore, we should aim at building others up, rather than pulling them down.

One commentary says, 'Every person you meet today is either a demolition site or a construction opportunity. Your words will make a difference'. How about you? Will your words destroy or build someone up today? Will you speak caring and loving words to others, or careless and hurtful ones?

King Solomon says, 'Gracious words are as honeycomb, sweet to the soul and healing to the bones'. (Proverbs 16:24) May your words be gracious today and as sweet as honey from the honeycomb.

Today's prayer: Father, forgive me if I have destroyed others with my words. Please let my words be tools for construction so that your name will be glorified. Amen.

January 24

GENUINE FRIENDSHIP

'A friend loves at all times, and a brother is born for a time of adversity.' **(Proverbs 17:17)**

The story of David and Jonathan is a story of two friends whose friendship was based on love, a love that David described as wonderful, 'Your love for me was wonderful, more wonderful than that of women'. (2 Samuel 1:26) In his lament over the death of his best friend, Jonathan, David was expressing 'the deep brotherhood and faithful friendship he had with Jonathan'. 'Jonathan became one in spirit with David, and he loved him as himself'. (1 Samuel 18:1) Their friendship was based on their love, loyalty, and commitment not just to each other but to God. How about you? What kind of friend are you?

David and Jonathan didn't just know each other socially; they were true friends. They remained loyal to each other throughout their lives, unlike the kind of friendship we sometimes see today. Fair-weather friends are those who will be your friend when everything is going well. However, the moment they feel they have nothing to gain from the relationship, they forsake you.

Are you a loyal friend, one that sticks closer than a brother? Solomon says, '...but there is a friend that sticks closer than a brother.' (Proverbs 18:24)

Abraham was called God's friend. (Isaiah 41:8). Can you imagine yourself, a mere human being, called a friend of God? Being friends with God, creator of the universe, means to spend quality time with him, studying his word, and being obedient: "You are my friends if you do what I command you". Abraham obeyed God even when he did not understand how God could ask him to sacrifice his only son, but because of his obedience, he became God's friend.

As a result of what Jesus did for us on the cross, we too can become God's friends. But why would God even want us as friends? Sinful mortals like us? We are sinners and therefore His enemies. But because He loves us so much, He cannot afford not to have us as friends. No matter how sinful we are, because He is a loving God, He has the power to transform enemies to become friends. St. Paul says, "Once you were alienated from God and were enemies in your minds because of your evil behaviour." (Colossians 1:21). However, when we accept that we are sinners and cannot save ourselves, and depend totally on God's grace and His power to forgive our sins, we too can become His friend.

Allow Jesus into your life today to be your friend, so that you can be a genuine friend to others and, in so doing, introduce them to Jesus, the dearest friend there is.

Today's Prayer: Father, help me to be a true friend. Amen.

January 25

FOLLOWING JESUS

"Come, follow me," Jesus said, "and I will send you out to fish for people." (Mark 1:17)

The chapter begins by telling us that as Jesus was walking by the Sea of Galilee, He saw Simon and his brother Andrew fishing, and asked them to follow Him, and without hesitation, they left their nets and followed Him. It is interesting to note that they immediately responded to the call of Jesus. They were fishermen, fishing was their livelihood, and yet they were willing to follow Jesus, not even thinking about how they would support their families.

As Scripture suggests, Simon and Peter had already encountered Jesus, so He was no stranger to them (John 1:35-42). They knew who He was; had John the Baptist not said, "Look, the Lamb of God!" John had been pointing people to the Messiah, so it might have been easier for Simon and Andrew to follow Jesus, because that was what John wanted them to do. They were influenced by the 'Baptist'. He was pointing people to Jesus. He was merely a 'voice in the wilderness', introducing others to the Messiah.

However, could it be that Simon and Andrew might have seen something in Jesus that drew them to Him like a magnet - his love and His compassion? They probably felt a sense of security as He bid them follow Him.

When Jesus called them, He said, "I will send you out to fish people." What did He mean? This was their call to discipleship. When we believe and accept Jesus as our Saviour, it is our responsibility to tell others about Him too. Jesus' commission to all His disciples is that after receiving Him in their lives, they should go and make disciples of others. Like Simon and Andrew, we must be eager to introduce others to Jesus. How eager are you to tell others about Jesus? Do your friends, colleagues and family know about Him? How many people in your life have heard you speak about Him? Does your behaviour reflect the loving, humble, caring character of Jesus? Or are you afraid or embarrassed to speak about Him?

The call to make fishers of men is no less pertinent today, and possibly more challenging. Fishing with a net is synonymous with the gospel, the gospel being a net lifting people from the dark waters of sin into the glorious light of God's majesty, bringing them hope and security. Are you a fisher of men, and where are you casting your net? Are you truly following Jesus?

Today's Prayer: Father, you have called me to be a fisher of men, to proclaim your message to those lost in sin. Help me to be eager like the disciples of old to introduce others to you. Amen.

January 26

GO AND DO LIKEWISE

'The expert in the law replied, "The one who had mercy on him." Jesus told him, "Go and do likewise." (Luke 10:37)

Sebbie Hall was just 17 years old when he decided to dedicate his life to helping others. And it took only three years to recognise him as a hero, as the UK's kindest person. During his three years of good work, he donated 400 coats and blankets to homeless charities, gifted 800 toys to children's homes, and even used his own pocket money to pay for strangers' coffees.

Sebbie, who was born with a chromosome anomaly, initially started spreading kindness during the Covid 19 lockdown, after discovering that some of his classmates didn't have access to a computer, and raised money and bought laptops for them.

In 2023 Sebbie was crowned the UK's Kind Hero and honoured with a statue near Tower Bridge in London alongside the likes of Captain Cook, and Winston Churchill. (goodnewsnetwork.org)

This story highlights the very lesson Jesus told in the parable of the Good Samaritan in Luke 10: 1-37. In His discourse with the lawyer, he tells of the man who was attacked by robbers and left to die by the wayside. A priest and a Levite passed by, crossed over to the other side of the road, and did not offer help to the man. However, it was a Samaritan who helped the injured man. Jesus asked him who he thought was a neighbour to the injured man, to which he responded, "The one who had mercy on him." Jesus said, "Go and do likewise. " (Verse 37)

Have you ever walked away from a homeless or impoverished person as you go about your daily activities? Have you made excuses for not helping those who are poor and needy? The way we act and treat others does not escape the eyes of God. Jesus expects us to care for the poor and needy. He says we should feed the hungry, give those who are homeless somewhere to stay, look after the sick, and visit those in prison. In Matthew 25: 31-35 we are being told that we should treat others kindly, for in doing so, we are treating them as if they were Jesus. "Truly I tell you, whatever you did for one of the least of these brothers and sisters of mine, you did it for me."

Today's Prayer: Lord, help me not to walk away from those who need my help. Amen.

January 27

NO GREATER LOVE

"Greater love has no one than this: to lay down one's life for one's friends." (John15:13)

Have you ever stopped to contemplate God's love for you? I guess one can scarcely take it in. For God to love us to the extent that He gave His only Son to die for us is truly amazing and difficult to comprehend. 'When we were yet sinners, Christ died for us. Very rarely will anyone die for a righteous person, though for a good person, someone might possibly dare to die. But God demonstrates His own love for us in this: while we were still sinners, Christ died for us'. (Romans 5:7). What matchless love! 'While we were still sinners', these words should really stop us in our tracks. We were helpless and unable to save ourselves from our sins, and so Jesus, God's only son, came on a rescue mission to earth to rescue us. Why? 'For God so loved the world that He gave His one and only Son, that whoever believes in Him shall not perish but have eternal life' (John 3:16).

Abraham was willing to sacrifice his only son, although He was surprised that God should ask him to do such a thing. He had waited all those years for a son, and it was when he was a hundred years old that God fulfilled His promise when Isaac was born. Abraham's willingness is remarkable; this was because he loved God and trusted Him. Abraham did not have to sacrifice his son because the angel stopped him, but God offered up His only Son to die in your place and mine, not because there was anything good in us, but just because He loved us.

Can anyone love you more than Jesus? No. He showed us the greatest kind of love. The songwriter Frederick Lehman expresses this so well, 'The love of God is greater far, than tongue or pen can ever tell; it goes beyond the highest star and reaches to the lowest hell...To write the love of God above would drain the ocean dry, nor could the scroll contain the whole, though stretched from sky to sky.'

The love of God for us is the greatest love story there is. Jesus chose to die for us, not because we loved Him, but because He first loved us. The challenge for us today is, how can we show love to those around us? Jesus says, "A new commandment, I have given you, that you love one another."

Prayer: Father, I thank you for your love for me. Help me to love others as you love me. Amen.

January 28

THE DANGER OF SELF-RIGHTEOUSNESS

'To some who were confident of their own righteousness and looked down on everyone else, Jesus told this parable. "Two men went up to the temple to pray, one a Pharisee and the other a tax collector."' (Luke 18:9-10)

In this parable, Jesus addresses those who were 'confident of their own righteousness' and thought themselves better than others. The Pharisees were the spiritual leaders who obeyed the very letter of the law. They looked down on others who failed in keeping the law. They were the elite of Jewish society and revered by all. However, Jesus' words were directed at them.

In Bible times, people would often go to the temple in Jerusalem to pray, so it wasn't unusual to find those two men praying there. One can imagine the Pharisee praying loud enough so others could hear how good he was. With pride in his heart, he lifted his voice and prayed, "God, I thank you that I am not like other people – robbers, evildoers, adulterers – or even like this tax collector. I fast twice a week and give a tenth of all I get." (Verse 11 and 12)

The Pharisee wasn't really praying; neither was he praising God; he was praising himself. By contrast, the tax collector recognised that he was a sinner and prayed a prayer of confession. 'But the tax collector stood at a distance. He would not even look up to heaven, but beat his breast and said, "God have mercy on me, a sinner." (Verse 13)

The Pharisee really believed he was better than the tax collector. Tax collectors were hated in those days and were regarded as sinners. They were hated by fellow Jews because they worked for the Romans and were seen as traitors. The Romans hired them to collect taxes from the people who resented paying taxes to their foreign rulers. The Pharisee was obsessed with self-righteousness, which led to pride, which is dangerous. In his prayer, he was congratulating himself for all the sins he had not committed; however, he did not realise that he was guilty of spiritual pride.

The Bible tells us that God hates pride. 'There are six things the lord hates, seven are detestable to Him, haughty eyes...' (Proverbs 6:17). The Pharisee's disingenuous prayer showed the extent of his pride; sadly, he seemingly didn't even realise that pride was his problem. As far as he was concerned, the problem was with the tax collector and not with himself!

Jesus' assessment of the situation shows us how He views self-righteousness and pride. He says, "I tell you that this man, rather than the other, went home justified before God. For all those who exalt themselves will be humbled, and those who humble themselves will be exalted." (Verse 14)

Today's Prayer: Father, give me a spirit of humility and sincerity. Amen.

January 29

A GRACIOUS AND COMPASSIONATE GOD (1)

... "I knew that you are a gracious and compassionate God, slow to anger and abounding in love, a God who relents from sending calamity." (Jonah 4:2).

The story of Jonah is an intriguing one. Here is a prophet actually running away from God and the assignment given to him. God sent him to Nineveh in Assyria, but he chose to go in the opposite direction. Why was Jonah reluctant to take God's message to Nineveh? We shouldn't be too hard on him; he had every reason not to want to go, for the Assyrians were very wicked, and he had grown up hating them. He hated them so much that he didn't want to go to Nineveh just in case they repented from their sins. However, Jonah chose to run away from God rather than obey Him.

Although Jonah headed in the opposite direction, he couldn't run from God. David tells us in Psalm 139:7-10 that we cannot run from God: 'Where can I flee from His presence? If I go up to the heavens, you are there, if I make my bed in the depths, you are there.' (Verse 7- 8) Jonah knew that God had called him to deliver a specific message to the citizens of Nineveh, but he didn't want to do it.

Are we sometimes like Jonah? When God gives us an assignment through His word, are we reluctant or fearful at times and make excuses? Or do we complain that the task is too hard and that God should ask someone else? Whatever way we choose to respond, it's still disobedience.

Disobedience can affect others, too. In the case of Jonah, his disobedience endangered the lives of the entire crew on the ship that was bound for Tarshish. By disobeying God, we can cause hurt to others. Disobedience is sin and will ultimately have consequences. As a result of his disobedience, the ship was caught in a storm, and Jonah was willing to give his life to save the crew. The irony is that Jonah was willing to give up his life for the sailors but was unwilling to do the same for the Ninevites.

Today's Prayer: Father, please forgive me for my reluctance to spread your word. Help me not to make excuses but to carry out the assignments you have given me. Help me to learn to trust you, knowing you are a loving and compassionate God. Amen.

January 30

A GRACIOUS AND COMPASSIONATE GOD (2)

It is interesting to note that when Jonah asked to be thrown into the sea, the soldiers were reluctant to do so; they did everything possible not to, and they seemingly showed more compassion for him than Jonah did for the people of Nineveh. They were pagans, and yet they showed more compassion than Jonah, who believed and later admitted that God was compassionate… "I knew that you are a gracious and compassionate God, slow to anger and abounding in love, a God who relents from sending calamity." (4:5)

When Jonah finally delivered God's message to the Ninevites, after being swallowed by a fish, he became angry because they repented of their sins. It is hard to understand Jonah; after all that God had done for him, he dared to be angry with Him!

In this narrative, we see a God who is gracious and compassionate, a God of love and mercy. It is not His desire that any of us should perish, but that all should come to repentance. As wicked as the Ninevites were from a human standpoint - they did not deserve to be saved, but God is merciful and compassionate and loving; they, too, needed salvation. The story shows that no one is beyond redemption. The gospel is for all of us as long as we are ready to repent of our sins and accept God in our lives.

God has commissioned all of us to take the message of salvation to a sinful world. Are you running in the opposite direction like Jonah, or are you making excuses? Remember that God's message of love and forgiveness is for all people. The people of Nineveh did not deserve it, but our compassionate and loving God spared them when they repented.

We, too, are undeserving, but God loves us so much that He sent His only Son, who did not deserve to die, so that we can live eternally. Although Jonah ran from Him, God accepted him, for God loves us all even when we fail Him.

Today's prayer: Dear God, forgive me for the times I have fallen short of your expectations. I know it is better to obey than to run away from you, because you love me and want me to be saved in your kingdom. Amen.

January 31

BETRAYED!

'Even my close friend, someone I trusted, one who shared my bread, has turned against me.' (Psalm 41:9)

Have you ever been betrayed? One writer says, "It's often the people we love most and trust implicitly who have the greatest power to betray us." It is thought that when David wrote those words, he was alluding to Christ's betrayal by Judas. Judas, one of Jesus' disciples, had spent three years travelling and eating with Him. He was one of the inner circle who managed the finances of the group and was therefore very close to Jesus and knew Him well.

Matthew records the details: 'then one of the twelve – the one called Judas Iscariot - went to the chief priests and asked, "what are you willing to give me if I deliver Him over to you?"' (Matthew 26: 14). It is hard to think why Judas would want to betray Jesus; he had everything to gain from being a disciple of Christ. He, like the other disciples, believed that Jesus would overthrow the wicked Romans and that they would all be given positions in Jesus' government. He would probably retain his position as treasurer, yet out of greed and love of money, he betrayed the innocent One.

If you've ever been betrayed, you can, no doubt, recall the painful emotions of hurt and anger you felt, for when trust is shattered and demoralised, then hurt, anguish, and pain remain, leaving you crushed and battling with the struggle to forgive. David expressed his hurt when he said, 'Even my close friend, someone I trusted, one who shared my bread, has turned against me.' (Psalm 41:14)

At some time in our lives, we might be betrayed. St. Paul speaks of a time when he was "in danger from false believers," (2 Corinthians 11:26); he must have had his fair share of betrayal, too. What do we do when we've been betrayed? We cannot afford to remain angry and hurt for the rest of our lives. Jesus expects us to forgive, however difficult that is, and move on. You would have lost confidence in that friend or loved one who violated your trust, but God will remove the pain if you let Him.

Today's Prayer: Father, you know how hurt and angry I feel. Help me to forgive so healing can begin. Amen.

60

February 1

THE LEPROSY OF SIN

A man with leprosy came to Him and begged Him on his knees, "If you are willing, you can make me clean." (Mark 1:40)

In this story recorded by Mark, a leper asks Jesus to heal him. Leprosy, also known as Hansen's disease, is a long-term infection caused by the bacterium, Mycobacterium leprae. It is a highly infectious disease, and dreaded by all. In keeping with the law in Leviticus 13 & 14, lepers were seen as ritually unclean and were declared unclean by Jewish leaders. Lepers were deemed unfit to participate in any religious or social activities. The law stated that if anyone had contact with leprosy, they themselves would be contaminated and therefore deemed unclean. As a result, people kept as far away as possible from lepers. In fact, lepers were relegated to living in their own communities.

As Jesus was travelling throughout Galilee, a leper approached Him and asked to be healed. Here is the dilemma: because the leper was ritually unclean, he must avoid contact with others. What will Jesus do? Filled with compassion, Jesus reached out His hand and touched the man. "I am willing," he said. "Be clean!" Immediately, the leprosy left him (Verse 41 and 42). This action on the part of Jesus meant that He would have been deemed unclean until evening and would be required to bathe to become ritually clean again. However, Jesus was not defiled by touching the leper.

What can we learn from this story? One commentary says: 'The real value of a person is inside, not outside. Although a person's body may be diseased and deformed, the person inside is no less valuable to God.'

Sin is like leprosy, and everyone is contaminated, diseased, and deformed by the ugliness of sin. Lepers were alienated from society; we, too, because of sin, have become alienated from God. Leprosy deforms the sufferer, and we, too, as sinners, are all deformed by sin and cannot heal ourselves. We have sinned and come short of the glory of God. Jesus touched the leper, who exercised faith in Him, and was healed immediately.

Are you like the leper, wanting to be healed? He came to Jesus because he had had enough of his miserable life and could no longer continue to live in isolation. You, too, must come to Jesus for healing from your sin. He will have compassion on you and will forgive you of your sin. He desires that you will be cleansed from the disease of sin.

Today's Prayer: Father, I need healing like the leper in the story. I would like to hear those words, 'Be clean.' I thank you for sending your Son, Jesus Christ, through whom I have the opportunity to be healed. Amen.

February 2

CAUGHT IN A STORM

"I have told you these things so that in me you may have peace. In this world, you will have trouble. But take heart, I have overcome the world." (Matthew 16:33)

Have you ever been caught in a storm, a crisis in your life? A storm that found you frantically trying to keep your head afloat, for fear you would drown. We know that storms will arise from time to time, but they should serve to deepen our faith and trust in God. However, they can become so severe that if we keep focusing on them, we can lose hope.

Think of Job, the storm that he went through was relentless and fierce, his pain and suffering were unbearable. However, his anguish was not so much the pain of his affliction, but being unable to understand why God allowed him to suffer. He was "blameless and upright, he feared God and shunned evil." (Job 1:1) Why was he suffering? Why does God allow His children to suffer?

Have you ever been in a situation where you were unable to understand why God allowed you to go through your storm? Although He may not explain it to you, you must understand that as a child of God, trials will come, storms will most certainly appear; however, we must be prepared for the testing of our faith. Jesus knew that His children would be sorely tested, and before He left for heaven, He told His disciples that "In this world you will have trouble, but take heart, I have overcome the world." (John 16:33)

What about Joseph? He was hated by his brothers, who tried to murder him. When that failed, he was sold as a slave to a foreign land. It was in Egypt that his storm grew fiercer; lies and seduction, which ended with him spending two years in prison for a crime he had not committed.

How we respond during times of storm is crucial. Job never lost his faith in God and boldly proclaimed, "Though He slay me, yet will I hope in

Him." (Job 13:5). Although there were times when Job wished he were dead, because of his suffering, he never sinned against God. However, he was faced with two choices: He could curse God and die, or he could trust God and draw strength from Him. He chose the latter, and God rewarded him beyond his greatest expectations. "The Lord blessed the latter part of Job's life more than the former part." (Job 42:12)

It is often in the storms that we are being purified when God shows us who we really are and clears the dross from our lives to make way for complete trust in Him.

Today's prayer: Lord, as I go through the storms of life, I am thankful that you are with me. Help me to realise that you seek to purify me so my life can bring honour and glory to you. Amen.

February 3

HOW TO OVERCOME GUILT (Part 1)

"The man and his wife heard the sound of the Lord God as He was walking in the garden in the cool of the day, and they hid from the Lord God among the trees of the garden." (Genesis 3:8)

After sinning, Adam and Eve felt guilty and, because of their guilt, they hid from God. If you have ever experienced guilt, you will agree that it is a very uncomfortable feeling. All of us at some time in our lives have done wrong and have suffered guilt. Guilt is defined as a painful emotion that people experience when they believe their actions, whether real or imagined, have violated a moral personal standard.

Guilt was the first adverse emotion felt by the human race. Soon after Adam and Eve sinned, their behaviour changed. They hid among the trees in the garden (Genesis 3:8). After sinning, they felt guilt and embarrassment, and as a result, they tried to hide from God. This unprecedented reaction indicated fear of their heavenly Father and Friend who visited daily in the garden.

Can you imagine walking with God in the Garden of Eden? It must have been such a wonderful experience for Adam and Eve. I can only imagine how they woke up every morning anticipating His visit. However, when they disobeyed Him, this beautiful bond of friendship was severed; they felt shame and sorrow as they were made aware of the terrible consequences of their sin, and even before they heard Him approaching them in the garden, they were overcome with guilt.

Guilt is like a corrosive which burns deep into our heart and soul. It is what robs us of peace with God; it is what separates and alienates us from Him. It severs our friendship and relationship with Him. Sin had broken Adam and Eve's close relationship with God just as it has broken our relationship with Him.

Guilt and shame can destroy us and harm others too. Some have committed suicide because of guilt. It is a common emotion that all of us experience at times in our lives, because we are all sinners. It stops us from living our lives to its fullest. Guilt can result in both physical and mental health conditions: cancer, stomach ulcers, obsessive-compulsive disorders, and other anxiety disorders. However, God wants to set you free from guilt today.

Today's Prayer: Father, you know I cannot be healthy and happy as long as I am burdened with the load of guilt. I seek your forgiveness as I repent of my sins. Amen.

February 4

HOW TO OVERCOME GUILT – (PART 2)

"Therefore, there is now no condemnation for those who are in Christ Jesus." (Romans 8:1)

How can you overcome guilt? If you were guilty of committing a crime and sentenced to die, how would you feel if the judge commuted your sentence and told you that you were no longer guilty? You are free to go! What would those words mean to you? The same as it would mean for all humanity, for everyone is guilty, because we have been justly condemned for repeatedly breaking God's law. "For all have sinned and fall short of the glory of God." (Romans 3:8) However, there is good news! "Therefore, there is now no condemnation for those who are in Christ Jesus, because through Christ Jesus the law of the Spirit who gives life has set you free..." (Romans 8:1-2)

When King David had an adulterous affair with Bathsheba and subsequently murdered her husband Uriah, he never for a moment thought of the consequences. It even caused the death of an innocent child! This is what sin does; we sometimes have to pay a high price for our actions. Can you imagine the enormous guilt that David felt? Psalm 51 gives us an insight into his feelings of guilt and also, importantly, his expression of repentance. Although he had sinned with Bathsheba, David acknowledged that he had sinned against God. "Against you, you only have I sinned and done what is evil in your sight." (Psalm 51:4)

David repented of his sins, and God in His mercy forgave him, and he was set free from his guilt and his sins. You might be thinking that you have done something very wrong and that God will not forgive you. These thoughts are from the evil one who wants us to constantly live in a state of guilt, because he wants us to perish in our sins. God will forgive you of any sin as long as you confess them and ask for forgiveness, and when He does, you are no longer shackled by guilt. He is longing to restore your relationship with Him. Not only did David confess his sins and ask for forgiveness, but he was also genuinely repentant. In his desperate prayer in Psalm 51, he cried out to God. "Restore to me the joy of your salvation and grant me a willing spirit, to sustain me." (Psalm 51:12)

Without Jesus in our lives, we would be in a constant state of guilt; without Him, we would be without hope, lost in our trespasses and sin. But thank God, He has set us free, and we are no longer guilty. He has given us power through His Holy Spirit to overcome sin and to do His will. This is indeed good news!

Today's Prayer: Father, please deliver me from guilt and 'restore unto me the joy of your salvation'. Amen.

February 5

DO YOU WANT JESUS TO SHOW UP IN YOUR LIFE?

'Then He got into the boat and His disciples followed Him.' (Matthew 8:23)

Sometimes Jesus shows up when we least expect. As His disciples were making their way across the lake, a storm arose, and their boat was being tossed about by the wind and the waves. It must have been a frightening storm in which they must have thought they would not make it back safely to shore, as they feared for their lives.

The Sea of Galilee is actually a large lake, and even to this day, it is the scene of fierce storms, sometimes with waves as high as six meters. The disciples were not frightened without cause; even those who were expert fishermen and knew how to handle a boat in a storm feared for their lives too.

As we read the narrative, we realise that they were now losing hope as they struggled through the night. Are there times in your life when you are so overwhelmed with challenges that you feel like giving up as you begin to lose hope? Are there times when you lie awake all night asking, "God, where are you?"

Just when the disciples feared that they would go under, Jesus showed up. The Bible tells us that He showed up in the 'fourth watch'. However, they were in such a state of heightened anxiety and fear that they didn't even recognise Him until He said "It is I do not be afraid."

It was in the darkest hour that Jesus showed up for His disciples. Many times, He shows up at the darkest time in our lives just when all seems hopeless. In the Hebrew culture, there are four watches in the night: First watch: 6-9 pm; Second watch: 9 pm-midnight; Third watch: midnight to 3 am; Fourth watch, being the last watch before dawn, which is the darkest time. It was in the darkest hour that Jesus showed up for the disciples. Maybe you are going through terrible storms in your life right now, but keep holding on, for Jesus will show up for you, too. "Weeping my last for a night, but joy comes in the morning." (Psalm 30:5)

You might be in a desperate situation today and feel that God has abandoned you, don't despair, for He has heard your cry and will show up. Whatever is holding you captive, rest assured, He can set you free if you let Him. He showed up for the man at the pool of Bethesda (John 5) and asked him if he wanted to get well. He had been disabled for 38 years, and all attempts at being healed were futile. He had no hope of being healed until Jesus showed up. No matter how trapped you are in your illness or your situation, God can minister to your deepest needs. Don't let problems such as sickness and hardship cause you to lose hope, for when Jesus shows up, He can heal you like He did for the man at the pool.

Today's Prayer: Father, please show up in my life today. Amen.

February 6

MY GRACE IS SUFFICIENT

'But He said unto me, "My grace is sufficient for you, for my power is made perfect in weakness." Therefore, I will boast all the more gladly about my weaknesses, so that Christ's power may rest on me.' (2 Corinthians 12:9)

In verse 8 of the chapter, Paul apparently had a debilitating condition which he referred to as a "thorn in his flesh." While we are unsure of the nature of his ailment, he asked God three times for healing, but God refused to heal Him. However, God reassured him that His grace would be sufficient for him. That is, during his affliction, God would demonstrate His power, and Paul would have to depend more on God than at any other time in his life. It is through our weaknesses that God's character can be developed in us, and this is what He wanted for Paul and for us, too.

God told Paul that His grace was more than enough for him. How do we respond to our weaknesses and our limitations? Do we spend our time focusing on them rather than allowing God to use them so we can trust Him more? The moment Paul recognised that he had no power in himself to change his situation, he had to accept that God knew what was best for him. There are times when God, for reasons best known to Him, chooses not to heal some of His followers from physical ailments, but rather uses them so they can depend more on Him, to develop good Christian characters and to deepen their relationship with Him.

Once Paul had come to the realisation that God's grace was indeed sufficient for him, he was able to say, "Therefore I boast all the more gladly about my weakness, so that Christ's power can rest on me."

As believers, it is not God's intention for us to be weak and ineffective, but that, despite our challenges, we can become strong and bold. It is because of His grace we can delight in "weaknesses, in insults, in hardships, in persecutions, in difficulties. For when I am weak, then I am strong." (2 Corinthians 12:10)

As a result of his acceptance that he had no real power in himself to change his situation, Paul was able to affirm God's strength.

Are you ready to accept that you have no power in yourself to change your situation? Is there something that is a hindrance to your ministry? If so, take everything to God in prayer. When you pray for healing, accept that God is more concerned about healing you spiritually than physically. Our spiritual condition is of far more importance than our physical condition. It is not God's desire that we perish in our sins, but that all of us should come to repentance.

Today's Prayer: Dear Father, may my life reflect your grace today. Amen.

February 7

FORGIVENESS

"But you are a forgiving God, gracious and compassionate; slow to anger and abounding in love." (Nehemiah 9:17)

Someone once said that forgiveness is like a rose that blesses the foot that crushes it. It has been explained as: 'Just as a rose would leave its scent on the boot that aggressively crushes it, forgiving someone influences the one who is forgiven, no matter how harsh or cruel his act has been.'

Alexander Pope wrote, "To err is human, to forgive is divine." This simply means that everyone commits sins and makes mistakes and needs to be forgiven, and God is the only one who can forgive sins. It is also saying that as humans we are not capable of forgiveness; however, when we realise and accept the extent of God's forgiveness, it will enable us to forgive those who have hurt us.

Nevertheless, it is very difficult to forgive someone who has hurt you, and it does not happen overnight; it may take months or even years! Jesus gives a stark warning about un-forgiveness in Matthew 6:14 &15. He says, "For if you forgive other people when they sin against you, your heavenly Father will also forgive you. But if you do not forgive others their sins, your Father will not forgive your sins." In other words, if we refuse to forgive others, God will also refuse to forgive us. Can you imagine not being forgiven by God? It is easy for us to ask God to forgive us when we sin, yet we find it hard to forgive others. Before we even ask God for forgiveness, we should ensure that we have forgiven the people who have wronged us, or who we have wronged, before going to God to ask forgiveness.

The story is told of Methode, who survived the genocide in Rwanda. His father was shot in church, his mother was killed by a machete, and his brother and two other siblings were also killed. He started a hit list of people he planned to kill when he grew up. However, with help and support from trauma counsellors, with time, he took the painful but healing steps toward forgiveness. As healing and forgiveness took place, he was able to discard the list of people he had planned to kill. He slowly began to accept God's love for him and accepted His forgiveness and extended love to those he once hated. It must have been a painful journey for him, but God set him free.

If you are struggling today with not being able to forgive, you might be asking yourself, how can I forgive someone who hurt me so deeply? It is difficult, however, you must. It was C.S. Lewis who said, "Everyone says forgiveness is a lovely idea until they have one thing to forgive."

Today's Prayer: Father, help me to learn to forgive. Amen

February 8

THINKING BEYOND EARTHLY RICHES (1)

"This is how it will be with whoever stores up things for themselves but is not rich towards God." (Luke 12:21)

In Luke 16-21, Jesus tells the parable of the rich fool whose farm yielded an abundant harvest. He had so much that he did not have a place to store his crops. Rather than share what he had with others, he decided to tear down his existing barns and build bigger ones so he could store his surplus grain. He thought to himself, "You have plenty of grain laid up for many years. Take life easy, eat, drink and be merry." (Verse 19) He was sure he would live to enjoy his riches; however, God said to him, "You fool! This night your life will be demanded from you. Then who will get what you have prepared for yourself?" (Verse 20)

The rich man was greedy, selfish, and very foolish. He thought that he would live a good life because he had riches. However, he died before he could enjoy his riches. Unfortunately, he was more concerned about accumulating wealth for himself. God expects us to be generous and share what He has blessed us with. In 1 Timothy 6:18 we are told, "Command them to do good, to be rich in good deeds, and be generous and willing to share."

How about you? Are you storing up earthly goods that will soon perish? The Bible tells us not to "store up treasures for yourselves where moths and vermin destroy, and where thieves break in and steal. But store up for yourselves treasures in heaven, where moths and vermin do not destroy, and where thieves do not break in and steal." (Matthew 6:19 & 20)

In this story, Jesus is helping us to understand that being rich in earthly goods is not as important as living a fulfilled life in Him. He challenges us to think about our motivation in acquiring wealth. If we are more concerned about accumulating wealth to enrich ourselves without concern for others, we are merely storing up treasures on earth and not in heaven. A truly fulfilled and wealthy life is lived for Christ. Jesus tells us to seek Him first (not earthly riches), to "Seek His kingdom and His righteousness, and all these things will be given to you." Matthew 6:33) In other words, He is saying we are to put Him first in our lives; this should be our first priority, not being materialistic. A far as the rich man was concerned, he had everything; however, in reality, he had nothing!

Today's Prayer: Father, help me to understand that nothing matters more than having a relationship with you. For what will it profit me if I gain the whole world and lose my soul? Thank you that my salvation is secure in you. Amen.

February 9

THINKING BEYOND EARTHLY RICHES (2)

"No one can serve two masters. Either you will hate the one and love the other, or you will be devoted to the one and despise the other. You cannot serve God and money." (Luke 16:13)

In this parable, Jesus was speaking to those who loved money. The Pharisees, in particular, loved money, and when Jesus made this statement, they were very disparaging of Him. They were a very pious sect who loved to be praised by others. They gave the impression that they were more righteous than others. Having great wealth was important too, because they considered that their wealth was a sign of God's approval of their righteousness. Jesus was certainly not impressed. He said to them, "You are the ones who justify yourselves in the eyes of others, but God knows your hearts. What people value highly, is detestable to God." (Luke 16:14-15) Because of their love for money, and self-righteous attitude, they did not take kindly to Jesus' teaching.

What Jesus said is also a lesson for us today. Do we love money more than God? Do we spend all our time accumulating wealth and have no time to do His work? Our love for money and how we use it is an indication of where our allegiance lies. Jesus says it clearly, "No one can serve two masters. Either you will hate the one and love the other, or you will be devoted to the one and despise the other. You cannot serve God and Money." (Luke 16:13)

Jesus is not saying that possessing money is bad; it is how we use it that matters. He is the one who has gifted it to us; it belongs to Him and not to us, therefore, we should use it wisely. Money can easily become our 'god' when it takes God's place in our lives. One commentary says that "Money is a hard and deceptive master. Wealth promises power and control, but often it cannot deliver." Riches can be lost overnight. In one of the thirty sayings of the wise, it says, "Do not wear yourself out to get rich; do not trust your own cleverness. Cast but a glance at riches, and they are gone, for they will surely sprout wings and fly off to the sky like an eagle." (Proverbs 23:4 & 5)

What is the lesson for us today? Let us use money carefully and wisely, and don't allow it to replace God in our lives. Money can buy all you need, but it doesn't buy happiness. Use your wealth to help those in need. Invest in others who need your help; in so doing, you are laying up treasures in heaven and not on earth.

Today's prayer: Father, help me to make wise use of the resources and financial opportunities that you have gifted me with, not to be selfish but to share with those who are in need. Amen.

February 10

HOW WILL YOU MANAGE?

"If you have raced with men on foot and they have worn you out, how can you compete with horses? If you stumble in safe country, how will you manage the thickets by the Jordon?" (Jeremiah 12:5)

In Jeremiah 12:5, the prophet is complaining to God and asking Him, "Why does the way of the wicked prosper?" (Verse 1-6) Whilst Jeremiah realises that God is just, he seemingly wanted the wicked to be dealt with and that justice should come quickly to them.

We sometimes feel that way too, especially for those who have hurt us; we want God to punish them then and there. When we see the wicked prospering, like Jeremiah, Job, and Habakkuk did, we question God. Habakkuk asks God, "Why do you tolerate wrongdoing?" (Habakkuk 1:3). Like the prophets, we are concerned and saddened by the violence, corruption, and injustice that is happening in our society, and wonder why God allows it. However, we might not understand why God does, but He will act in His own time. However difficult it might be, we must trust Him and not allow our concerns to doubt Him.

We can therefore understand Jeremiah's complaints. He found himself in a situation where his very life was threatened. The people in his home town of Anathoth were plotting to kill him because they did not want to hear his message or heed his warnings. He openly condemned their idol worship, and they hated him for pointing out their sinful behaviours. What was Jeremiah to do? How would he handle this situation? There are times when we are in challenging situations and need to make decisions. Do we run away, or deal with them ourselves, or do we call on God for help? When faced with problems such as discrimination, injustice, threats, or hostility from others, do we run away, or do we call on God? In chapter 12, Jeremiah chooses to call on God and remain faithful to Him.

God answered Jeremiah, but when we read the answer, we can assume that Jeremiah was not anticipating such a response. "If you have raced with men on foot and they have worn you out, how can you compete with horses? If you stumble in safe country, how will you manage in the thickets by the Jordon?" God is actually saying to the prophet, "If you think what you are going through now is bad, how are you going to cope when it gets worse?" If we are anything like Jeremiah, we might be thinking, "Lord, I thought you'd get rid of those who are hurting me." We might be surprised at God's answer to Jeremiah's complaints; however, we might not always like His answers, they might not be easy to deal with, but we can be assured that God knows best and He will work things out for our best good.

Today's Prayer: Dear God, I might not always understand the answers to my prayers, but help me to remember that when things get tough and when you answer in ways that seem hard to handle, I must trust you anyway. Amen

February 11

GRACE, HOW AMAZING! (1)

"And should I not have concern for the great city of Nineveh, in which there are more than a hundred and twenty thousand people who cannot tell their right hand from their left – and also many animals?" (Jonah 4:11)

In this amazing story, we are introduced to Jonah, the reluctant prophet who chose to run away from God and dared to disobey Him. However, the story is a profound example of God's love, mercy, and grace.

God had given Jonah a mission to preach to the people in the Assyrian city of Nineveh, but instead of doing as God had instructed, he chose to run away. The people of Nineveh were very wicked. Nahum, the prophet, in his book gives us some insight into their wickedness. He says they were guilty of evil plots against God (Nahum 1:9); exploitation of those who were helpless (Nahum 2:12); cruelty in war (Nahum 2:12-13); idolatry, prostitution, and witchcraft (Nahum 3:4). Despite their wickedness, God told Jonah to warn them of judgment if they did not repent of their evil ways. However, because he hated the Ninevites, Jonah responded to God's message with anger and reluctance.

It is easy for us to condemn Jonah for not wanting to deliver God's message to the Ninevites; however, we must understand his reluctance. The Assyrians were Israel's worst enemy; they had committed many atrocities against them. Jonah hated them and wanted vengeance. He couldn't understand why God would want to extend mercy to them, let alone show them love and compassion, so he decided to run away. This is what happens:
- God sends a violent storm as Jonah makes his way by boat to Tarshish.
- He's thrown overboard, and God prepares a fish to swallow him.
- After spending three days and three nights in the belly of the fish, God orders the fish to vomit him out.

- Jonah finally goes to Nineveh, and the Ninevites repent and are spared God's judgment.

One would have thought that Jonah would have been happy that the people repented, but not so; he continues to sulk and keeps complaining to God. "I know that you are a gracious and compassionate God, slow to anger and abounding in love." (4:2) Jonah is self-centred and lacks compassion, and cannot even appreciate what God has done for the Ninevites. He wants them to be destroyed. He cannot accept that the gospel is for everyone; God does not want any of us to perish in our sins. Are we sometimes like Jonah, wanting swift judgment to overtake those who have wronged us?

Today's Prayer: Lord, help me to be obedient even when you may ask me to do things that I am afraid to do and I feel like running away from you. Make me willing to respond to your call. Amen.

February 12

GRACE, HOW AMAZING! (2)

'But the Lord replied, "Is it right for you to be angry?"' (Johan 4:4)

Jonah finally delivers God's message to the Ninevites, and they repent. Believe it or not, he is furious! He didn't want God to forgive them. He was so mad with God for His mercy and compassion and grace that he asked God to take his life. "Now, Lord, take away my life, for it is better for me to die than to live." (4:3) Isn't it strange how happy he was when God saved him from the belly of the fish, but in his selfishness, he was angry that God had saved the Ninevites.

Jonah is not unlike us in his transparency; we can see so much of ourselves in him. One commentary says, "We can see right through him and most of what we see we don't like. He reminds us too much of ourselves, fearful, selfish, spiteful and proud." We always want to get even with those who hurt us.

Jonah begins to argue with God; however, he acknowledges that He is a "gracious and compassionate God, slow to anger and abounding in love, a God who relents from sending calamity." But, as far as he was concerned, God should not have saved Nineveh. Why was he so angry? He, like his fellow Jews, did not want to share the gospel with the Gentiles and felt that God should not freely offer salvation to the wicked Ninevites.

What are so amazing in this narrative are God's patience, love, mercy, and grace towards Jonah. Although he ran away from God, Jonah was given a second chance. The same applies to us today, for God in His mercy is willing to forgive us and give us a second chance, no matter how much we have messed up. God was patient with Jonah and did not reject him, but was teaching him that everyone deserves forgiveness and salvation. His message is for everyone.

Are you running away from God today? Are you saying no to His call? Are you refusing to repent of your sins because you think they are too many and that God won't forgive you? Remember that God loves and cares deeply for each of us, even when we disappoint Him.

The word for today is: We have a great responsibility to obey God, because our disobedience and sin can prevent us and others from being saved in His kingdom. God's purpose will always be accomplished with or without us. Jonah could not outrun God's purpose; he tried and failed and suffered the consequences. However, through it all, God's love and compassion shone through because He loves us and wants to save us.

Today's Prayer: Lord, you know I have been running away from you. I surrender all to you so you can use me to accomplish your mission. Amen.

February 13

HEART TRANSPLANTS

"I will give you a new heart and put a new spirit in you. I will remove your heart of stone and give you a heart of flesh." (Ezekiel 36:26)

A heart transplant is sometimes given to patients to replace their damaged or failing heart. This usually happens for severe heart conditions when other methods fail. Physically speaking, not everyone requires a heart transplant. In Ezekiel 36: 25-27 God, through the prophet, promised to restore His people Israel, not only physically but also spiritually. He would give them a new heart and put His Spirit in them, meaning a transformation would take place as a result.

Like Israel, you too need to be transformed; you need a new heart, so your life can be changed and you can be empowered to do God's work. However, being born in sin and shaped in iniquity, we all have an incurable heart condition needing an operation that only the Master Surgeon can perform.

Is your heart hardened by sin? No matter how sinful your heart is right now, God can perform heart surgery on you and replace your old heart with a new one. He will give you a fresh start. You can have all your sins washed away, and if you are willing to accept Him, He will put His Spirit in you. You might think you can change yourself or even patch up the old heart, but not so; where God is concerned, you have no power in yourself to bring about the change that you need.

Jeremiah the prophet says it like this, "The heart is deceitful above all things and beyond cure, who can understand it?" You cannot even patch up that old heart; it needs to be changed by God Himself. God makes it clear that the sin problem is a matter of the heart. Your heart is inclined towards sin from the moment you were born. King David expresses the sin problem quite succinctly when he says, "Surely I was sinful at birth, sinful from the time my mother conceived me." (Psalm 51:5) He meant that he was not just a sinner by practice but also by nature.

The only one who can perform heart surgery on you is the One who was not born in sin, Jesus Christ, the only sinless One! He was sinless from the time of conception. We are told by Peter that, "He committed no sin and no deceit was found in His mouth." (1 Peter 2:22). It is therefore reassuring that you can put all your trust in the Master Surgeon to perform heart surgery on you because He is the sinless One.

Today's Prayer: Father, I recognise that you are the only one who can offer me a new heart, help me to accept your promise so my sins can be washed away and I can begin a fresh start in my life. Amen.

February 14

DO NOT BE AFRAID

"Have I not commanded you? Be strong and courageous. Do not be afraid; do not be discouraged, for the Lord your God will be with you wherever you go." (Joshua 1:9)

We all have fears of some kind; however, there are individuals whose fears can prevent them from doing what they want to do. Some are afraid of flying, afraid of speaking in public, or afraid of spiders. When fears become irrational, they are referred to as phobias. "A phobia is an anxiety disorder, defined by an irrational, unrealistic, persistent and excessive fear of an object or situation..."

Some people's lives have been crippled by fear. It was the billionaire Warren Buffett who admitted that he was once terrified of speaking in public, and he knew that if he didn't do something about it, it would end his career. Franklin Roosevelt, one-time president of the United States of America, once had a fear of fire. He was severely disabled after having been affected by polio. His fear developed when he became obsessed with the thought that he would probably not be able to escape because of his disability. However, both these individuals were able to overcome their fear and became successful.

When Joshua succeeded Moses as Israel's leader, he must have been fearful when he realised the enormity of the task that lay ahead of him. His job consisted of leading more than two million stiff-necked and rebellious people into a strange country and conquering it. He knew how difficult and troublesome they were. He had witnessed the challenges Moses had faced.

However, before Joshua became obsessed with fear, he knew he had nothing to fear, unless he had forgotten how God had led Moses. It seemed that God did not even allow him to think about fear, for the chapter opens with these words of reassurance and promise, "Be strong and very courageous. Be careful to obey all the law my servant Moses gave you: do not turn from it to the right or to the left...Do not be afraid, do not be discouraged, for the Lord your God will be with you wherever you go." (Joshua 1:7-9)

Are you afraid of moving forward in life because you are crippled by fear? The good news is that you needn't fear, for the solution is found in God's word; obedience to Him, reading and studying His word and trusting Him. Psalm 118:6 says, "The Lord is with me; I will not be afraid. What can mere mortals do to me?" Through the prophet Isaiah, God reminds us that He will help us. "For I am the Lord your God who takes hold of your right hand and says to you, do not fear; I will help you." (Isaiah 41:13) What beautiful imagery, God holding you by the hand when you are fearful.

Today's Prayer: Lord, help me to put my hand in yours when I feel afraid. You have promised that you will never leave me or forsake me. Amen.

February 15

GOOD NEWS

"Today in the town of David a Saviour has been born to you; He is the Messiah, the Lord." (Luke 2:11)

When we receive good news, it makes us feel happy because our bodies produce hormones that result in a feeling of happiness, stress levels decrease, and we experience an increase in overall heart health.

When the angels appeared to the shepherds on that eventful night, the greatest event in history had just taken place. The Messiah, Saviour of the world, had been born! The Jews had waited for ages for this momentous event. However, there was no fanfare on the streets of Bethlehem; the announcement came to humble shepherds. They were terrified at first, but their fear soon turned to joy when they heard the good news of the Messiah's birth, accompanied by rapturous music from the heavenly choir.

"Now there was a man in Jerusalem called Simeon, who was righteous and devout." (Luke 2:25) He too was awaiting good news of the birth of Christ, but on the eighth day after His birth, Simeon, to whom God had revealed that he would see the Messiah before dying, was privileged to take the baby Jesus in his arms and praise God. What an honour! Can you imagine the joy that filled his heart when he held the baby Jesus in his arms?

There was yet another who would experience similar joy – Anna the prophetess. The Holy Spirit had revealed to her that she would also be privileged to see the Messiah before she died. What good news! She could hardly wait for His arrival, so much so that "she never left the temple but worshipped night and day, fasting and praying." (Luke 2:3) When the baby Jesus arrived at the temple that day with His parents, like Simeon, her heart was full of joy as she gave thanks to God for the fulfilment of His promise.

There's still more good News, Jesus is coming back for the second time, and His coming is nearer than when we first believed. He will be coming back 'with power and great glory'. One writer says, "It will not be a secret event but rather the most incredible event that the world has ever seen..."

This is good news; in fact, the best news that we have heard. Are you willing to spread the good news? There is so much bad news these days; people want to hear some good news, so go and tell them that Jesus is coming again. It's the best news they will hear. He is coming back again, and no one or anything can stop Him.

Today's Prayer: Lord, I have heard the good news of your return, and while I am waiting, give me the courage to tell others that your coming is soon. Amen.

February 16

WHO IS JESUS?

"The beginning of the Good News about Jesus the Messiah, the Son of God..." (Luke 1:1)

Mark did not doubt at all who Jesus is. He is the Messiah, the Son of God. Who do you say He is? In fact, Jesus asked that very question to his disciples. 'When Jesus came to the region of Caesarea Philippi, He asked his disciples "Who do people say the Son of Man is?" They replied, "Some say John the Baptist, others say Elijah and still others, Jeremiah or one of the prophets."' (Matthew 16:14) Even to this day, many are still asking who Jesus is. In the book of Mark, Jesus is presented as:

The Son of God. He demonstrates his divinity by overcoming disease and death. Mark also describes Jesus as a human being, but not before telling us that he is divine first of all.

Jesus is the Holy One of God. (Mark 1: 24) We must also recognise Him as the holy one of God. In the book of Mark, we find that even demons recognised Him.

Jesus is both Teacher and Itinerant Preacher. While here on earth, He spent time teaching His disciples and the people. He was also found preaching wherever He went. 'Jesus replied, "let us go somewhere else to the nearby village, so I can preach there also."' Mark 1:38 Jesus preached and taught about the kingdom of heaven. He was the Master Teacher. His teaching and preaching, states one Christian writer, "had a divine seal, being rooted in revelation, which He sought to make relevant and meaningful to His audience."

Jesus the Healer: Everywhere He went, He healed the people, healing physical and mental diseases and bringing hope to those dying in sin. He made the blind man see, healed the crippled man, and healed and liberated the demon-possessed. His ministry brought restoration and hope.

Who is Jesus to you? To Peter, he was the Messiah, the Son of the living God. (Matthew 16:13-20) He confessed Jesus as divine and as the promised and long-awaited Messiah. If Jesus were to ask you this question, how would you answer? Is He your Lord and Saviour?

Today's Prayer: Lord, I acknowledge that you are my Saviour and Redeemer. Amen.

February 17

YOU WILL MEET WITH OPPOSITION (1)

"I am carrying on a great project and cannot go down." (Nehemiah 6:3)

The narrative begins with Nehemiah weeping when he hears the disturbing news that the walls and gates of Jerusalem were broken down. Why was he so upset? In Nehemiah's day, the walls of a city offered safety from intruders. Walls also symbolised strength, peace, power, protection and beauty; therefore, the broken-down walls meant that the people were vulnerable and defenceless.

Rebuilding the walls of the city became a priority for Nehemiah, and so he prayed to God for direction. Not only did God put a desire in his heart to rebuild the wall, but also a vision for the work. Knowing that it was God's will for him to rebuild the walls, he asked permission from King Artaxerxes, whom he served, for leave of absence. Arriving in Jerusalem, he found the people disorganised, without a leader, and broken-down walls and a defenceless city.

Nehemiah did not begin working straightaway, but spent several days carefully observing and assessing the damage to the walls. Once completed, he was then able to plan his next move. He then shared his vision, plan, and strategy with the leaders of Jerusalem, with passion and enthusiasm. Therein lies an example for us; we should plan with God's help and present our plan with confidence to others.

This story presents us with several themes:

i) **Vision** – God put the desire in Nehemiah's heart and gave him a vision for the work.
ii) **Prayer** – Nehemiah spent quality time in prayer as he consulted God's guidance. When faced with problems, he responded with prayer.
iii) **Leadership** – Nehemiah demonstrated excellent leadership skills, planned in advance, team player, problem solver,

iv) **Repentance and revival:** after the wall had been rebuilt, Nehemiah recognised that the people also needed to rebuild their lives. They had wandered far away from God, and as a spiritual leader, he encouraged them to repent of their sins and return to God. As a spiritual leader, you must be committed and lead by example, as you seek to lead others to Christ so they, too, can experience Him for themselves.

showed courage and did not fear opposition and threats. He led the entire rebuilding project and also worked alongside the others. He led by example.

Today's Prayer: Dear God, help me to respond to your call. Give me a vision of what I need to do to rebuild my life, so that others will be encouraged to rebuild their lives too. Amen.

February 18

YOU WILL MEET WITH OPPOSITION (PART 2)

"I am carrying on a great project and cannot go down." (Nehemiah 6:3)

As the work progressed, Nehemiah and his team met with great opposition from their enemies, who tried every possible way to stop the construction of the wall. They tried several strategies to stop the wall from being built. When they failed, they began personal attacks on Nehemiah. However, Nehemiah and his team stood firm and resolute in the face of opposition and criticism. "I am carrying on a great project and cannot go down," says Nehemiah.

If you are doing God's work, you must accept that you will face opposition; you may even receive personal attacks on your character, like Nehemiah did. When you work for God, you will be insulted and ostracised. Follow the example of Nehemiah; despite opposition, he kept going, and so must you, for God will help you to accomplish the task He has called you to do.

When others oppose and criticise you because you are doing God's work, it is easy to want to give up. Personal attacks can be very hurtful, especially when criticisms are unjustified and false. It is sometimes tempting to ask God to remove you from the situation. However, like Nehemiah, pray for strength to surmount life's challenges and He will give you the strength, courage, and determination to overcome them. You might even be opposed by those who are closest to you. In Nehemiah's case, he did not get the full support of the people; some who should have been working with him were among his greatest opponents.

Despite the challenges that Nehemiah faced, he did not give in to fear or intimidation; instead, he showed courage and tremendous determination to complete the work regardless of threats. Nehemiah knew that God was with him. It was God who had given him this vision, and nothing would hinder him from completing it. Nehemiah was able to accomplish this mammoth task in record time; the wall was completed in fifty-two days. What an accomplishment! One commentary puts it this way, "What a tremendous monument to God's love and faithfulness". Supporters and enemies alike recognised that this was God's plan; therefore, it had to succeed.

The story of Nehemiah challenges us to use our God-given talents to accomplish the work God has called us to do. It challenges us to confront biases, injustice, and challenges with prayer and determination, to courageously be the leaders He wants us to be.

What about you? Has God given you a vision of what He wants you to do? Are there walls in your life that need to be rebuilt? If you recognise that God is calling you for a specific task, are you committed to rising to the challenge?

Today's prayer: Father, strengthen me, so I can carry out your work. Amen.

February 19

LESSONS FROM NATURE: ANTS (1)

'Go to the ant, you sluggard; consider its ways and be wise.' (Proverbs 6:6)

According to the National Geographic magazine, ants are the longest living insects and one of the strongest creatures in relation to their size. They can carry 50 times their own bodyweight, and they'll even work together to move bigger objects as a group!

Ants are social insects that live in colonies where you'll find three types of adults living: the queen, female ants, and male ants. The queen ants are the largest in the colony. Ants are highly organised. They work tirelessly as billions of them work together to build colonies. The largest ant's nest ever found was over 3,700 miles wide! (National Geographic)

Research shows that because of their collective behaviour, coordinated actions, and interactions in their colonies, we can learn about their remarkable abilities to solve complex problems, adapt to environmental changes, and thrive as cohesive societies without central control. (insectlore.com)

Ant colonies also teach us about division of labour, where individual ants specialise in specific tasks. "This specialisation ensures that all essential functions of the colony are fulfilled efficiently, maximising overall productivity and survival." (insectlore.com)

Research is not telling us anything new, for King Solomon, the wisest man who ever lived, tells us that the ant "has no commander, no overseer or ruler, yet it stores its provisions in summer and gathers its food at harvest".

What lessons can we learn from ants? They are organised, they are united, and work as a team, and in spite of their size, can accomplish great tasks, teaching us that if we follow their example, together we too can accomplish much.

In Proverbs 6:6-11, Solomon uses the ant as an example to show us how it utilises its energies and resources economically. He warns about laziness and the importance of working hard. God has called you and me to work for Him.

Today's Prayer: Father, I thank you for the creatures you have created. As I learn from them, I marvel at your greatness, your might, and your power. Thank you for these creatures. Amen.

February 20

LESSONS FROM NATURE: ANTS (2)

"But ask the animals and they will teach you…" (Job 12:7)

My uncle, who was a bee farmer, once told me the following lesson he learnt from ants. One morning, he awoke and, as he sat wondering how he would feed his family (they did not even have food for breakfast that morning), he noticed a swarm of ants transporting their food. Although he had jars of honey waiting to be sold, no one purchased his honey that week.

As he sat observing those small creatures, he suddenly thought, 'if God can provide for a swarm of ants, surely He would provide for him and his family.' He became so excited when he thought about what God would do for him. He knew within his heart that God would birth a miracle that day. As he sat there thinking he became even more animated, for when he looked up, there was a long queue of people coming towards his shop to purchase honey. To his utter amazement, at the end of that morning, he had sold more honey than he ever did in a week! God heard and answered his prayer.

There are so many lessons you can learn from nature. God wants us to appreciate even the small creatures He has created. It is in nature that He often reveals so many aspects of His creative power, knowledge, goodness and the extent to which He loves and cares for us. By observing the complex systems of nature, the creatures that He has made, you can be inspired and learn lessons that will strengthen your faith. Only a powerful and intelligent Creator would even use a swarm of ants to demonstrate that He cares for those He has created and provides for their needs.

The lesson my uncle learnt that day shaped his life, whereby he always depended on God to supply all his needs. He also learnt about how much God cares for us and that His creation teaches us so much about His character, that He loves us immeasurably.

As you consider God's creative power and His promise that He will take care of all your needs, you need not worry because He cares for you. "Speak to the earth, and it will teach you." (Job 12:8) As you recognise God's might and power as the Creator of all things, this should serve as a compelling invitation to trust Him, especially when you are being challenged in life.

Today's Prayer: Lord, help me to appreciate and learn from nature lessons that you want to teach me. Amen.

February 21

LESSONS FROM NATURE: EAGLES (3)

'But those who hope in the Lord will renew their strength. They will soar like eagles; they will run and not grow weary, they will walk and not faint.' (Isaiah 40:31)

Eagles are such beautiful, strong and majestic birds, and from them we can learn many lessons. The eagle eye is the sharpest in the animal kingdom, with eyesight estimated at 4 to 8 times stronger than that of the average human eye.

As the eagle descends from the sky to attack its prey, the muscles in the eyes continuously adjust the curvature of the eyeballs to maintain sharp focus and accurate perception throughout the approach and attack. Eagles have accurate vision and will remain focused no matter what obstacles they encounter. It will not move its focus from the prey until it grabs it. We too must remain focused on God and His word so we do not fall prey to the evil one. Do you have a vision? Remain focused like the eagle.

Eagles fly alone and at high altitudes; they don't fly with sparrows, ravens, and other small birds. Eagles fly with eagles. You can learn from the eagle to aim high and stay away from those who might try to bring you down. We should keep company with like-minded people.

It is said that the raven is the only bird that dares to peck an eagle. It sits on the eagle's back and bites its neck. However, the eagle does not respond or fight with the raven; it just opens its wings and begins to fly higher and higher in the sky. The higher the flight, the harder it is for the raven to breathe, and it eventually falls due to lack of oxygen. You, too, should aim high and reach your full potential despite the challenges you may face along the way. From the eagle, we can learn to develop a clear vision, keep going higher even if others try to pull you down, rise above challenges, soar to great heights, and show courage. Rise to a higher level, because that is what God expects of you. You must grow in Him daily.

Today's prayer: Lord, when I feel crushed in my spirit, help me to remember to call upon you to renew my strength. Take me to a height where it will be difficult for the enemy to peck me. Amen.

February 22

LESSONS FROM NATURE: HENS (4)

"Jerusalem, Jerusalem, you who kill the prophets and stone those sent to you, how often I have longed to gather your children together, as a hen gathers her chicks under her wings, but you were not willing." (Matthew 23:37)

In this verse, Jesus is expressing His grief over His people's sins and their stubbornness. Their sin: killing and stoning the prophets; their stubbornness: refusing to accept God's love and protection. He wanted to gather His people together as a hen protects her chicks under her wings.

According to one source, in the first century AD, the Greek historian Plutarch praised the many ways in which mother hens cherish and protect their chicks, "Drooping their wings for some to creep under, and receiving with joyous and affectionate clucks, others that mount upon their backs, or run up to them from every direction; when a predator threatens the life of her chicks, she will gather them under her wings".

The story is told of a forest fire, when, after firefighters had eventually brought the fire under control, a firefighter found the charred remains of a large bird that had been burned halfway through. He wondered why the bird hadn't flown away from the fire. Perhaps the bird had been sick or injured, he thought; however, he soon discovered when he kicked the carcass away. As soon as he did, he was startled as there was a flurry of activity around his feet. Four baby birds came out of the dust and ash, and then scurried down the hillside. The bulk of the mother's body had protected them from the fire.

This is such a beautiful picture of God's protection. In this verse, Jesus wanted to gather His people that He loved so much together, as a hen protects her chicks, but they would not let Him. Jesus also wants to protect you. Will you stubbornly refuse His protection? How many times have you been hurt or traumatised and don't know who to turn to? Yet

Jesus is always there for you, waiting with open arms like the hen extending her wings to protect her chicks, yet you stubbornly reject His help, because you don't think He can solve your problems.

If you are hurting today, do not reject God's invitation to be gathered under His wings of protection, for those who do will find comfort and security from the only one who can.

Today's prayer: Thank you, God, for your protection. Help me understand that I am always safe with you. Amen.

February 23

GONE FISHING

'"Come follow me," Jesus said, "and I will send you out to fish for people." At once they left their nets and followed Him.' (Matthew 4:19-20)

Have you ever gone fishing? I can't say that I have. However, those who do say it is therapeutic as it offers significant mental health benefits, such as stress reduction, improved focus, it's relaxing, and it gives one a sense of accomplishment. However, when Jesus spoke those words, He was sending His disciples to fish for people and not fish.

We can almost visualise Jesus walking that day by the Sea of Galilee, and as He was walking, He saw two brothers, Simon Peter and his brother Andrew. They were casting a net into the lake, for they were fishermen. He asked them to follow Him. 'At once they left their nets and followed Him.' (Matthew 4: 18 &19)

Why would they readily leave their fishing business and follow Jesus? According to John 1:34-42, they had already met, and knew, Jesus. He had previously spoken to them when He preached in the area where they were. Jesus was no stranger to them, and they were willing to follow Him. By the same token, Jesus has called you to go fishing, too. Are you willing to become a fisher of men? Being a true disciple of Christ calls for 'radical commitment'; it means giving up all, especially those things that are dear to us. It means not questioning the call even when it doesn't seem to make any sense at all. One source says, "It involves leaving comfort and prior attachments to embrace His new way of life and share His message."

Are you willing to give up your well-paid job and travel to some distant land to bring others to Christ? In fact, you might not be required to go to some far-flung country as a missionary, but to go to your town, city, or to your next-door neighbour, or a family member. Once He calls you to become His disciple, He demands a response from you. Is He calling you to go fishing today? What will your response be? Peter and Andrew immediately followed Him, abandoning their fishing nets and their livelihood. The call of Jesus is clear, powerful and direct. It is a call to a new way of life, it is a call to a transformed life, to embrace His love and share the message of His coming soon to others. Just as Peter and Andrew used nets to catch fish, in the same way, when you accept the call to go fishing for Jesus, your newfound faith and the good news of the gospel will draw others to Him. If you are willing to go fishing today, respond to His call, for He wants to shape and mould you into a new person, one who will be His disciple, proclaiming the message of salvation to others.

Today's Prayer: Heavenly Father, I am ready to go fishing so others will be drawn to you. Amen.

February 24

ARE YOU WILLING TO GO WHERE GOD SENDS YOU?

'Now an angel of the Lord said to Philip, "Go south to the road – the desert road – that goes down from Jerusalem to Gaza."' (Acts 8:26)

The story of Philip and the Ethiopian official is an intriguing one. Philip was called to a specific mission. In Acts 8:26-40, we find Philip successfully preaching to crowds of people in Samaria. However, in verse 26, God sends him on a mission. Without hesitation, Philip obeys and 'so he started'.

Here he was in Samaria enjoying a successful ministry where many accepted Jesus as their Lord and Saviour, now he is being called to go to a desert where there weren't any people. At face value, this looks like a demotion, but God knew what He was doing. Philip would meet someone who needed to know about the true God, so he obediently followed God's leading.

There in the desert, he encountered the Ethiopian official reading the Scriptures (the book of Isaiah), and asked him if he understood what he was reading. Not understanding what he was reading, Philip takes the opportunity to explain about the gospel and under the guidance of the Holy Spirit, he explains about the Messiah as found in the book of Isaiah. Once convinced, the official asks to be baptised – baptism being a sign of identifying with Christ, showing others that you have decided to leave your life of sin and embrace your new life in Christ. Although Philip was the only witness to his baptism, this was an important step for the official.

Are you willing to go where Jesus sends you? You may not understand His plans or even know why you are asked to leave a successful ministry to travel to a 'desert land', or to faraway places; however, like Philip, obey God's leading because there are others who also need to hear the gospel.

Today's Prayer: Dear God, please help me to be willing to go where You want me to go. I may not understand at first, but you alone know the way I should go. Amen.

February 25

CHOSEN BY GOD

'They presented these men to the apostles, who prayed and laid hands on them.' (Acts 6:6)

In the book of Acts, we learn how the early church grew under the influence of the apostles as they were led by the Holy Spirit. They had been baptised by the Holy Spirit on the day of Pentecost and had received power to spread the gospel. In chapter 5:41, we learn that, 'day after day, in the temple courts and from house to house, they never stopped teaching and proclaiming the good news that Jesus is the Messiah'.

However, as the early church grew, so did its needs. One of the needs concerned the distribution of food to the poor. The Hellenistic Jews complained against the Hebraic Jews because their widows were being overlooked in the daily distribution of food. It could be that this favouritism might not have been intentional; however, it caused a problem in the early church. We must understand that there is no perfect church; we will encounter problems and disagreements. However, how we deal with these problems is important. The apostles dealt with the situation by choosing seven men who were known to be filled with the Holy Spirit and wisdom.

The food programme might not have appeared as important as preaching; however, each person has a role to play in God's work. This administrative task was not taken lightly. Notice the requirements for the task. "Brothers and sisters, choose seven men from among you who are known to be full of the Holy Spirit and wisdom." God's work calls for committed and dedicated individuals. Leadership is a serious business which should be seen as a privilege and therefore should be treated as such. God's work must be led by men and women who should have these qualities, those who are wise and spiritually mature. Leadership is never without its challenges; however, once the situation was resolved, the apostles were able to focus on their ministry, teaching and preaching the good news about Jesus.

Leaders can sometimes find themselves overwhelmed by their responsibilities, but like the early church leaders, they must always seek God's guidance and direction. The apostles recognised that their God-given ministry should not suffer because of internal church problems and administrative burdens. They realised that they could not do everything, and so it was important to utilise the skills of others. Leaders today should do likewise so that the spreading of God's word is not hindered in any way. Once the early church got over these hurdles, the Bible tells us that 'the word of God spread and the number of disciples in Jerusalem increased rapidly and a large number of priests became obedient to the faith'.

Today's Prayer: Father, help me to go out and make disciples. Amen.

February 26

STANDING FOR GOD

"If we are thrown into the blazing furnace, the God we serve is able to deliver us from it, and He will deliver us from Your Majesty's hand. But if He does not, we want you to know, Your Majesty, that we will not serve your gods or worship the image of gold you have set up." (Daniel 3:17-18)

This was not the first time Shadrach, Meshach and Abed-Nego's faith would be tested. They had been tested on the point of appetite, and now it was about worship; to whom would they show allegiance?

In ancient Babylon, statues were frequently worshipped. One commentary says that Nebuchadnezzar hoped to use this huge image that he had made to unite the nation and solidify his power by centralising worship. As the supreme ruler of Babylon, this proud monarch expected everyone to obey him. As the proclamation went out, nations and people of every language were commanded to fall and worship the image of gold that he had set up. As the nation's ruler of Babylon, he expected everyone to obey him. If anyone dared to disobey, they would be immediately thrown into a blazing furnace. The fire was made so hot that no one could survive.

Would anyone dare to disobey the king whose demands were extreme and cruel? In the narrative, we are not told if there were others who did not obey the king's command; however, we are told that the three Hebrews, Shadrach, Meshach and Abednego, defied the king and refused to bow down to the image. Furious with rage, the king questioned their actions and told them categorically that no god would be able to deliver them out of his hands. They were determined to be true to their God and were determined to worship none other. Not knowing whether they would be delivered from the fire, they told the king that the God they served was able to deliver them; even if He didn't, they would not serve his god or bow down to his image.

Although given a second chance by the king, they still refused. However, they could have made excuses, such as: 'we'll fall, but not actually worship', or 'we won't become idol worshipper, but will worship just this once and then ask God to forgive us'. They knew better than to violate God's law, which clearly states we should have no other gods before Him, so they chose to remain faithful to Him no matter what happened.

These men were ready to stand for God, not knowing whether He would deliver them or not, but God did. And He will deliver you too if you remain faithful.

Today's prayer: Dear God, help me to live a godly life in this sinful world and when I go through trials, grant me the courage to remain faithful. Amen.

February 27

FROM PRISON TO PALACE

'The Lord was with Joseph so that he prospered, and he lived in the house of his Egyptian master.' (Genesis 39:2)

The story of Joseph is told in Genesis chapters 30-50. These chapters catalogue the many hardships he experienced in his early years. His brothers hated him, conspired against him, and tried to kill him. He was betrayed and deserted by them, and sold into slavery, and taken to Egypt. In Egypt, he was exposed to sexual temptation by his master's wife, who lied and accused him. Although he maintained his integrity, he was falsely imprisoned and forgotten in prison by those he had helped.

As the narrative unfolds, you will notice that he did not complain or keep feeling sorry for himself, nor did he spend time asking, "Why me?" He had every reason to despair and give up. However, with each setback, Joseph appears more positive, more resilient, and stronger. How did he manage to do that? The answer is repeated four times in Genesis chapter 39, "The Lord was with Joseph so that he prospered..." Joseph knew and acknowledged that God was with him and those who met him were also aware of that. He was known for his personal integrity. Knowing that God is with you makes you confident that, whatever the challenge or setback, He will sustain you through things that would most certainly destroy your faith in Him and cause you to lose hope.

Rather than become resentful and unforgiving, Joseph chose to forgive. As a slave and prisoner, he was diligent and had a positive attitude. He knew that God was with him and that one day he would prevail, and he did! He eventually left prison to become one of the most powerful rulers in Egypt, and under his rulership and unwavering trust in God, he saved the nation from a dreadful famine.

Are you facing a challenging time in your life? Does your predicament seem hopeless? Are you feeling helpless? Learn lessons from Joseph's life. He remained faithful and steadfast during his trials and was able to say to his brothers, "You intended to harm me, but God intended it for good to accomplish what is now being done, the saving of many lives." No matter what happens, God's purpose will ultimately prevail. He can use any situation for good, even when others intend it for evil, as we can see in this story. Joseph made the right choices despite being tempted to sin against God. What emerges from this story is that, despite the circumstances in which we find ourselves, it is the way we respond to them that will determine the outcome. We must recognise God's hand at work in whatever situation we find ourselves, knowing that He is with us, He's in control, and that He has a plan for our lives.

Today's Prayer: Lord, help me to remain positive and focused, and use failures as stepping stones to success. Amen.

February 28

THE RETURN OF THE PRODIGAL. (1)

"I will set out and go back to my father and say to Him: Father, I have sinned against heaven and against you." (Luke 15:18)

In Luke chapter 15:11-31, Jesus tells the parable of two sons and their father. The younger one said to his father, "Father, give me my share of the estate." So, he divided his property between them. Not long after that, the younger son got together all he had, set off for a distant country and there squandered his wealth in wild living.

Asking for his share of his father's estate was unthinkable and disrespectful, especially when we consider the culture and norms of the Middle Eastern country in which the story is set. As the younger son, he was entitled to one-third, with the elder son receiving two-thirds. The younger son's behaviour showed arrogant disregard for his father; in fact, it was tantamount to him wishing his father were dead. The boys' inheritance would happen after their father's death. However, the younger son took action and demanded his portion of the father's estate.

He received his share of the inheritance, left home and went as far away as possible. He wanted to be free to live as he pleased. In chapter 15:13, we are told that he sets off for a distant country and there squandered his wealth in wild living, partying, and having a good time.

'After he had spent everything, there was a severe famine in the entire country, and he began to be in need'. (Verse 14) He was now jobless, penniless, and friendless; his fair-weather friends were nowhere to be found. When he managed to find a job, it was feeding pigs. For a Jewish boy to find himself feeding pigs was such a humiliation, and to eat pigs' food was most degrading. The boy had really sunk to the depths; however, like many who are rebellious and want to have their own way, he had now hit rock bottom and began to realise the error of his ways, and came to his senses. Sometimes it might take hardship or even tragedy for some people to realise that they cannot get themselves out of the rut in which they have found themselves. It is in times of utter despair that they will turn to God for help. If you are trying to live your life in the fast lane, you had better come to your senses before you hit rock bottom.

Jesus paints a beautiful image of the boy's return journey. "But while He was still a long way off, his father saw him and was filled with compassion for him; he ran to his son, threw his arms round him and kissed him". (Verse 20) In the same way, God our heavenly Father is waiting patiently for us to return to Him.

Today's Prayer: Father, please forgive me for wandering away from you. Amen.

February 29

THE OTHER PRODIGAL WHO DID NOT RETURN (2)

"Meanwhile, the elder son was in the field. When he came near the house, he heard music and dancing. So, he called one of the servants and asked him what was going on." (Luke 15: 25 & 26)

In the parable, we are told of two sons. The younger brother, as we know, asked for his share of the father's estate, left home and squandered his wealth in wild living. When he reaches rock bottom, he comes to his senses and returns home, only to be met by his loving and forgiving and compassionate father. The father is so happy that his prodigal son has returned, that he welcomes him home, putting the best robe on him and a ring on his finger. He throws a party as everyone rejoices and celebrates the son's return.

Unfortunately, his older brother was far from being happy. Was his father out of his mind? How could he welcome his brother back, after all he had done? The older brother is angry and will not participate in the celebrations; he even refused to go into the house. However much his father pleads with him, the more he complains and accuses his father of being unkind to him. "Look, all these years I've been slaving for you and never disobeyed your orders. Yet you never gave me even a young goat so I could celebrate with my friends. But when this son of yours who has squandered your property with prostitutes comes home, you kill the fatted calf for him!" (Verse 29 & 30) The older son, unlike his father was unforgiving. The father forgave because of his love for his son. The older son refused to forgive his brother. In fact, he even disowned his brother, referring to him as "this son of yours". His angry and resentful spirit rendered him just as lost to the love of his father as his younger brother had been.

In this parable, the older brother is not unlike the Pharisees in Jesus' day. They were angry and resentful that sinners were accepting Jesus. They were self-righteous and could not accept that Jesus came to save sinners.

The older could not rejoice at his brother's return because of his self-righteousness and unforgiving nature.

Is our self-righteousness and unforgiving spirit preventing us from rejoicing when a sinner turns to God? The older brother wants his younger brother to be punished, but the father forgives and welcomes his younger son with open arms. He extends grace to him. Just like God, whose love is unconditional, patient and welcoming. Like the father in this story, God is patiently waiting for us to return to Him, no matter what we have done. He expects us to accept repentant sinners in love and support them as they grow in Christ.

Today's Prayer: Dear Jesus, give me a heart of love and compassion. Forgive me for being judgmental of those whom you have rescued from the pigpen of life. Help me like the father in the story to extend loving and welcoming arms to them. Amen.

March 1

KEEP YOUR EYES ON JESUS

"But when he saw the wind, he was afraid and, beginning to sink, cried out, Lord, save me". (Matthew 14:30)

Matthew records the story of Jesus walking on water. One night, His disciples were in a boat on the lake, trying to get to the other side, but Jesus was not with them. However, just before dawn, He went out to them, walking on the water. When they saw the figure coming towards them, they were terrified and thought it was a ghost. However, straightaway Jesus calmed their fears, saying, "Take courage it is I, don't be afraid". (v.27)

Peter, the ever-impulsive disciple, said to Jesus, "Lord, if it is you, tell me to come on the water, Jesus tells him to come. When Peter said these words, he was not putting Jesus to the test; he was the only one in the boat who exercised faith, so he got out of the boat and began to walk on water! He was doing well until he took his eyes off Jesus and immediately began to sink, and in terror cried out, "Lord, save me". His faith wavered the moment he took his eyes off Jesus.

Therein lies a lesson for us; we might not walk on water, however, we can sometimes find ourselves in stormy and frightening situations in our lives. The truth is, if we keep focusing on the difficulties, we will lose our focus on Jesus and go under. It is not easy to maintain our faith in God during trying times. It is so human to focus on the mountains in our lives and not focus on Jesus the mountain mover.

When Peter's faith faltered, he called out to Jesus, "Save me". Our faith can falter during difficult periods in our lives, too, but remember that Jesus is always walking alongside us. He says He'll never leave us or forsake us. If your faith falters, it doesn't mean you have failed. Peter's faith faltered because he took his eyes off Jesus; consequently, all he saw at that moment were the high waves ready to engulf him as he began to sink. In the same way, we too can sink below the waves of difficult circumstances whenever, we lose our focus. Like Peter we must look to Jesus for help when our faith falters.

When you face challenges in your life, remember Jesus is an ever-present God and the only one who help us. Do you want to walk on water? Get out of the boat and walk with Jesus, and never lose sight of Him. Keep your eyes focused on Him and you'll be able to ride every storm that comes your way.

Today's Prayer: Dear Jesus, help me never to become distracted but to always focus on you. Amen.

March 2

CHOICES

"But if serving the Lord seems undesirable to you, then choose for yourselves this day whom you will serve, whether the gods your ancestors served beyond the Euphrates, or the gods of the Amorites in whose land you are living. But as for me and my household, we will serve the Lord." (Joshua 24:15)

Joshua, the great military leader who succeeded Moses, in his farewell speech to the children of Israel, tells them they would have to decide whether they would obey God, who had been faithful to them, or obey the local man-made gods.

By taking a definite stand for the Lord, Joshua told the people that he had made a commitment to God and was determined that he and his household would set an example by living by that decision.

It is easy to go about life doing our own thing, because God has granted humans freewill to the point at which we can choose to act directly against His will. However, there comes a time when you have to choose who you want to serve. Is it God or the gods of materialism, selfishness, pleasures, greed and hate? You have to make the choice now, for tomorrow may be too late. In his appeal to Israel, Joshua said they shouldn't wait to make a decision the next day, but "today", meaning they had to make their decision there and then.

What about you? The time comes when you will have to choose who will be first in your life. The choice is yours; will it be the true God, or some other god? It was John Maxwell who said, "Life is a matter of choices and every choice you make eventually makes you."

What is your number one priority in life? Make God your number one choice for "No one can serve two masters. Either you will hate the one and love the other, or you will be devoted to the one and despise the other..." (Matthew 6:24)

God has given us the power to make choices regarding our ultimate destiny. Adam and Eve chose to disobey God, which led to the entrance of sin and its subsequent consequences. Today, you, too, have been granted freewill and the ability to choose. "Choose life, so that you and your children may live and that you may love the Lord your God, listen to His voice and hold fast to Him…" (Deuteronomy 30:19-20)

Today's Prayer: Dear God, help me to make the right choice. You have proven your trustworthiness and power in my life. I choose you this day. Amen.

March 3

PROMISES

"Do not let your heart be troubled. You believe in God, believe also in me. My Father's house has many rooms; if that were not so, would I have told you that I am going there to prepare a place for you? And if I go and prepare a place for you, I will come back and take you to be with me, that you may be where I am." (John 14:1-3)

Are you feeling troubled? Jesus' promise is sure. He will never go back on His word. He asks us to trust Him and to have total confidence and reliance on Him, for He has our best interests at heart. Jesus knew that living in a sinful world such as ours would cause us 'heart trouble', that's why He has given us this beautiful promise. In Philippians 4:6, Paul tells us that we should not be anxious about anything, "but in every situation, by prayer and petition, with thanksgiving present your requests to God". Is Paul actually saying you should never feel anxious at all? Surely this is not possible! How often are we worried about our jobs, our finances, our families, our children? However, Paul admonishes us to stop worrying, stop being anxious and start praying.

God's promises never fail; however, He knows that there will be times when you will become anxious, fret, and worry, and that's the reason He tells us not to let our hearts be troubled with the things of this life because He has something better in store for us - mansions! In His promise, He is telling us that there is much more to life than what we currently have. He tells us that the way to eternal life, which He has promised to the faithful, is secure. We can trust Him to fulfil His promises. These words of Jesus are such rich promises that should make us determined to seek after those things that are eternal.

He promises everlasting happiness, and all of us can share in this happiness too. He has even promised accommodation in His Father's house, which has many rooms. In speaking about our eternal home, we can only see it by faith now; however, it is secure because He has promised it. Do you believe that one day His promise will be fulfilled?

Have you ever been promised a gift and never received it? I can still remember as a child being promised something and never receiving it. After those many years, I can still recall the disappointment I felt. However, when Jesus promises, we can be sure that it will be fulfilled. "And if I go and prepare a place for you, I will come back and take you to be with me that you also may be where I am." What a rich promise! He has already prepared the way for us to live with Him eternally. You can look forward to eternal life because Jesus has promised it.

Today's Prayer: Dear God, although the way to eternal life I cannot see, I know I can rest secure in your promise, because your word is true. Amen.

March 4

SINGLE-MINDEDNESS

"However, I consider my life worth nothing to me; my only aim is to finish the race and complete the task the Lord Jesus has given me – the task of testifying to the good news of God's grace." (Acts 20:24)

In the Cambridge dictionary, single-mindedness is defined as 'the quality of being determined and thinking only about achieving a particular thing'.

We find this character trait in St. Paul. In Acts chapter 20:23, although warned by the Holy Spirit of prison, danger, and hardships, he was not deterred; his only purpose, as he says, was to tell others of Jesus Christ. In Philippians 3:7-9, he says: "But whatever were gains to me I now consider loss for the sake of Christ. What is more, I consider everything a loss because of the surpassing worth of knowing Christ Jesus my Lord, for whose sake I have lost all things. I consider them garbage that I may gain Christ."

Paul gave up everything, family, friendship and freedom in his single-minded pursuit of the gospel. Because of his love for others, he became the greatest missionary who ever lived. God is looking for men and women who, like Paul, are single-minded in accomplishing much for Him. Do you desire to do His work? He is looking for someone like you who will focus on the Great Commission that He has given to everyone to make disciples of all.

You might feel frustrated or feel you have failed in life. You might not be getting the recognition or praise for your accomplishments, or the fun or money or success you crave. However, make God the priority in your life and, like Paul, focus on the task He has given you. If you are to do God's work, you will have to develop an attitude of single-mindedness; it is the quality that is needed if you are going to do the work God has called you to do. Paul's quality of single-mindedness is needed by those who wish to carry out God's work. Paul considered that his life was worth nothing unless He used it for God's work.

Are you willing to sacrifice all for Christ? Is it time you examined your priorities? Will you make Christ first? Will you put His work in first place where it belongs?

Today's Prayer: Father, help me to forget about myself and make you first in my life. Amen.

March 5

OVERWHELMED BY GIANTS

David said to the Philistine, "You come against me with sword and javelin, but I come against you in the name of the Lord Almighty, the God of the armies of Israel, whom you have defied." (1 Samuel 17:45)

In 1 Samuel 17:50 we read about Goliath, a giant with a big attitude. He was a Philistine who was their champion. Everyone feared him, especially the armies of Israel. As both armies camped on opposite sides of a valley, each side waited for the other to attack first. Goliath derided, taunted and intimidated the army of Israel, defying the army of the Living God. Clad in his armour and his physical height and strength, Goliath obviously had the advantage over Israel. He was certainly a force to contend with; his strategy being fear and intimidation.

One can only imagine the fear that gripped and paralysed Israel; however, only for a short time, for here comes David. David, a young shepherd boy, could no longer bear the insults and criticisms of the giant against God. He could no longer stand by and hear Goliath defying God; he had to take action. As Goliath continued his taunts, God instructed David to use a most unusual strategy to defeat the enemy. From a human standpoint, Goliath had the advantage over David, however, he didn't realise that in fighting David, he was really fighting against God.

As David runs toward Goliath, he says, "You come against me with sword and spear and javelin, but I come against you in the name of the Lord Almighty, the God of the armies of Israel whom you have defied." With only a 'sling and a stone, without a sword in his hand, he struck down the Philistine and killed him.' (1 Samuel 17:45 & 50)

When the giants of despair, fear, and hopelessness overwhelm you, when you have no more fight left in you, when the enemy comes in like a flood, remember the battle is not yours, it is God's. "For our struggle is not against flesh and blood, but against the rulers, against the authorities, against the powers of this dark world and against the spiritual forces of evil in the heavenly realms." (Ephesians 6:12) We face a very powerful army that seeks to destroy us, and although God has promised victory, we must engage in warfare until Jesus returns to take us home.

If today you are facing a giant in your life, remember David, he conquered Goliath with only a sling and a stone, by calling upon God, and he was victorious. Victory can be yours too if you hand your giant over to God. He will fight **for you.**

Today's Prayer: Father, you know I have no power to overcome the enemy. Thank you for providing me with the Holy Spirit, who will defeat the foe. Amen.

March 6

THE OTHER SIDE OF MORIAH

'Then God said, "Take your son, your only son, whom you love – Isaac- and go to the region of Moriah. Sacrifice him there as a burnt offering on a mountain that I will show you." (Genesis 22:2)

God sometimes asks us to do some very strange things. I imagine Abraham was alarmed and perhaps thinking, after having waited all this time for my son, I am now being asked to sacrifice him. He had waited almost all his life for the promised and long-awaited son, and now God was asking him to sacrifice him. However, he knew better than to question God.

One can only imagine the pain and anguish in Abraham's heart as he travels the 50-60 miles from Beersheba to Mount Moriah with Isaac, the unsuspecting son. It must have been an extremely difficult time for him, knowing that he would soon be sacrificing his beloved son. Over the years, Abraham had learnt some hard lessons about the importance of obeying God. This moment was possibly the hardest challenge he had to bear, but he knew he had to go through with it. He recognised that obeying God could sometimes be a real struggle. In this narrative, it meant Abraham had to give up someone he really loved and desperately wanted.

That night on Mount Moriah, as young Isaac slept, his father could not sleep, knowing what he had to do in the morning. It is very difficult to give up what you really love, especially your child whom you dearly love. However, no matter what you lose God will always provide and bless you with even more. Unknown to Abraham at the time, God did not want Isaac to die, but as one commentary says, God wanted Abraham to sacrifice Isaac in his heart so it would be clear that Abraham loved God more than his promised son. However difficult it was for Abraham, on the other side of Mount Moriah was another Father who would one day sacrifice His only begotten Son. In Abraham's case God stopped him from sacrificing his son, but God did not spare His own Son, Jesus, from dying on the cross, "He who did not spare His own Son, but gave Him up for us all…" (Romans 8:32). "For God so loved the world that He gave His only Son, that whoever believes in Him shall not perish but have eternal life." (John 3:16). It was hard for Abraham, but it was even harder for God. What are you willing to give up?

Today's Prayer: Father, thank you for your sacrifice of love. Amen.

March 7

LIVING IN A STATE OF READINESS

"This is how you are to eat it with your cloak tucked into your belt, your sandals on your feet and your staff in your hand. Eat it in haste; it is the Lord's Passover." (Exodus 12:11)

During the Israelites' 400 years of slavery by the Egyptians, they were oppressed by Pharaoh, the king and treated cruelly. The people cried out to God for deliverance, and He delivered them. In the case of Israel, God sent Moses, a Hebrew who was once an Egyptian prince (having been adopted by Pharaoh's daughter), to deliver them. He pleaded with Pharaoh to free the people, but to no avail. It was after a series of ten plagues and many broken promises that the people were finally freed.

During the falling of the plagues, God instructed Moses to tell the people that their deliverance was nearer than before, and they should be ready at any time to leave Egypt. Exodus chapter 12:11 captures their state of readiness – they were to eat the Lord's Passover in haste, standing, dressed, and with their bags packed and ready to depart from Egypt anytime. This readiness - eating the Passover feast while wearing travelling clothes, was a sign of the Hebrews' faith. Although they were still waiting to be freed, they were to prepare themselves for departure. God had said that He would one day deliver them, and they believed Him. Their preparation was an act of faith. Jesus left us a wonderful promise in John 14:3, "And if I go and prepare a place for you, I will come back and take you with me that you also may be where I am." We should also be prepared to meet Him.

Are you living in a state of preparedness to leave this sinful world? God has promised that one day soon He will return to deliver us just as He did for Israel when they were enslaved in Egypt. Right now, ask Him to deliver you from a life of sin as you prepare for His coming, "For in just a little while, He who is coming will come and will not delay." (Hebrews 4:30)

The final day of deliverance will take place. "He will send His angels and gather His elect from the four winds, from the ends of the earth to the ends of the heavens." (Mark. 13:27) Will you be ready on that final deliverance day when Jesus will come to take His people from this sinful world? The word for today is: Live in a state of readiness.

Today's Prayer: Father, help me, by faith, to live in a state of readiness until you come. Amen.

March 8

COMPASSION

"When Jesus landed and saw a large crowd, He had compassion on them, because they were like sheep without a shepherd…" (Mark 6:34)

The crowd must have looked lost and pitiful to Jesus, scattered like sheep without a shepherd. He, being the Good Shepherd, seeing their lost condition, had compassion, that is, sympathetic pity and concern for their suffering or misfortunes. In Matthew 9:36, the writer also gives us a beautiful picture of Jesus, the loving and compassionate God, "When He saw the crowds, He had compassion on them, because they were harassed and helpless, like sheep without a shepherd." In both the gospels of Matthew and Mark, we find Jesus overwhelmed with compassionate pity for the people. His response really shows the depth of God's love for His people.

How do you respond to people around you, especially those on the fringes of society, the homeless, the alcoholics, the poor and needy, those going about aimlessly in life, those living lives of desperation? Is your response sometimes like that of the Levi and the priest in the parable of the Good Samaritan as told by Jesus in Luke 10: 31-32? They were full of bigotry because of their membership in their religious group or sect, and for this reason, they showed no compassion for the wounded man. The legal expert in the parable viewed the wounded man as a topic for discussion; the robbers saw him as an object to rob and exploit, the priest saw him as a problem to avoid, and the Levite, as an object of curiosity. However, it was only the despised Samaritan who showed compassion and treated the wounded man with kindness, a person to love and to be cared for.

As a follower of Christ, are you showing compassion to others? Or do you cross over to the other side of the road to avoid the beggar or homeless person? In this parable, Jesus is telling us that everyone is our neighbour regardless of ethnicity, race, or social standing. Wherever you go today, there will be poor and needy people. Jesus says, "You will always have the poor among you." (Matthew 12:8). God expects us to show love and compassion and care for the needs of others less fortunate than ourselves. We have no excuse to neglect those who have deep needs, and we shouldn't have the attitude that says, the church will care for them. It is also our individual responsibility to care for others.

Jesus says in Matthew 25: 35-36, "For when I was hungry you gave me something to eat, I was thirsty and you gave me something to drink, I was a stranger and you took me in, I needed clothes and you clothed me, I was ill and you looked after me, I was in prison and you came to visit me." If we show compassion, Jesus says, "Truly I tell you whatever you did do for one of the least of these you did do for me". (Matthew 25:45)

Today's Prayer: Dear God, help me to be personally involved in caring for the needy, for in so doing, I am doing it for you. Amen.

March 9

IS YOUR WORSHIP JUST A PERFORMANCE? (1)

"God is Spirit, and His worshippers must worship in the Spirit and in truth." (John 4:24)

Someone once said "Performance has no place in God's house. God wants a surrendered heart with which to work".

When you come before Almighty God to worship, do you come to perform to let everyone know how well you can sing or speak? Is your focus on yourself and your abilities? When you worship, do you approach God in a spirit of humility, penitence, and reverence? Is He the central focus of your worship? It has been said that worship is a heartfelt response to God's presence, while performance is a means of drawing attention to oneself or the activity. True worship involves humility, sincerity, and a focus on God, whereas performance often prioritises technique, spectacle, and the audience's reaction.

Focusing on one's self can lead to arrogance and pride and a sense of self-importance, because the focus is not on God. Worship should always be directed towards God and not towards the audience or yourself. Authentic worship is not how well you perform; it is characterised by respect, humility, and recognition of God's awesome power. Worship is about a genuine expression of one's faith, while performance is an outward display of one's talent or abilities; it lacks true spiritual conviction. Genuine worship allows us to connect with God; performance, on the other hand, connects us with the audience. It makes you feel good as you try to impress others, as you receive their praise and accolades.

Performance is self-centred, whereas worship is God-centred. Worship can result in a personal encounter with God. The woman at the well in John chapter 4 had a personal and intimate encounter with Jesus. True worship is authentic; it reflects a heart that is honest and sincere, a heart that seeks a lasting relationship with God. Performance can lead to self-adulation and pride; pride wants to be admired and always seeks self-gratification and a desire to be recognised by others. If your worship is about how well you can perform, such 'worship' is not acceptable to God, as it brings glory to self and not to God.

John, in verse four, makes it clear that God is Spirit. He is not a physical being and therefore not limited to time or place. It is not where or when you worship, but how you worship. Worship emanates from the heart. Is your worship from your heart? Is it genuine? Or is it about self and recognition? Make the decision today to worship God in Spirit and truth. After all, your aim should be to cultivate a heart that is surrendered to Him and a worship that will bring glory to Him and others.

Today's Prayer: Father, may my worship of you be a genuine expression of my love for you. Amen.

March 10

IS YOUR WORSHIP JUST A PERFORMANCE (2)

'Come let us bow down in worship, let us kneel before the Lord our maker. For He is God and we are the people of His pasture, the flock under His care.' (Psalm 95:6-7)

What is worship? True and acceptable worship emanates from the heart. It is when we give our deepest and highest praise to God. It is an indication of our love for Him. It is when He is placed above everyone and everything else. He is the first in our hearts. There is no other worthy of worship. God and no one else must be the centre of our worship. John tells us that "God is a Spirit and His worshippers must worship Him in the Spirit and truth." (John 4:24). We know that God is not a physical being but spiritual. He is **Omnipotent** (having unlimited power), **Omniscient** (all knowing), **Omnipresent** (present everywhere at the same time).

Humans worship because worship is innate; we were created for worship. We worship God because He alone is worthy of our worship and praise. We worship Him because He is holy and just. The psalmist David says, we are to bow down to worship the Lord our Maker. It is He who has made us and not we ourselves. Therefore, your worship should be focused on God alone and not yourself. Worship should not be self-centred as it often is today. Could it be that we have forgotten how to worship or don't really know how?

When you worship, you should get a sense of who God is, you should experience His presence which should bring about a change in your life. There is no way in which you can come into the presence of God and remain the same. It is in His presence that you can receive the outpouring of His Holy Spirit.

In his book, Dan Lucarin states, "We have seen the worship of God too often made into a human-centred entertainment event." It is only when you have truly received Christ into your life that your worship will become authentic and God-focused. Worship must begin in the heart and as you experience God's power in your life you will have a greater appreciation of who He is and desire to worship Him".

"Worship is love responding to love, it is obeying the first four commandments, it is expressing admiration to the One we adore, it is recognising God's supremacy and our dependence on Him..." (Cynthia Brown). Do you long to experience the presence of God in your life? Then forget about yourself, take your mind off your problems and make Him the centre of your worship.

Today's Prayer: Lord, as I worship you today help me to appreciate your majesty and change my perspective from an earthly one to a heavenly one. Amen.

March 11

THE JOY OF WALKING WITH GOD

"Enoch walked faithfully with God; then he was no more, because God took him away." (Genesis 5:24)

When I read this verse of Scripture my imagination begins to run wild. In the King James Version it says, 'Enoch walked with God and he was not for God took him'. It is such a mysterious text. I imagine Enoch going out for a walk one day and God said to him, Enoch you have been so faithful to me, why don't you just come home and live with me? And that was it, no one saw him anymore – gone, a missing person!

This is such an amazing and unusual event that it is almost impossible to process it. However, whilst we are unable to understand this phenomenon, what we do know is that Enoch walked with God. What a testimony! This is such a vitally important point that it is stated twice. In verse 22 we are told, 'Enoch walked faithfully with God'. This was obviously no ordinary walk, because to walk with God means to have a relationship with Him, that is a life dedicated wholly to Him. Enoch's experience is truly unique and unusual; however, the message is clear: God wants us to 'walk worthy of the calling with which you were called'. (Ephesians 4:1 NKJV) We must have such an intimate relationship with Him that we will go wherever He leads. As we walk with God, we might not always know the direction in which He leads us, but we must follow in faith. Enoch did. In Hebrews 11:5 we are told, 'By faith Enoch was taken up so that he should not see death, and he was not found because God had taken him. Now before he was taken, he was commended as having pleased God'. This is what it means to walk with God, to please Him and in faith stay in step with Him, put your hands in the hands of Him who is the way, the truth and the life. Enoch's life pleased God, and because of this, God prevented him from seeing death. One day, we too will pass from death to life if we remain faithful.

Today's Prayer: Dear God, help me to walk with you as Enoch did. Amen.

March 12

A NEW CREATION

'Therefore, if anyone is in Christ, the new creation has come: the old has gone, the new is here!' (2 Corinthians 5:17)

Are you happy with yourself? Is there something about yourself you would like to change? It might be your physical appearance, or it could be a habit. If so, how would you go about making these changes? If you have tried, you might have failed miserably and ended up frustrated when you discovered that it's impossible to change yourself.

The prophet Jeremiah, in the book named after him, says we cannot change ourselves. "Can the Ethiopian change his skin or a leopard its spots? Neither can you do good who are accustomed to doing evil." (Jeremiah 13: 33). The children of Israel had wandered so far away from God and had become so used to doing evil that they could not change; in fact, they had no power in themselves to change from doing evil. Had they found themselves in a hopeless situation? No, for God through the prophet had been warning His people to repent before it became impossible to change. If one continues to sin and refuses to change, it may become impossible to change. We must be willing to change and not put off until tomorrow what can be done today. God is waiting for us to submit to Him. He is the only one who can bring about change in our lives.

It is dangerous when we become so set in our sinful ways that we lose all desire to change; that is why the prophet said, "Neither can you do good who are accustomed to doing evil." If we allow God to change us, He will, and when He does, He transforms us completely. In 2 Corinthians 5:17, we'll find that He changes us from the inside; we become brand new people! It is the Holy Spirit who gives us new life, and when He does, we are not the same anymore. Those looking on will see the difference in us. Paul makes it clear that not only are believers changed from within, but a whole new order of creative energy begins when we allow Christ to change us.

There is a new covenant, a new perspective, a new body, a new church. All of creation is being renewed. This change is not temporary or superficial; it is a recreation, it is about being born again in Christ. The Holy Spirit now dwells in you; therefore, you cannot be the same person that you were. Paul knew what it meant to be a new creature in Christ. When as Saul he persecuted and killed those who believed in Jesus, when he encountered Jesus on the Damascus Road, he was no longer the same person. He became a new creation in Christ. Will you commit your life to Him today?

Today's Prayer: Lord, I realise I have no power to change myself. I humbly submit myself to you, so I can become a new creature in you. Amen.

March 13

CARING FOR OTHERS

"Is it not to share your food with the hungry and to provide the poor wanderer with shelter – when you see the naked, to clothe them, and not to turn away from your own flesh and blood?" (Isaiah 58:7)

The UK homeless charity Shelter, estimated in 2004 that the number of people in England who were entirely homeless or in temporary accommodation was 354,000. However, rough sleepers are only a small proportion of the homeless. In 2022/23 the number of children living in poverty increased by 100, 000 from 4.2 million in 2021/22 to 4.3 million children, that's 30% of children in the UK! 69% of poor children live in working families. 46% of children in families with three or more children were in poverty, up from 36% in 2011/12. Poor families have fallen deeper into poverty. 36% of all children in poverty were in families with the youngest child aged under five. These statistics are alarming, considering we are living in an affluent society. Have you ever been poor? Have you ever wondered where your next meal will come from? Have you ever wondered if you'll have somewhere to sleep tonight? Have you ever had to flee from your country and become a refugee in a foreign land? If you haven't experienced these things, it is hard to identify with those who find themselves in such situations.

How do you as a Christian respond to the needs of the poor, the marginalised and the disadvantaged in your community? Do you behave like the priest or the Levite in Jesus' parable about the Good Samaritan? Do you cross over on to the other side when we see a homeless or needy person begging for food? God expects us to care for each other, especially the poor and needy. As a Christian God expects you to demonstrate your love and your faith in Him through positive actions, like sharing what you have with the needy, showing compassion for the poor, helpless and oppressed in society. He wants you to have a heart for the disadvantaged and the broken lives in our society.

Loving God is not about going to church and going through routines or rituals, it means loving God and loving our neighbours as ourselves. He wants our Christianity to go beyond our selfish motives and behaviours to acts of service and kindness, charity and generosity to others; "...Spend ourselves on behalf of the hungry and satisfy the needs of the oppressed". (Isaiah 58:10) You have a duty of care to those less fortunate than yourself. In Psalms 82: 3-4 we are told to "Deliver the poor and fatherless, do justice to the afflicted and needy. Deliver the poor and needy: free them from the hand of the wicked."

Today's Prayer: Father, give me a heart to love and care for those who are poor and needy. You have a heart for them and so must I. Forgive me if I have not been as loving and caring as I should be. Amen.

March 14

PUT ON THE WHOLE ARMOUR (1)

"Put on the full armour of God, so that you can take your stand against the devil's schemes." (Ephesians 6:11)

Soldiers need to prepare thoroughly to fight the enemy. They need training before they can enter the battlefield. Training which includes weapon drills, marksmanship, combat simulations, safety and strategy training.

However, the battle that Paul speaks about in Ephesians chapter 6 is no ordinary battle, and the armour worn by soldiers in his time and indeed today will not suffice. Everyone on planet Earth is involved in a battle so fierce that you need a special kind of armour. This battle is a cosmic conflict that has impacted and continues to impact every human being daily. This is no skirmish; it is a fight against good and evil, a conflict between God and Satan, and we are caught in the middle. It is a conflict that cannot be fought with man-made skills and armour. St Paul tells us that "our struggle is not against flesh and blood, but against the rulers, against the authorities, against the powers of this dark world and against the spiritual forces of evil in the heavenly realms." (Ephesians 6:12) It is a conflict between God's kingdom of light and Satan's kingdom of darkness. However, you should not be fearful, for God has equipped you with the armour with which to fight. We are in a spiritual combat with Satan and the evil forces of this world, and for this reason, Paul urges us to "be strong in the Lord and in His mighty power. Put on the full armour of God, so that you can take a stand against the devil's schemes." (Ephesians 6:10 &11)

We have no power to fight the evil one; we must keep our focus on Jesus and resist the devil. James says, "Submit yourselves, then, to God. Resist the devil and he will flee from you." (James 4:7) However, we must be armed with spiritual armour if we are to resist the devil. Paul itemises six pieces of this spiritual armour. The first being the **'belt of truth'**. This means that to withstand the enemies' onslaught, we must depend on

God's strength. The belt of truth is central to the Christian's faith; without it we will not be able to withstand the enemy. We must therefore embrace God's truth, for He is the God of truth.

Are you willing to fasten God's truth around your waist? It is His word of truth that will give us hope as we engage in battle. Truth must be central to our lives.

Today's prayer: Dear God, help me to stand firm and fasten your belt of truth so I will not fall for the lies of the evil one. Amen.

March 15

PUT ON THE FULL ARMOUR (2)

"Stand firm then, with the belt of truth buckled round your waist, with the breastplate of righteousness in place." (Ephesians 6:14)

The second piece of armour: the breastplate of righteousness. If a soldier does not wear a breastplate, he will be vulnerable to an attack, for it is the breastplate that protects the heart. It is the breastplate of righteousness that will guard the heart against sin.

The third piece of armour: Feet fitted with the readiness of peace (v.15). Soldiers in battle are always on their feet; therefore, they need good shoes. God's people cannot become frozen by fear because of the enemy; therefore, having a sense of God's peace in our lives will help us to move forward despite the battle.

Fourth piece of armour: The shield of faith (v16). Faith is needed to "extinguish all the flaming arrows of the evil one". Faith in God and His word is the only way we will be able to extinguish the fires of the evil one.

Fifth piece of armour: The helmet of salvation. It will protect you from discouragement and doubts that the evil one will hurl at you. He battles for the mind. You will recall how he tempted Jesus by creating doubt in his mind, "If you are the Son of God". We must have no doubt that we are God's children bought by His blood.

Sixth piece of armour: Pray in the Spirit at all times (v.18). How can anyone pray in the Spirit at all times? St. Paul tells us we are to pray without ceasing. The battle is so fierce that if we neglect prayer, we will lose, and the enemy will gain control. One writer says, "Only through prayer do you become clothed for spiritual warfare, so don't go into battle undressed." If you are going to survive in this warfare, your very life must become a prayer.

The message for today is: put on the armour of God and you will not be discouraged or defeated, you will be victorious, for Jesus is the one who fights for you.

Today's Prayer: Father, I know that a battle is being waged for my soul, and the only way to withstand the attacks of the evil one is to put on the whole armour so I can be strong in you and in your mighty power. Amen.

March 16

THE BEST LOVE STORY EVER TOLD

'For God so loved the world that He gave His one and only Son, that whoever believes in Him shall not perish but have eternal life.' (John 3:16)

No, the greatest love story in the world is not William Shakespeare's fictional Romeo and Juliet's love story, but God's real love for us, and nothing in this world can compare to it. It is a love that is unconditional, not static, or self-centred; it is real and it is the foundation of His law. God's love for us goes beyond our human comprehension; it transforms us and sets us free from the bondage of sin. His love is the basis of all relationships, says one writer, for "when you love someone dearly, you are willing to give freely to the point of self-sacrifice." That is what God did for us: He sacrificed His only Son; that being the highest price He could have paid for humanity. Jesus, the sinless one died in our stead. He was innocent and did not deserve to die.

In sending His Son to die for us, God could not have done more. He paid dearly with the life of Jesus; no higher price could have been paid. When we come to terms with what happened at Calvary, it should bring us to our knees in gratitude. In fact, there are no words in our human vocabulary to fully express our thankfulness for what He has done for us. John says it so beautifully, "Greater love has no one than this: to lay down one's life for one's friends." (John 15:13)

We are to love each other as Christ loves us. The story is told of two soldiers, lifelong friends who joined the army during World War 1. One day, one of the friends saw his other friend badly wounded on the battlefield, and, putting his own life at risk, went to rescue him. Although his lieutenant told him that it would not be worth his putting his life in danger by rescuing his friend, who was probably dead anyway, he insisted that he had to. He knew he had to go to his friend. Eventually, he managed to bring him back to the company's trench.

On return, the lieutenant checked the wounded soldier and then said to his friend, "I told you it would not be worth it, your friend is dead, and you are mortally wounded." The soldier replied. "Sir, it was worth it." "What do you mean?" replied the lieutenant, "Your friend is dead." "Yes, sir," he answered, "It was worth it. When I got to him, he was still alive, and I heard him say, 'Jim, I knew you'd come!'" What love! But God's love is even greater.

What about you? Are you willing to accept God's love and love others as God loves you? Are you willing to sacrifice the things that mean so much to you? Are you willing to give up your comfort and security and tell others of God's everlasting love for them so they, too, can have eternal life?

Today's Prayer: Thank you, Father, for loving me, a love that I do not deserve. Help me to love others as you love me. Amen.

March 17

IS THERE NO BALM IN GILEAD?

'Is there no balm in Gilead? Is there no physician there? Why then is there no healing for the wound of my people?' (Jeremiah 8:22)

Gilead was a place in Bible times famous for its healing balm or medicine. The Balm was a substance used to heal and smooth. Jeremiah asks this question: is there no balm in Gilead...? Israel had sunk so deep in sin, they had repeatedly disobeyed God and had reached an all-time low. They had deceived themselves into thinking that they could do as they pleased, stopped their ears from hearing God's messages to them through the prophets, and thought that there would be no consequences for their actions.

They had completely forgotten God, who had brought them out of Egyptian bondage. Things had gotten so bad that God said, "Even the stork in the sky knows her appointed seasons, and the doves, the swift and the thrush observe the time of their migration. But my people do not know the requirements of the Lord." (Jeremiah 8:7) The people of Judah were told by God through the prophet Jeremiah that only the Balm in Gilead (Jesus himself) could save them.

The answer to Jeremiah's question, "Is there no balm in Gilead?" is as true today as it was then. Yes, there is a Balm in Gilead, as the songwriter says, "There is a Balm in Gilead to make the wounded whole, there is a balm to heal the sin-sick soul." Although God's people in Jeremiah's time had lost sight of Him, their spiritual sickness could be healed. Sadly, they refused the medicine. A doctor can prescribe as much medicine as he likes, but if the patient refuses to take it, his health will only worsen. Regrettably, Jeremiah could not get the people to repent; rather, they chose to follow the stubbornness of their hearts. As you read the book of Jeremiah, you can almost feel his hurt and disappointment. He responded with anguish at their rejection of God.

How about you? Is your heart not broken for those in your community who do not know or have failed to accept God? How about your friends and family members who are struggling in this lost world of ours? Be like Jeremiah, show love and compassion for others and tell them that Jesus loves them and wants to save them from their sin. Can you imagine Jeremiah's pain when he experienced the people's rejection of God? Similarly, Jesus expressed His emotions when He experienced the people's rejection of God. "Jerusalem, Jerusalem, you who kill the prophets and stone those sent to you; how often I have longed to gather your children together as a hen gathers her chicks under her wings, and you were not willing." (Matthew 23:37) Here we can see the depth of Jesus' anguish for His people. He wanted to protect them and wants to do the same for you today.

Today's Prayer: Father, I thank you that you are the answer to all our needs. Help me not to reject your offer to heal and protect me. Amen.

March 18

THE POWER OF THE MIND

"...Have the same mind-set as Christ Jesus." (Philippians 2:5)

The smartphone has revolutionised our lives, so it would appear. Our mobile phones include functionality beyond making calls and sending messages. Most smartphones have the capacity to display photos, play videos, check and send emails and surf the web. This is truly an amazing man-made miracle, yet cradled in our cranial cavity, God has created a living computer, the human brain, to which there is no comparison. The brain is the most complicated mechanism known. It is beyond human comprehension. When we consider the intricacies of the brain, there has to be a great designer who has put it all together. Little wonder, the psalmist David proclaims, "I will praise you because I am fearfully and wonderfully made, your works are wonderful, I know that full well." (Psalm 139:14) The mind can be described as the capital of our body, and it is where our thoughts develop. The mind and the body are strongly related, and when one is affected, the other is also affected.

The following story shows the power of the mind. Liu Shih-Kun was an esteemed concert pianist in China until the Cultural Revolution banned all things of Western influence. He was imprisoned because he would not give up his music. In prison, he had no music book or piano on which to practise; however, six years later, for propaganda reasons, he was asked to play in Beijing with the Philadelphia Orchestra. After years of imprisonment and no piano to practise on, he performed brilliantly! How did he manage to do that? For seven and a half years, Liu disciplined himself to shut out negative thoughts and practised hour after hour on an imaginary piano. Such is the power of the mind.

Each of us has the capacity to control our thoughts and therefore can direct the course of our will. We decide whether we do right or wrong. Since the mind is so powerful, we need God's help in controlling our thoughts. In Philippians 2:5, Paul says: "...Have the same mind-set as Christ Jesus."

Today's Prayer: Father, please help me to control my mind. Fill it with pure thoughts. Amen

March 19

FORGET WHAT IS BEHIND

"Brothers and sisters, I do not consider myself yet to have taken hold of it. But one thing I do: forgetting what is behind and straining towards what is ahead. I press on towards the goal to win the prize for which God has called me heavenwards in Christ Jesus." (Philippians 3:13-14)

St. Paul had every reason to forget what was behind. He had persecuted God's followers, he even held the coats of those who stoned Stephen to death, the very first Christian martyr. Have you done things in the past that you have regretted? We have all done wrong in the past, for which we are ashamed. Have you experienced disappointments and setbacks in life? It could be the loss of a job or the failure to secure that job you needed so badly, or that house you longed for?

Life is filled with disappointments and failures. However, you should see failure as a stepping stone to success. You must stop looking back and start looking forward. Quite often, when you look back, all you can see are the scars from the battles you have been through. However, when you look back at the battle scars, do you see the victories too that God has won for you? Jesus tells us that to enter the kingdom, we must go through great tribulations. These tribulations could be the loss of a job, injury, or sickness. Don't look back, look forward, for the best is yet to come. When Paul asked God to remove the 'thorn in his flesh', God told him that His grace was sufficient for him, for His power was made perfect in weakness. (2 Corinthians 12:9)

There are times when, like Paul, you'll be tormented in some way by Satan, and you'll plead with God until you are exhausted. However, your focus should be on what God can and will do in your life or in that situation. He will give you the strength and courage to look forward and leave those things that trouble you behind. The Bible tells us that we are to be strong in the Lord and in His mighty power.

Let us forget what is behind and look forward to what God has in store for us. He has great things in store for us, He says: ..."my Father's house has many rooms; if that were not so, would I have told you that I am going to prepare a place for you? And if I go and prepare a place for you, I will come back and take you to be with me that you also may be where I am." What a beautiful promise!

Although we don't know very much, the little that we know is enough to know that spending eternity with God will be more wonderful than we can ever imagine. So, forget what is behind and start looking forward. Don't dwell on the past; let go of those things that might have affected your relationship with God. Ask Him to forgive you, and move on to a faith-filled and more meaningful life with Christ.

Today's Prayer: Lord, help me to look forward to what you want me to become. Help me not to dwell on the past, for according to your word, the best is yet to come. Amen.

March 20

TAKING GOD FOR GRANTED

'Then she called, "Samson, the Philistines are upon you." He awoke from his sleep and thought, "I'll go out as before and shake myself free." But he did not know that the Lord had left him.' (Judges 16:20)

Do you take God for granted? Well, Samson did, and it cost him his life. Through cunning and deceit, Delilah was able to cause his demise. One commentary says, "with honey on her lips and poison in her heart, cold and calculating, she toyed with Samson, pretending to love him while looking for personal gain." Delilah, after putting Samson to sleep on her lap, called for someone to shave off seven braids of his hair, and so began to subdue him. And his strength left him (v.19).

How could Samson be so foolish? Delilah had taken advantage of him four times, and he still hadn't seen through her. Samson was chosen by God before birth to lead Israel to victory, but instead, because of pride and disobedience fell helplessly into the hands of his enemies. God had delivered him many times from the hands of his enemies until he began taking Him for granted. Samson thought he could go out "as before, at other times" and defeat his enemies, thinking that God would come through for him yet again, but this time, he had gone too far.

Are there times when you have taken God for granted, thinking you can play into the hands of the enemy and get away with it? "Do not be deceived: God is not mocked. A man reaps what he sows." (Galatians 6:7) Samson did, and so will you. If you have taken God for granted, think about Samson; he made the wrong decisions because he had taken God for granted. He thought he could disobey His commands and God would turn a blind eye to his wrongdoing. Samson had many opportunities to refrain from doing wrong, and while he didn't choose to be captured by the Philistines, he chose to be with Delilah, who deceived him; consequently, he could not escape the consequences of his decision.

If you are taking God for granted, it is not too late to ask forgiveness. Samson did, and despite his past, God heard and answered Samson's prayer. He will do the same for you, too. No matter how long you have walked away from God because you have taken Him for granted, He is waiting patiently for you and will restore you.

Today's Prayer: Dear God, I am sorry for having taken you for granted. If you answered Samson's call for help, you can also do the same for me and make me worthwhile in your sight. Amen.

March 21

LORD SEND ME

'Then I heard the voice of the Lord saying, "Whom shall I send? And who will go for us?" And I said, "Here am I send me!"' (Isaiah 6:8)

The prophet Isaiah has a vision of God; however, seeing and listening to the praise of the seraphim, he realises his own sinful condition, he is unclean in the presence of a Holy God. His first response is found in verse five, "Woe is me!" he cries. "I am ruined! For I am a man of unclean lips, and I live among a people of unclean lips, and my eyes have seen the King, the Lord Almighty." However, when the angel touches his lips with a live coal, he is cleansed of his sins, and God asks, "Whom shall I send? And who will go for us?" Isaiah immediately responds by saying, "Here am I, send me." Have you responded to God's call? He is calling you today. However, like Isaiah, you must first seek cleansing of your sins before you can proclaim God's message to others. Are you ready for this cleansing, which is required before you can accept His call to speak on His behalf? Before you can accept His call, you must be cleansed like Isaiah, before you can truly represent God to others.

Jesus left us a commission in Matthew 28:19-20. "Therefore, go and make disciples of all nations, baptising them in the name of the Father and the Son and of the Holy Spirit. And teaching them to obey everything I have commanded you. And surely, I am with you always to the very end of the age." Jesus left His last words of instructions to all His followers. It is not an option, but a command to all believers.

Are you willing, like Isaiah, to be God's spokesperson to tell the world that Jesus loves them and He wants everyone to be saved in His kingdom? Are you ready to be purified from your sins today? Will you, without hesitation, when God calls you, accept His call and say, 'Here I am. Send me'? Isaiah did, and fearlessly and courageously proclaimed God's message, calling Judah back to repentance.

Prayer: Lord, I accept your call. Please send me. Amen.

March 22

ARE YOU DISTRESSED FOR THE LOST?

'While Paul was waiting for them in Athens, he was greatly distressed to see that the city was full of idols.' (Acts 17:16)

Paul had travelled to Athens on one of his journeys, and while there, he observed that the city was full of idols. This troubled him greatly. Athens, with its magnificent buildings and many gods, was at the centre of Greek culture, philosophy, and education. Philosophers would often gather at the Areopagus, the high council of the city, to discuss and exchange thoughts and opinions and debate.

It was during his visit to the city, in the market place that Paul met some Epicurean and Stoic philosophers who began to debate with him. They were the dominant philosophers in Greek culture. The Epicureans, according to one source, believed that seeking happiness or pleasure was the primary goal of life. The Stoics, by contrast, placed thinking above feeling and tried to live in harmony with nature and reason, suppressing their desire for pleasure. They were highly disciplined. However, on hearing Paul preach the good news about Jesus and His resurrection, they ridiculed him and referred to him as a 'babbler'.

Paul was later taken to the Areopagus, where he met other philosophers who said he was bringing strange ideas to them. However, Paul was well prepared to speak to them about the true God. As he explained to them about the one true God, although they were religious men, they still had not heard of the one true God.

Many in your community do not know the true God. You need to proclaim Christ to them as Paul did to the Athenians. You must be distressed like him when he saw the number of gods the Athenians believed in and worshipped. Although you may live in a 'Christian' society, you should not assume everyone knows the true God, even though they say they are religious. They may not truly understand who Jesus is or let alone the importance of faith in Him.

Paul's speech to the Philosophers received a mixed reaction – some laughed and ridiculed him, while others wanted to know more, and a few believed and accepted God as the only true God. You are called to proclaim Christ to everyone, whether they want to accept or not. Do not expect everyone to listen, but even if one person believes it will be worth your effort.

Today's Prayer: Lord, I realise that although I live in a 'Christian' society, you are still unknown to many. Let me not hesitate to tell them about the only true God. Amen.

March 23

ARE YOU ONE OF THE TEN OR ONE OF THE TWO?

..."We seemed like grasshoppers in our own eyes, and we looked the same to them." (Numbers 13:33)

The children of Israel, who were enslaved in Egypt for over four hundred years, had, after many wanderings due to their disobedience, now approached the borders of Canaan, the Promised Land. The excitement must have been palpable as they eagerly awaited the day when they would finally enter the land God had promised them. Instructed by God, Moses sent twelve men as spies to gather information about the land. On their return, ten of them gave good reasons why they should enter the land. However, they could not stop focusing on their fears of giants and fortified cities. "We can't attack these people; they are stronger than we are, and they spread among the Israelites a bad report about the land they had explored." (Verse 31)

However, the two other spies, Caleb and Joshua, tried to reassure the people that "it was not impossible and said, "We should go up and take possession of the land, for we can certainly do it." Can you imagine standing before a crowd and disagreeing with your colleagues and voicing what was seemingly an unpopular opinion? However, Caleb was willing to defy the naysayers and negative ten, because he could not help but focus on God's promises. The other ten spies apparently lost sight of the promise and, because of fear, magnified the problem and minimised the power of God who had led them for over forty years.

It is one thing to go against the grain of popular opinion; however, you must have the facts – Caleb did, he had been to the land and seen it for himself. You must have a positive attitude, Caleb did; he trusted God's promise that He would one day give them a land flowing with milk and honey. Caleb believed in God. The people, by contrast, believed the negative report of the ten, became disappointed and angry, blamed Moses and accused God, and were ready to return to Egypt, where they had been enslaved for over four hundred years. By contrast, Caleb and

Joshua gave a different report and were ready to go up and take the land. This was the day the people had been longing for; now they were being told that they could not enter the land. No one had paid attention to Caleb and Joshua's report. All they could think about was the negative report from the ten leaders. The people were disappointed. This then turned to anger, which led them to blame Moses for bringing them out of Egypt to die in the wilderness. They went as far as saying that they should choose leaders to take them back to Egypt.

Have you, like Israel, forgotten the way God has led you? Are you one of the ten or one of the two? Are you listening to the voices of dissent and negativity? Don't be like Israel of old and accept the negative opinion of others.

Today's prayer: I am too near the finishing line to turn back now. Help me never to lose my focus on you. Amen.

March 24

WHICH FIVE ARE YOU?

"Five of them were foolish and five were wise." **(Matthew 25:2)**

Jesus told the parable of the ten bridesmaids. On the wedding day, the bridegroom went to the bride's house for the ceremony. Later, the bride and groom, along with a great procession, returned to the groom's house, where a feast took place. This feast would often last for an entire week.

The ten bridesmaids who were waiting to join the procession and to participate in the wedding banquet got tired of waiting and fell asleep. (The groom's arrival was delayed.) They awoke only to find that the groom had arrived, but five of them were out of oil. The wise bridesmaids had ensured they had enough oil; however, the foolish ones hadn't, resulting in them not being able to attend the banquet. By the time they had managed to purchase extra oil, it was too late for them to join the banquet.

In this parable, Jesus was helping His listeners to understand the importance of being spiritually ready for His second coming. He has left us in no doubt that He will return. The parable highlights the facts that while ten bridesmaids were waiting to attend the feast, only five were ready to attend at any time. They had taken extra oil; however, the foolish ones were not careful to take an additional supply, suggesting they were not really prepared. You may be anticipating the return of Jesus, but are you really ready?

The oil mentioned in this parable symbolises what we now understand to be the Holy Spirit. It therefore means you must be ready spiritually to meet Jesus when He returns. Spiritual preparation cannot be bought or borrowed. Our relationship with God must be our own. Each person must have a personal relationship with God that will enable their own personal preparedness. The parable also draws our attention to the fact that you must remain vigilant and prepared for the coming of Christ, especially when we do not know when He will come. "For you know very well that the day of the Lord will come like a thief in the night." (1 Thessalonians 5:2)

The Lord will return suddenly and unexpectedly. Paul, in the above text, is warning us to be ready, because no one knows when Jesus will return to earth; we should be prepared at all times. The foolish bridesmaids were not prepared and missed out on the banquet. Which five are you? Are you ready to meet Jesus when He comes?

Today's Prayer: Father, help me to live prepared each day to welcome you when you return. Amen.

March 25

TRUST GOD – REGARDLESS

"Though He slays me, yet will I hope in Him…" (Job 13:15)

The story of Job is a fascinating one. He was tempted severely, lost his family and friends, lost all his possessions, yet he still trusted God. Through no fault of his own we find Job suffering physically and mentally. Here was a good man suffering for no apparent fault of his own. He must have struggled to understand what was happening to him. There were no answers to his questions – God is silent from chapter one until He speaks in chapter thirty-eight.

Job was the model of faith, trust, and obedience to God. However, God allowed Satan to attack him with temptation, pain, and adversity, beyond anything that you can imagine. It is hard to imagine how Job could have written words such as "though He slays me, yet will I trust in Him." Satan's attacks were relentless and vicious, yet Job never sinned against God. He just kept on trusting and exercising faith in Him. If you were Job, what would you have done? Are you experiencing trials and grief in your life? It is hard to imagine if your grief and suffering can be compared with Job's. The depth of his suffering is hard to contemplate, yet he remained faithful to God.

When you have setbacks and tragedies in your life remember how Job dealt with his. How do you respond? Do you ask God, why me? Or do you respond like Job, "I know that my Redeemer lives." (Job 19:25). "I myself will see Him with my own eyes – I, and not another…" (Job 19:27) When we consider Job's situation, it appears unlikely that he would ever see God, that he would be restored. Job was looking through the eyes of faith and was confident that God would be just and he would be vindicated. We should learn from this story that God is in control of our lives and He is the only one who understands why good people are allowed to suffer. However, even if we don't understand, we must courageously, like Job, trust Him anyhow.

Today's Prayer: Dear God, as I often do not understand the way you act, I will continue to trust you. Amen.

March 26

JESUS SPEAKS TO A PROSTITUTE

"Therefore, I tell you, her many sins have been forgiven – as her great love has shown..." (Luke 7:47)

Jesus was not afraid to go against the norms of society. One day, He was invited to dinner with a Pharisee called Simon. While there, a woman in that town who had lived a sinful life learned that Jesus was eating at Simon's home, so she went there with an alabaster jar of very expensive perfume. It is quite clear that the woman had not been invited; she gate-crashed the dinner party to anoint the feet of Jesus.

You can imagine what the guests were thinking, however, Simon could not help himself. He said, "If this man were a prophet, He would know who is touching Him and what kind of woman she is, that she is a sinner." (Verse 39) Simon had got it all wrong; after all, the Pharisees believed that only God could forgive sins. Jesus knew about the woman. He knew about her sinful lifestyle – but that did not matter to Him because His response was the very reason why He came. "I tell you, her many sins have been forgiven as her great love has shown." (Verse 47)

The woman left His presence forgiven, restored, and looking toward a bright future. He will do the same for you, too. All you have to do is accept His forgiveness. One writer says, "Only those who realise the depth of their sin can appreciate the complete forgiveness that God offers to them." This woman did, and Jesus lifted her out of a life of sin and despair. His love, mercy, and forgiveness can be yours too if you accept Him in your life today.

This is an amazing story of God's love for sinners, showing us that no one, regardless of how sinful, is beyond the reach of salvation. It is interesting to note that it was the sinful and immoral woman who was forgiven and not the self-righteous religious leader.

If you are weighed down with sin today, remember this: Jesus came to save sinners, and like the woman, He can forgive and restore you, for He is not looking at your past but your future.

Today's Prayer: Dear God, thank you for your love and forgiveness, and your desire to save me. Amen.

March 27

LEADERS' INFLUENCE

"Woe to the shepherds who are destroying and scattering the sheep of my pasture!" (Jeremiah 23:1)

The leaders of Israel who were responsible for leading God's people were the very ones who led them astray. As a leader, you are accountable and will be held responsible for those whom God has entrusted to your care; you are ultimately accountable to Him.

During Jeremiah's time as a prophet, he repeatedly warned the leaders of their sins. However, they continued to disobey his warnings, and for this reason, God judged them ever so severely. Throughout the Scriptures, we find accounts of the consequences of the failures and mistakes of leaders who should have known better but instead chose to trust in themselves, rather than trust God.

The leaders and the false prophets alike prophesied and told the people what they wanted to hear. "Both prophet and priest are godless; even in my temple I find their wickedness," says the Lord through the prophet Jeremiah. (Jeremiah 23:11) They were so influential that the people preferred to accept their lies rather than the truth of God's word. The false prophets had a large following and were very popular because they gave the people a false sense of security. By contrast, Jeremiah's message from God was not met with enthusiasm from the people. He showed them how far they had sunk into sin, and rather than turn from their wicked ways, they sought to kill Jeremiah; such was the influence the leaders had on them.

If you are a leader in God's church today, you have a great responsibility, and Satan knows this and will target you. He knows that if he brings you down, he'll also bring the people down too. For this reason, you must influence for good, remembering that you are accountable to God for those you lead and influence. This is why God said, "Woe to the shepherds who are destroying and scattering the sheep of my pasture."

Today's Prayer: Lord, I understand the great responsibility I have as a leader. Let me not just speak your message but live it. Amen.

March 28

HOW CONTROLLED ARE YOU?

St. Paul speaks about the fruit of the Spirit being the spontaneous work of the Holy Spirit in our lives. The fruit of the Spirit has different 'segments'; each segment comprises a different trait, for example, love, joy, peace, forbearance, kindness, goodness, faithfulness, gentleness and self-control. (Galatians 5:22)

One writer says, "Our character is based on self-control, and self-control is about making the right choices." You can choose how to deal with situations; however, sometimes people make excuses for their lack of self-control. For example, 'It's a family trait', or 'I just can't help myself from flying off the handle'. To be self-controlled is to be disciplined. What about the times when you have faced temptation? Do you just give in regardless of the consequences, or do you throw caution to the wind? A lack of self-control can result in failures in your personal life, failure at work, and failure in relationships and in other areas of your life.

Research shows that the same part of the brain that controls empathy also controls self-control. How then can you exercise self-control? St. Paul reminds us that it is the Holy Spirit that produces the character traits that he mentions in Galatians 22 & 23. They are the by-products of Christ's Spirit dwelling in our lives. You cannot obtain them by trying to get them without His help. If you want the fruit of the Spirit, including self-control, to be manifested in your life you must first grow in Christ. After all, "He is the vine, and we are the branches. If you remain in Me and I in you, you will bear much fruit; apart from Me you can do nothing." (John 15:5) Remaining in Christ means we must accept and believe that God is who He says He is.

Do you want to move from a lack of control to a controlled life? Spend time in God's word for there you will find answers to life's challenges. Spend quality time in prayer and build a relationship with Him so you will gain strength to overcome temptation.

Today's Prayer: Father, give me the strength to remain controlled. Amen.

March 29

DO YOU HAVE A HABIT THAT IS HARD TO GIVE UP?

"I can do all things through Him who gives me strength." (Philippians 4:13)

Habits are easily formed but are hard to break. Do you have a habit that you are trying to break? No matter how hard you try you just cannot break it. We all have habits that we would like to break but find we just cannot break free of them. It has been suggested that to break a habit you can take the following steps:
Identify cues: Something has to trigger a habit; stress for example can make you crave chocolate.
Disrupt: Once you discover the cues you can disrupt the bad habits. In other words, stop focussing on the triggers – don't focus on the chocolate, but on something else.
Replace: Research shows that 'replacing a bad behaviour with a good one is more effective than stopping the bad behaviour alone. The new behaviour interferes with the old habit and prevents your brain from going into autopilot'. Deciding to eat an apple instead of a chocolate, substitutes a positive behaviour for the negative habit.

The above may or may not work, however, why not go to Jesus in prayer instead? Focus on Him and draw strength from Him. It could very well be that a sinful habit is stunting your growth in Christ, so seek His help. It might not happen overnight, it might be difficult to break that habit, because the evil one does not want you to be victorious, he wants to hold you captive. You may recall how he kept tempting Jesus, but Jesus was victorious because He called upon His Father. You too must call upon your Heavenly Father if you are to break that sinful habit. It will be a struggle at first because Satan will try his utmost to keep you bound by that habit. He seeks to enslave you in more ways than one, but God wants to set you free.

Regardless of what psychologists suggest you do to break your habits, it is only as you submit them to God that you will break free of them, you will become more than conquerors in Christ Jesus.

Today's Prayer: Dear God, I pray for your Holy Spirit's power in my life to break the habits that are holding me captive. Amen.

March 30

GOD PROVIDES FOR ELIJAH

'The ravens brought him bread and meat in the morning and bread and meat in the evening, and he drank from the brook. Sometime later, the brook dried up because there had been no rain in the land.' (1Kings 17:6 &7)

Elijah the prophet had been hiding by the brook Cherith when God provided for his needs. He sent ravens that brought bread and meat in the morning and evening, and he drank water from the brook. Who would have thought that God had used a raven, a most unlikely source, to provide for the prophet! However, this is God, Jehovah Jireh, the one who provides. He is God and can use any means to provide for His children.

When Jess, the little four-year-old asked her mother what they would be having for Sunday lunch, her mother's reply was, "God will provide." Unknown to Jess, there was no food because both her parents had lost their jobs and were barely surviving. Like Elijah, God provided for their needs most miraculously. On returning from church that Sunday, they found a bag with groceries with enough food to last for two weeks! This is the God we serve, who provides for all our needs.

Elijah's brook dried up because there was no rain on the land. How would he manage now? God tells the prophet to go to Zarephath, and he does. You must always be willing to do as God says, even when you do not know where He will lead you. Elijah arrives in Zarephath, where God provides a widow who was down to her last meal to provide for him; all she had left was a little meal in her barrel and a little oil. (Verse 13-16) "The jar of flour will not be used up and the jug of oil will not run dry until the day the Lord sends rain on the land," (Verse 14) she was assured.

If you are down to your last meal or your last penny, do not worry, Jesus says, "Ask and it will be given to you." Just as God provided for the prophet and the widow, He will provide for you, too. This widow's simple act of faith produced a great miracle that day. She trusted the prophet and gave all she had to eat to him. This is the kind of faith and trust you must have in God, for He can work miracles in your life. However, without faith, nothing can be accomplished. "But without faith it is impossible to please Him: for he that cometh to God must believe that He is, and that He is a rewarder of them that diligently seek him." (KJV)

Today's prayer: Dear God, thank you for providing for all my needs. Amen.

March 31

ANOTHER MIRACLE

'Sometime later, the son of the woman who owned the house became ill. He grew worse and worse, and finally stopped breathing.' (1Kings 17:17)

The widow of Zarephath (1 Kings 17) had experienced God's miraculous provision of food for her family and for the prophet Elijah. God delivered them from an impossible situation. However, unknown to her at the time, God was about to do even greater miracles in her life.

Elijah the prophet had been staying at her house when it happened - her only son became ill and died. (1 Kings 17:17) You can imagine the depth of this woman's grief. Being a widow in those days was hard enough, and not having a son to care for her compounded the problem even more. In her grief, she questioned the prophet. "What do you have against me, man of God? Did you come to remind me of my sin and kill my son?" (Verse 18)

Little did she know that God was about to perform yet another miracle. Elijah took her son from her arms, laid him upon his own bed and cried out to God to bring the child back to life. 'The Lord heard Elijah's cry, and the boy's life returned to him, and he lived.' Elijah brought the child back to his mother, and said, "Look he is alive!" Can you imagine the joy of that mother when her son lived again! She praised God and said, "Now I know you are a man of God and that the word of the Lord from your mouth is the truth."

God had performed yet another miracle. All we need to do is call upon Him, for He specialises in things deemed impossible. Is He not the one who healed the blind man, cleansed the lepers, made the disabled walk again, and raised Lazarus from the dead after three days?

Is there an impossible situation in your life? Can you see no way out? As humans we have no power in ourselves to change our situations, so hand them over to God who can. When you face difficult challenges in your life that seem impossible, all you need to do is to call on God; there is nothing too hard for Him. Knowing that God can do the impossible in your life there is no need to worry about your present difficulties for He will make the impossible possible. He did it for the widow, He released Peter from prison, He elevated Joseph from prisoner to prime minister, and Sarah conceived a child when she was well past child-bearing years. He did it for them and He'll do it for you, so expect a miracle today.

Today's Prayer: Lord Jesus, I am struggling to find a way out of what appears to be an impossible situation. Thank you for making the impossible possible. Amen.

178

April 1

PRAYER 1

"Lord, teach us how to pray." (Luke 11:1)

Do you know how to pray? In Luke 11:1 we are told that one day Jesus had been praying and when He had finished, His disciples asked Him to teach them how to pray, just as how John taught his disciples to pray.

Luke, more than any other apostle, demonstrates the importance of prayer in the life of Jesus and His ministry. If prayer meant so much to Jesus then we too should feel the need for prayer in our lives. It is obvious that the disciples' request meant that Jesus' prayer had impacted them so much that they felt a great need to know how to pray.

You must understand that it is through prayer that God's power is released into your life. It is through prayer that He makes the impossible possible. According to John Maxwell, "Prayer changes us by drawing us closer to God, changing and moulding us into His likeness in the process." For this reason, you should allow God to teach you how to pray. The lives of many have been transformed because they prayed. In order to learn you must be teachable, and when you are, you will experience spiritual growth in your life. In Psalm 25:4-5 we find David praying, "Show me your ways Lord, teach me your paths. Guide me in your truth and teach me, for you are God my Saviour and my hope is in you all day."

Here David expresses his desire for guidance; so must you if you are to navigate your way around this sinful world. David knew the importance of being taught by God. "When God shows me, He has my heart. When God teaches me, He has my mind. When God guides me, He has my mind. When God guides me, He has my hand." (John Maxwell)

When you consider the three and a half years the disciples spent with Jesus, and the times they saw Him praying to His Father, it must have motivated them to ask Him to teach them to pray. How privileged they were to have been taught by the Master Himself as He provided the model prayer for them found in Matthew 6:9-13 and also recorded in the book of Luke. Jesus provided this model prayer so we can duplicate it. In His prayer you will learn that God is majestic, holy, and worthy to be praised. When you pray the 'Lord's Prayer' you learn to honour His holy name.

Do you want to learn how to pray? Spend much time in prayer. The lives of many have been transformed because they prayed.

Today's Prayer: Father, I realise that is through prayer that my relationship with you will grow, so teach me how to pray. Amen.

April 2

PRAYER (2)

..."Men ought to pray and not faint." (Luke 18:1)

His daughter had become a paraplegic following an accident. After the accident the doctors did all they could, but finally gave up all hope and told her father that she would never be able to walk again. The father, however, refused to accept the doctor's prognosis and said that his daughter would walk again, for he believed in the power of prayer and would not stop praying until God healed her. This father had learnt to pray and not give up, God heard and answered his prayer and today his daughter is no longer confined to a wheel chair, but is able to walk and run. This is the power of persistent prayer. James says, "The prayer of a righteous person is powerful and effective." (James 5:18) Being able to commune with God through prayer is a privilege and an honour for the Christian. It is during prayer that you can be in close contact with God the Creator.

When Jesus told his disciples that 'men ought to pray and not faint', He meant that they should not give up praying, however, He did not mean they should keep repeating the same things over and over again. Constant prayer means to be in communion with God all the time, bringing our requests before Him and giving thanks for all He does for you. Praying constantly means getting to know God and forming a relationship with Him. You may not get answers to your prayers straightaway; however, by waiting patiently on Him, your faith is being strengthened.

The story told in Luke 18:1-5, about the widow and the judge, teaches us that we should persist in prayer. Although the judge kept sending her away, she kept going until one day the judge eventually responded to the widow's persistence. Have you experienced the power of prayer in your life because you never gave up? The father in the story who refused to give up praying for his daughter experienced the power of prayer in his life. As humans we expect God to answer as soon as the prayer has been uttered. However, He will respond in His own time, He loves you and wants you to grow in character to be like Him. Keep praying and don't give up, for in due course you will experience the power of prayer in your life.

Today's Prayer: Father, forgive me for the times when I have given up praying because I did not get the answers straightaway. Lord, I want to experience the power of prayer in my life. Amen.

April 3

PRAYER (3)

'And the prayer offered in faith will make the sick person well; the Lord will raise them up...' (James 5:15)

James is referring here to someone who is physically ill, that the prayer of faith will heal the sick person. However, as believers we should not separate the physical healing from the spiritual healing because God wants to heal us both physically and spiritually.

James is saying that 'the prayer of faith' does not refer to the faith of the sick person as much as the one who is offering the prayer. God expects you to pray in faith; it is a vital element in prayer. If we don't believe that Christ can heal the sick then it is pointless praying. It is not faith that heals, but God; however, our prayers of faith are all part of the healing process.

The account of the healing of the Roman centurion's faith speaks to the importance of exercising faith when we pray. The centurion had heard about Jesus and His power to heal and therefore believed that Jesus could heal his sick servant. He was so confident that Jesus could heal his servant that he even sent a message to Jesus saying, "Lord, don't trouble yourself, for I do not deserve to have you come under my roof...but say the word, and my servant will be healed." Jesus was amazed when He heard this, and said to those around Him, "I tell you, I have not found such great faith even in Israel." (Verse 7&9) The centurion's faith was even more amazing because he was a Gentile who did not know about a loving God.

This is the kind of faith that you must have; it is what James means when he says, "the prayer of faith will heal the sick." Are there situations in your life that call for you to exercise faith and you find yourself lacking? Is there a sick person that you need to pray for, but have doubts whether they will be healed? You must believe that God is waiting for your prayer of faith before intervening. Paul says, "And without faith it is impossible to please God, because anyone who comes to Him must believe that He exists and that He rewards those who earnestly seek Him." (Hebrews 11:6) Prayer is an act of faith, demonstrating that we believe that God exists and nothing is impossible for Him. What He has promised that is what He will do.

If you are praying for healing today, remember that your prayer is part of the healing process, but it is God who heals. Belief, faith and trust are what enable God to make the impossible situations in your life possible.

Today's Prayer: Dear God help me to exercise faith in you and learn to take everything to you in prayer. Amen.

April 4

PRAYER (4)

"Come near to God and He will come near to you." (James 4:8)

How can you draw near to God? It is through prayer that you can draw near to Him. It is through prayer that you can form a relationship with God and get to know Him.

Sometimes, even Christians can find it hard to draw near to God, because they do not pray as often as they should. Research shows that many Christians spend as little time praying as non-believers. Is it because they are too busy to pray, or they feel they can get along without God, especially when things are going well in their lives? Do you lack faith, and doubt whether God really hears and answers prayer? Often people pray when they can see no way out when a crisis arises. As long as everything is going well in their lives most people see no need to pray. They treat God as if He is there for their convenience. However, this is not the kind of relationship God desires. In James 4:8 he says, "Come near to God and He will come near to you." When you yield to His authority and will, when you commit your life to serve Him, and are willing to follow where He leads you, and resist the devil, that is, not allow him to distract you or lead you into temptation, then and only then will you be able to draw near to God.

Do you want to have a closer relationship with God? Draw near to Him, and when you do your relationship with Him will deepen and the more you will grow to love Him.

When you spend time with God you will live a successful life that will bring glory to Him. However, drawing close to Him will take time and effort, but it is through a dedicated prayer life that you will develop the kind of relationship that God wants to have with you. "But what in this life – and for eternity could be better than developing a relationship with a Father who loves us perfectly and who wants to know us and grow us into the people He created us to be?" (John Maxwell)

If you are feeling lonely or lost today, try drawing near to Jesus, He'll never turn you away. Surrender all to Him today and your life will never be the same again.

Today's Prayer: Dear God, it is my desire to have a lasting relationship with you. Help me to yield myself completely to you and no other. Amen.

April 5

BEHOLDING HIS GLORY

"And he said, 'the Lord our God has shown us His glory and His majesty'..." (Deuteronomy 5:24)

The composer Friedrich Handel was bankrupt in 1741 when a group of Dublin charities offered him a commission to write a musical work. It was in aid for the freedom of men from debtor's prison.

Handel composed his well-known masterpiece, The Messiah, which contains the Hallelujah Chorus, in just twenty-four days. Recounting his experience he wrote, "Whether I was in my body or out of my body as I wrote it, I know not, God knows. I did think I did see all heaven before me and the Great God Himself."

St. Paul in 2 Corinthians 12:3 recounts a most extraordinary experience about being 'caught up to the third heaven' where he received a divine revelation. "And I know that this man whether in the body or a part from the body I do not know but God knows." Paul beheld God's glory and this experience transformed his life. When you have an experience with the Lord you will never be the same again. When you behold His glory, your life will bring glory to others. Handel's Messiah is still being played and sung all over the world and giving glory to those who experience this God-given heavenly music.

What an awesome opportunity for St. Paul and Handel to have seen a vision of God and of heaven. When Moses saw God's glory, Scripture tells us that his face shone. Not to mention the prophet Isaiah who testified that he had seen the "King, the Lord Almighty." You too, if faithful, will one day see God's glory when you see Him face to face in all His glory.

Are you longing to see God face to face? In the hymn, 'Face to Face with Christ', Carrie Breck the writer expresses the joy that will be experienced by those who are faithful. 'Face to face with Christ, my Saviour, face to face what will it be? When with rapture I behold Him, Jesus Christ who died for me? Face to face in all His glory, I shall see Him by and by!'

Do you want to see His glory? Make the decision today to accept Him and faithfully serve Him until He comes.

Today's Prayer: Lord, I want your glory to be revealed in me so that my life will bring glory to others. Amen.

April 6

EXCUSES

"Alas Sovereign Lord," I said, "I do not know how to speak: I am too young." (Jeremiah 1:6)

Are you making excuses when sensing that God is calling you to ministry? Are you happy to sit back and do nothing for God? Perhaps you are feeling inadequate, thinking others are more talented and gifted, more educated, and would do a better job. Or are you lacking self-confidence? Jeremiah thought that he was just a boy, and too young to be used by God, that was his excuse. Moses too felt he was not qualified for the job of leading God's people out of Egypt. In Exodus 4:10 we read his excuse: "Pardon your servant, Lord, I have never been eloquent, neither in the past nor since you have spoken to your servant. I am slow of speech and tongue." Like Jeremiah he felt unqualified for the task, hence the excuses. Moses might have felt that someone else would do a better job, or because of his lack of eloquent speech he would embarrass himself.

Do you sometimes make excuses because you are focusing on your weaknesses? Remember, God will not call you to do something you cannot do. It is said that He always equips those He calls. If you are making excuses because of your weaknesses or inabilities He promises to strengthen you. St Paul writes: "My grace is sufficient for you, for my power is made perfect in weakness..." (2 Corinthians 12:9). Although God did not remove Paul's physical ailment, He promised to demonstrate His power. By the same token God will give you the strength and all you need to accomplish the task He has given you. Therefore, there is no need for you to make excuses. It is His grace that will benefit you in your weakness and lack of confidence. Answer His call today,

Once Moses and Jeremiah recognised that God would enable them, look at what they accomplished for Him! Jeremiah was one of the most successful prophets in all of history, and Moses was one of the greatest leaders the world has known, because they were both guided by God.

When Maud Kells, who grew up on a farm in Northern Ireland, realised that God was calling her to work as a missionary in Africa, she too made excuses, saying, "Lord, I can't, I'm too weak and nervous. I could never stand in front of people and speak. I couldn't do all the things that missionaries do." However, God kept on speaking to her, until one day as she read her Bible and prayed the Lord spoke to her in the words found in Revelation 3:8, "See, I have placed before you an open door that no one can shut. I know that you have little strength, yet you have kept my word and have not denied my name." With that reassurance from God, Maud decided to go where God wanted her to go and became a missionary to the people of Zaire.

Today's Prayer: Lord, please forgive me if I have been making excuses. Help me to say like Isaiah, "Lord, send me." Amen.

April 7

TELL IT TO YOUR CHILDREN

'Impress them on your children. Talk about them when you sit down at home and when you walk along the road, when you lie down and when you get up.' (Deuteronomy 6:7)

The children of Israel were instructed in so many ways in making their religion an integral part of their lives. God told them through His servant Moses about the importance of educating their children, and how they should teach them about Him. He wanted parents to teach their children to make Him known to them from one generation to the next. One commentary highlights the fact that the Israelites were extremely successful at making religion an integral part of life. They were successful because their religious education was life-oriented, not information-oriented. They used the content of daily life to teach about God, as they were instructed to impress the commandments on their children, "Talk about them when you sit at home and when you walk along the road, when you lie down and when you get up." (Verse 7) They were to constantly teach their children about God. In other words, parents used the content of their daily life to teach their children about Him. They didn't just tell their children, they practised what they preached.

You might be struggling with teaching your children about God, however, according to the instructions given in these verses, if you want them to know Him you must make Him the central focus of your life too, and your everyday experiences. It is by setting the right examples that children will learn from their parents. You must also teach your children diligently to learn about God in every aspect of life, not just about going to church, but how to care for others, how to care for the environment and for those living in your community; these are examples of an education that is life-oriented and not just information based.

The central theme of verses 4-9 is that God expects you to set the right examples for your children, and as you relate to His word in your daily life you will create an environment that is conducive to learning. You should love God, think constantly about His commandments and teach them to your children. "Write them on the door-frames of your houses and on your gates." God is emphasising the responsibility that you have of teaching His word to your children.

The children of Israel were constantly being reminded about the importance of teaching their children; this reminder is for you too. Teach them to see God in every aspect of their lives, teach them about His love and faithfulness.

Today's Prayer: Lord, help me to make you part of my everyday experiences so that my children can learn to follow you too. Amen.

April 8

BROKEN CISTERNS

"My people have committed two sins: they have forsaken me, the spring of Living Water, and have dug their own cisterns, broken cisterns that cannot hold water." (Jeremiah 2:13)

The children of Israel seemingly did not appreciate what God had done for them. He had freed their ancestors from four hundred years of bondage in Egypt, and parted the waters of the Red Sea as they crossed over on dry land. After much wandering because of disobedience, they were finally settled in the Promised Land.

However, they were never satisfied with what they had, but wanted what other nations had, even their gods! They wanted a king like the surrounding nations, and worshipped the gods that the pagans worshipped, which resulted in them turning their backs on God, 'The Spring of Living Water'. In verse 11, through the prophet Jeremiah, God asks, "Has a nation ever changed its gods?" God is saying that the pagans remained loyal to their gods, but Israel had abandoned Him, the one and only true God.

Who would want to discard a splashing fountain or a spring of fresh, clean water for a broken cistern – used for collecting rain water that leaked and couldn't hold water? Surely this does not make much sense. However, this was the very thing Israel had done when they turned their backs on God, the Spring of Living Water, to worship idols. "They had built religious systems in which to store truth, but these systems were broken; they were useless," according to one commentary.

Have you turned your back on Jesus, the Living Water? Are you clinging on to the 'broken cisterns' of wealth, power, broken promises, self-adulation, pride and self-importance, education, creating and serving other gods, rather than serving the true God? God is waiting to refresh you with Himself, 'The Living Water'. "If you knew the gift of God and who it is that asks you for a drink, you would have asked Him and He would have given you living water." (John 4:10) Jesus was offering the woman at the well water from the living spring, and He is still offering living water to you today to refresh your soul.

Have you, like Israel, abandoned the one and only true God who can satisfy your needs? Now is the time to turn to Him. Your broken cisterns will hold no water. You no longer have to dig broken cisterns, for God is ready to forgive you if you repent and turn to Him. He promises to give you Living Water, Himself! And you will no longer thirst or be hungry for He satisfies.

Today's Prayer: Dear God, help me not to cling to the broken cisterns in my life, cisterns that cannot hold water. I want to be refreshed daily by you, the only one who can satisfy my soul. Amen.

April 9

A LIFE OR DEATH DECISION

'And they said, "Believe in the Lord Jesus, and you will be saved – you and your household."' (Acts 16:31)

It was in 2009 when the 'Hudson River Miracle', took place. Flight 1549 had not long taken off from La Guardia airport in New York with 155 passengers and crew, when it struck a flock of Canada geese causing the engines to lose power.

The pilot knew it was impossible to return to any nearby airport; this was a life-threatening situation and he had to make a quick decision. He decided to land on the river. With masterful and expert skill, he smoothly and gently guided the plane on to the water's surface, saving everyone on board. They were evacuated on to the wings of the plane and then into life boats. Indeed, a heroic action!

Have you ever had to make a life or death, decision? Has there ever been a time in your life when a situation or a crisis arose and you had to make a quick decision knowing the likely consequences of your action?

After having trained and worked as a general nurse and midwife, there were times when I had to make decisions to save a patient's life. You might not have to make such decisions, but there comes a time when each individual living on this planet will have to make the decision to either follow Jesus Christ, or not. This will not be a heroic decision, but one that will be made to determine your eternal salvation. There comes a time in everyone's life when they will have to decide whether they want to spend eternity with Christ or not.

If you are currently in the 'valley of decision', make the decision to follow Jesus today. He says He does not want anyone to perish, but that everyone to come to repentance. (2 Peter 3:9) You may be praying for someone, maybe a child, a spouse, family member or friend to make the decision to follow Christ and it appears that nothing is happening. You might even be thinking that God is taking His time, but God is not slow in what He is doing, He does not work with our timetable. He is waiting for your loved one to repent and turn to Him - a decision that only they can make. If the pilot had not made the decision to land the plane on the river that day, the consequences would have been catastrophic.

Making the decision to follow Christ is crucial, because it involves a commitment to leave behind your current lifestyle and embrace a new life in Him. He is waiting for you to make that decision today. The jailer made the decision to follow Jesus when he witnessed the might, and power of God, and how He delivered Paul and Silas.

Today's Prayer: Dear God, I want to be transformed by you, help me to make the decision to follow you all the way. Amen.

April 10

WAITING ON GOD

'Wait for the Lord; be strong and take heart and wait for the Lord.' (Psalm 27:14)

David knew from experience what it meant to wait for the Lord. He had been anointed king at a young age but did not ascend the throne until many years later. After experiencing various battles and threats to his life, being chased by Saul, he had to wait on God for the fulfilment of the promise that one day he would become king of Israel.

Abraham and Sarah waited until well past child-bearing age for Isaac the promised son. Abraham was actually one hundred years old when Isaac was born. In fact, Sarah could not wait and encouraged Abraham to run ahead of God, resulting in dire consequences. King Charles waited seventy years since his birth to become king. He acceded to the British throne on the death of his mother.

As humans we find it hard to wait, however, when we are asked to wait upon God, we must understand that when we pray and wait, God is developing our character. It is during the waiting time that we learn patience and trust in God. It is during the waiting time that you will grow spiritually. While you are waiting on God stop focusing on the request or the problem that you have brought to Him in prayer. If you focus on yourself or your problems you might very well miss the blessings God promises to bestow upon you during the waiting time. You might even miss the answers to your prayers!

Waiting for God is not easy. You may have been waiting months, or perhaps years without answers from Him. It might even appear that He hasn't even heard you. You might even be asking yourself whether He understands your dilemma, or the urgency of your situation. It is not unnatural to have these feelings; however, you must learn to wait on Him, no matter how long it takes. When you begin to think that God is doing nothing about you situation, it is almost as if you are saying, that

God is not in control, He is not fair, He is selective, He answers other people's prayers, but not mine. However, no matter how long it takes, God is worth waiting for. You stand a good chance of losing hope and confidence in God when you cannot wait on Him. The prophet Jeremiah says, "The Lord is my portion; therefore, I will wait for Him. It is good to wait quietly for the salvation of the Lord." (Lamentations 3: 24 & 26) After all that Jeremiah went through, it must have been very difficult for him to wait upon the Lord, but He waited on the Lord, and was one of the most successful people in all of history, because He was obedient and faithful to God.

The word for to today is: Learn to wait on God.

Today's Prayer: Lord, please help me to be patient and learn to wait on you. Amen.

April 11

CAST YOUR CARES UPON HIM.

'Cast all your anxiety on Him because He cares for you.' (1 Peter5:3)

I received the following from a most unexpected source: "Balancing life, chasing dreams, showing up for others – and still finding time to take care of you, we know that's not easy."

"Sometimes, a few words are all it takes to feel lighter. If today feels heavy, let these words be a gentle reminder for your heart to keep going. Even slow steps forward are still progress – don't stop now. You've made it through hard days before. You will again. Keep moving, even if it is one small step. You are not behind – you're building something beautiful, at your own pace. You've already come so far – don't lose sight of that."

Life isn't always smooth; it comes with its challenges. There are times when you feel like giving up. Coping with difficult situations and circumstances can make it hard to balance your life. You can become overwhelmed with the demands placed on you, it could be work and family issues that seem to weigh you down, and if you are not careful, you can't even find time for yourself.

In 1 Peter 5:7, Peter tells us not to be anxious about anything; we are to cast all our anxieties on God because He cares for us. If you carry your worries, stresses, and daily struggles by yourself, it shows that you have not trusted God fully in your life. It takes faith to accept that He really cares.

If God has come through for you in the past, chances are, He'll come through for you again if you only trust Him. The songwriter says: "You may feel down and feel like God has somehow forgotten that you are faced with circumstances that you can't get through. But right now, you're going under, God's proven time and time again, He'll take care of you. He'll do it again." So cast all your cares upon Him, He can take care of you. Jesus says, "My grace is sufficient for you, for my power is made perfect in weakness." (2 Corinthians 12:9)

Today's Prayer: Dear God, thank you for grace. Help me not to worry, but to trust you and cast all my anxieties upon you. Amen.

April 12

COME ALIVE

'He asked me, "Son of man can these bones live"?' (Ezekiel 37:3)

In Ezekiel 37 God gives the prophet a vision showing him that the nation of Israel would be restored not just physically but also spiritually. The dry bones Ezekiel saw in a vision represented God's people in captivity, like the dry bones they were scattered, and dead. The dry bones also represented the spiritually dead condition of Israel.

You can only imagine how Ezekiel felt when he preached to the people who would not respond to him. He must have felt he was preaching to the dead. However, in the vision God showed him that the bones would respond meaning that the nation would turn to Him again. Just as how God brought life to those dry bones, He would also bring life again to spiritually dead Israel.

In the vision, God told the prophet to prophesy to the bones and say, "Dry bones hear the word of the Lord", and when he did, breath entered them; they came to life and stood on their feet. They were a vast army.

Does the vision of dry bones represent your present condition? Do you attend church each week, but you are spiritually dead? Have you lost your first love for Christ? Have you lost your way? Is your life in despair and disarray, so that you have no more life left in you? Although you still attend church does it seem like a heap of dry bones to you, lifeless and pointless?

Currently, you might be experiencing a shaking up in your life; could it be that God is about to change your situation? He really wants you to come alive because He wants to restore you just the way He promised to restore the nation of Israel. Trust Him because He wants to restore you if only you will let Him. Don't give up on Him as you go through your period of dryness. When you feel like a walking dead, a dry bone, when you feel like giving up because you are overwhelmed with life's challenges, go to

God in prayer and pray for renewal instead. He will breathe new life into you. Spend time studying His word and you'll never feel dried up and hopeless, for God is still at work restoring His people and He will do the same for you.

Today's Prayer: Father, breathe new life in me so I can come alive in you. Amen.

April 13

GOD THE SOURCE OF ALL POWER

'Now I know that there is no God in all the world except in Israel.' (2 Kings 5:15)

The story of the healing of Naaman is a wonderful reminder of not only the existence of God, but of a God who is all powerful and worthy to be praised and worshipped. Naaman was a mighty warrior who seemingly had wealth, power, and prestige. However, despite his wealth, connections, and no doubt, fame and political power, and being one who controlled others, he had a major problem in his life, one that he could not control, nor could his wealth or political standing help. The Bible tells us that he was a leper. He had no power over this terrible disease; it controlled him.

Leprosy was one of the most feared diseases at that time. You can imagine how difficult it must have been for Naaman, a man of such standing, to be afflicted with this extremely contagious and in most cases incurable disease. Since he was still able to serve the king and his country it could be that he might have had a mild form of the illness, however, he was still a leper.

When his Jewish servant girl told him that Elisha could heal him, Naaman set out to find the prophet, who treated him like an ordinary person. Naaman was outraged and refused to do as the prophet instructed. Being a proud man, he expected royal treatment. Pride has no place where God is concerned. Naaman soon realised he had to humble himself and obey the prophet's commands. One writer says, "Obedience to God begins with humility."

Do you have a sin problem in your life that has become chronic like leprosy? Why not humble yourself before God and experience His mighty healing power not just to heal you of a disease, but to heal your sin-sick soul. The same God who healed Naaman of his leprosy after he dipped seven times in the river Jordon can also transform your life too. We are told that when Naaman was healed 'his flesh was restored and became clean like that of a young boy.' (Verse 14)

God expects obedience more than anything else. Nothing is impossible for Him, and just as He healed Naaman of his leprosy, He can heal you physically and spiritually because He is the source of all power.

Today's Prayer: Lord, I acknowledge that there is none greater than you. Amen.

April 14

THE LEGACY

"I have fought a good fight. I have finished the race. I have kept the faith." (2 Timothy 4:7)

As Paul neared the end of his life, he could say quite confidently that he had been faithful to God and to His call. He was not afraid to die for he knew that there was a reward, a crown of righteousness awaiting him when he would finally see Jesus. How about you, can you confidently say as Paul did that there is a crown waiting for you? Have you done the work the Lord has asked you to do? Paul's devoted life to Christ was a legacy to all believers.

According to one source a person's "legacy refers to a lasting impact and the way they will be remembered for generations to come. Legacy can be career accomplishments, financial assets, or a loved one's incredible character." The Oxford dictionary defines legacy as "The long-lasting impact of particular events, actions, etc. that took place in the past, or of a person's life."

What legacy will you leave behind? I can recall my father's words to me while he was in hospital. It fell on me to break the news to him of his terminal illness. The cancer had now spread and from the doctor's perspective there was no hope. When I told him his prognosis, he looked me in the eye and without hesitation told me that he had finished his work and that the Lord was calling him home to rest until His return. Like Paul, my father had faithfully carried out the work God had entrusted him with and was ready to go. He would leave a legacy of a life well lived and devoted to God.

My father's final words to my siblings and I were such powerful words of encouragement to us. He said he and our mother (who had preceded him in death) would be leaving us a legacy, and that legacy was Jesus Christ. As I reflect on those words, what greater legacy could a father leave for his children?

St. Paul gave his words of comfort to young Timothy to encourage him and to us too, so no matter how difficult the task or your situation might appear, you must faithfully carry out what God has entrusted to you and leave a legacy that will be a lasting impact on others.

Today's Prayer: Father, help me to live a life that will bring glory to you and one that will impact others. Amen.

April 15

DISCONNECTED

"I am the vine; you are the branches. If you remain in me and I in you, you will bear much fruit; apart from me you can do nothing." (John 15:5)

There are times when you might have wondered why your phone was dead, only to find that the plug had become disconnected from the socket. Not being plugged into the main source of power means it will be useless trying to connect with another person. Jesus says in John 15:5 that He is the vine, which suggests that the connection between Himself and believers is vital if we are to remain in Him and bear fruit. When believers are truly connected to Christ, there can be no disconnection, and they can draw strength and spiritual nourishment from Him, the true vine, and the source of your growth.

If you are not connected to Christ, you will merely be going through the motions; you'll be like the bones that Ezekiel saw in a vision. When the bones came together, they were organised, they looked good, but had no breath in them. When you become disconnected from the vine, you might be convicted, but not converted. You will not have the Holy Spirit dwelling in you because He cannot dwell in a disconnected body.

The metaphor of Christ as the vine and believers being the branches illustrates the relationship that must exist between them. In the same way, the branches that are connected to the vine for sustenance must remain connected or else they will die. Believers who are connected will learn to depend on Jesus for life and fruitfulness. When you are connected to Him, you will bear much fruit.

Are you feeling disconnected from Him today? Ask God to impress upon your mind the importance of being connected to Him. Through prayer and study of His word, you can remain connected to Him. If you are to experience spiritual growth you must tap into the Source of all power.

Today's Prayer: Father, I want to remain connected to you so I can experience spiritual growth and bear much fruit for you. Amen.

April 16

ARE YOU A GOSSIPER?

'A gossip betrays a confidence, but a trustworthy person keeps a secret.' (Proverbs 11:13)

What is gossip? One definition states that it is "Information about the behaviour or personal life of other people often without the full truth revealed or known". Gossip is a deadly sin. However, it is not one of the sins that is considered a sin; it is not usually on the list of sins like adultery, lying, or murder. In the eyes of God there is no big or little sin - sin is just sin. Gossip is destructive for the gossiper reveals secrets, speaks badly of someone, especially about their character. The gossiper's intention is to hurt or even destroy another person.

Are you a gossiper? Someone once said, "Gossip is spread by wicked people; they stir up trouble and break up friendships." In Proverbs 18: 8 Solomon says, "The words of a gossip are like choice morsels, they go down to the innermost parts." It is not easy to ignore rumours and gossip. It is so tempting to listen and hear more. One commentary says, "It is as had to ignore rumours and gossip as it is to turn down a delicious dessert. Taking just one morsel of either one creates a taste for more. You can resist rumours the same way a determined dieter resists chocolates – never even opening the box. I you don't nibble on the first bite of gossip you can't take the second and the third."

God wants us to stay away from people who gossip. We are to guard our words and be careful what we say about others. 'A gossip betrays a confidence; so, avoid anyone who talks too much.' (Proverbs 20:19) Gossiping should not be found among God's people. Unfortunately, this is not the case. During the time of the early church, it was a concern and St. Paul in his list of sins that were evident in the early Christian church, pointed to gossip as one of them. He speaks of discord, jealousy, fits of rage, selfish ambition, slander, gossip, arrogance and disorder. (2 Corinthians 12:20)

God expects you to live differently from unbelievers and not allow the secular society in which you live to influence you. God hates sin and gossip is a sin against Him, for all the sins of the tongue are deadly: profanity, insults, lying, backbiting, slandering, complaining, and criticising others are harmful and displease God.

Today's Prayer: Father, let me praise you at all times, let your praise be continually on my lips so I can refrain from gossiping. Amen.

April 17

CAN OTHERS SEE JESUS IN YOU?

"You should show that you are a letter from Christ, the result of our ministry, written not with ink but with the Spirit of the living God, not on tablets of stone but on tablets of human hearts." (2 Corinthians 3:3)

Paul is telling the Corinthian believers that they are a 'letter of commendation' written not with ink but with the Spirit of God. He meant that their transformed lives, rather than their previous lives, are the true testament to God's power and grace, and that He is the one who wrote that letter through the Spirit of God.

Does your life reflect Christ? Can others see a change in you? Once you have met Jesus there must be a visible change in you. You cannot be the same person any longer. Letters are written to be read and by the same token, your life will be read by others like a written letter. The question is what are they reading, do they see kindness, selflessness, and love in you? Do they see someone who reaches out to the disadvantaged and marginalised in society?

When Paul met Jesus on the Damascus Road he was transformed by God. Those who knew him as Saul when he was 'breathing out to murderous threats' against the Lord's disciples, could hardly recognise the transformation that had taken place as they heard him proclaim the word of God, with Spirit-filled boldness. In Acts 1:1, similarly, we read, "When they saw the courage of Peter and John and realised that they were unschooled, ordinary men, they were astonished and they took note that these men had been with Jesus."

Has your life been changed as a result of having encountered God? One writer says," One changed life convinces people of Christ's power." What is your testimony today, can others see Jesus in you, the newly created you, for the old has gone?

Today's Prayer: Father, may my life reflect you in all I do. Amen

April 18

REASONING WITH GOD

"Come now, let us settle the matter," says the Lord. "Though your sins are like scarlet, they shall be like wool." Isaiah 1:18

In Isaiah 1:1-15, God, through the prophet Isaiah, catalogues Israel's sinful state. The prophet presents a blistering and sharp indictment of Judah and Jerusalem. God's chosen people had sunk so low in sin, yet they were still going through their religious practices, no doubt thinking their worship was acceptable and meaningful to God. Somehow, they thought that as long as they were going through the rituals, God would be pleased with them. However, God's response to them showed His displeasure; in fact, He was disgusted with their behaviour and compared it as "the whole head is sick, and the whole heart is faint, from the sole of their feet..." (Isaiah 1:5&6)

What is so amazing though, after all God's scathing indictment of His people, in His love and forgiveness, He calls them to repentance. "Wash you, make you clean..." (Verse 16) Despite their sin and rebellious lifestyle, He offers forgiveness. (Verse 18) He says, "Let us reason together," let's talk about it, just like any loving Father would. He offers hope to a nation without hope. "Though your sins be as scarlet, they shall be as white as snow; though they be red like scarlet, they shall be as wool." Scarlet and crimson were the colours of a deep-red permanent dye, their stain being virtually impossible to remove from clothing. The stain of sin is impossible to remove from our lives; it is equally permanent, and only God can remove it. After all, according to the psalmist, we are all sinful from the time we are conceived. (Psalm 51:5)

If you have rebelled against God, if you have turned your back on Him, all is not lost; He wants you back. It is not His desire that any of us should perish in our sins, but that all should come to repentance. (2 Peter 3:9) Make the decision today to return to God, and He will transform you and make you to become a 'new creature'.

Today's Prayer: Father, I want to live a life of obedience to your will. Amen.

April 19

CONTROL YOUR ANGER

'Fools give vent to their rage, but the wise bring calm in the end.' (Proverbs 29:28)

If you cannot control your anger, you are as helpless as a city without walls, open to attack. 'Better a patient person than a warrior, one with self-control than one who takes a city.' (Proverbs 16:32) Self-control is superior to conquest is what Solomon is saying here.

You must learn self-control rather than become angry. In controlling your temper, you can win personal victories. One writer says, "When you feel yourself ready to explode, remember that losing control may cause you to forfeit what you want the most."

Are there times when you feel angry? The maxim 'count to ten' before you react is a good principle to abide by. James tells us to be "quick to listen, slow to speak, and slow to become angry, because human anger does not produce the righteousness that God desires." (James 1:19-20) When you feel angry because someone has hurt your feelings or when your ego has been bruised, it is easy to lash out at others; however, you need to control your anger. "The giving way to violent emotions endangers life; many die under the burst of rage and passion." (E. G. White) If you fail to control or deal with anger properly, it often leads to bitterness, which can destroy you.

Dr Redford Williams, professor of Psychiatry and Behavioural Science at Duke University, states, "The hostility and anger associated with Type-A behaviour is a major contributor to heart disease. People who struggle with anger are five times more likely to suffer coronary heart disease, and people with heart disease double their risk of a heart attack when they get angry." When your temper gets the better of you, it reveals the worst of you.

If you are struggling to control your anger, you might like to consider the following:

   i)   Think before you act. King Solomon says, 'Fools give vent to their rage, but the wise bring calm in the end.' (Proverbs 29:11) Confess your sins. 'He that conceals their sins does not prosper...' (Proverbs 28:13)

   ii) Pray without ceasing. Talk to Jesus about your anger problem, and with God's help, you will be victorious.

Today's Prayer: Dear God, help me to be slow to anger. Give me the ability to respond to those who might cause me to get angry, with patient, gentle words, grace seasoned with salt. Amen.

April 20

IS GOD TRYING TO GET YOUR ATTENTION?

'There, the angel of the Lord appeared to him in flames of fire from within a bush. Moses saw that though the bush was on fire it did not burn up. So, Moses, thought "I will go over and see this strange sight – why the bush does not burn up?"' (Genesis 3:2&3)

God had been trying before this to get Moses' attention; but now He uses a dramatic method to do so. He spoke to Moses from quite an unexpected source: a burning bush which was not consumed. When Moses saw it, he went to investigate. Finally, God had caught his attention! Is God trying to communicate with you? Is He trying to get your attention? As in the case of Moses, He may use unexpected sources or people to get your attention. Like Moses, be willing to investigate and be open to what He has in store for you. Little did Moses know that his encounter with God at the burning bush would transform his life forever. In fact, his encounter with God was the most transformative experience that Moses had because this was his own personal experience with God, an experience that changed his life completely.

Can it be that God is trying to get your attention, too? Like Moses, He has a plan for your life and wants to save you. He wants to change your life. Can it be that you once walked with the Lord and no longer do? Perhaps you have become entangled with the things of this world that are of no eternal value, and God is calling you away from them. I recall the testimony of a young woman who had walked away from God. One night as she was about to enter the club that she often frequented, a sudden feeling came over her of not wanting to go inside. So strong was the pull away from the club that she had no other option but to return home and to return to God. God may be trying to get your attention, too and will sometimes use unexpected sources to communicate with you.

The message for today is: Be willing to listen and to investigate, and be open to His surprises, and when He gets your attention, be ready to go where He sends you.

Today's Prayer: Dear God, help me to remain focused on you so I can recognise when you are trying to get my attention. Amen.

April 21

JUSTICE

"He has told you, O man, what is good; and what does the Lord require of you but to do justice, and to love kindness, and walk humbly with your God." (Micah 6:8)

Justice, according to the dictionary, means: "the quality of being fair and reasonable." This is a quality we can attribute to God. He is perfect and loves us and dispenses perfect justice. However, although He loves us with an everlasting and immeasurable love, His love does not tolerate sin and will therefore deal with you in a just manner. He cannot and will not overlook those who deliberately sin against Him. Jesus showed and pursued justice while He was here on earth. He is our example, and therefore we too must pursue justice. In Psalm 82:3 we are told to 'Give justice to the weak and the fatherless; maintain the right of the afflicted and the destitute.' 'Learn to do good; seek justice, correct oppression; bring justice to the fatherless, and please the widow's cause.' (Isaiah 1:17)

In the book of Ezekiel chapter 18 we read about God's justice. The children of Israel, despite being warned about their sins, still chose to continue in their sin, and when punished thought that God was not fair.
They believed they were being punished for the sins of their ancestors and not their own and concluded that God was not being just. Israel continued to sin although God sent warning after warning through His prophet Ezekiel. However, He cannot overlook sin, and sinners have to be punished; He would much prefer if they would turn to Him. "As surely as I live," declares the sovereign Lord, "I take no pleasure in the death of the wicked, but rather they turn from their evil ways and live. Turn, turn from your evil ways! Why will you die, people of Israel." (Ezekiel 33:11)

God is just and impartial and wants us to deal justly with others. Even the unjust judge mentioned in Luke 18:1-8 had to show justice in the end to the widow, after having succumbed to pressure.

You might be experiencing a situation in your life, whereby you feel you are being treated unjustly. Our world is filled with injustice, the wicked seem to prosper and the righteous suffer, however, you must continue to trust God for His justice will prevail. When you experience injustice at the hands of others, you want to see them punished. We all want justice. However, we too must exercise justice to others. Micah emphasises that it is important to show mercy, justice, and humility in our relationship with God and others. Micah's message stands as a challenge, especially to those who profess to love God.

Today's Prayer: Father, forgive me if at any time I have failed to act justly. Amen.

April 22

GREED

'Then He said to them, "Watch out! Be on your guard against all kinds of greed; life does not consist of an abundance of possessions."' (Luke 12:15)

Greed and the desire to be wealthy can bring ruin and disaster to your life. Jesus warned against all kinds of greed and that you should be on your guard against it, that is, desiring what you don't have. You can live a happy and comfortable life without being rich. However, society would make us believe that we should all aspire to be rich. Advertisers spend time and money enticing us to buy their products, promising that we can live happier and more fulfilled lives. Sadly, this is not the case.

The rich fool in the parable told by Jesus in Luke 12:16-21 helps us understand that amassing wealth is pointless. The man, rather than give to others, decides to build larger barns to store his grain. He had so much that he decided to retire early and enjoy life. However, that same night, he died and left everything behind. God expects you to share what you have with others and not keep it all to yourself.

Greed is an 'insatiable' desire for something; it could be wealth, food or fame. The story of Balaam tells of someone who was tempted by the promise to be rich. He was driven by greed and would do anything to make a profit in any situation. In this story, Balaam was ready to obey God's command as long as he could make a profit. However, his heart was consumed with greed, especially when he thought about how he could gain much by obeying Moab instead of God. Balaam was willing to curse God's people because of his desire for wealth and honour. Balak, the king of Moab, promised Balaam riches and honour if he cursed the Israelites. Motivated by greed, he tried to curse them; however, he found himself blessing them instead.

Balaam was so blinded by greed and the desire for wealth that he couldn't even recognise that God was stopping him when he set out on his donkey to curse Israel. God had to make a donkey speak to Balaam to help him realise that what he was doing was wrong.

Are you sometimes blinded by the desire for wealth and fame? Are you greedy for gain? You can avoid Balaam's mistake by not allowing yourself to be consumed with greed, but by acknowledging that all that you have are gifts from God to be shared with others. Do not allow yourself to be tempted by fame, money, or status, but focus on the benefits from serving God. Think about the riches that God has in store for those who love and serve Him. One commentary says: "If you accumulate wealth only to enrich yourself, with no concern for helping others, you will enter eternity empty-handed."

Today's Prayer: Dear God, help me to think beyond earthly riches and learn the importance of living, serving, and obeying you which will bring richness to my life while here on earth. Amen.

April 23

HANNAH GAVE UP WHAT SHE WANTED MOST

'And she made a vow, saying, "Lord Almighty, if you will only look on your servant's misery and remember me, and not forget your servant but give her a son, then I will give him back to the Lord for all the days of his life, and no razor will ever be used on his head." (1 Samuel 1:11)

Hannah had been unable to conceive, and in Old Testament times, a woman was considered a failure if she was unable to conceive. Socially, it was also an embarrassment for her husband, too, who, by law, could divorce his barren wife. You can therefore understand Hannah's plight, which was made even more painful by the insensitive Peninnah, Elkanah's other wife. Hannah was mocked and jeered at by her daily. In fact, her criticisms, taunts, and ridicule continued for years. You can imagine the pain and hurt that Hannah endured. The Bible tells us that 'Whenever Hannah went up to the house of the Lord, her rival provoked her till she wept and would not eat.' (1 Samuel 1:7)

Although Peninnah did much to destroy any self-confidence Hannah might have had, Hannah seemingly chose the best way to react. She took her problems to God, spending much time in prayer when she visited the temple. You might not be able to silence those who criticise you; however, you can choose how you will react to the hurtful words and behaviours of others. Despite the behaviour of Peninnah, Hannah persisted in prayer to God. At times, you might experience challenges in your life from others, but like Hannah, you must persist in prayer to God. You might currently be going through a period of barrenness; that is, you might conclude that nothing is going right for you, everything and everyone is against you; however, keep praying until God answers. You might not feel like praying; however, you should not give up on God for He will come through for you.

Hannah persisted in prayer, even the very priest who should have supported her, misunderstood her motives. It must have been very hard and discouraging for her, yet her overwhelming desire for a child seemed to have strengthened her faith, and the more she prayed the more confident she became that one day God would grant her request. In her desperation she promised God that if He gave her a son, she would give him back to Him. To Hannah's credit, she kept her promise and when Samuel was weaned, she gave up what she wanted most, her son, to serve in the temple.

Are you willing to give your best to the Lord? Are you willing to give yourself to Him? Hannah gave what she wanted most. God is not interested in tokens, or broken promises. He wants our love. He wants you to give your life wholly to Him.

Today's Prayer: Father, I want to give my entire life in service to you. Amen.

April 24

YOU ARE NOTHING WITHOUT LOVE.

"...If I have a faith that can move mountains, but do not have love, I am nothing." (1 Corinthians 13:2)

In 1 Corinthians 13, Paul helps us to understand that we are nothing without love. He says you may even give your body to be burned, have the gift of prophecy, knowledge, and faith even to remove mountains, but without love it means nothing. You could be well learned, have all the degrees that the best university can bestow on you, but if you lack genuine love for others, it is meaningless. However, before you can love others you must first love and accept God's love.

Paul is not saying that having these gifts are not good in themselves, but that their true value and impact are realised when they are exercised in love. He stresses that of all the virtues we possess, love is the foundation upon which all other virtues and actions should be built.

It is difficult to understand how one can profess to love God and not love others. Jesus says that the greatest commandment is love; first you should love God with all your heart, soul and mind, and when we do, we should love others as ourselves. (Matthew 22: 36-39) Paul suggests that love is the ultimate expression of the Christian life. We are nothing without love because it requires us to put the needs and well-being of others above our own.

Matthew Henry in his commentary on chapter 13 says that, "You can speak all the languages on earth and that with the greatest propriety, elegance, and fluency, you could talk like an angel and yet without love, it would be empty noise, mere un-harmonious and useless sound, that neither profit or delight." The love that St. Paul is talking about is genuine and pure love which is demonstrated in how we treat others. God's love is a love that is directed towards others and not to ourselves, and we can only manifest this love when we fall in love with Jesus. The more you love Jesus and become like Him the more you will show more love to others.

The message for today is, love God and you will learn how to love others, for without love you are nothing.

Today's Prayer: Dear God, please help me to learn to love as you love, for it is the only virtue that surpasses others. Amen.

April 25

TURN AND RUN

..."How then could I do such a wicked thing and sin against God?" (Genesis 39:9)

Joseph had no idea when he was sold by his brothers that he would have to face some of the greatest challenges of his life in Egypt. However, God was with Joseph and what could have ended in tragedy and disaster brought triumph, not just to himself but to his family and the Egyptians. Joseph, who had been sold into slavery by his brothers, found himself living in Potiphar's home as his servant. Joseph was committed and diligent in his work and soon won the favour of his master, and became his attendant. 'Potiphar left everything he had in Joseph's care; with Joseph in charge, he did not concern himself with anything except the food he ate.' (Genesis 39:6) Such was his trust in Joseph.

The Bible tells us that Joseph was 'well-built and handsome', and that became a problem, because Potiphar's wife 'took notice of Joseph' (Verse 7), and tried to seduce him. However, she failed; Joseph resisted this temptation by saying it would be a sin against God if he did such a thing, and for this reason avoided Potiphar's wife as best as he could. He kept on refusing her advances and finally ran from her. Sometimes merely trying to avoid temptation is not enough, there might be times when you have to turn and run like Joseph did.

Joseph was a young man of integrity; he knew that succumbing to Potiphar's wife would be an act of disobedience to God. Although he was far away from home, he had not forgotten the good values he had been taught, and therefore chose to run away from temptation.

The temptation of Joseph was not an isolated case; we are all tempted on a daily basis. Paul addresses the matter of temptation with the Corinthian believers who lived in a culture filled with all kinds of moral depravity. He states: "No temptation has overtaken you except what is common to man. And God is faithful; He will not let you be tempted beyond what you can bear. But when you are tempted, He will also provide a way out so that you can endure it." (1 Corinthians 10:13) Paul is saying that temptation happens to everyone, so if you are currently being tempted, don't feel that you are being singled out, others are also being tempted. However, you can resist temptation by calling on God for He will help you to resist by helping you to recognise what is wrong from what is right. You must also, like Joseph choose to do what is right and turn and run from temptation. Some might think that running away is a cowardly act, however, if you are wise, you will realise that removing yourself from the source of temptation is not a cowardly act. It is by running away that you will gain the victory. If you are being tempted today, turn and run, this will be the most courageous action that you would have taken. Jesus told Peter, "Watch and pray that you will not fall into temptation..." (Matthew 26:41) You must do likewise.

Today's prayer: Father, when tempted, help me to find the way of escape that you have provided. Amen.

April 26

THE STILL SMALL VOICE

'After the earthquake came a fire, but the Lord was not in the fire. And after the fire came a gentle whisper.' (1Kings 19:12)

Elijah, the prophet, experienced times of great spiritual victories and times of discouragement and depression. In 1 Kings 19: 17 -22 we read about his conflict with King Ahab and his evil wife Jezebel. Throughout his trials, Elijah stood for God, and despite opposition from both of them, he showed that with God on your side, no one can be against you. (Romans 8:31) Elijah now finds himself running away from Jezebel when he has a profound encounter with God. After a period of intense fear and despair, God reminds him of his mission. Elijah was depressed and had no energy to continue his mission. However, God confronted him, telling him to return to his mission.

It is interesting to note that when God told Elijah to stand on the mountain in His presence that there was a 'great and powerful wind, an earthquake and a fire; however, none of these contained God's presence. Elijah did later hear a gentle whisper and recognised it as the voice of God. Why didn't he hear God in the wind, earthquake and fire? It is because God does not only reveal Himself (as one writer states), "in powerful and miraculous ways. It is in the stillness of the moment that you can hear Him speaking to your heart." It is easy to get caught up in the singing, the concerts, or other church activities and not hear Him speak to you. In trying to hear Him at these events, you might just miss His voice because it is often heard gently whispering to our hearts in the quietness of the moment.

There are times when you might find yourself busy at work or getting on with life and become so engrossed with your daily activities, and amid the din and clamour of your surroundings you cannot hear Him, because He is often found whispering in a gentle voice as He tries to get your attention. Are you hearing His whisper? Can it be that you might need to step back and listen as He whispers His plan for your life? God is waiting for you to come away from your busy schedule, listen and pay attention and await His instructions and guidance. Will you hear His gentle whisper today?

Today's Prayer: Father, help me to hear your gentle whisper as you reveal yourself to me. Amen.

April 27

ALL THAT SHE HAD

"Truly I tell you", He said, "This poor widow has put in more than all the others. All these people gave their gifts out of their wealth, but she, out of her poverty, put in all she had to live on." (Mark 12:41-44)

You can imagine the scene as the worshippers gathered in the temple as they worshipped God with their offerings. Quietly, a poor widow reaches the offering box and places all she has in the box - two small coins. Jesus, who was present, noticed and remarked about the stark contrast to those of the wealthy and affluent worshippers. "All these people gave their gifts out of their wealth, but she, out of her poverty, put in all she had." (Luke 21:4)

The widow gave of her poverty, whilst the rich gave from their abundance. The amount they gave would not have made much difference to their bank account, unlike the widow who knew that after giving all that she had, she would have to exercise faith, knowing that God would provide and supply all her needs. What she did was a demonstration of her faith, love, and trust in God. In His comment to His disciples, Jesus was telling them that it is not the amount we give but the spirit with which we give, that is, our motives. In 2 Corinthians 9:7, we are told, 'Each of you should give what you have decided in your heart to give, not reluctantly or under compulsion, not grudgingly, for God loves a cheerful giver.'

God commends the poor widow's offering because she gave more than anyone else, she sacrificed all she had, and she gave out of her poverty all that she had. Giving from a heart of love and generosity despite her poverty was acceptable to God. He places no value on the amount you give, but the heart of sacrifice behind the gift is of more value to Him. True generosity is not measured by the amount you give, but by your motive.

How about you? Do you give because you can afford to give from your abundance, or do you give because of your love for God? Consider your attitude behind your gift. Giving back to God is not just about money; it is about the giving of yourself, your time, your abilities, your talents, and your acts of service to others. Whatever you do, you must give glory to Him.

In John 3:1, we are told, "For God so loved the world that He gave His one and only Son, that whoever believes in him shall not perish but have eternal life." This was the ultimate sacrifice. He gave himself willingly so that you could have everlasting life. Are you prepared to give all you have to God?

Today's Prayer: Dear Father, thank you for your great sacrifice of love. Amen.

April 28

JESUS BRINGS SALVATION

"Today salvation has come to this house, because this man, too, is a son of Abraham." (Luke 19:9)

The story of Zacchaeus is well-known. He was a tax collector who worked for the Romans. To finance their world empire, the Romans levied heavy taxes on Israel, which was under their control. The Jews hated this system because the taxes supported a secular government and its pagan worship. For that reason, if you were a tax collector for the Romans, you would be hated by your fellow Jews. Tax collectors were the most hated and unpopular people in Israel. Quite apart from working for the Romans, it was common knowledge that tax collectors were making themselves rich by overcharging or swindling their own people.

When Jesus said he wanted to visit Zacchaeus in his home, the crowd was horrified. How could He? Did he not know that he was a cheat and a turncoat? However, Jesus said Zacchaeus was a son of Abraham who needed to be saved. The crowd must have been shocked to hear this and said, "He has gone to be the guest of a sinner." Jesus loved Zacchaeus and wanted to save him.

After Zacchaeus encountered Jesus, he realised that he could not continue to live as he did. He needed to change his lifestyle. "Look, Lord! Here and now, I give half of my possessions to the poor, and if I have cheated anybody out of anything I will pay back four times the amount." His conversion was genuine because Jesus did not just enter his house; he entered his heart, and an inner change took place, which was consistent with his outward actions.

Will you allow Jesus to come into your life today? He wants to change you. Despite his dishonest behaviour, Jesus loved Zacchaeus and wanted to save him. He wants the same for you too. You must genuinely want to change your sinful ways; you cannot afford to have only a head knowledge of God you must have a heart experience with Him evidenced by a changed behaviour.

What changes do you need to make in your life? Do you need an encounter with Jesus to bring about change?

Today's Prayer: Come into my heart, Lord Jesus, and bring about the change that is so badly needed. Amen.

April 29

YOU LACK NOTHING

'The Lord is my shepherd, I lack nothing.' (Psalm 23:1)

Living in a world of greed, selfishness, and consumerism, you might feel that you don't have enough and desire to have more. This is what some people believe and will spend countless hours trying to amass wealth and possessions thinking that having more will bring them happiness. They are never content with what they have, and feel they don't have enough.

The psalmist says, 'The Lord is my shepherd, I lack nothing.' (Psalm 23:1) To believe that God is your Shepherd and that you lack nothing is to come to the realisation that you do not have to worry about anything. You can feel secure, confident, and content that He will supply all your needs. Accepting that you will lack nothing also means that you have no need to worry about your needs not being met, because God is your Shepherd who provides the love and tender care that you need and seek.

When you think of this metaphor, 'the Lord is my shepherd, I lack nothing.' it is easy to think that it refers to just your physical needs; it means more than that. God provides for all your needs, physical, emotional, and spiritual. He is a relational God and for this reason as He supplies your needs; you can also enjoy a personal relationship with Him.

Like the Good Shepherd that He is, He will shower you with abundant blessings of joy, peace, and love. Therefore, knowing you lack nothing should fill you with hope and anticipation, and being one of His sheep should make you appreciate how special you are to Him. You should understand how cherished and valued you are in His sight. One commentary's overview of this text states that "It establishes a core relationship between the believer and God, portraying God as a shepherd who provides and cares for His people. It signifies a state of contentment and completeness, where all needs are met through God's provision, highlighting divine sufficiency and personal relationship with God."

Aren't you thrilled to know that because God is your Shepherd, you have need of nothing and you lack nothing. Are you happy to be counted as one of His sheep, totally dependent on Him?

Today's Prayer: Heavenly Father, thank you for being my shepherd, I can now live a life of security and contentment. Amen.

April 30

GOD'S ASSURANCE

"And if I go and prepare a place for you, I will come back and take you to be with me that you also may be where I am." (John 14:3)

It was nearly time for Jesus to return to His Father. His disciples were sad, but Jesus assured them that one day they would all be reunited. He comforts them and tells them that He would be going to prepare a place for them to live with Him. This assurance was not just for the disciples but for all believers everywhere. He then comforts them with these words, "Do not let not your hearts be troubled." Jesus knew that they would feel the pain of separation, they would miss him, after all they had spent three and a half years together and now, He was leaving. Can you recall a time when you had to say goodbye to a loved one or a friend?

It was hard for the disciples, yet the assurance and the comfort of His promise made it easier for them to accept His soon departure. We too have been given this same promise, a promise that relates to an eternal home and not a temporary one. Are you longing to see the home He has prepared for you? The grandest mansion on earth is like a shack compared to what God has in store for us. Paul expresses it so beautifully, "What no eye has seen, what no ear has heard, and what no human mind can conceive – the things that God has prepared for those who love Him." Knowing the wonderful and eternal future that awaits you should fill you with joy untold.

No matter how hard you try, you cannot imagine what God has in store for you. He says He will create new heavens and new earth (Isaiah 65:17), and we won't have to make the journey alone, for He promises to return to take us home. You can, without any doubt, look forward to eternal life because Jesus has given us His promise; He is not a human that He should lie, not a human being, that He should change His mind. Does He speak and then not act? Does He promise and not fulfil? (Numbers 23:19)

With such promises, do you not feel a longing for home? Although we don't know all the details, we do know that our homes will be found in the New Jerusalem. A city of pure gold, walls of jasper, gates made of pearl. In Revelation chapter 21, John does his best to describe the grandeur of what awaits us; however, the half has not been told!

Jesus is preparing to welcome us home one day; do not disappoint Him.

Today's Prayer: Father, I know your promises are true. Help me to live in anticipation of your soon return. Amen.

May 1

THE LORD WILL FIGHT FOR YOU

"Stand firm and see the deliverance the Lord will bring today. The Egyptians you see today you will never see again. The Lord will fight for you: you need only to be still." (Exodus 14:17)

The Hebrews were enslaved in Egypt for four hundred years; at last, they were free. However, after the excitement of finally leaving Egypt their first challenge is encountered at the Red Sea. This was an impossible situation; they could not go forward because of the sea, nor backwards because of Pharaoh and his army, who had pursued them. They were in an impossible and desperate situation. Their joy had now turned to despair, and when they looked behind and saw Pharaoh's army approaching, they were terrified and cried out to God. However, with the same breath they began to complain and blame Moses, saying he had brought them out of Egypt to die. In fact, they were blaming God and not Moses.

Although the people became hostile towards Moses and Aaron, Moses encouraged them to watch the marvellous way in which God would rescue them. From the people's standpoint they were trapped and could see no way out. Moses called upon God to intervene. He told them, "The Lord will fight for you." And with a mighty hand God led them through the Red Sea on dry ground. One writer says, "The Exodus is the most dramatic and glorious experience of God's people in the Old Testament."

Have you ever experienced a time in your life when all seemed hopeless? A time when the situation appeared impossible, when you had no answers, when God seemed far away. Is there a time when you lost hope? You may not have had a literal Red Sea experience or have been chased by an army, however, you may be feeling trapped by situations in your life and have forgotten how God has fought for you in the past. Israel had apparently forgotten how God had led them out of Egypt. They had given in to despair. If you are feeling helpless and hopeless, and living a life of quiet desperation, be like Moses who adopted a positive attitude and implicit trust in God. That's why he was able to say to the Israelites, "Stand firm and you will see the deliverance the Lord will bring you today."

Although you may be feeling trapped in your situation today, do not give in to despair for God will fight for you.

Today's Prayer: Heavenly Father, help me not to despair when trials assail me but to stand firm and experience your deliverance. Amen.

May 2

A GOOD SHEPHERD LOOKS AFTER HIS SHEEP

'For this is what the Sovereign Lord says: "I myself will search for my sheep and look after them."' (Ezekiel 34:11)

I recall the time I met a shepherd, and couldn't help but think of Jesus, our Shepherd. A shepherd's role is to care for the sheep, ensuring their safety and general well-being. Shepherds protect the sheep from harm and danger. One of the most important roles of the shepherd is to lead, guide, and teach the sheep to follow his voice, and direct them to new pastures. Shepherds are known to have a close relationship with their sheep, learning their personalities and needs.

Jesus is not just a shepherd; He is the Good Shepherd. His role is that of a loving and protective Saviour who has sacrificed His life for His people. "I am the good shepherd. The good shepherd lays down His life for the sheep." (John 10:11) As the Shepherd, Jesus is not just doing a job, He is committed to loving and saving us in His kingdom.

A shepherd has a great responsibility. In Ezekiel 34:9-10, the prophet refers to Israel's spiritual leaders who were to shepherd the people, but failed to do so. They became more concerned about themselves and neglected to serve the people. God told Ezekiel that the shepherds who failed the flock would be removed and held accountable, and He promised that He would shepherd the people himself. The spiritual leaders in Israel who had the responsibility for shepherding the people had "ruled them harshly and brutally so they were scattered because there was no shepherd..." (Ezekiel 34:4&5) God was displeased with the leaders and said He would "remove them from tending the flock..." (Verse 10)

One commentary says, "Spiritual leaders must be careful not to pursue self-development at the expense of the broken, lost people they are meant to help." When we give too much attention to our own needs and ideas, it's easy to push God aside and abandon those who depend on us.

If you are a spiritual leader, are you being led by the Good Shepherd, or are you failing the people He has entrusted in your care? True leadership is dependent on guidance from Jesus and on helping others. What do you do when your leader fails you? You might become disappointed and disillusioned; however, do not despair, trust God because He is the Good Shepherd.

Today's Prayer: Heavenly Father, I thank you for being my shepherd. Wherever you lead, I will follow. Amen.

May 3

NUDGED FROM YOUR COMFORT ZONE

'Like an eagle that stirs up its nest and hovers over its young, that spreads its wings to catch them and carries them on its pinions.' (Deuteronomy 32:11)

Eagles make their nests (eyries) using large sticks and branches, which they weave together to form a sturdy platform. They line it with softer materials such as grass and moss to create a comfortable nest for the eggs and the eaglets. You can imagine the young ones being so comfortable that they might sometimes be reluctant to leave the nest. However, there comes a time when they have to leave the comfort of their nest. Although they are born with an innate ability to fly, and also learn by observing their parents, it could be that sometimes they might just need a little nudge from their parents to leave the comfort of the nest. "Like an eagle that stirs up the nest..." (Verse 11)

The children of Israel had sinned against God and had become comfortable in their sin, and as a result, they had abandoned Him. He had been to them like an eagle that protects and cares for its young. Have you become so comfortable in your comfort zone that you have lost all motivation to witness for God? You have probably been in the church for thirty, forty years, a long time and no longer feel the need to tell others about God and what He has done for you. Before Jesus went back to heaven, He gave the commission to everyone: "Therefore, go and make disciples of all nations..." (Matthew 28:219) Here, Jesus is telling us that there is much work to do; therefore, we cannot afford to remain in our comfort zones. Each person has been called to action, whereby they should be actively engaged in sharing the Good News about Jesus.

Are you content to attend church every week, going through the motions and doing nothing for God? Have you remained in your comfort zone because you are afraid of being ridiculed or mocked? Do you lack courage and confidence? Or are you ashamed of the gospel? In Romans 1:16, Paul says, "For I am not ashamed of the gospel, because it is the power of God that brings salvation to everyone who believes." Paul knew that the gospel has life-changing power. Accept God's message to you, do not be afraid to leave your comfort zone, for Jesus says, "...But take heart! I have overcome the world." Will you leave your comfort zone today and, with courage, proclaim the good news of salvation to all who will hear? Could it be that God is giving you a nudge to do the work He has called you to do?

Today's Prayer: Dear God, I have become comfortable in my comfort zone. Help me to respond to your call for there is work for me to do. Amen.

243

May 4

THE GREATEST MISCARRIAGE OF JUSTICE

"...I am innocent of this man's blood," he said. "It is your responsibility!" (Matthew 27:24)

In 1974, six men were wrongly convicted of the Birmingham pub bombings, serving seventeen years in prison for crimes they did not commit. Their convictions were quashed in 1991. Also in 1974, four other men were wrongly convicted of pub bombings – one of the UK's worst miscarriages of justice. They saw their convictions quashed after new evidence emerged. The Guildford Four suffered a similar fate; theirs too was a case of a miscarriage of justice, and in 1974 they were wrongly convicted and imprisoned.

However, over two thousand years ago, the greatest miscarriage of justice took place on planet earth when Jesus, the sinless and innocent Son of God, was nailed and crucified to the cruel cross. He was falsely accused of usurping the throne, the Jews believed belonged to the 'true' king; as far as they were concerned, Jesus was not their king. He was accused of stirring up the people with His teachings and claims to be God. He was brought before Pilate, who could find no fault in Him, nor could Herod. This displeased the Jewish leaders, who, with the riotous mob, demanded the release of the criminal called Barabbas and called for the crucifixion of the innocent Jesus. The trial was a travesty.

Pilate, after succumbing to the cries of the people, proclaimed, "I am innocent of the blood of this just man." This miscarriage of justice took place because of God's love for us. "For God so loved the world that he gave his one and only Son, that whoever believes in him shall not perish but have eternal life." (John 3:16). Think of the great price that was paid for your sin and mine, an innocent Man!

Today's Prayer: Dear God, there are no words in my human vocabulary to fully express my gratitude for what you did for me on the cross of Calvary. Amen.

May 5

A RED SEA EXPERIENCE

'So, God led the people around by the desert road towards the Red Sea...' (Exodus 13:18)

The crossing of the Red Sea is a well-known story of God's deliverance of His people since leaving Egypt, where they had been enslaved for over four hundred years. You can only imagine the joy and excitement of the Hebrews as God delivered them from captivity. However, their joy was short-lived when they found themselves facing a dilemma, an impossible situation – the Red Sea before them and Pharaoh's army behind them. They were well and truly trapped.

Stop and reflect on the last time you faced an impossible and perhaps terrifying situation in your life. What was your initial response? How did you react? We know from Exodus 14 how the Hebrews reacted. "For it had been better for us to serve the Egyptians, than that we should die in the wilderness," was their reaction. These were the same people whom God had freed from Egypt. They had been spared the terrible plagues and had witnessed the dramatic might and power of God, but now, faced with their current dilemma, they had forgotten how God had rescued them from the hand of Pharaoh. Instead of guiding the people along the direct route from Egypt to the Promised Land, He took them the longer route to avoid fighting with the Philistines, hence the Red Sea experience.

Sometimes, God does not answer our prayers or always work in a way that seems best to us. He knows the beginning and the end and will always lead us the best way, His way. Do not grumble or complain like the Israelites did when they encountered the Red Sea. If God does not answer your prayer in the way you want it, or if He does not lead you along the shortest path to your desired destination, don't complain or resist. Follow Him willingly and confidently, and He will lead you safely around unseen obstacles.

It is so easy to forget the way in which God has led in the past. If you are enduring a Red Sea experience in your life today, remember that God led Israel through the Red Sea on dry land, and He will do the same for you.

Today's Prayer: Heavenly Father, forgive me for having forgotten the way you have led me in the past. Amen.

May 6

SING THE SONG OF MOSES AND THE LAMB

'... They held harps given by God and sang the song of God's servant Moses and the Lamb.' (Revelation 15:2)

After the miraculous crossing of the Red Sea, the children of Israel sang a song of victory, led by Miriam. It was a song of deliverance from the Egyptians at the Red Sea. The song was a song of praise and thanksgiving. It celebrated God's victory over Pharaoh and his army. It also celebrated God's might and power to lead His people out of slavery.

You can only imagine the joy and happiness when the people burst into a mighty chorus of praise and gratitude to God for their deliverance. This song became known as the song of Moses because it speaks about God's love for His people and His ability to save. It was a song of the past, but also of the future, as it points us to the time when the redeemed of all ages will sing the song of Moses and the Lamb in the earth made new. In Revelation 15:2-4, John, in a vision, describes a scene yet to come, when the faithful ones of all ages will be gathered around the throne of God and sing this song. The song of Moses celebrated the Hebrews' deliverance from Egyptian slavery. The song of the Lamb (Jesus Christ), will celebrate the ultimate deliverance of God's people from the power of the archenemy, Satan. The songwriter Johnson Oatman, in collaboration with John R Sweney, wrote this beautiful song, "Holy, Holy, is what the angels sing [...] but when I sing redemption's song, angels will fold their wings for angels never felt the joy that our salvation brings." This song gives credit to Moses and Jesus the Lamb for the triumph over evil. This song is not exclusive to a few people; you, too, can be a part of that mighty heavenly chorus as the redeemed of all ages join their voices together and sing redemption's story. Isn't this worth looking forward to?

Today's Prayer: Father, help me to remain faithful to you, for I want to join that heavenly choir one day to sing the song of Moses and the Lamb. Amen.

May 7

GOD REVEALS SIN

"There is nothing concealed that will not be disclosed." (Luke 12:2)

Ezekiel the prophet when in a vision was taken to the temple in Jerusalem. God showed him the great wickedness that the leaders and the people were practising. In scene after scene God revealed to Ezekiel the extent to which the people had embraced idolatry and sin. Similarly, God's spirit works within us, revealing sin that lurks in our lives. How comfortable would you feel if God held an open house in your life today?

In Luke 12:2 we are told, "There is nothing concealed that will not be made known." When the Holy Spirit reveals sin in your life you must confess and repent from them. When Nathan the prophet confronted King David about his secret sin, he was truly sorry for having sinned against God. "Against you, you only have I sinned and done what is evil in your sight." (Psalm 51:4). David did not continue to dwell on his sin, but returned to God and God forgave him, thus opening the way for him to begin life anew. When we return to God, accept His forgiveness and change our ways, He gives us a fresh start.

Like David you must realise that sin in any form is rebellion against God, therefore when tempted to do wrong, remember that you will be sinning against God. If you are concealing a sin you have committed against God, confess it today, ask for forgiveness, repent and ask God to cleanse you from within.

Today's Prayer: Father, create in me a pure heart and restore unto me the joy of your salvation. Amen.

May 8

DON'T GIVE WAY TO BITTERNESS (1)

"And now, do not be distressed and do not be angry with yourselves for selling me here, because it was to save lives that God sent me ahead of you." (Genesis 45:5)

Have you ever met a bitter person? An angry person who is resentful and whose anger has accumulated over time that they can no longer forgive? Bitterness is defined as 'anger and disappointment at being treated unfairly'. It is synonymous with resentment and envy. The story of Cain and Abel is an example of bitterness that led to Cain killing his brother.

Some people think they have every reason to be bitter; the heartache of a tragedy when a loved one has died; being robbed of what was rightly yours. Bitterness can also be the result of hurtful or unkind words spoken about you. You might also be bitter after losing your job because you felt that you had been treated unjustly. You might think you have every right to be bitter, but do not succumb to this toxic spirit.

Joseph could have been bitter; he certainly had every reason to be angry and bitter, almost everyone he knew betrayed him. His own brothers hated him and plotted to kill him. Think about all he had been through in Egypt, seduced by his master's wife, imprisoned for something he hadn't done. He had every reason to be bitter, but God was with Joseph. If he had grown resentful and bitter as a result of his circumstances, he would not have become second to Pharaoh and preserve the lives of his family. He saved Egypt and prepared the way for the beginning of the nation of Israel. Joseph did not give way to bitterness because he knew God was with him and for that reason, he was able to say to his brothers, "Do not be distressed and do not be angry with yourselves for selling me here, because it was to save lives that God sent me ahead of you." (Genesis 45:5) "You intended to harm me, but God intended it for good to accomplish what is now being done." (Genesis 50:20) Today, if you have bitterness in your heart, pray to God and ask Him for release.

Today's Prayer: Heavenly Father, release me from any bitterness that might be destroying me. Amen.

May 9

OVERCOMING BITTERNESS (2)

'My times are in your hands; deliver me from the hands of my enemies, from those who pursue me.' (Psalm 31:15)

David expresses his belief that whatever was happening to him he knew God was in control. Knowing that God loves and cares for you should bring joy to you rather than bitterness.

In order to overcome bitterness, stop focusing on your circumstances, stop being angry with those who hurt you. Bitterness can cause anxiety, depression, and other mental and physical conditions. Bitterness is like a corrosive that can impact your spiritual life. You experience no joy in serving God because the heart is filled with anger and resentment. Even if the one who has hurt you never repents, forgive them, for this will free you from the heavy load of bitterness.

You might be thinking that you have every reason to be bitter. The family whose ten-year-old died in an accident, or the family who lost both children through drowning, may all have reasons to be bitter, however, God is waiting to bring joy to lives embittered, therefore to overcome bitterness you must first acknowledge and share your feelings with others. Forgive yourself and others.

As a believer in Christ, seek His forgiveness by praying for those who have hurt you. Although it might be difficult to forgive, you must remember that as a believer, forgiveness is not an option, it is a command from God. "Bear with each other and forgive one another. If any of you has a grievance against someone, forgive as the Lord forgave you." (Colossians 3:13)

Today's Prayer: Thank you, Lord for the joy of forgiveness which can rid me of bitterness. Amen.

May 10

RESTORATION

"But I will restore you to health and heal your wounds." (Jeremiah 30:17)

Everyone born on planet Earth needs to be restored because we are all suffering from the terminal disease called sin. Sinners cannot cure themselves, neither can anyone be cured by being good or by being religious. Why? "Because everyone has sinned and come short of the glory of God." (Romans 3:23) Because God loves us so much, He does not want any of us to die in our sins, and is waiting for us to ask for forgiveness, so He can restore us.

After Israel sinned against God so many times, and suffered the consequences, He said He would restore them if they turned away from their sins. In Ezekiel chapter 43 we read of God's restoration of the Temple. In chapter 30:17 the prophet speaks of God's power to heal His people both physically and spiritually - those who have been wounded by sin. In Psalm 51:12 David's prayer of repentance expresses the joy of restoration. "Restore to me the joy of salvation and grant me a willing spirit to sustain me." Sin had driven a wedge between David and God and that was why he sought restoration. His sin had severed the relationship he had with God.

If you are feeling alienated from God because of your sins, confess them to Him and He will restore you.

Today's Prayer: Father, restore unto me the joy of your salvation. Amen.

May 11

HIDDEN TREASURE

'For prophecy never had its origin in the human will, but prophets, though human, spoke from God as they were carried along by the Holy Spirit.' (2 Peter 1:21)

Some claim that the Bible is a fairy tale book, although they might not have even read it. Others believe that since it was written by man, it could not possibly be true. However, it was God who instructed men to write; it was not the work of the prophets; it was God who inspired them to write, and for that reason, what they have written is genuine, authentic, and reliable.

The Bible can be seen as a storehouse of hidden treasures. The story is told of an elderly lady who left her nephew twenty thousand dollars and her Bible and all it contained. The young man didn't bother to open the Bible, let alone read it. He left it on a shelf in his house and went to Las Vegas to live the high life. Before long, he had squandered all his money. He lived as a pauper for the next sixty years of his life. One day, he decided to open the Bible, and as his trembling hands reached for it, it fell to the floor and to his utter amazement, falling from each page were one-hundred-dollar bills. What a disappointment! He had lived the life of a pauper, not knowing how rich he was, all because he failed to open the Bible and read its truths.

I once heard a pastor describe the Bible as an acronym: **'Basic Instruction Before Leaving Earth'**. That might be so; however, the Bible is much more than that; it is no ordinary book. If you want to know about history, astronomy, science and other topics, you will need to study the Bible. For example, there are many scientific facts contained therein. The Earth hangs in space. 'He spreads out the northern skies over space; He suspends the earth over nothing.' (Job 26:7) Centuries ago, it was argued that the earth sat on a large animal or giant. However, it was not until 1650 that science discovered that the earth does not sit on anything but 'floats' in space.

People used to believe that the earth is flat; however, both the Bible and science describe a spherical earth. Isaiah 40:22 states, 'He sits enthroned above the circle of the earth...' The word circle suggests that the Earth is round and not flat. Arguments that state that the Earth is flat contradict the Biblical and scientific evidence that the Earth is indeed round. The Bible is to be believed because it is divinely inspired by God. There is scientific, historical, and archaeological evidence and accounts that verify its authenticity. There are so many hidden treasures contained in the Bible; however, you will only find them when you study it. As you study and learn about God, you will be pointed to Jesus Christ, and you will learn truths that will build your life in Him. Are you ready to find those hidden treasures? Begin reading and studying God's word, for it will "make you wise for salvation through faith in Christ Jesus." (2 Timothy 3:15)

Today's Prayer: Father, help me to spend more time studying your word. Amen.

May 12

FINDING COMFORT IN GRANDMA'S PSALM (1)

'Wait on the Lord, be of good courage, and he shall strengthen thine heart, wait, I say, on the Lord.' (Psalm 27:14)

I cannot recall a time when I did not hear my grandmother reading, reciting, or having this psalm read to her. It was her daily mantra. There were times in her life when she endured sickness and hardship, and this psalm became her pillar and anchor of faith. I can still see the expression of joy reflected on her face as she repeated the first verse, 'The Lord is my light and my salvation, whom shall I fear?' Like David, she was expressing total confidence in God.

In this Psalm, David declares his trust and confidence in God and because of that, he had no fear, for he knew that God would always be there for him. Can you, like David, feel no fear, even though you may be walking 'in the shadow of death'? There might be times in your life when you despair, when you 'hit rock bottom'. These are times of urgency when you need to call out to God. David did, "Hear, O Lord, when I cry with my voice." "When the wicked, even mine enemies and my foes, came upon me to eat up my flesh, they stumbled and fell." (Verse 2 &7)

If you are going through a difficult time in your life, learn from this psalm to trust God and wait upon Him. Feel no fear; fear sometimes gets the better of us and can imprison us. However, you can conquer fear by trusting in God. Remember what the psalmist says, "The Lord is my light and my salvation." He is your light in the darkness of fear. Ensure that you are in God's presence every day so when trouble comes your way, you will have already been in His presence.

Today's Prayer: Dear God, thank you for your guiding light in my life. Amen.

May 13

FINDING COMFORT IN GRANDMA'S PSALM (2)

'The Lord is my light and my salvation – whom shall I fear?' (Psalm 27:1)

I recall the summer holidays spent with my grandmother, when, during evening and morning worship, she would request that my cousins and I read Psalm 27. As we read, she would repeat the entire psalm word for word. She often commented on certain verses and what they meant to her. She would speak about how the psalm inspired and brought comfort to her.

In the psalm, David acknowledges reliance on God's help as he pleads for His continual presence. He shows unwavering confidence in God, which is our antidote for fear and loneliness. David realised the importance of seeking God's presence in his life; this is what brought him comfort. Do you sometimes run to God only when you experience difficulties in your life, or when you are sad and need comfort? Psalm 27 offers comfort when you, like David, acknowledge God as the only source of comfort in your life. As you go through difficulties, he is your 'light and your salvation', and a protective stronghold when fearful and frightened.

You can find comfort in the psalm as it encourages you to call on God for help. However, you should be mindful to call on Him at all times and not only when you are facing challenges. In this psalm, we find David seeking God's guiding presence every day, not just when he encountered difficulties. When trouble came his way, he was able to handle it because he was already in God's presence and was therefore prepared to handle any trial that assailed him. In verse 10, he was confident that 'though my father and mother forsake me, the Lord will receive me'. Having such confidence brought him much comfort.

You may have had a sad experience of abandonment or being forsaken by those you love and may still be bearing the scars today; however, take comfort in this verse. David assures us that the pain of being forsaken or rejected can be healed because God, your Heavenly Father, can take the place of a mother or father in your life. He can fill that void, ease your pain and heal your hurt. This should bring you reassurance and much comfort. Despite what you might be going through right now, seek comfort from God's word. The psalms are a good place to start. He will bring comfort and hope if you let Him. You should remain confident that you will 'see the goodness of the Lord in the land of the living'.

Today's Prayer: Father, thank you for the comfort I find in your word. Amen.

May 14

DO NOT PITCH YOUR TENT IN SODOM (1)

'Abram lived in the land of Canaan while Lot lived among the cities of the plain and pitched his tents near Sodom.' (Genesis 13:2)

When God called Abram to move from Ur to Haran, and ultimately to Canaan, his nephew Lot also accompanied him. However, a quarrel arose between Abram's herdsmen and Lot's. Facing a potential conflict with Lot, Abram took the initiative in settling the dispute. He gave Lot the first choice of which part of the land he should have. (See chapter Genesis 13). However, Lot should have considered that Abram, out of respect and seniority, should have had first choice. However, for the sake of peace, Abram allowed Lot to have first choice.

In Genesis 13:10 11 we read, 'Lot looked around and saw that the whole plain of the Jordon towards Zoar was well watered, like the garden of the Lord, like the land of Egypt. So, Lot chose for himself the whole plain of the Jordon and set out toward the east. The two parted company, and Lot pitched his tent towards Sodom. Abram went to live near the great trees of Mamre at Hebron, where he pitched his tents. There, he built an altar to the Lord.' (Verse 18)

Lot's character was revealed by his choice. He took the best share of the land. He did not consider the needs of Abram, nor did he exercise fairness. Each of us has choices to make; you can be like Lot and choose the best for yourself while ignoring the needs of others. Sadly, Lot suffered the consequences of his choice. Sodom was a wicked place, yet he chose to pitch his tent nearby. He finally moved to Sodom. (See chapter 19). Lot thought he was making a wise decision when he pitched his tent towards Sodom. He probably thought he was strong and would not be affected by the sins of Sodom.

Have you pitched your tent in Sodom? Have you considered that this wicked Sodom in which you now live can provide temptations strong enough to destroy you and your family? Are your children in Sodom because you chose to pitch your tent there? You might be saying you pitched your tent in Sodom to reach the people there. Be careful you do not become like the very people you are trying to reach.

Today's Prayer: Father, guide me to where you want me to pitch my tent. Amen.

May 15

DO NOT PITCH YOUR TENT IN SODOM. (2)

'So, Abram went to live near the great trees of Mamre of Hebron, where he pitched his tents. There he built an altar to the Lord.' (Genesis 13:18)

What a contrast to Lot, who pitched his tent towards Sodom. Not only did Abram pitch his tents, but he also built an altar for worship, showing his relationship with God. One writer says, "Building an altar is a crucial act of devotion, signifying Abram's thankfulness to God for His faithfulness and renewed promises. The altar serves as a public declaration and a constant reminder of God's presence and promises to Abram and his descendants."

Abram built an altar to worship God and to show his gratitude to Him. Lot, on the other hand, was more concerned about the fertile Jordan Valley and owning that land. However, it turned out that his decision to pitch his tents there led to his spiritual ruin, but Abram found spiritual security where he pitched his tent. Lot chose material things above God.

Are you building altars to honour and worship God, or are you choosing to pitch your tent in Sodom? Sodom was so appealing to Lot until he eventually found himself living there. He had no business in Sodom. As a believer, you are called to establish and maintain an altar, a place of daily devotion where you commit yourself to God's guidance. You are called to choose God's unseen promises rather than the visible and temporary things of this world. Everywhere Abram went, he built an altar; he understood the importance of being in the presence of God.

Like Abram, you need to establish a family altar, where "each morning consecrate yourself and your family to God for that day…Surrender all your plans to God, to be carried out or given up, as His providence shall indicate. In this manner, you may day by day be giving your life with its plans and purposes into the hands of God, accepting His plans instead of your own…" (E.G. White)

Will you build an altar in your life today? Abram's "life was one of prayer and humble obedience, and he was a light in the world. Wherever he pitched his tent, close beside it was set up his altar, calling for the morning and evening sacrifice of each member of his family." By building altars, you will be setting examples for your children, and you will be the light shining in this dark world of Sodom.

Today's Prayer: Lord, I want to consecrate myself and family to you on the altar I have erected. Amen.

May 16

DO NOT BE DECEIVED (1)

"For false messiahs and false prophets will appear and perform great signs and wonders to deceive, if possible, even the elect. See I have told you in advance." (Matthew 24: 24 & 25)

Jesus warns us that before He comes, false prophets will arise, performing great signs and miracles to deceive many. In Biblical times, including when Jesus lived on earth, there were false prophets - a false prophet, such as Balaam, who was hired to curse Israel. False prophets during the time of Jeremiah, who led the people away from God, the four hundred prophets of Baal, are just some examples.

There are modern-day examples too, like Jim Jones, the founder of the Peoples Temple, whose false prophecies led to the mass murder-suicide of over nine hundred followers in Jonestown, Guyana. And not forgetting David Koresh, leader of the Branch Davidian, whose deception resulted in the death of his followers, after a deadly standoff with American federal agents. False prophets are good at delivering false or misleading information. They come in many guises today, especially on the internet, where conspiracy theories are prevalent. People are confused and don't know what truth is from what is falsehood. The use of AI has even intensified their confusion.

However, in today's text, Jesus is telling believers to remain vigilant and not be misled by those claiming to be Christ. He wants His followers to be alert, and spend time studying His word and getting to know His voice. In Matthew 10:27, He says, "My sheep listen to my voice: I know them, and they follow me." Believers need to rely on God's wisdom, guidance and the truth of His word and not be deceived. Jesus warns us against false teachings and, like the Bereans in the early church, to search the Scriptures for ourselves. Believers should be careful not to trust human authority or interpretation over God's word.

You might say those who were deceived by Jim Jones, Koresh, and others must have been very trusting, or else very gullible, to have fallen prey to their deceit. However, false prophets are usually very persuasive and therefore believable, and for this reason, Jesus stresses in His warning that if it were possible, even the very elect will be deceived.

Avoid deception by studying God's word and seeking His wisdom; be alert to the deceptive schemes of false prophets; guard against self-deception, too, and surround yourself with those who uphold truth.

Today's Prayer: Heavenly Father, it is so easy to be deceived. Let me learn to trust you more, and give me the spirit of discernment. Amen.

May 17

DO NOT BE DECEIVED (2)

"For such people are false apostles, deceitful workers, masquerading as apostles of Christ." (2 Corinthians 11:13)

When St. Paul made this statement, he might have been thinking of Satan masquerading as an angel. He might have been referring to Satan's deceptive character. Satan is the master of deception, and as a child of God, he seeks to destroy you through this evil device. Paul was saying that in the same way, these false apostles were pretending to be servants or apostles of Christ, 'servants of righteousness', but were in fact agents of the devil.

Look what happened in heaven. Lucifer, as he was known then, managed to deceive a third of the angels! 'Its tail swept a third of the stars out of the sky and flung them to the earth.' (Revelation 12:4) The stars here refer to the angels that were cast out of heaven with Satan. He continues to deceive; the Bible says he is a liar, and the Father of Lies. The truth is not in him. He focuses on lies, half-truths, and appealing falsehoods to lead people away from God's truth. This is why Jesus warns us about his deception, especially in the end times in which we live.

Satan uses several evil devices to deceive, some of which can be identified in society today, as 'Psychological operations'. The media often employs these same methods to change people's thinking or opinion. If you look in Genesis chapter 2, you will find the master deceiver at work using these very tactics to cause our first parents to sin against God. Some examples are, firstly, creating curiosity in Eve's mind, he then creates doubt: "Did God really say you must not eat from any tree in the garden?" He continues his heinous, deceptive attack when he finally undermines God's authority and destroys Eve's trust in Him, and presents God as an oppressor and her enemy. (You can read the narrative in Genesis chapter 3). Satan was successful in reframing Eve's mind, which ended in the fall of our first parents.

Do not think that you cannot be deceived by Satan. Our salvation is not in his best interest. In John 10:10, we are told that "the thief comes only to steal and destroy..." and Satan is not just a liar but also a thief. As a believer, you must rely on the truth of God's word and test all teachings against the word of God. '...If anyone does not speak according to this word, they have no light of dawn.' (Isaiah 8:20) Satan will even make you believe he does not exist; this is probably his greatest deception.

Today's Prayer: Lord, help me to remain vigilant in prayer and living my life rooted in you. Amen.

May 18

ROVER AND SEPARATION

"Then I saw a new heaven and a new earth, for the first heaven and the first earth had passed away, and there was no longer any sea." (Revelation 21:1)

In John's time, the sea was viewed as dangerous and changeable. I have often wondered why John mentioned that there was no longer any sea. Some commentators interpret the absence of the sea to mean that the source of evil in the world will be no more. No longer will there be opportunity for rebellion in God's creation. Others interpret it to mean that the New Earth will not be a place of turmoil or fear. Psalm 46 speaks of the sea's waters roaring and foaming, and the mountains quaking with the surging. However, the absence of the sea could also mean there will be no more separation. John had been exiled on the island of Patmos, and of course, he was separated from his homeland by the Mediterranean Sea. To be separated from loved ones must always be a painful experience, especially if death is the reason for the separation.

I recall an experience of separation that happened in my family. I grew up with three brothers and two sisters, two dogs, two cats and later two budgerigars. Because our father had immigrated to the United Kingdom, the time had come when we had to join him. By now, the only pet that remained was our dog, Rover. Regretfully, we were unable to take him with us. As we said our goodbyes to our neighbours, my younger sister said she could not help but see the sadness in the eyes of our beloved Rover. When she called him over to her, he gazed at her with such sadness that it nearly broke her heart, and then, taking one last look, he walked away completely broken as he sensed he would never see us again.

If our separation caused so much pain to our dog, can you imagine the pain God felt when Adam and Eve sinned against Him, when that beautiful and loving relationship was broken? My sister could do nothing to relieve the pain that our dog felt. However, because God loves us so much, he cannot bear to be separated from us, and that was why He sent His Son, Jesus Christ, to sinful Earth to save us from sin that separates us from our loving Heavenly Father. Before Jesus ascended to heaven, He left us a beautiful promise which stands as a constant reminder that the separation will not be forever. He says, "...I will come back and take you to be with me that you also may be where I am." (John 14:3) What a beautiful promise, that one day we will be reunited with our heavenly Father. When you reflect on what John says in Revelation 21:1, that there was no longer any sea, it should be a constant reminder to us that one day soon, we will never be separated from God and our loved ones. We should therefore look forward to that time as much as He does with great anticipation, when, according to the songwriter, "We will never part again, no, never part again."

Today's Prayer: Dear Father, thank you for your promise of eternal life with you. Amen.

May 19

BUILD ON THE ROCK

"Therefore, everyone who hears these words of mine and puts them into practice is like a wise man who built his house on the rock." (Matthew 7:24)

A builder knows **the** importance of building on a firm foundation. Rocks are therefore essential because they provide materials for the construction of buildings. According to one definition, rocks denote 'strength, steadiness, and permanence due to their inherent durability and foundational nature'. Rocks also symbolise an unwavering quality and resilience.

Matthew 24 describes two types of people who are likened to builders who build their homes, one on a solid foundation of rock, the other on an unstable foundation of sand. In verse 24, we are told that the person who hears God's word and puts it into practice is compared to a wise builder who builds on a strong foundation; a foundation that will withstand the storms and challenges of life that you will sometimes face. By contrast, some will hear the word of God but disobey it. They are like a foolish builder who builds on the sand, whose house collapses during a storm.

What can we learn from the analogy of the two builders? One writer says, "that true wisdom lies not in mere intellectual acknowledgement of Jesus' teachings but in faithful obedience and application of them to one's life." It is therefore important to put into practice what we learn from the Scriptures; simply listening or reading His words is not enough; we must apply the truths learnt to our lives.

Are you a wise builder? Are you building your life on God's word? If you are, you are building on Jesus, the solid rock of stability and security. In this world of challenges and insecurities, what better place to build than on the rock and not on the shifting sand of insecurity. It is foolish to build on the sand, as the sand represents a life that is without a firm foundation. When trials, hardships, and difficulties arise in your life, you will not be able to stand. A life that is grounded in Christ, the rock, will withstand the storms of life, for a life that is grounded in obedience to Him will exercise faith and dependence, and hope as they look forward to a secure future in His kingdom.

Today's Prayer: Father, thank you for being my rock and my salvation on which I can build. Amen.

May 20

DRAW NEAR TO GOD

"Come near to God and He will come near to you." (James 4:8)

How can you draw near to God? In this text, James is suggesting that you can yield to His authority and will, obey His commands, and let Him have control over your life. However, you must be willing to submit to His leading. In verse 7, he says you are to resist the devil. You might say, 'I am no match for the devil, how can I resist him?' - By drawing near to God. Satan will try to entice and tempt you; however, you do not have to fall for his enticements if you draw near and stay close to God.

It is such a wonderful experience that when you draw near to God, He will not push you away because you are a sinner; on the contrary, He reciprocates by drawing near to you too. However, do you want to draw near to Him? To draw near to God requires a broken spirit and a contrite heart, a humble and repentant heart. Drawing close to God is a reciprocal relationship; therefore, you must allow Him to rid you of the sins that so easily beset you. Any movement towards Him requires seeking forgiveness and cleansing of sinful habits. James continues to say, "Wash your hands, you sinners, and purify your hearts, you double-minded." (Verse 8) That is, 'replacing your desire to sin with a desire to experience God's purity'. You cannot approach a holy God with unconfessed sins. To purify one's heart is not just about a physical preparation, but also, importantly, the necessary spiritual preparation that is needed before approaching God.

Drawing near to God suggests that you must be sincere and genuinely want to be near Him. Some believers believe that by going through the motions, attending church, singing in the choir, and using the right clichés will guarantee God's favour, which means they are drawing near to God. However, this is the surest way of moving away from Him. In John 6:37, Jesus says, "All those the Father gives me will come to me, and whoever comes to me I will never drive away." He desires that all, regardless of ethnicity, class, status, gender or any other qualification, draw near to Him. Will you draw near to Him today?

Today's Prayer: Heavenly Father, I want to draw near to you so you can draw near to me so that we can have an intimate relationship. Amen.

May 21

DO YOU WANT DIRECTION IN YOUR LIFE?

'In all your ways submit to Him, and He will make your paths straight.' (Proverbs 3:6)

After having been an educator for over twenty-five years, I encountered a number of students who had no idea what career path they should choose, and some had no idea what direction they should take in life. These students needed help and guidance. As believers, we too need guidance because we do not know what is best for us. God, who is a better judge and all-knowing, knows what is best for us. He is a better judge of what we want than even we are! He knows the beginning from the end. While God has given us the ability to think and reason, we should not rely on our own judgment but learn to trust Him.

In all our ways submit to Him means we must not be wise in our own ways. "We should always be willing to listen to and be corrected by God's Word and wise counsellors. Bring your decisions to God in prayer; use the Bible as your guide, and then follow God's leading. He will make your paths straight by guiding and protecting you," says one writer. However, according to Solomon in this verse, to receive God's guidance, you must acknowledge God in all ways. This means that you should turn every area of your life to Him and allow Him to take full control.

If you are in the process of deciding the way you should take, are you seeking counsel and guidance from your friends? Have you made wrong decisions in the past and are afraid that you might fail again? Do what Solomon is suggesting: submit your ways to God. First, examine your priorities and values. What is important to you? What do you hope to achieve? Where is God on your list of priorities? Have you failed in some areas of your life because you have not submitted to Him?

You may think you have all the answers and insist that you want to do it your way. It is like trying to help a young child with a task that you can clearly see that she or he is unable to manage; however, no matter how much you try to help, the child will insist, "I can do it." You cannot afford to ignore God's guidance; otherwise, it will be to your detriment. Make Him a vital part of everything you do in your life so that He will guide you to accomplish His purpose in you.

Make the decision today to trust God and acknowledge Him in all your ways. You were placed on this earth to accomplish His will and not yours. 'Hold on to instruction, do not let it go; guard it well, for it is your life.'

Today's Prayer: Heavenly Father, let me always consult, listen, and submit to you so you can direct my path. Amen.

May 22

SHE LOVED TO LAUGH

'A cheerful heart is good medicine, but a crushed spirit dries up the bones.' (Proverbs 17:22)

My mother loved to laugh. I'll always remember the times when she and her siblings would sit in my grandmother's kitchen, and it was laughter all the time.

What is Solomon saying? He is saying that laughter is the best medicine. One writer says, "Cheerful people are as welcome to others as pain-relieving medicine." Solomon recognised that the connection between one's mental state and physical health is important. We are encouraged to cultivate a positive mind-set. One study shows the effect of laughter on the body and mind. It shows that laughter "swaps the stress-inducing cortisol in our bloodstream for a cocktail of feel-good neurotransmitters, dopamine and oxytocin."

'Endorphins in the body will trigger feelings of pleasure. Laughter is a natural mood booster; it also increases oxygen intake to muscles and heart and raises endorphin levels released in the brain. It also increases circulation and facilitates muscle relaxation. Laughter is certainly the best medicine, for it promotes overall well-being and vigour, contrasting with the debilitating effects of a dejected spirit, which can lead to emotional and physical ailments,' notes one commentary.

In another study carried out by Zander-Schellenberg et al (and others) in 2020, they found that the more participants laughed, the less stress they reported. Laughter can leave us feeling more content with our lives. Research agrees with what Solomon says in Proverbs 17:22, that a cheerful heart benefits health, acting as 'good medicine', while a spirit crushed by sorrow and despair causes physical deterioration, described as 'drying up the bones'. We can therefore see the powerful mind-body connection and how laughter can impact every aspect of our body.

Jeanne Calmont, who died at the age of 122 and was entered in the Guinness Book of Records as the oldest woman, was asked the secret of her longevity, "laughter," she replied.

God expects his people to be filled with joy and happiness, as it encourages a resilient spirit and shows His goodness toward them. Even in the face of trials and difficulties as a child of God, you can maintain an inner joy. As you go out today, remember to laugh and bring a smile to others. What better way to witness for Christ?

Today's Prayer: Father, I thank you for giving me the ability to laugh. Amen.

May 23

THE RACE IS NOT FOR THE SWIFT

'...The race is not for the swift.' (Proverbs 9:11)

You can no doubt recall Aesop's fable about the 'Tortoise and the Hare'. The hare, who was the faster runner, was so confident that he would win the race, took time out to rest. While he was sleeping, the tortoise kept plodding on. This account, although a fable, holds spiritual significance. It teaches lessons of perseverance, humility, and the importance of being consistent in working towards your goals. The story symbolises the Christian journey where believers need to be focused on their eternal home. It also embodies steadfastness and faith that is required. The tortoise embodies these qualities, showing that to win the race of life, "It is not just about physical speed but about maintaining a steady inner rhythm and peace," says one writer.

By contrast, the hare represents pride, overconfidence, and self-assuredness. The hare's arrogant belief sadly can be seen in some who profess to know God, and yet are prideful and arrogant in their behaviour. Self-assurance without humility can become an obstacle in life's journey. Pride, which God hates, can lead to spiritual apathy and decline.

The tortoise won the race, and the hare lost. This reflects the unpredictable nature of life. Believer's success is not guaranteed by their own abilities or effort. Total dependence on God and exercising faith in Him, and trusting in His power, will bring success in life. Matthew Henry, in commenting on this text, says, "Men's success seldom equals their expectations. We must use means, but not trust in them: if we succeed, we must give God praise..."

When we think of the Christian race we are running, it is clearly not about how swift or how strong we are; it is about enduring to the end. We need to run with the prize in mind, the hope of eternal life; this must be our focus. Our motivation in serving God means much more than anything this world offers. We don't run for a temporary crown, but an eternal one. Paul, in 1 Corinthians 9:24-25, helps us to understand that the race we are running requires purpose and discipline. For the Christian life, it takes hard work and determination. The tortoise knew the hare was much faster than he; however, he was prepared to run the race.

If you have not yet made up your mind to run the race for Christ, now is the time to decide whether you seek earthly accolades or are looking for that blessed hope. In running this race, you are called to ask others to join you and complete the task God has given you, the task of making disciples and testifying to the gospel of God's grace and mercy. God expects you to put every effort into the work of proclaiming the gospel of salvation to a dying world. Are you prepared to run the race of life despite challenges? Focus on the goal like athletes do.

Today's Prayer: Father, I know I cannot win the race without you. Amen.

May 24

PROCRASTINATION

'As Paul talked about righteousness, self-control and the judgment to come, Felix was afraid and said, "That's enough for now! You may leave." (Acts 24:25)

Procrastination is defined as 'the act of unnecessarily delaying or postponing something despite knowing that there could be negative consequences for doing so'. Someone once said, "Procrastination is the thief of time." Procrastination might also be the result of laziness. In Acts 24:25, however, when Paul began to get personal, Felix was frightened and became uncomfortable and asked Paul to leave; he would call for him at a convenient time.

Like Felix, some people might be happy to discuss the gospel, but if it touches their personal lives, they might not wish to hear, or make excuses not to listen. Felix delayed his decision about his faith, and so did King Agrippa (See Acts chapter 26). When Paul explained the gospel to him, Agrippa exclaimed, "Do you think that in such a short time you can persuade me to be a Christian?" He did not commit to becoming a Christian, and neither did Felix. The people in Noah's day heard him preach for one hundred and twenty years, and not one of them entered the ark. Could it be that many were convicted when they heard Noah's message, but kept procrastinating, saying, it might not rain in their lifetime, or they just kept putting off responding to Noah's message?

If God is calling you to respond to His message or to work for Him today, what will your response be? Do not procrastinate. As a child of God, you cannot afford to delay any longer. You have been called to share the gospel with others. Paul reminds us in 2 Corinthians 6:2 that "now is the time of God's favour, now is the day of salvation."

Today's Prayer: Father, I know there is no time like the present; let me not put off deciding for you today. Amen.

May 25

THE WAY OF TRANSGRESSION IS HARD

'Good judgment wins favour, but the way of the unfaithful leads to their destruction.' (Proverbs 13:15)

When we transgress God's Word and disobey His commands, we must suffer the consequences. Solomon says, in Proverbs 13:15, that the way of transgression is hard. Take David, for example, in the well-known narrative found in 2 Samuel 11:27, about David and Bathsheba, we read, 'But the thing David had done displeased the Lord'. This is the same David that God said was a man after his own heart; now God is displeased with him.

When David committed adultery with Bathsheba and she became pregnant, he tried to cover up what he had done by having her husband killed and then marrying her before the child was born. It seemed David had forgotten that his sin would find him out. The same applies to us too; we cannot sin and believe that God does not see. You can only imagine God's displeasure and His disappointment in David. God reminds him, "I anointed you king over Israel, and I delivered you from the hand of Saul. I gave your master's house to you, and your master's wives into your arms. I gave you all Israel and Judah, and if all this had been too little, I would have given you more." (2 Samuel 12:8)

By sinning against God, the judgment meted out to David made him realise the magnitude of his sin. As a result, God would bring calamity on him before all Israel (2 Samuel 12:10-12). David had committed his sin in secret; however, his punishment would be open for all to see. Tragedy and turmoil plagued his family. The way of transgression is hard, but God, in His mercy, accepted David's confession and repentance.

God will treat our sins the same way he treated David's; however, the Bible tells us that "If we confess our sins, He is faithful and just and will forgive us our sins and purify us from all unrighteousness." (1 John 1:9)

If you have unconfessed sins in your life that you need to deal with, go to God, confess and ask Him for forgiveness. You don't want to displease God, do you?

Today's Prayer: Father, I confess my sins and ask for your forgiveness. Amen.

May 26

A GENTLE ANSWER

'A gentle answer turns away wrath, but a harsh word stirs up anger.' (Proverbs 15:1)

What does Solomon mean by a gentle answer turns away wrath? Have you ever tried to argue in a gentle or soft tone? It is equally hard to argue with someone who insists on speaking quietly or gently. On the other hand, if someone speaks harsh and angry words, you are not likely to respond in a gentle voice because abrasive words will always trigger an angry response. Harsh words will only escalate anger, and before you know it, you may say things you will later regret.

This verse helps us to understand that speech can either harm or heal, and for that reason, Solomon is encouraging individuals to learn to control their speech and choose to exercise wisdom and gentleness when communicating with each other. We should not let our words cause conflict, anger, or hostility; we should always aim to promote peace. Therefore, if someone speaks angrily to you, it is much wiser to respond with kindness and gentleness and grace as you learn to turn away wrath with peaceful and gentle words.

You probably know of individuals who are known for their 'sharp tongue', or you might have a sharp tongue too. Solomon tells us how we are to behave in such situations. Before you speak or respond to someone who speaks harshly to you, think about the impact of your words on the outcome of the interaction and how it might affect your relationship with them. If you are a parent, you must be careful how you speak to your children; speak to them with kindness so that they in turn, will cultivate a gentle spirit.

If someone speaks angrily to you, how will you respond? Pray for heavenly wisdom before you respond. When you respond with gentle words, you demonstrate wisdom, control, and emotional maturity. Choose kindness and a calm spirit rather than an angry response. Do not view gentleness as a weakness; it is strength. The verse encourages individuals to respond in a measured and thoughtful way, to think before they speak and ask themselves: 'Will my words cause damage to the relationship that I have with this person?'

Although you might be provoked by what the other person might say, choose a calm and respectful response. When Jesus was here on earth, He interacted with love, grace, and humility with those who treated Him unkindly. The word for today is: speak words that give grace to others, and, "Live a life worthy of the calling you have received. Be completely humble and gentle, be patient, bearing with one another in love." (Ephesians 4: 1 & 2)

Today's Prayer: Father, help me to be gentle and respectful in my speech. Amen.

May 27

THE BIRTHRIGHT

'...So Esau despised his birthright.' (Genesis 25:34)

A birthright was a special honour given to the firstborn son who would receive a double portion of the family inheritance. It also meant that they would become the family's leader.

In the book of Genesis, chapter 25, we read the story of how Esau, Jacob's firstborn, lost his birthright to his younger brother Jacob. He sold his birthright to his brother for a meal. Esau seemed to have lost control of his appetite. The Bible tells us in verse 34, 'So Esau despised his birthright.' His problem was not just about a lack of control of appetite; it was a much deeper-seated problem. He had a profound misunderstanding and a lack of appreciation of his heritage; he did not value his birthright, nor did he understand 'the spiritual significance of his heritage'. Commentators highlight the fact that the birthright was not just about an inheritance, but it signified spiritual privileges and the continuation of the covenant with God.

Have you traded your birthright? Don't be like Esau, who allowed the pressures of the moment to cause you to lose sight of your rich heritage as a son or daughter of God and heir to His kingdom. The pressures of the moment can distort your perspective and cloud your judgment, causing you to make wrong choices and yield to temptation. You should recognise that you are special to God. "You are a chosen people, a royal priesthood, a holy nation, God's possession." (1 Peter 2:9) Your birthright is found in Jesus Christ. When you trade Him and the gifts and blessings, He has bestowed upon you for the meaningless and inconsequential things of this world, you are despising your birthright.

Today's Prayer: Heavenly Father, help me to remain faithful to you and not trade your blessings for the things of this world. Amen.

May 28

NO OTHER GODS

"You shall have no other gods before me." (Exodus 20:3)

After all God had done for the children of Israel, you might wonder why He commanded them not to have any other gods when they crossed over the Red Sea on dry land. They had experienced many miracles. He even fed them manna, angel's food, when they were in the wilderness. Surely, they would not even dare think of serving other gods. However, this was not the case. They promised to serve only God and told Moses that they would do everything the lord said.

Their promise to obey God was short-lived; their good intentions did not last long. Time and again, they broke the covenant that they made with God and worshipped other gods. They forgot God's goodness and substituted idols for Him. Instead, they should have made Him first in their lives, but failed to do so and suffered the consequences.

Are you worshipping other gods, gods of possession, money, education, celebrities, or your achievements? Anything that is loved or admired more than God is your idol. The things that you spend more time doing can also become your idol. How many hours do you spend on your phone or watching television compared to the time you spend in prayer or study of His word? God is the only one worthy of our worship and devotion. When He says, "Have no other gods before me," He means that He must be the central focus in our lives; therefore, make a conscious decision to let Him be the central part of your life today.

Today's Prayer: Dear God, there is none greater than you; let me worship you and no other. Amen.

May 29

REPENTANCE

'From that time on, Jesus began to preach, "Repent, for the kingdom of heaven has come near."' (Matthew 4:17)

Have you ever found yourself confessing the same sins repeatedly? God wants us to be truly repentant, that is, grieving over sins we have committed, turning away from them and turning to Him. *Godly sorrow brings repentance that leads to salvation and leaves no regret, but worldly sorrow brings death." (2 Corinthians 7:10)

We are all sinners and in need of God's forgiveness. He wants us to turn away from our sins and turn to Him, for He is the only one who can save us. Asking for forgiveness is the first step; however, we must be repentant; that is, we must feel sorrow, regret, and remorse for our sinful behaviour. Repentance is about turning away from sin and a commitment to put away our sinful ways. True repentance means acknowledging the weight of your sin.

In David's prayer of confession, you can almost feel the gravity of his sin as he expresses grief over his actions. He agonises with God, "Have mercy on me, O God [...] against you, you only, have I sinned. Cleanse me with hyssop and I shall be clean, wash me and I shall be whiter than snow." (Psalm 51: 1, 4, & 7)

It was Charles Stanley who said, "Repentance is a change of mind, a change of heart, a heart that is going to result in a change of conduct..." Although David had sinned against Bathsheba, he said he had sinned against God. All sin hurts us and others, but ultimately it is against God that one has sinned. Sin is offensive to Him because sin is rebellion against Him. Our behaviour can sometimes be like that of a child who has been scolded for wrongdoing and promises not to repeat the behaviour. However, they soon forget and can be found doing the same thing again. Isn't that just what we do, promising God we will not repeat our sinful actions, but later find ourselves doing the same thing again?

How many times have you told God how sorry you were, and you wouldn't do it again? However, God calls us to repentance. When tempted to sin, remember that you will be sinning against God. When we repent, restoration takes place.

God is waiting to forgive you of your sins. He says, "If we confess our sins, He is faithful and just and will forgive us our sins and purify us from all unrighteousness." (1 John 1:9) True confession of sin involves a commitment not to continue in sin, but to repent and move on.

Today's Prayer: Heavenly Father, give me strength to defeat temptation so I do not keep sinning against you. Amen.

May 30

DOING THE RIGHT THING

"If anyone then knows the good they ought to do and doesn't do it, it is sin for them." (James 4:17)

You might think that doing wrong is a sin, and quite rightly so; however, James is telling us that sin is also not doing right. He highlights the fact that the sinfulness of not acting when it is right to do so is also a sin. You might have heard of someone who has suffered workplace harassment, and their colleagues, instead of supporting them, choose not to intervene. This is an example of not acting when it is the right thing to do.

Are there times when you have witnessed wrongdoing but chose not to help? Was your lack of intervention due to fear, or was it just a case of not wanting to get involved? Whatever the reason, not doing what is right is sin. God expects His children to do what is right at all times. A believer knowing the right thing to do and failing to do it is clearly sinning against God.

It is also a sin to know the truth and withhold it. James defines this sin as the sin of omission; that is, when you know the right thing to do but refuse to act. Your intervention might help exonerate someone who has been wrongfully accused. You should be ready to help as guided by the Holy Spirit. One source states that verse 17 "challenges believers to move beyond mere knowledge and actively demonstrate their faith through action, realising that inaction in the face of known good also constitutes a violation of God's law and a form of rebellion."

There is also the sin of commission, which is when we do something that we shouldn't do. For example, lying or stealing, or deliberately hurting someone. We often tend to speak more about the sins of commission, and not the sins of omission. Another example of the sin of omission is not helping someone whom you recognise as needing help. In the teachings of Jesus, there are several examples of sins of omission. "For I was hungry and you gave me nothing to eat, I was thirsty and you gave me nothing to drink. I was a stranger and you did not invite me in, I needed clothes and you did not clothe me, I was ill and in prison and you did not look after me." (Matthew 25:42 & 43) Jesus demands our personal involvement in caring for others; anything short of that is a sin. He expects us to do what is right because it is right.

Today's Prayer: Father, forgive me for not acting when I should. Amen.

May 31

THROWING IN THE TOWEL

"Let us not become weary in doing good, for at the proper time we will reap a harvest if we don't give up." (Galatians 6:9)

Have you ever felt that nothing is going well in your life? It could be at work, church, or at home; things have become overwhelming, and you want to give up, you want to throw the towel in. Perhaps there are times you have worked hard, made sacrifices, and you didn't even receive thanks, just criticisms. You have gone the second mile and see no tangible results. You become discouraged and frustrated and want to give up.

Think about great leaders and the prophets of old, Jeremiah, Ezekiel, and Moses. Take Moses, for example; the odds were stacked heavily against him when he decided to give up his place in Pharaoh's palace. What about the grumbling and complaining Israelites, the criticisms from his siblings, Aaron and Miriam, and the negative reports from the spies. He had every reason to give up, but he didn't.

It is discouraging when you have worked hard and put effort into all you have done; it is easy to give up. In the text (Galatians 6:9), Paul challenges the Galatians to keep doing good and trust God despite what others say.

If you are in a situation today where you have been thinking of throwing in the towel, think again. Keep your eyes on the fixed prize, don't give up and like Paul, "... press towards the goal to win the prize for which God has called me heavenwards in Christ Jesus." (Philippians 3:14). "Do not become weary in doing good."

Today's Prayer: Heavenly Father, when the going gets tough, help me to look forward to a more meaningful life because of my hope in you. Amen.

June 1

LOVE YOUR ENEMIES

"But I tell you, love your enemies and pray for those who persecute you." (Matthew 5:44)

When Jesus spoke these words to his Jewish listeners, it must have sounded unbelievable or even offensive to them. As far as they were concerned, you should love your neighbour and hate your enemy (verse 43). I can imagine them thinking it was easy for Jesus to do, for after all, He was the Messiah, for those who believed. It was easy for Him to do good to those who wronged Him, but that would be asking too much of them, as far as they were concerned. (This statement, although centuries old, still applies to us today.)

What Jesus was saying did not make sense to them. Any Messiah who spoke like Jesus was certainly not the military leader they were waiting for to come to overthrow their Roman oppressors; they wanted to get even with their enemies.

Jesus' approach in dealing with enemies went against the grain; it was a radical one. However, His message was clear. Instead of demanding your rights, Jesus was saying; give them up freely, for it is more important to give justice and mercy than to receive it. One writer says, "True perfection is to love, to be forgiving and to be merciful even to those who do not deserve it. This principle and the actions are what it means to reflect God's character."

You might have been badly hurt by someone whom you now consider an enemy. Can you find yourself doing what Jesus suggests? He is actually saying do not retaliate, but show love instead? I know this is a hard thing to do, but you should, for it is by loving and praying for your enemies that you will overcome evil with good. This act involves death to self.

Today's Prayer: Heavenly Father, you know I have been wronged, help me to forgive and respond with love to those who have hurt me. Amen.

June 2

ACTS OF KINDNESS (1)

"Be kind and compassionate to one another, forgiving each other, just as God in Christ forgave you." (Ephesians 4:32)

A story is told of a mother whose six-month-old baby suffering from cancer was hospitalised. On leaving the hospital to go home, she tried to pay for parking, but the machine did not accept her card, and she had no cash with which to pay. Soon a security guard came along and kindly paid for her parking. She offered to repay however, he refused.

In this text Paul commands the believers to show kindness and compassion to others, for this is what God expects. For believers, kindness is not an option. One preacher says, "Kindness is a supernatural expression of God into your world." Because we are sinful beings, we do not naturally display kindness in our lives. Being kind means caring for others, bearing their burdens (showing empathy), and valuing them above ourselves. In Ephesians 4:32, Paul tells the believers to put away sinful attitudes and behaviour. We should act kindly to others.

In Colossians 3:12, believers are encouraged to live the way God expects them to live. If we expect to receive kindness from others, we must demonstrate it to others. Mother Theresa gave her life to the people of Calcutta – she lived simply so that others may simply live. In 2 Samuel 9:7 David showed kindness to Mephibosheth (Jonathan's son), for the sake of his father. You too might have been shown kindness because your parents showed kindness to others.

Think about it, do you naturally display kindness in your life? Emulate Christ for He shows us first-hand how to live.

Today's Prayer: Father, help me to show kindness to those around me. Amen.

June 3

ACTS OF KINDNESS (2)

"But the fruit of the spirit is love, joy, peace, forbearance, kindness, goodness, faithfulness..." (Galatians 5:22)

Do you find it hard to be kind? St. Paul mentions kindness as being one of the segments of the fruit if the spirit. Kindness cannot be achieved by human methods because it is a divine quality. Kindness is really love in action. People will know who you are by your actions. "By their fruit you will recognise them." (Matthew 7:16)

Are you selective in your kindness? Your acts of kindness should be motivated by love. However, there are people who are motivated sometimes, not by love; their primary motivation might be as a result of fear or guilt, or about trying to impress others, or to show how generous they are. In 1 Corinthians 13:3, Paul says, "If I give all I possess and give over my body to hardship that I may boast, but do not have love, I gain nothing." To be kind is to be motivated by love for others.

The parable of the Good Samaritan is an example of someone whose kindness was motivated by love. (You can read the story in Luke 10:25-37.) The injured man is ignored by the Levite and the priest, the very ones who should have shown kindness. However, the despised Samaritan, because of his ethnicity, stops to provide attention and care to the wounded man. Yet the two religious leaders who should have cared behaved differently; they lacked compassion, love, kindness and empathy. This parable of Jesus challenges us to look deep within ourselves to see whether our biases and prejudices are preventing us from showing genuine kindness to others. In the account, Jesus tells the lawyer to go and do likewise, to show love and kindness to others. Will you go out and do likewise?

Today's Prayer: Father, let my kindness be motivated by a genuine desire to serve others. Amen.

June 4

FLOODGATES OF BLESSINGS (1)

"Test me in this," says the Lord Almighty, "and see if I will not throw open the floodgates of heaven and pour out so much blessing that there will not be room enough to store it." (Malachi 3:10)

Floodgates are barriers that control the movement of water, typically to prevent it from entering an area during a flood, for example, the Thames barrier, which is one of the largest movable barriers in the world. Can you imagine if there were a flood in London and there were no floodgates? The city would most probably be completely flooded.

In Malachi 3:10, God says if you are faithful in returning a tenth of your earnings, He will "throw open the floodgates of heaven and pour out so many blessings that there will not be room enough to store them." Can you imagine being blessed by God? When He says He'll open the floodgates of heaven and pour out His blessings upon you, that is exactly what He will do. Your blessings will be so abundant that you won't have enough room to store them.

Are you struggling financially, or otherwise? Read this very powerful promise, meditate upon it. However, to have the floodgates of heaven open for you, you must be obedient and faithfully trust God to provide for you. When He opens the floodgates of heaven for you, your blessings won't be just financial; you will experience success and an enriched life, physically, spiritually and emotionally. You will experience joy, peace, and well-being in your life. God says, put Him to the test in this, so go ahead and see what He has in store for you. He is asking you to step out in faith and obedience; trust Him to deliver, for He is always faithful.

Today's Prayer: Father, thank you for your promise to bless me abundantly. Amen.

June 5

FLOODGATES OF BLESSINGS (2)

"Bring the whole tithe into the storehouse, that there may be food in my house. Test me in this, says the Lord Almighty, and see if I will not throw open the floodgates of heaven and pour out so much blessing that there will not be room enough to store it." (Malachi 3:10)

My aunt's two neighbours each had a lychee tree. One neighbour's tree would only produce a few lychees, whereas the other neighbour's tree produced so many year-on-year that customers would flock to his farm to purchase his lychees. As customers' cars parked outside the farm, my aunt often wondered why this neighbour's lychee tree was so productive. One day, she decided to ask, and to her utter amazement, he told her that the more tithe he returned to God, the more lychees his tree bore. In today's text, God promises to throw open the floodgates of heaven and pour out multiple blessings so that there will not be room enough to store them.

The people in Malachi's day ignored God's command to return a faithful tithe of their income. They might have been afraid of not having enough left for themselves. Or they probably lacked faith and therefore would not take God at His word. They doubted that He would supply all their needs like He said He would. They misunderstood God's might and power to bless their faithfulness, and for that reason, found it difficult to return a faithful tithe.

God always keeps His promises. In Luke 6:38, we read His promise: "Give, and it will be given to you. A good measure, pressed down, shaken together and running over will be poured into your lap. For with the measure you use, it will be measured to you." Talk about multiple blessings!

God is waiting to pour out His blessings upon you, so make the decision today to become a faithful and cheerful giver. "Each of you should give what you have decided in your heart to give, not reluctantly or under compulsion, for God loves a cheerful giver." (2 Corinthians 9:7)

Today's Prayer: Father, help me to cheerfully return a tenth of my income to you. I want to receive the multiple blessings you have promised. Amen.

June 6

WHAT IF GOD WERE TO TAKE ALL YOUR POSSESSIONS?

"The Lord gave and the Lord has taken away, may the name of the Lord be praised." (Job 1:21)

If you had all your possessions taken away, what would you do? Job lost his possessions and his family, but was still able to praise God. Satan took all he had. He even took his body. The Bible tells us that Job was covered with sores from the crown of his head to the soles of his feet. Yet Job was able to say, "...The Lord gave and the Lord has taken away." (Job 1:21)

Despite his devastating loss, Job still praised God. Although he was a very wealthy man, he did not allow his possessions to define him. If you had everything taken from you, would you still trust and praise God? Job did not understand why he was suffering so much. In Job 1:1 he is introduced as a man who was blameless and upright; he feared God and shunned evil.

Like Job, you must understand that everything you have comes from God and can be taken away at any time, for He is the one who sustains and provides for you; the one who controls your life and your possessions.
Can you still praise God in the midst of loss? Job did and he was able to, because he had learnt to trust God in both the good and the bad times.
You might be suffering loss today; read the story of Job again. It is hard for us to put ourselves in his place but praise God anyhow. Job's loss would have caused many to despair, but despite his loss, Job's faith sustained him, to the point where he was able to say, "Though He slay me, yet will I hope in Him..." (Job 13:15)

Today's Prayer: Father, even if I lose everything, I will still trust you. Strengthen my faith. Amen.

June 7

JESUS THE MIRACLE WORKER

'Taking the five loaves and the two fish and looking up to heaven, he gave thanks and broke the loaves.' (Matthew 14:19)

Matthew records this amazing and miraculous account of the feeding of the five thousand. How could two fish and five loaves feed five thousand or more people? The disciples must have wondered at that, too. However, Jesus had already worked out the maths. After giving thanks, He proceeded to break the loaves and the two fish. He then asked for baskets, and one by one, each was filled until there were twelve baskets full, and the people ate to their fill. Afterwards, the disciples picked up twelve baskets of broken pieces that were left over.

Can you imagine being there and seeing Jesus breaking bread and fish and filling up basket after basket? His maths was flawless. He certainly knew about multiplication! This miracle speaks of Jesus' power, His ability to do the impossible. One writer says, "The most obvious aspect of the miracle is Jesus' ability to increase food miraculously, showcasing his authority over the natural world."

If you are struggling with meeting your daily needs, learn from this account that just as Jesus used something small to accomplish something big that day, He can do the same for you today. Place the little you have in His hands and with faith and trust in Him, watch Him do great things with the little that you have.

Today's Prayer: Lord, may I be willing to give what I have to you, for even when my resources are insufficient; I know you will multiply what I have. Amen.

June 8

THE GIFT OF HEALTH

"Do you not know that your bodies are temples of the Holy Spirit, who is in you, who you have received from God? You are not your own; you were bought at a price. Therefore, honour God with your bodies." (1 Corinthians 6:19-20)

Have you ever heard someone say that their body belongs to them; therefore they have the right to do whatever they want with it? This is contrary to what Paul is saying in this text: our body belongs to God. Health is a gift from God, and as such, we should treasure our bodies and take care of it. One writer says, "If you don't take care of your body, where are you going to live?" Paul says our bodies are temples of the Holy Spirit. That is, when we accept Christ in our lives, the Holy Spirit comes to live in us, and for this reason, you should not violate His standards or commands for living. In 1 Corinthians 10:31, Paul says, "So whether you eat or drink, or whatever you do, do it all for the glory of God." This should be our guiding principle, that is, whatever we do should bring glory to God.

We should stop and think about whether our lifestyle is a healthy one. Doctors are becoming concerned about the significant rise in the incidence of some early-onset cancers, particularly in the under-fifties. Research shows that this increase is linked to factors such as diet, environmental exposures and lifestyle changes. Diet plays a crucial role in your health. Unfortunately, modern diets are far from being healthy, foods are highly processed, contain too much sugar, salt and fats. Because we were bought with a price, the blood of Jesus Christ, we should therefore dedicate our bodies to glorify and serve Him. We do not own our bodies; God does. The moment we accept Christ, and the Holy Spirit dwells in us, He now owns us; it is as if He places a seal on us. We now belong to God. The moment we are redeemed by Christ, there is a transfer of ownership. We belong to none other than Jesus Christ.

Today's Prayer: Father, I dedicate my body to you, so I can bring glory to you. Amen.

June 9

THE NEED FOR SELF-DISCIPLINE

"Do you not know that in a race all the runners run, but only one gets the prize? Run in such a way that you get the prize." (1 Corinthians 9:24)

Paul uses the analogy of athletes running a race to help us understand the importance of being disciplined. Winning a race requires purpose and discipline. Using this analogy, he helps us to understand that the Christian life takes effort and hard work. It is known that athletes are highly self-disciplined. They develop positive daily habits, set themselves clear goals, exercise mastery over unhealthy foods and adhere to a strict diet, and set themselves clear goals. Athletes maintain focus and do not allow themselves to be distracted, and are consistent in what they do, cultivating mental toughness and fortitude. They do not allow themselves to accept defeat, but to see defeat as a stepping stone to success.

Paul continues in verse 25 saying that those who compete in a race "go into strict training, they do it to get a crown that will not last, but we do it to get a crown that will last forever." He is saying that the Christian life cannot be left to chance; we, too, are in a race; we are running toward our heavenly home. This race, like the athletes', requires hard work, self-discipline and exhausting preparation. In the heavenly race, all will receive a crown that will last forever. How are you running your race? Are you focused and self-disciplined? There will be challenges and obstacles along the way; however, according to Matthew, "... he that shall endure to the end, the same shall be saved." (Matthew 24:13 KJV) What are the essentials needed for Christian discipline? Prayer, study of God's word, and meaningful worship. One writer says, "Don't merely observe from the grandstand, train diligently – your spiritual progress depends upon it."

Today's Prayer: Father, help me not to lose focus, let me keep my eyes on you so I can run the race to the finishing line. Amen.

June 10

THEY HAD BEEN WITH JESUS

'They took note that they had been with Jesus.' (Acts 4:13)

The narrative in Acts chapter 4 chronicles the challenges the apostles faced as they proclaimed the gospel of the risen Christ. The religious leaders were amazed at the boldness and how well the apostles spoke. They knew Peter and John were uneducated and untrained, or so they thought; however, little did they know that these men were trained by Jesus, the Master Teacher Himself. The change that the religious leaders witnessed in the apostles resulted in them concluding that Peter and John had been with Jesus.

Can others looking on say the same of you that you have been with Jesus? Are you keeping company with Him? Peter and John's behaviour showed that they had been keeping company with Jesus; however, it was far more than that, they had experienced the transformation that comes only from Jesus, they were empowered by the Holy Spirit and therefore spoke with boldness and confidence about Jesus Christ.

Can it be said that you have been with Jesus because of your changed life, because of the boldness with which you communicate the gospel of Christ to others? When others see the change in you, it should convince them of God's love. Being with Jesus means His light will shine through you. Spending time with Him will affect others. Like Moses, whose face shone with God's glory, so radiance will be stamped on your face too, and others will be able to tell that you are abiding in the presence of God. Acts chapter 4:13 is a powerful reminder of the transformative power of Jesus Christ and the Holy Spirit. It challenges societal norms and expectations, emphasising the importance of faith, boldness, and the influence of Jesus in the lives of believers. It serves as an encouragement for believers to seek a close relationship with Jesus.

Today's Prayer: Father, may I live my life so others can see that I am living in your presence. Amen.

June 11

PERSEVERANCE (1)

"If we endure, we will also reign with Him…" (2 Timothy 2:12)

If you are facing hardships; if life appears to be a series of failures and disappointments, God promises that one day you will live eternally with Him. This is why you should not give up, for God has promised a wonderful future with Him. Henry Wadsworth Longfellow once said, "Perseverance is a great element of success. If you knock long enough and loud enough at the gate, you are sure to wake up somebody." But how does one develop the ability to persevere?

Paul tells us in Romans chapter 5:3 that although we might encounter pain and suffering in the process, it is suffering that produces perseverance. Therefore, the problems that you encounter will help you to develop perseverance. Athletes, for example, will go through gruelling moments of pain to win the race; however, despite the pain, they never give up. You will hear them say they leave everything on the field, that is, they did all they could, they persevered to the end.

It is by persevering that your character will be strengthened and you will experience a deeper trust in God. As a believer, do you persevere even when the odds are against you? It is only through faith in God and dependence on the power of His Holy Spirit that you will persevere. It is through prayer and study of His word that you will be enabled to carry on as you draw strength from His word.

Scot Wylie once said, "Perseverance is the ability to endure and persist through challenges, difficulties and setbacks with steadfastness, determination and resilience." If you are to be successful, focus on the prize, like an athlete does, and never give up.

Today's Prayer: Dear God, give me the strength and determination to persevere to the end. Amen.

June 12

PERSEVERANCE (2)

"Let us not become weary in doing good, for at the proper time we shall reap a harvest if we do not give up." (Galatians 6:9)

Paul challenges the Galatians, and he also challenges us not to give up but to keep trusting God. It is not easy for believers though, however, Paul assures us that in due time we will reap a harvest of blessings.

Are there times when you have tried and failed; you have become disappointed and disillusioned, and want to give up? Paul is saying here that you must persevere, although the going is rough. Take my nephew, who does not believe in giving up. He wanted to do a particular course in college; however, he did not have the grades he needed to qualify to do the course. However, he presented himself at the college on the day of enrolment and was told several times that he could not be enrolled on the course. However, he persisted and was eventually enrolled on the course by the course tutor, who commended him for his persistence.

As believers, we have every reason not to quit. The Bible tells us to persevere because Jesus did. When He was agonising in the Garden of Gethsemane, He could have given up, but man's life hung in the balance. He had to go to Calvary to save us, so there was no way He would give up. We are to "run with perseverance the race marked out for us, fixing our eyes on Jesus, the pioneer, and perfector of our faith." (Hebrews 12:1-2)

If you feel like quitting today, remember that 'Blessed is the one who endures trials, because when he has stood the test, he will receive the crown of life that God has promised to those who love Him.' (James 1:12)

Today's Prayer: Father, when life gets tough, help me to persevere because you have promised a glorious end. Amen.

June 13

BLESSED ARE THE MEEK

"Blessed are the meek, for they will inherit the earth." (Matthew 5:5)

The Beatitudes found in Matthew 5, constitute a code of ethics as a standard of behaviour for believers. In His sermon on the mount, Jesus described how His hearers should conduct themselves.

What does Jesus mean by being meek? Does He mean you should be submissive and allow others to treat you like a doormat? Should we remain passive when others are unfair to us? On the contrary, 'to be meek is to be humble and patient under adversity,' says one writer. Meekness describes a quality of controlled strength, discipline, and humility. As a believer, God expects you to endure wrongs without bitterness, anger, or malice.

You might be thinking, how can Jesus expect me to show meekness when it is so much easier to do otherwise, seeing that I have the capacity to express anger, especially when I am treated unfairly. This beatitude comes with a promise, the promise of inheriting the kingdom. Jesus is saying that if you are to gain heavenly citizenship, being meek is one of the characteristics you must possess. He doesn't ask us to do anything that He won't give us the strength to do. All you need to do is to make Him your example, for He is the very model of meekness. In Mathew chapter 11:29, we read these words, "Take my yoke upon you and learn from me, for I am gentle and humble in heart, and you will find rest to your souls."

Today's Prayer: Heavenly Father, thank you for your promised inheritance. Teach me how to be meek. Amen.

June 14

WHO DO YOU SAY JESUS IS?

"Who do people say the Son of Man is?" (Matthew 16:13)

Matthew records this conversation between Jesus and His disciples. He first asks, who do people say He is, and then asks them who they think He is. It was a commonly held view then that Jesus was one of the prophets. In reply to the first question, the disciples said some people said John the Baptist, others said Elijah, and still others said Jeremiah. However, when Jesus asked the disciples, "Who do you say I am"? (Verse 15) Peter declared, "You are the Messiah, the Son of the living God." His answer was a confession that Jesus was indeed divine, and He was truly the Messiah they were waiting for.

If Jesus were to ask you this question, "Who do you say I am?" How would you respond? Would you like Peter, proclaim that He is your Lord and Saviour, and would you boldly state this fact? If indeed He is your Lord and Saviour, are you faithfully fulfilling the Commission He gave you? "Therefore, go and make disciples of all nations…" You cannot accept Him as your Lord and Saviour and fail to proclaim Him. Believe it or not, you answer this question every day, sometimes consciously or unconsciously. For it is your lifestyle that will tell others who you say Jesus is.

Paul says, "You yourselves are our letter, written on our hearts, known and read by everyone." (2 Corinthians 3:2) If you really believe that Jesus is who He says He is, it will affect the way you live. Does your life bring glory to Him? Does your behaviour demonstrate to others that Jesus is the Son of God? The fact that you know who Jesus is does not need to be written on paper for others to read, but by your lifestyle, it will be evident that, because of your transformed life, others will see Jesus in you.

Today's Prayer: Lord, make me a living epistle empowered by your Holy Spirit. Amen.

June 15

BE AN ENCOURAGER (1)

'Gracious words are a honeycomb sweet to the soul and healing to the bones.' (Proverbs 16:24)

Words have a profound influence on others; therefore, you must speak kindly to others. Solomon uses the word 'gracious', which means to speak with kindness and compassion, and love; speaking words of encouragement that will build others up.

You might be able to recall people who have encouraged you, perhaps, your parents or teachers, who have helped you to succeed. We all need encouragement, and we, in turn, should not fail to encourage others. Have you noticed that when athletes run, the stadium is always full of supporters cheering them on and encouraging them. As a runner, especially those who run the marathon near the end of a long and exhausting race, their body aches and cries out for them to stop; however, the cheers of fans and spectators encourage them to keep going.

Just as fans encourage the athlete, so also should believers encourage others by speaking words of kindness and complementing them. It is so easy to criticise others, especially leaders. However, a kind word of encouragement can make a difference between them finishing well or being burnt out. Paul encourages the believers in Thessalonica to build each other up. He emphasises the importance of doing so as it creates an environment of love, faith, and trust. It is conducive to spiritual growth and the success of the gospel. Why not become an encourager today and experience the impact it will have on you and others around you? Or, if you have been encouraged, go out of your way to be an encourager today; be aware and be sensitive to the needs of others, offer a kind word and give support to those who need it.

Today's Prayer: Heavenly Father, I like to be encouraged, please help me to be an encourager to others. Amen.

June 16

BE AN ENCOURAGER (2)

"And let us not weary in well doing: for in due season we shall reap, if we faint not." Galatians 6:9)

Have you ever felt discouraged when you have put a lot of effort into what you have done, and no one seems to recognise or appreciate your efforts? In Galatians 6:9, Paul encourages the believers not to give up but to continue to do good despite being challenged. He uses the analogy of farming. If you have planted anything, you will know that it takes time, effort, and consistency to tend to your plants until they mature and are ready for harvest. In the same way, as believers, if we are to grow spiritually, it will take time and patience. We can sometimes be impatient, especially with new believers and expect too much of them. Instead, we must give them time and support and mentor them, just as you need to tend to your plants to help them to grow, and just as the seeds you have planted need time to grow so does one need time to grow spiritually.

Paul encourages believers to remain faithful and not weary in well doing; that is, never give up, don't lose heart, but to continue doing good, for in due season, you receive a harvest of blessing. It is discouraging to continue to work and do what is right and receive not even a word of thanks. Paul challenges and encourages the Galatians to continue to do good. We too should be challenged in a similar way. We should always encourage others and not take them for granted. As believers we should be actively building each other up and not tearing each other down. We should encourage each other by being honest, by speaking the truth, and helping them to see themselves as children of God with potential to carry out His mission. In the New Testament we have the example of Barnabas, nicknamed the 'son of encouragement' for his support of Paul and Silas, and who was a great encourager to the early church. We cannot forget Job, although he was suffering did not fail to encourage his friends.

Jesus is the ultimate encourager; He offered hope and assurance to those He met. In John 16:33 we read His words of encouragement to His disciples: "I have told you these things, so that in Me you may have peace. In this world you will have trouble. But take heart! I have overcome the world." What words of encouragement!

If you are feeling disheartened, weary and fatigued, be encouraged today as you reflect on the promises of God. Become an encourager too.

Today's Prayer: Dear Father, thank you for those you have placed in my life to encourage me and help me to be an encourager too. Amen.

June 17

UNBELIEF

"Help me overcome my unbelief." (Mark 9:24)

Living in a world of conspiracy theories, it is sometimes hard to believe all the information that circulates in the media. Belief is an attitude of trust and confidence in what you hear or read. However, faith plays an important role in believing, especially in the Bible, the word of God. Unfortunately, society is filled with people who often express unbelief in the Bible, even though truth has been presented to them. Take Nebuchadnezzar, for example, who praised Daniel's God, yet still did not believe in Him completely or submit to Him. Sadly, this attitude still prevails today. Some people profess to believe in God, yet they have not submitted themselves to Him. They attend church, say the right words, and use spiritual language, use the appropriate clichés, but they don't really believe and give honour to God, as they should.

Do you profess to be a believer but have not fully submitted to Christ? One writer says, "Profession doesn't always mean possession." Unbelief is destructive because it prevents you from having a fulfilling relationship with God. The preacher Martyn Lloyd-Jones describes unbelief as "a dangerous enemy to God's plans; an active force that keeps people from receiving God's promises and experiencing spiritual freedom." Unbelief will separate you from God, causing you to remain in spiritual darkness. Unbelief is a sin that paves the way for other sins. It will prevent you from receiving God's saving grace. Failure to believe in God can cost you your eternal life.

If you are struggling with unbelief, pray and ask God to help you overcome your unbelief.

Today's Prayer: Lord, I realise that unbelief is a sin. I want to experience spiritual freedom. Help me to overcome my unbelief. Amen.

June 18

GET SOME REST

"Come with me by yourselves to a quiet place and get some rest." (Mark 6:31)

Do you lead a busy life and have little time to rest? We live in a fast-paced world where we are constantly being kept busy and have little or no time to rest.

In this text, we find Jesus telling his disciples that they need to take a rest after having just returned from their mission. Mark tells us that there was so much going on around them, people were going and coming, that the disciples and Jesus were perhaps not even getting time to eat. Jesus knew the importance of rest. At creation, He instituted the Sabbath day of rest. God had been creating for six days, but on the seventh day Sabbath, He rested from all His work. Being God, the Creator, He was clearly not tired; however, He established the day of rest for mankind. In Mark chapter 2:27, we read, "The Sabbath was made for man, not man for the Sabbath." That is, He created it for our benefit. We are restored, not just physically, but also spiritually.

The disciples were tired on their return from their mission, and so Jesus took them away from the crowd to rest. Doing God's work is vitally important; however, you need to take time to rest. Jesus invited His disciples to rest because He knew that without adequate rest, they would not be effective in their mission. We too need to plan rest periods in our daily schedules. Do you find yourself rushing around and not getting time to rest? If God felt He needed to rest after creation, how much more do we, as humans, need to rest? Remember that rest is crucial, not just for your physical health, but also for your spiritual health. If you are not getting enough rest, make it a priority today, and by so doing, you will be honouring God with your body.

Today's Prayer: Father, help me to make rest a priority in my life, for both my physical as well as for my spiritual well-being. Amen.

June 19

HE WILL DELIVER YOU TOO

"My God sent His angel, and he shut the mouths of the lions." (Daniel 6:22)

Daniel, that great statesman and servant of God, found himself in a dilemma. He occupied a high position during the reign of Darius the Mede. Because he was a diligent and responsible worker, he made many enemies at work, and this led his enemies to plot against him as they tried to bring him down. You might have had a similar experience, whereby others have tried to bring you down. They were probably jealous, not wanting you to prosper, and did everything in their power to destroy you. Daniel finds himself in this situation; however, his enemies could not find anything with which to destroy him, so they attacked his religion. (You can read the account in Daniel chapter 6) Daniel's enemies appealed to the king's vanity by getting him to sign a law that no one should worship any other god but the king. (He had set himself up as a god for thirty days.) This did not deter Daniel; he kept praying as he always did. 'Three times a day, he got down on his knees and prayed, giving thanks to his God, just as he had done before.' (Verse 10)

What do you do when you are persecuted? What do you do, when you find yourself in the lion's den? Daniel kept praying even when he was thrown into the lion's den. He had a disciplined prayer life and continued to pray because he knew the only one who could deliver him was his God, whom he kept praying to, and in a mighty way, God delivered him. He was able to pen these words, "My God sent his angel, and he shut the mouths of the lions." (Verse 22) Whatever your situation is today, trust God; he delivered Daniel, and He will deliver you too. One writer says, "The person who trusts and obeys God is untouchable until God takes him or her. To trust God is to have immeasurable peace...", the kind of peace that Daniel had even in the lion's den.

Today's Prayer: Father, thank you for my deliverance from the enemy. Amen.

June 20

DO YOU KNOW GOD, OR KNOW ABOUT HIM?

"Now this is life eternal that they know you the only true God and Jesus Christ, whom you have sent." (John 17:3)

Do you know God, or do you just know about Him? There is a crucial difference between the two. To know God is to have a personal relationship with Him. You can read or hear of Him and know that He exists and not really know Him.

In this text, John defines eternal life as a deep personal relationship of knowing God and Jesus Christ, whom He sent. Knowing God goes beyond a mere intellectual understanding of Him. It is an experiential understanding of a life that characterises a profound relationship with Him. Moses' life serves as a good example. In Exodus 33:12-17, we find him desiring to know God. You would have thought that, having spent time in God's presence on the mountain for forty days and nights and more, Moses would have known God; however, he desired to know God's character in a real way. He realised that although he had spent time in God's presence, he still needed to have a genuine and intimate relationship with Him, and that was his reason for asking God to teach him His ways. "If you are pleased with me, teach me your ways so I may know you and continue to find favour with you." (Verse 13)

Everyone has the opportunity to know God because He has made Himself known by sending His only Son to be known to mankind when He took on humanity and became one of us.

Today's Prayer: Father, like Moses, my prayer is: show me your way, that I may know you. Amen.

June 21

LEST YOU FORGET

"These stones are to be a memorial to the people of Israel forever." (Joshua 4:7)

God had miraculously parted the Jordan River for the children of Israel. After crossing, God commanded that a pile of stones should be placed in a particular spot as a permanent reminder of what God had done for them. This memorial was intended to remind the people of God's mighty and powerful deeds. It was to be a constant reminder that they would not forget His goodness to them. The pile of stones was to serve as a lasting testimony of God's faithfulness to them, not just to them but to succeeding generations. "So that when your children ask you, what do these stones mean? Tell them that the flow of the Jordon was cut off before the ark of the covenant of the Lord."

Like the children of Israel, we too should build memorials. God wanted His people not to lose focus on Him; they were to remember who had guided them as they journeyed. How about you? Are you building memorials as you work for the Master? As you carry out God's work, set aside time to build your own memorials to God's power so that your loved ones can appreciate His love and power in your life.

Jesus left an empty cross and an empty tomb as a memorial of His self-sacrificing love for us. The empty tomb stands as a memorial of His victory over death and sin for mankind. As you focus daily on what God has done for you, set up memorials in your home by spending time in the study of His word with your family, and spend time in prayer and testify to His goodness to you and live a life of praise and thanksgiving. Do not forget the way God has led you.

Today's Prayer: Lord, let me remember to build my own memorials of your guidance throughout my life. Amen.

June 22

THE SCHOOL OF HARD KNOCKS

'But how is it to your credit if you receive a beating for doing wrong and endure it? But if you suffer for doing good and you endure it, this is commendable before God." (1 Peter 2:20)

Have you ever experienced trials and sufferings in your life and told yourself, I never signed up for this, I didn't apply to the school of hard knocks? You haven't done anything wrong to deserve this. 1 Peter 2:20 highlights the difference between suffering for doing wrong and suffering for doing good. You expect to be punished for doing wrong but not for doing good. How do you respond when you are treated unjustly for doing good? I once met someone who was extremely efficient in her work; whatever task she had to accomplish was done with diligence. However, her colleagues did not like her because they felt she was showing those up who were less efficient. As a result, they made her life very difficult. However, she continued to endure the injustice that was meted out to her. 1 Peter 2:20 should bring hope and comfort to those who are suffering and being treated unjustly, or punished for good behaviour. Peter says that if you suffer for doing good, you will gain significant favour and credit with God. Even in the face of injustice, the child of God must be patient and continue to do good, trusting that God will vindicate them and they will be victorious.

One commentary states that, "Enduring such unjust suffering for good deeds serves as a witness to the nature of Christ, who suffered unjustly for others, but entrusted Himself to God." This patient endurance also plants seeds against institutions of unjust treatment. So, if you are currently in the school of hard knocks for doing good, endure it, for you will be commended by God.

Today's Prayer: Father, you have said I must be of good courage even if I am in the school of hard knocks, because you have overcome the world. Amen.

June 23

ROYAL BLOOD

"But you are chosen people, a royal priesthood, a holy nation, God's special possessions, that you may declare the praises of Him who called you out of darkness into His wonderful light." (1 Peter 2:9)

The songwriter says, "I am a child of the King, His royal blood flows through my veins." You are of royal birth because your father is the King of Kings, Monarch of the universe. In 1 Peter 2:9, we are reminded that we are a 'royal priesthood.'

Being a member of an Earthly royal family means that you have a hereditary connection to a reigning monarch, either by blood or marriage, and this typically bestows titles, social standing, and specific public duties. To be a member of a royal family means you are likely more privileged than ordinary citizens. However, being a child of the King of Kings, being of God's royal priesthood, sets you apart from others, because you have been chosen by God as His very own – His blood flows through our veins. Like the earthly royal family that represents our country, as a child of the King of Kings, you should represent Him to others.

As a child of the Creator King, you must value your worth. Your value comes from being one of God's children, not from your achievements or your earthly heritage. You are royal; you have worth because of what Jesus has done for you on the cross of Calvary.

Today's Prayer: Father, I am thankful that I am your child and that I am a member of the royal family of heaven. Amen.

June 24

GOD DOES THE IMPOSSIBLE (1)

'So, the sun stood still and the moon stopped, till the nation avenged itself of its enemies.' (Joshua 10:13)

God did that which was scientifically impossible. Verse 13 describes God's miraculous intervention during the battle of Gibeon. Joshua commanded the sun and the moon to stand still, thus prolonging the day, so that there was enough daylight to finish the battle.

How did the sun stand still? There are various interpretations of the text; however, when these celestial bodies stood still, it was because of divine intervention. We know that in relation to the Earth, it is the sun that stands still; the Earth travels around the sun. However, what happened that day was a miracle; the day was prolonged. God did the impossible for His people. We don't know what method God used to prolong the day; however, the Bible is clear that God did the impossible and Israel won the battle.

Some believe this phenomenon was a literal stoppage of the sun and the moon, while others suggest that it could have been a more general 'long day' occurrence. Regardless of the speculations, it is clear from the text that God intervened that day in answer to Joshua's prayer.

We should learn from this that God can do the impossible in our lives too. After all, as He says in Jeremiah 32:17, "Nothing is too hard for me." You might be going through what appears to be an impossible situation in your life right now, but learn from this story that God can make the impossible possible. Joshua exercised faith when he made such a bold request, which, from a human standpoint, was impossible, but God came through for him, and He'll do the same for you.

Today's Prayer: Father, I have every reason to believe that you can intervene in my situation, too and make the impossible possible. Amen.

June 25

GOD DOES THE IMPOSSIBLE (2)

'The waters divided, and the Israelites went through on dry ground, with a wall of water on their right and on their left.' (Exodus 21:22)

You can imagine it, thousands of people fleeing from Egyptian bondage, only to find all their hopes shattered when they discovered that there was no escape route – the Red Sea before them and Pharaoh's army behind them. There was no apparent way to escape, but the God of the impossible opened up a dry path through the sea, where they witnessed the miraculous power of God. Commanded by God, Moses stretched out his rod and the waters of the mighty sea divided, and the people crossed over on dry ground. The dividing of the sea was an act of God's supernatural power to do the impossible, even defying the laws of nature.

If you have found yourself today caught in a situation that seems impossible, you cannot see any way out, don't panic. Be assured that the same God who parted the Red Sea for the people and made a way for them is the same God who will intervene in your situation and open up a way for you. When Israel saw no way of escape, the God who created the earth and the water performed a mighty miracle and demonstrated His power, love, and mercy for His people. Never fear, He'll do the same for you too.

Today's Prayer: Heavenly Father, in the times when things seem impossible, help me to exercise faith in you, because you can do the impossible things in my life. Amen.

June 26

GOD DOES THE IMPOSSIBLE (3)

'The water from upstream stopped flowing.' (Joshua 3:16)

'Now the Jordon is in flood all during harvest, yet as soon as the priest's feet touched the water's edge, the water from upstream stopped flowing. It piled up in a heap a great distance away.' (Joshua 3:15 & 16) Here again, God did the impossible for His people under the leadership of His faithful servant Joshua. After all their wanderings, the Israelites were now on the brink of Canaan, the promised land; however, they had to cross the Jordon River. You can only imagine what was going through the people's minds; no doubt panic began to set in. Had they already forgotten what Joshua had said the day before? "Consecrate yourselves, for tomorrow the Lord will do amazing things among you."

When faced with an impossible situation in your life, do what Joshua commanded the people to do: consecrate yourself, that is, ask God to forgive you of your sins. We all need to be forgiven of our sins before we approach God. Only then will He hear our cry.

God gave Joshua specific instructions about what the people should do as they prepared to cross the flooded river. If you are to cross the flooded rivers in your life, you must follow God's instructions. Through the miraculous parting of the river, God made the impossible possible for His people. Once more, they could testify to His might and supernatural power. When God leads you out of the waters that seem to engulf you and delivers you, you will have a testimony to share with others. God was always faithful to Israel, and He always keeps His promises. He was with His people through impossible situations from the time they left Egypt until they entered Canaan, demonstrating His might, His power, and His faithfulness to them. He will do the same for you.

Today's Prayer: Father, thank you for making the impossible in my life possible. Amen.

June 27

SELF-DENIAL

"Greater love has no one than this: to lay down one's life for one's friends." (John 15:13)

What is self-denial? It means the denial of one's interest and needs. According to the text, self-denial is motivated by love. We are to love each other as Jesus loves us. You may not have to give your life for someone, but there are so many ways in which you can deny yourself in order to show love to others.

Self-denial is a concept that is deeply rooted in the teachings of Christ; it is the fundamental principle by which believers should live. One writer says, "Self-denial involves a conscious effort to reject the natural human inclination towards selfish desire, choosing instead to live according to the word of God." You cannot claim to be a disciple of Christ and be selfish. In Matthew 16:24, Jesus told His disciples, "Whoever wants to be my disciple must deny themselves and take up the cross and follow me". When He said this to His disciples, they understood what He meant. Crucifixion was a common method of execution, and criminals had to carry their cross through the streets so all could see. Jesus was telling His disciples that self-denial came with a cost, even the risk of death.

Taking up your cross to follow Christ means a genuine commitment and a willingness to endure suffering and even rejection for the sake of Christ. However, no one wants to deny themselves; it's only human that we want to preserve ourselves. It was A.W. Tozer who said, "Odd thing that Jesus should place such an obstacle before people and that He should lay down a condition to follow Him, a condition contrary to human nature. No one wants to deny him or herself, we want to preserve ourselves." Is your life one of self-denial? Are you willing to give up comforts, desires, habits, or your time to serve others? Are you ready to prioritise God's will and desires and not your own? Christ challenges you to set aside your own concerns and align your life with His teachings and will.

Today's Prayer: Father, help me to live a selfless life, a life of self-denial. Amen.

June 28

WALKING IN THE LIGHT

"I am the light of the world. Whoever follows me will never walk in darkness, but will have the light of life." (John 8:12)

I remember leaving my grandmother's house one night to visit my aunt. I had forgotten how early it gets dark in the Caribbean. Although I had a torch, its light seemed inadequate, for there were no street lights, and the darkness that surrounded me was almost palpable.

When Jesus proclaimed that He was the light, He was telling the truth about His divine nature, that He is the source of spiritual truth. He is the only one who can dispel the darkness of sin from this world and from our lives. He is the only source of truth that is available to mankind. In verse 12, He is telling us that when we follow Him, we are no longer in darkness. Reflecting on my experience of walking in the dark to get to my aunt's house, I had to follow the light of my torch. In the same way, we should follow Jesus, who is the light and the way. Because of sin, this world is in darkness; however, the presence of Jesus brings us out of darkness into His marvellous light, and we are protected and guided by Him. John says, "The light shines in the darkness, and the darkness has not overcome it." (John 1:5) The darkness has not overcome it because the darkness of this evil world cannot and will never extinguish God's light. When we accept Him in our lives, the darkness of sin will vanish. When we follow Jesus, we no longer stumble in darkness; we can avoid walking blindly and not fall into sin. Just as the torch lit the way for me, in the same way God lights the way ahead for us, so we can see where we are heading. As we trust Him to lead and guide our lives, He will remove the darkness of sin from us. Is Jesus the light of your life? In what ways have you allowed the light of Christ to shine into and out of your life? If you have not yet allowed the light of Christ to shine in your life, let Him, for when you do, you will no longer stumble in darkness.

Today's Prayer: Father, I acknowledge that you are the true light. Shine in my life today so I can be a reflector of your light to others. Amen.

June 29

TRUST GOD'S PLAN

"For I know the plans I have for you, declares the Lord, plans to prosper you and not to harm you, plans to give you hope and a future." (Jeremiah 29:11)

Do you know that God has a plan for your life? As you go through life, you make plans, and you must do so, for it is foolish to go through life aimlessly. When you read this chapter in the book of Jeremiah, you will find these words were spoken to the Jews living in bondage. You can only imagine the emotional pain of living under the domination of another. For the Jews, it was a hopeless situation; however, throughout all of this, God told Jeremiah He had a plan for His people. This meant a future and a hope for the exiled people. They most probably had lost all hope, but God reassured them through the prophet that, despite their suffering, they would be free one day. As long as God was in control, they would have nothing to fear.

Just as He did for Israel, He also has a plan for you. God's plan for the people was about their well-being. God intended to give them a bright future and hope, and His plan is the same today as it was then. However, His plan does not exclude pain, suffering, and hardship; but He says He will be with you throughout, because He will never leave you or forsake you.

You might be going through a difficult time right now, but take comfort from this beautiful promise from God: despite your challenges, He has a plan to make your future brighter and to give you hope. Put your trust in Him and seek Him even in the difficult times in your life.

Today's Prayer: Father, I thank you for your plan for my life. Amen.

June 30

IS THE OLD MAN DEAD?

"For I know that our old self was crucified with Him so that the body ruled by sin might be done away with, that we should no longer be slaves to sin – because anyone who died has been set free from sin." (Romans 6:6-7)

I was at a gathering recently when a pastor spoke about an injustice that someone had endured at the hands of another. Sitting behind me was someone who, on hearing, made the most unpleasant and shocking remark, I had ever heard from a spiritual leader. Then and there, my mind went back to the text above. The 'old man' of aggression had not yet died in this individual. Sadly, our sinful nature sometimes takes a long time to die, and from time to time will rise up in us.

The 'old man' refers to humanity's fallen nature and the inherited tendency to sin. Paul refers to it as the body ruled by sin, which describes "our rebellious and sin-loving nature inherited from Adam." However, as a result of Jesus' death on the cross, the power of sin over us died with Him on the cross; therefore, we no longer live under the power of sin.

Are there times in your life when you feel like doing the wrong thing, and sometimes do? Before you accepted Christ, you were a slave to sin, but now you have chosen to live for Him; He makes all the difference in your life now. The things you used to do, you do them no more, the reason being that you have been crucified with Christ and you no longer live, but Christ lives in you. The life that you now live, you live by faith in the Son of God who loved you and gave Himself for you. (Galatians 2:20) Do you want to say hallelujah? Then do, for the old man is dead!

Today's Prayer: Heavenly Father, thank you for your power over sin. Help me to put off the old man and walk in newness of life. Amen.

July 1

PENTECOST

'All of them were filled with the Holy Spirit and began to speak in other tongues as the Spirit enabled them.' (Acts 2:4)

The text describes the event of the outpouring of the Holy Spirit on the disciples, causing them to speak in other languages. This phenomenon took place at Pentecost when the believers were unitedly awaiting the promise that Jesus had given them. They were now experiencing the fulfilment of that promise. The fact that they could speak in different languages was a miracle in itself. God wanted everyone from different nations and languages to hear the gospel. There were many foreigners assembled in Jerusalem at that time, and God wanted them to hear the message of salvation.

It was at Pentecost that the early church was born. God made His presence, His might and power known dramatically. Would you like God to reveal Himself to you today? It might not be as dramatic as Pentecost, but He is waiting to reveal Himself to you in whatever way He chooses. Do you want the presence and power of the Holy Spirit in your life? All you need to do is make yourself available, spend time in prayer and ask him to prepare your heart to receive Him. God had to prepare His disciples for the work He had called them to do, and being filled with the Holy Spirit, they took the world by storm, and the Christian church was established.

The disciples were commanded by Jesus to go and make disciples of all nations, baptising them in the name of the Father, and the Son and the Holy Spirit (Matthew 29:19). You, too, are called to become a disciple and make disciples, but first you must experience Pentecost in your life. Are you ready for Pentecost? May you be filled with God's Spirit today as you witness to others.

Today's prayer: Heavenly Father, I pray for the presence of your Holy Spirit in my life today. Amen.

July 2

THE LITTLE FOXES

'Catch for us the little foxes, the little foxes that ruin the vineyards, our vineyards that are in bloom.' (Song of Solomon 2:15)

I must confess, foxes are far from being my favourite animals. We have an entire family living in our garden. The little ones are particularly destructive. One day, as I was looking out onto the garden, I saw one digging up the lawn with all its might. Suddenly, my mind went back to the words of Solomon, where he speaks about the little foxes that ruin the vineyards.

One writer explains the 'little foxes' as the kinds of problems that can disturb or destroy a relationship. The 'little foxes' can sometimes be the biggest problems in our lives. They could be minor irritations that you might not like in an individual or your spouse; however, these must be dealt with before they create bigger problems. Solomon is saying that we should consciously and actively address these small irritations or threats to relationships before they become stumbling blocks. The 'little foxes" can cause the biggest problems in your relationship with others. The 'little foxes' in your life can also destroy your relationship with God. Your 'little foxes' might be: telling a white lie, pride, selfishness, covetousness, jealousy or backbiting, among others. Remember that God hates sin, and these 'little foxes' represent sinful things that we must get rid of. There are no little sins in the sight of God; sin is just what it is, sin. Do not allow the 'little foxes' to undermine your relationship with God. You must not minimise or ignore them, for if you do, they will become huge problems that will be harder to deal with. The 'little foxes' can impact your spiritual life and cause you to lose sight of God's blessings. They will destroy your connection to the vine, Jesus Christ.
What are the 'little foxes' that nibble away at the tender grapes of your life? Ask God to rid you of them.

Today's Prayer: Dear God, show me the 'little foxes' in my life today and help me deal with them. Amen.

July 3

FREEDOM FROM SIN'S GRASP

"What shall we say, then? Shall we go on sinning, so that grace may increase? By no means! We are those who have died to sin: how can we live in it any longer?" (Romans 6:1-2)

Do you really understand the seriousness of sin? Paul in Romans 8:7 tells us that, "The mind governed by the flesh is hostile to God; it does not submit to God's law, nor can it do so." Paul addresses the misconception that some believers had about God's forgiveness and His grace; that is, if God is forgiving, then we can keep on sinning because He will forgive us. Of course not, says Paul. You should not think that because God is forgiving, it makes sin less serious. Sin is the very reason that caused the death of Christ on the cross; Jesus, knowing that we would otherwise perish in sin, died for our sakes. "For God so loved the world that He gave His one and only Son, that whoever believes in Him shall not perish but have eternal life. For God did not send his Son into the world to condemn the world, but to save the world through Him." (John 3:16 &17)

Being freed from sin because of what Jesus has done for us should lead to a new life in Him; we no longer continue in sin, and we leave our past life behind. God offers us grace as a gift; however, it does not mean we can sin as much as we like because He forgives us every time we ask for forgiveness. It is presumptuous to think this way. Do you want to be free from sin's grasp? If you do, you must understand the seriousness of sin and hate it as much as God does. Accept God's grace, stop and contemplate the amazing sacrifice that has been made for you at Calvary. You cannot free yourself from sin; it is only through God's grace and His power to save that you can be set free. The message for today is: a life of sin is unacceptable to God; in fact, it is offensive to Him. Would you be free from your burden of sin? There's power in the blood of Jesus. Accept Him today if you want to be truly free.

Today's Prayer: Father, I desire to accept the freedom that you offer, through grace, for I have no power over sin. Amen.

July 4

THE BLESSED HOPE

"...while we wait for the blessed hope, the appearing of the glory of our great God and Saviour, Jesus Christ." (Titus 2:13)

The blessed hope should fill you with joy and anticipation as we await the coming of our Lord and Saviour Jesus Christ. The world in which we live has become a hostile place. The condition of the world should make us long for His coming. In 2 Timothy 3, 1-5 Paul describes the very time in which we are living. "But mark this; there will be terrible times in the last days. People will be lovers of themselves, lovers of money, unforgiving, slanderous, without control, brutal, not lovers of good, treacherous, rash, lovers of pleasure rather than lovers of God, having a form of godliness but denying its power. Have nothing to do with such people." What a horrifying and gloomy picture of our world!

I am sure you can see the kinds of behaviour outlined in the text, happening all around you. One writer says, "Courage is needed to stand between two extremes of current troubles and ultimate triumph." It is indeed frightening to see the things happening in our world today. However, the Bible is clear that these are the things we will experience as His coming draws nearer. "People will faint from terror, apprehensive of what is coming on the world..." (Luke 21:26)

However gloomy and frightening things might sound, they should not cause believers to worry; on the contrary, they should be a cause for great joy because these are signs of the coming of Jesus, the blessed hope. We are reminded by Luke that "when you see these things begin to take place, stand up and lift up your heads, because your redemption is drawing near." (Luke 21:28) Waiting for the blessed hope should fill you with hope and great anticipation, rather than being fearful and terrified by what is happening in our world. We should confidently await the coming of our lord Jesus Christ, for He will put an end to sin and restore the earth to its former state. A perfect earth, as there will be no more sin to contaminate it.

Today's Prayer: Father, I know that the only answer to the problems of this world is the blessed hope. Help me to live in expectation of your soon coming. Amen

July 5

YOUR RESPONSE TO SUFFERING

"Though He slay me, yet will I hope in Him." (Job 13:15)

How do you respond to suffering? Do you exercise faith and trust in God despite your suffering? Job suffered greatly at the hands of Satan; he lost everything, even his health. He was covered in painful sores from the crown of his head to the soles of his feet. Yet he was able to say, "Though he slay me, yet will I hope in Him." It is easy to lose hope when everything has been taken from you.

I reflect on the story behind the words of the hymn, "It is well with my soul," written by Horatio Spafford. He suffered a series of personal tragedies, and the loss of his fortune in the Great Chicago Fire in 1871, the death of his son, and the death of his four daughters in 1873 at the sinking of the ship on which they were travelling. Spafford suffered great financial ruin and the loss of his family, yet he was able to pen the words of this now well-known hymn, 'It is well with my soul'. Despite his grief, he was able to express faith in God and found peace and solace in Him. He understood the goodness of God and that He would never leave or forsake him when he needed Him most. You might be suffering a tragedy or a sickness which is causing you great distress; however, read the words of this hymn and draw strength from the words. Regardless of what you are going through, still trust God. Spafford had every reason to be bitter, yet he expressed a trust in God like Job's when he wrote, "Christ hath regarded my helpless estate and hath shed His own blood for my soul." Not only does he express his faith in God, but also hope and a longing when his "faith shall be sight". You, too, can find hope and peace in the profound message of this hymn if you are currently going through pain and suffering. Meditate on the promises of God and the words of this hymn; trust God, and He will help you to overcome. He will bring you 'peace like a river'.

Today's Prayer: Father, I seek your peace amid the storms and turbulence in my life. Amen.

July 6

IS JESUS YOUR FRIEND?

"I can no longer call you servants, because a servant does not know his master's business. Instead, I have called you friends, for everything that I have learned from my Father I have made known to you." (John 15:15)

What an honour it is to be called a friend of Jesus. Being His friend suggests that one has an intimate relationship with Him. With this elevated status from servants to friends comes the responsibility of being true and willing to love Him and others. Abraham in Isaiah 41: 8 is referred to as a friend of God. Being a friend of God implies actively and purposefully doing His will and being motivated by love for Him. One writer says that "the relationship places you in the 'inner circle' of God's confidence, giving you a profound opportunity to know and experience God intimately."

Being a friend of Jesus does not mean you won't have challenges along the way, or even personal loss. However, when you come through your challenges, does your friendship remain intact? Joseph Scriven did not stop being friends with God, despite his personal losses. His life was marred by tragedies after having lost his fiancée on the eve of their wedding, and later, the death of another fiancée to pneumonia. Yet, after such heartbreak and loss, he was able to write the words of the hymn "What a friend we have in Jesus, all our sins and griefs to bear, what a privilege to carry everything to Him in prayer."

Do you have such a friend in Jesus, the only one to whom you can take all your troubles? A faithful and genuine friend who will never leave you in times of loss and distress. You will find in Him comfort, solace, and hope.

If you are feeling that no one cares, or if you are hurting because a friend has disappointed you, do not 'forfeit' your peace by not carrying all your troubles to God, for He is a friend who really cares.

Today's Prayer: Father, thank you for making me your friend. Amen.

July 7

FAITHFULNESS

'Therefore, know the Lord your God, He is God, the faithful God who keeps covenant and mercy for a thousand generations with those who love Him and keep His commandments.' (Deuteronomy 7:9)

God is calling you to faithfulness. What does faithfulness mean? "Faithfulness is defined as being loyal and steadfast." It means that one is 'consistently loyal and true to a person, commitment, or principle, and demonstrates this devotion through consistent actions and adherence to promises, even in difficult circumstances'.

Thomas Chisholm, the writer of the hymn 'Great is Thy Faithfulness', understood what it meant to remain loyal and committed to God during difficult circumstances. He experienced a decline in health during his time as a Methodist minister. His poor health forced him to leave his congregation, and it was during this time of illness that he wrote the words of the hymn. He wrote the hymn despite financial struggles, too; he chose God's faithfulness, choosing to remain faithful to Him. Deuteronomy chapter 7:9 describes God's great and enduring faithfulness and loyalty to those who love Him and keep His commandments. Throughout Israel's history, they were constantly reminded of His faithfulness to them. However, they were not always faithful to Him in return; they were always breaking their covenant with Him. God's promises are trustworthy and He will not break them, but will always remain faithful.

Are you faithful to God? He has been faithful to you; however, His faithfulness is also conditional on your loyalty and obedience to Him. Do not break your covenant with Him like the children of Israel did. Chisholm, who had experienced God's faithfulness, wrote, "There is no shadow of turning with Thee. Thou changest not, thy compassions, they fail not; As thou hast been, thou forever wilt be." Make this your experience too and remain faithful to Him.

Today's Prayer: Lord, help me to remain faithful to you. Amen.

July 8

DOGS AND CRUMBS

"Yes, it is, Lord," she said. "Even the dogs eat the crumbs that fall from their master's table." (Matthew 15:27)

The encounter in Matthew 15: 24-28 between Jesus and the Canaanite woman can be easily misunderstood. His reply to this Gentile woman does not contradict the truth that God's message of salvation is for everyone, Jews and Gentiles alike.

The woman came to Jesus for help for her demon-possessed daughter when He told her that He was sent only to the lost sheep of Israel. However, the woman insisted that He helped her. When Jesus responded the way He did, He was not rejecting the woman, but showing that salvation is available to everyone regardless of ethnicity or background. He uses the analogy of taking the children's bread and tossing it to the dogs. Was he referring to the Gentiles as dogs? The Jews commonly applied this term dog to the Gentiles, because they were considered pagans and no more likely than dogs to receive God's blessings and His salvation. However, Jesus was not insulting or degrading the woman with what He said. He was reflecting the attitude of the Jews, but eventually showing the woman that He was not of that mind-set.

The woman responded by saying, "Even the dogs eat the crumbs that fall from the master's table," expressing a "profound faith, not demanding justice but appealing to mercy," says one commentary. In verse 28, Jesus affirms the woman's faith. "Your request is granted," and her daughter was healed at that moment.

As you read this story in Matthew 15, remember that God loves everyone and He desires to save us all. As His disciple, you have a responsibility to tell others about Him.

Today's Prayer: Father, thank you for your saving grace. Let me reach out to those who need to hear the gospel. Amen.

July 9

DON'T GIVE UP

"We are hard-pressed on every side, but not crushed; perplexed, but not in despair; persecuted, but not abandoned; struck down, but not in despair." (2 Corinthians 4:8&9)

In this text, Paul helps us to understand that although believers may go through hardships and suffering, we are not to give up, but that God will give us strength to endure. It's hard to believe what Paul went through for the sake of Christ: persecuted, abandoned, struck down, in danger, shipwrecked; these are just some of the many hardships that he went through.

It is so easy to give up when life gets rough. However, Paul assures us that while suffering is a reality for believers, we must not lose heart, "For our light and momentary troubles are achieving for us an eternal glory." (Verse 16 &17) Rather than quit when you're being crushed and in despair, do what Paul did. He didn't let his trials wear him down, but focused on the inner strength that he received from the Holy Spirit.

If you are going through hard times and being hard-pressed on every hand, remember that there is a purpose in your suffering. Can it be that God is building your faith and trust in Him as you go through your suffering? You might be feeling crushed right now, but don't give up, for God will sustain you and carry you through. He will never abandon you.
You might be struck down by circumstances in your life, but you are not destroyed. James tells us to "Consider it pure joy, my brothers and sisters, whenever you face trials of many kinds." (James 1:2)

Paul reminds us that suffering is part of the Christian experience, so we shouldn't be surprised or give up when they come our way. He says, "For our light and momentary troubles are achieving for us eternal glory that far outweighs them all." (2 Corinthians 4:17). In other words, our trials are small and will not last very long. Our troubles should not diminish our faith in God and should remind us of the suffering Christ went through to give us salvation. Troubles will also allow God to demonstrate His might and power in our lives, so our lives will then become living testimonies.

Today's Prayer: Father, let me see my trials as opportunities for you to demonstrate your power in my life. Amen.

July 10

UMBRELLAS

'Whoever dwells in the shelter of the Most High will rest in the shadow of the Almighty.' (Psalm 91:1)

As I went for my walk one day, I could not help but notice the two unusually shaped silver birch trees that lined the road. They were shaped like open umbrellas. I stood to admire those beautifully shaped trees, and the hymn, 'A Shelter In The Time Of Storm', came into my mind. I even imagined standing under the trees for shelter, should it begin to rain. The lyrics of the hymn were written by Charles Vernon Worth around 1880, and the tune was composed by Ira D Sankey. The hymn's text is based on Psalm 32:7. 'You are my hiding place; you protect me from trouble and surround me with songs of deliverance.'

The psalmist uses the metaphor of God as a 'hiding place' to help us understand that He is our refuge and He protects us from danger and surrounds us with joy, 'songs of deliverance'. The message of the song is that Christ will be a rock and shelter during the storms of life. It reminds us of God's protection and care. Just as the two trees would provide shelter if it rained, so God will provide shelter from the attacks of the enemy. In Psalm 61: 3, the psalmist says, 'For you have been my refuge and strong tower against the foe'. The psalm expresses deep trust in God; that one can feel secure in Him. He is your strong tower and an unshakable rock, especially in times of weakness, distress, and despair. If you are feeling unprotected or overwhelmed because of life's storms, let this psalm be a source of comfort and strength to you. God is your strong tower, and you can feel protected in Him. He is also your shelter; therefore, you can feel protected as you dwell in the shelter of the Most High. What better place to find shelter but under the shadow of God? There is no need to feel unprotected or vulnerable, for in Christ you can experience protection from harm and feel secure in Him.

Today's Prayer: Dear God, I want to continue to shelter and rest in you and feel protected. Amen.

July 11

NOBODY'S FAULT BUT YOUR OWN

'Whoever has ears, let them hear what the Spirit says to the church.' (Revelation 3:22)

There's a gospel blues song entitled 'Nobody's Fault But Mine' recorded by Blind Willi Johnson, which emphasises personal responsibility for one's soul, through failure to live for God. It says, 'Nobody's fault but mine; if I die and my soul be lost, ain't nobody's fault but mine.'

Each person has a responsibility for their spiritual salvation. When we know God, it is our duty to apply the truths of the Bible to our lives. If we accept God's word and do not live by it, we cannot blame Him if we are not saved in His kingdom. He gives us every opportunity to accept Him. The people in Noah's time had every opportunity to accept God. Although Noah preached to them for 120 years, they chose not to accept his message. They all perished in the flood. Whose fault was it? Not God's. It was nobody's fault but their own. When God warned of the coming disaster on Sodom and Gomorrah, He told Lot to leave with his family; however, his wife looked back after having been told not to, and was not saved. Whose fault was it? Not God's, but her own. Judas and Peter did not listen to Jesus or heed His warnings. Judas betrayed Him and later committed suicide. Peter denied Jesus three times. Both Peter and Judas could have blamed Jesus and said it was His fault; on the contrary, it was their fault.

How about you? Are you hearing God's last warning call to the world and ignoring Him? It is a call to repentance; it is His last warning message. "And this gospel of the kingdom will be preached in the whole world as a testimony to all nations, and then the end will come." (Matthew 24:14) In Revelation 3:22 God is telling us to listen and hear what He says. He wants to transform our lives because He desires that we are saved in His Kingdom. Remember, if your soul is lost, it's nobody's fault but your own.

Today's Prayer: Lord, I want to be saved in your kingdom. Amen.

July 12

JESUS TELLS IT LIKE IT IS (1)

"Those whom I love I rebuke and discipline. So be earnest and repent." (Revelation 3:19)

At times, the truth can make us feel uncomfortable. If a friend corrects you and tells you what you did was wrong, you might not want to hear it. However, your friend loves you, and they will point out when you have done wrong. In Revelation chapter 3, we find Jesus' message to the seven churches in Asia and all believers everywhere. He gives warning and hope to believers; however, He is forthright and tells it as it is.

He tells the church in Laodicea that although they are wealthy and they think they need nothing; He informs them that they are wretched, pitiful, poor, blind, and naked. What scathing remarks! He tells them that they would be disciplined if they did not take heed and turn from their complacency and indifference. Not only did Jesus tell them the truth of their condition, but He also provided hope for them. He counsels them to buy gold refined in the fire so that they can become rich, and have white clothes to wear, so that they can cover up their shameful wickedness, and salve to put on their eyes so that they can see.

God still speaks bluntly to His people today, because He loves us, and although the truth might hurt, He wants us to turn from our wicked and sinful ways. The pleasures of this world: money, status, education, and material possessions may satisfy, but they are only temporary. God wants you to seek the eternal things. Like it or not, He is telling you as it is. He is knocking at the door of your heart because He wants to save you. Will you respond to Him today?

Today's Prayer: Father, I know the truth sometimes hurts, but I need to hear it as it is. Discipline me, even if it is painful. I open my heart's door to you this day, for I desire to be saved in your kingdom. Amen.

July 13

JESUS TELLS IT LIKE IT IS (2)

"Those whom I love I rebuke and discipline. So be earnest and repent." (Revelation 3:19)

Although we do not enjoy being corrected, God corrects us because He loves us. In Revelation chapter 3:19, we find His urgent call to the complacent, self-sufficient church of Laodicea to repent and be earnest in their faith. He tells them that the reason for the rebuke is for their correction and spiritual growth. His words may appear harsh; however, God is never harsh or condemning. He corrects us for our good. This verse very clearly highlights the depth of God's love for His people; as a parent corrects an erring child, so does God our Heavenly Father. His purpose is not to punish us but to bring us back to Him when we have strayed.

You might be able to recall the time when you were disciplined by your parents and how you felt at the time. Now that you are older, looking back, you realise that when you were disciplined, it was because of their love for you. In Proverbs chapter 3:11-12, Solomon tells us that God's discipline is an expression of His love for His children. "My son, do not despise the Lord's discipline and do not resent His rebuke, because the Lord disciplines those He loves, as a father the son he delights in." This is such a beautiful picture of God's love for us! You might have had situations in your life that, looking back make you realise that God had been disciplining you. It might have been a painful experience, but God needs to rebuke you.

Is your spiritual life in a lukewarm state? Are you just going through the motions, going to church and not really doing anything for God? Can it be that God might be trying to discipline you out of your current lukewarm state, and you are not responding? He might be telling you like it is, but you are not listening. Spend some time reflecting on your life. Draw near to God, and He will draw near to you. Confess your sins and turn to Him.

Today's Prayer: Heavenly Father, thank you for your rebuke and discipline, which stem from your love for me. I repent of my sins today. Amen.

July 14

REVELATION BOOK OF HOPE

'Blessed is the one who reads aloud the words of this prophecy, and blessed are those who hear it and take to heart what is written in it because the time is near.' (Revelation 1:3)

I have met people who are afraid to read the book of Revelation. They are frightened of the graphic scenes and beasts. However, if they can get past their fears and read the words of this book, they will find it is a book of hope. As you read the book of Revelation, you will find John explaining how he received revelations from God. John is favoured by God, who reveals the full identity of Christ and brings us hope.

When John was exiled on the island of Patmos, little did he know that God would give him a wonderful panoramic view of God's end-time plans. As you study this book, you should be full of hope and know that you serve a God who holds the future, and that the future is secure in his hands. The book of Revelation constitutes the warnings God has given to believers to prepare them for the earth's final events. It is also a book of warnings to Christians who have lost hope and have become apathetic. It is also a book of encouragement to those who are faithfully serving and looking forward to the soon return of Jesus Christ.

Revelation is the book of hope, because you will discover that one day sin will be eradicated from the Earth, and good will eventually triumph over evil. If you are feeling discouraged and fearful of the present condition of the world, study the book of Revelation, and you will find hope and security in God's word. Hope that one day He will create a new heaven and a new earth where righteousness dwells, and there will be no more sin, for Satan's power is broken and his hosts will be destroyed. Be encouraged to study this book as we look forward to the blessed hope and the appearing of our Lord and Saviour, Jesus Christ. Eternity with Jesus should fill your heart with hope and joy beyond compare.

Today's Prayer: Father, thank you for the hope I find in you. Amen.

July 15

WALKING WITH JESUS

'As they talked and discussed these things with each other, Jesus Himself came up and walked along with them, but they were kept from recognising Him.' (Luke 24:15&16)

Two disciples returning to Emmaus, after the crucifixion of Jesus, are found discussing the events of the day, when Jesus appears and joins them on their walk. However, they did not recognise him. They were so wrapped up in their grief and despair and confusion about the death of Jesus, they failed to recognise the risen Saviour walking beside them. Not only did they not recognise Jesus, they were walking in the wrong direction, says one commentary on the story. They were walking away from the fellowship of the believers in Jerusalem.

How is your walk with Jesus? Is He walking beside you, and you are unaware of His presence? Are you so focused on other matters of earthly things and miss spiritual truths that will open your eyes to see Him, the only one who can take away all your sorrows and griefs? The two disciples were so preoccupied with the day's events, that is, the death of Christ that they failed to understand what had really happened in Jerusalem. Jesus walked with the two to clear up their misunderstanding. They were looking for truth, but were spiritually blind; however, those who are sincerely seeking truth, Jesus will draw near to them, as He did for the two disciples. After they had had an encounter with him, their eyes were opened, and everything changed. "Were not our hearts burning within us while He talked with us on the road, and opened the Scriptures to us?" (Verse 32) Is Jesus walking with you today, and you haven't recognised Him? It is only when you are looking for Him in your life that you will experience the change that needs to take place in your life. Only then will you experience the help and the blessings He can bring to your life.

Today's Prayer: Father, I want to walk with you as good friends do and should. Amen.

July 16

SITTING AT THE TABLE WITH JESUS

"...If anyone hears my voice and opens the door, I will come in and eat with that person, and they with me." (Revelation 3:20)

Picture this: Jesus knocking at your door, you wonder who could be knocking so gently, you look out the window and see him standing there. You open the door, and He tells you He wants to come in and dine with you. When Jesus says He wants to come in and dine with you, He means He wants to spend quality time with you, thereby expressing the closeness and intimate time He wants to have with you.

Do you want Him to come into your heart today? If you want Him to come into your heart, you must open the door to your heart and let Him in. You will notice that He knocks and politely waits, and asks if He can come in. He doesn't push or force his way in. He waits until you invite Him in. Be careful not to allow your busy work schedule or your worldly pleasures to absorb your time and not notice He's trying to enter. I am reminded of the song: 'The saviour is waiting to enter your heart. Why don't you let him come in there is nothing in this world to keep you apart.' What is your answer today? Are you willing to open the door and let Him in? If you feel alienated from Him, if you are feeling indifferent to the gospel, you might unknowingly be shutting Him out of your life. Today Jesus wants you to come in and dine with you so why not leave your heart's door open so He can come in? He is your only hope for a fulfilled life. Leave your door open, for one day soon not only will you sit with Him now, but you will in the New Earth, when you will gather around that great table, and dine with the Father, Son and Holy Spirit, the saints of all ages and your loved ones. Jesus is looking forward to dining with you when He will drink from the fruit of the vine, and He will drink it in His Father's kingdom with you. Surely, this is worth looking forward to!

Today's Prayer: Father, I am looking forward to dining with you at the Great Marriage Supper of the Lamb. Amen.

July 17

ARE YOU LOOKING FORWARD TO CHANGING YOUR NAME?

'Whoever has ears, let them hear what the Spirit says to the churches. To the one who is victorious, I will give some of the hidden manna. I will also give that person a white stone with a new name written on it, known only to the one who receives it.' (Revelation 2:17)

I have met people who were not happy with the names given to them at birth, and some have since changed their names by deed poll. Some countries have even changed their names. For example, Myanmar was once known as Burma, Iran was known as Persia, and Tanzania was once called Zanzibar. Your name identifies who you are.

In Revelation 2:17, we find God's message to the church in Pergamum; they were told that those who are victorious will be given a white stone with a new name written on it and a name that will be known only to the one who receives it. This refers to the time when those who are faithful to God will receive a new name when they get to heaven. While it is unclear what the white stones are, they are obviously significant because they bear the name of everyone who believes and accepts Christ and receives eternal life. Are you looking forward to heaven, and to receiving a new name?

In Roman times, white stones were used as admission tokens for banquets or public games awards for athletes and victors. Athletes, who won competitions, would be given a white stone as a token of honour and victory. These stones could grant them free entry to future events, free maintenance at the public's expense. Receiving a white stone was a sign of distinction, granting the holder special privileges, a new identity, and an elevated social honoured status.

Are you looking forward to receiving your white stone with your name engraved on it when you get to heaven? Jesus says we will be given a new name that is unique to the recipient. We will be given a new identity because we will be declared worthy to receive the name that God will give to those who have overcome. This will be a sign of divine acceptance, that God loves and values us as His very own.

Dear friend, remain faithful, for that's not all we will receive, for the Bible says, eye has not seen nor ear heard, about the joys that await those who are victorious.

Today's Prayer: Father, I am looking forward to having a new name and spending eternity with you. Amen.

July 18

GOD OF A SECOND CHANCE

"For it is by grace you have been saved, through faith, and this is not from yourselves, it is the gift of God." (Ephesians 2:8)

Peter denied Jesus three times, but Jesus gave him a second chance after all that he had done because God gave him a second chance and more. We read in Matthew 16:18, "I tell you that you are Peter, and on this rock, I will build my church, and the gates of Hades will not overcome it." Peter became the first leader of the Christian church because God gave him a second chance. God is a God who gives chances, not just one or two, but many more. The Bible refers to this as grace.

Grace is an unmerited gift, something you do not deserve. Have you ever received something you did not deserve? I recall a friend telling me how she lent a fellow shopper her loyalty card, which meant his shopping bill was reduced considerably. He did not expect this; this is what God's grace looks like, an unmerited gift. We receive what we don't deserve. My friend was also rewarded by getting more points on her card. Neither of them expected this.

Peter, having received a second chance, encouraged the church to grow in grace. "But grow in grace and knowledge of our Lord and Saviour Jesus Christ," he told them (1 Peter 3:18). The nation of Israel also experienced God's grace; a stiff-necked and rebellious people, whom God could have destroyed for their unfaithfulness, were given a second chance, and more. After forty years of wandering in the wilderness because of disobedience, God gave them yet another chance, and under the leadership of Joshua finally entered the Promised Land. You might be wondering if God will give you another chance, because you have been unfaithful to Him. He will, because He is the God of second chances. You'll need to confess your sins and ask for forgiveness, and be repentant, and He will extend His grace to you.

Today's Prayer: Father, thank you for your grace. Amen.

July 19

SALT OF THE EARTH

"You are the salt of the earth. But if the salt loses its saltiness, how can it be made salty again? It is no longer good for anything but to be thrown out and trampled underfoot." (Matthew 5:13)

Have you ever tasted bland food that has no salt or flavouring? You'll agree that it tastes unpalatable. Salt is known to be a precious commodity, and in the ancient world it was used to preserve food and to add flavour.

What did Jesus mean when He said you are the salt of the earth? He uses this metaphor to help us understand that if we are truly His followers, we should be like salt, making a positive influence on others. As a believer and a follower of Christ, are you impacting the world? Are you like salt that enhances the flavour of food? Are you positively influencing and engaging with others in your community? God expects you to live out your faith in your communities. Can others see Jesus in you?

If you are to be the salt of the earth, you cannot be like the world around you. You should be an example, and your life should bring glory to God. You must draw others to Him. If you make no effort to emulate Him and affect the world around you, you are useless and of no value to God, for if the salt has lost its flavour, it is no longer good for anything. God cannot work with those who have lost their 'flavour'. As a child of God, you cannot afford to lose your distinctive Christ-like character; if you do, you cannot disciple others. Go out today and influence the world for the cause of Christ and become salt of the earth.

Today's Prayer: Heavenly Father, help me to maintain my identity in you so I will be of value to you and those around me. Amen.

July 20

REFUSING TO BELIEVE

"Where did this man get these things?" they asked. "What's this wisdom that has been given Him? What are these remarkable miracles he is performing? Isn't this the carpenter? Isn't this Mary's son?" (Mark 6:2&3)

Mark highlights Jesus' return to His hometown in Nazareth. You would have thought they would be proud of Him as one of their own. Interestingly, they acknowledged His mighty works, the miracles He performed. As He taught them in the synagogue on the Sabbath, they were amazed at His knowledge and wisdom, and recognised that His wisdom was from above. However, they took offence because they knew who He was, the carpenter of Nazareth. They also knew His family. Because they knew Him as one from Nazareth, and knowing His background, they found it difficult to accept Him and questioned His authority; after all, He was the carpenter from Nazareth, and surely not the long-awaited Messiah.

The people of Nazareth had allowed their prejudice and their familiarity to blind their eyes to who He really was. Seeing how they behaved led Jesus to say, "A prophet is not without honour except in his own town among his relatives and in his home." (Verse 4) Although He was not honoured in His town that did not take away from the fact that He was the Son of God, nor did it make his work less important. Jesus could have done so much for the people of Nazareth, but because of their pride and unbelief, sadly, 'He could do not any miracles there except lay His hands on a few people who were ill and healed them'. He was amazed at their lack of faith. What missed opportunities for the people of Nazareth?

As a believer, you might encounter such behaviour as you witness for Christ, especially in your own community. Unfortunately, we live in a world where many have rejected Christ, and some do not even believe He exists. However, Jesus still seeks those who will respond to Him. One writer says, "The power of belief emphasises a willingness to see past familiar facades; belief is essential in experiencing the transformative power of God. Unbelief, on the other hand, is self-limiting because it prevents you from accepting Him."

Today's Prayer: Dear God, take away doubt from my mind, so I can respond to you. Amen.

July 21

REFLECTING ON GOD'S PROTECTION

'The angel of the Lord encamps around those who fear Him, and He delivers them.' (Psalm 34:7)

I recall a story of a missionary and his family who were threatened with death from those who were hostile to the word of God. While they were asleep, a mob with sticks and stones and spears came to attack them. As they approached the missionary's home, they saw the house surrounded and being guarded by soldiers with drawn swords. The terrified mob ran away in fear. The next morning, they recounted their experience to the missionary. (Little did the mob know that God had sent his angels to protect the family.)

Have you ever stopped to reflect on God's protection? It could have been an accident that you walked away from, or not being harmed by thugs or thieves or a fierce dog or being knocked over as you crossed the road. As believers, we do not seem to speak much about God's protection over us. The Bible tells us in Psalm 121:3-4, 'He who watches over you will not slumber; indeed, he who watches over Israel will not sleep.' My cousin's rather humorous interpretation of this text is that God does not put on pyjamas! Psalm 121 expresses so beautifully, assurance and hope in God's protection day and night. Does it not fill you with joy to know that someone as mighty and powerful as God, the monarch of the universe, would love and consider you so precious to Him that He watches over you every moment.

We are reminded in Psalm 34:7 that the angel of the Lord encamps around those who fear Him and He delivers them. Daniel in the lion's den was protected by the angels and was able to tell the king that God had sent His angels to deliver him and the lions had not harmed him. Peter's escape from prison also shows the remarkable power of God in protecting His people. An angel frees Peter by blinding him and guiding him past the guards and through the city gates, after which his chains fell off his wrists. What a mighty God! (You can read the story in Acts 12:5-17.)

Have no fear. Jesus will protect you from the traps of the enemy who seeks to destroy you, but God rebukes the devil for your sake. Remember, 'The Lord will keep you from all harm - He will watch over your life.' (Psalm 121:7)

Today's prayer: Father, thank you for protecting me. Amen.

July 22

NO WEAPONS FORMED AGAINST YOU

"No weapon forged against you will prevail, and you will refute every tongue that accuses you." (Isaiah 54:17)

Satan is our enemy, and he tries to lead us from God as he seeks to destroy us. In Isaiah 54:17 we are told that no weapon or false accusation against God's children will prosper. The enemy's schemes and efforts to destroy us will fail. He will use sickness, pain, and adversity and all the weapons from his arsenal, but he will fail.

The story of Job is a good example of Satan's efforts to destroy. Although Job suffered, Satan did not achieve ultimate success, for God was with Job throughout his sufferings. If you are going through a time of pain and suffering, rest assured that God's divine protection will prevail. It could be that your challenges are in the workplace, where someone is trying to ruin your reputation or trying to harm you in some way, but remember that God guarantees that He will protect and defend you, and you will suffer no harm.

Are you feeling that the odds are against you, and that your enemies are getting the upper hand and will bring about your demise? Paul, in his letter to the Romans 8:31, assures us that if God is for us, who can be against us? You can therefore be confident that God will fight for you, so trust Him and remain strong if you are feeling crushed and defeated by the enemy. Spend time in prayer and meditate on God's word, for He is your shelter and strength, and always ready to help you in times of trouble. Meditate on Romans 8:31. It is a declaration that you can have confidence that the God you serve can defeat the plans and weapons of the enemy. Go forward today in confidence, knowing that God is with you and 'stand like the brave, with your face to the foe'.

Today's Prayer: Father, thank you for your promise that external forces are powerless, and I will not be defeated because no weapons formed against me will prosper. Amen.

July 23

WHERE TO FIND GOD

'Because God said, "I will never leave you, never will I forsake you." (Hebrews 13:5)

Do you sometimes wonder where to find God? There are times when the pressures of life mount up like a mountain in front of you; you feel helpless, hopeless and lost, and seemingly cannot find Him. However, He says He is always with us even to the very end of the age. Perhaps you are looking for Him in the wrong places and cannot find Him; however, He is everywhere because He is the omnipresent God. You might have missed Him in the morning when you awoke, for He was in the birds that woke you up with their singing, or you could have missed His beautiful face in the face of the baby in the pram, for He reveals himself in so many different ways. You can find Him in nature.

In Romans 1:19-20, we read, "Ever since the creation of the world, God has made the knowledge of Himself evident to all people [...] For since the creation of the world God's invisible qualities, His eternal power and divine nature have been clearly seen." The beauty and splendour that you see all around you testify to God's existence, that He's always there for us. The Psalmist David says, "The heavens declare the glory of God and the skies proclaim the work of his hands. Day after day, they pour forth speech night after night, and they reveal knowledge." You can find God in the skies and see the wonders of creation as you look at the stars and the planets, and the constellations. One writer says that the revelation of God in creation is only a tiny glimpse, a small whisper of who He is and how He wants to be known by humans. God is not far from you, and if you look closely, you'll find He is right beside you.

Jesus says, if you seek Him, you will find Him (Luke 11:10). You must believe that His presence is always with you. You can find Him in His word, and as you pray to Him, you will have the opportunity to speak and to listen to Him.

You don't really have to look far to find God; just look again at the beauty and wonder of the world around you, and you'll see Him in every intricately formed flower and blade of grass. You can also find Him in love, compassion, and the love of others. You'll find Him in your family and loved ones, in your work and in your relationship with others. You'll also find Him in your joys and in your sorrows. He can be found in the person of Jesus Christ and the indwelling of the Holy Spirit in your life.

Today's Prayer: Father, I am so happy to know that I don't have to go on a pilgrimage to find you, for you are everywhere and you are with me. Amen.

July 24

DOES YOUR SPEECH BETRAY YOU?

'A servant girl saw him seated in the firelight. She looked closely at him and said, "This man was with Him." But he denied it. "Woman, I don't know Him," he said.' (Luke 22:56 &57)

You can't help but feel sorry for Peter. How could he have denied Christ? But he did; his speech betrayed him. The moment he uttered those words, "I don't know him," he betrayed Jesus, the Messiah, the only one who could save him from his sins. In stating that he didn't know Jesus, Peter was fulfilling Jesus' prophecy that he would deny Him three times. His denial of Christ should be a warning and a lesson for us that we should be careful about the things we say. If you profess that you are a child of God, you must ensure that what you say and do, even the way you dress, does not deny Christ.

Peter denied Jesus; he denied knowing Him and being one of his followers. How could he have denied Jesus, his friend who had loved and taught him for three years? He failed as a friend and as a disciple. You can also deny Christ, not just verbally but also through your lifestyle choices. You can also deny Him by speaking evil of others, or by lying and saying untruthful things about others. Living in a way that contradicts the profession of your faith by seeking after the pleasures of the world; remaining silent when the opportunity arises for you to stand for truth; failing to spread the gospel to others are yet other ways in which you can deny Jesus.

When Peter realised what he had done, the Bible tells us that he 'wept bitterly'. However, Jesus, in His love and mercy and compassion, forgave him, and Peter became a powerful mouthpiece and leader for God in the early church. God can forgive you, like He did Peter, if you have denied Him, so pray for forgiveness.

Today's Prayer: Dear Father, help me not to fall into sin by denying you. Amen.

July 25

GOD'S PLAN

"For I know the plans I have for you," declares the Lord, "plans to prosper you and not to harm you, plans to give you hope and a future." (Jeremiah 29:11)

Do you know God has a plan for your life? He has a purpose for everyone. He knows what is best for us. He knows the beginning and the end. In Jeremiah 29:11 we are assured that the plans God has for us are good and full of hope. Will you work with God's plan or your own? You might say I don't know God's plan for my life; however, you just have to ask Him and He will reveal it to you. He knows the future you don't, so it's best if you follow His plan, and He will give you the agenda, and better still, will work with you to complete it.

Have you ever questioned why your plan isn't working when everything seems to be going wrong? It could be an indication that you are not following God's plan. However, following God's plan does not mean you will be spared challenges, pain, suffering, or hardship. Rest assured, God will see you through. Take a look at Jeremiah, who worked with God's plan, read his book, and you cannot help but agonise with him, as he goes through periods of rejection, denial, and opposition.

Jeremiah was thrown into prison and into a cistern, and was taken to Egypt against his will. He was poor and underwent severe deprivation to deliver God's message to his people. However, the people preferred to believe false prophets rather than God's word as proclaimed by Jeremiah.

You might be thinking to yourself as you read the book, was this the plan God had for Jeremiah? You might even be thinking perhaps it's less painful to follow my own plan. However, do not be tempted to think this way, for as you understand what Jeremiah went through because he followed God's plan, you will find that he emerges as one of the most successful Old Testament prophets. His success can be measured by his faithfulness, commitment, and obedience to God, although the going was tough.

If you are suffering today because you are following God's plan, learn from Jeremiah, who, regardless of opposition and personal cost, faithfully carried out God's plan with courage and obedience. The end was a glorious one for him. If you are faithful to God's plan, you will also experience a glorious end when God will say to you one day, "Well done, good and faithful servant."

Today's Prayer: Lord, I want to follow your plan and not my own. Amen.

July 26

WALKING IN GOD'S LIGHT

'Then Jesus spoke again to the people. He said, "I am the light of the world. Whoever follows me will never walk in darkness, but will have the light of life."' (John 8:12)

What does it mean to walk in God's light? It means that once we accept Him in our lives, we will obey Him and live according to His will. You no longer walk in the darkness of sin. Jesus is the true light, and He is the one who will lead you out of darkness, so we can see our way to God. When you walk in the light of God, your light should reflect His light to an unbelieving world, a world in darkness. Because Jesus is the light, we always point others to Him, for He is the light and we are mere reflectors of His character.

God wants us to reflect Him in our homes and in our communities and become beacons of hope for a world in darkness. In John 8:12, Jesus is portrayed as the light of the world, the only one who can lead us out of spiritual darkness. Light symbolises truth, and Jesus says, 'He is the way, the truth, and the life' (John 14:6). Jesus is the way, and by uniting our lives with His, we are united with God. This is such a wonderful truth to know that once we begin to walk in the light of Christ, we are ushered into His divine presence. His light will illuminate our path and help us to understand God's plan for our lives.

Do you want to walk in God's light today? To walk safely in the dark, you need a light, so you don't trip over and fall. Our walk in this life is like walking in the dark, not knowing where to go. If you want to go through life safely, then you must receive the light of life. Therefore, to walk without stumbling, you should study God's word, which is your light to show you the way and to keep you on the right path. David says, 'Your word is a lamp to my feet, a light on my path' (Psalm 119: 105).

To walk in the light also means you will gain eternal life and have a place in God's kingdom. He has gone to prepare a place for those who love and serve Him. If He is calling you to walk with Him, decide today not to walk in darkness any longer, for those who reject Him will remain in spiritual darkness. Walk with Jesus, the light, for He is the only source of light, and the only one you can follow. Accept Him today, and walk in the light.

Today's Prayer: Lord, I want to walk in the light of your love. Amen.

July 27

LET THE CHILDREN COME

'Jesus said, "Let the children come to me, and do not hinder them, for the kingdom of heaven belongs to such as these."' (Matthew 19:14)

Matthew highlights Jesus' reaction to His disciples' attempt to prevent the children from coming to Him. The mothers brought their children for Jesus to bless them. Jesus wanted the children to come to Him because he loves them, and because they have an innocent trust in God. Jesus is helping His disciples to understand that the kingdom of heaven belongs to those who approach it with the humility and dependence of a child. It would seem that the disciples might not have understood what Jesus said about receiving the kingdom of God, like a child (See Mark 9:33& 36). Jesus was clearly disappointed with His disciples, who might have seen children as not important or as a distraction to their ministry.

Do we sometimes look down on those in our communities whom we perceive as inferior, or those marginalised in society? In 1986, there was a film entitled 'Children of a Lesser God'. Do you, at times, see others as undeserving? In this encounter, Jesus rebuked the disciples; they seemingly did not understand that the qualities of innocence, trust, humility, and dependence are qualities each must possess before we can enter the kingdom of heaven. Everyone needs a childlike faith if we are to enter heaven.

During the time of Christ, the religious leaders were arrogant and stubborn and allowed their education and status to get in the way of the simple faith that we all need. The humility and trust of little children are what God expects from believers. We are to value everyone regardless of status, race, or abilities, and embrace Christian values, rather than those of the world. No one is insignificant in the sight of God, for His love extends to all.

When the children came to Jesus, He blessed them, showing that parents and carers should teach their children about Him, and His love for them, give spiritual guidance and instil good Christian values in them. He loves us so much that He has given His life for us. He showed His love for the marginalised and vulnerable in society, and so should we.

Today's Prayer: Father, I pray for a childlike faith in you. Forgive me if at any time I have looked down on others. Amen.

July 28

ALTRUISM

'For God so loved the world that He gave His one and only Son, that whoever believes in Him shall not perish but have eternal life.' (John 3:16)

The definition of altruism is described as 'the behaviour that benefits others at some personal cost or risk to oneself, motivated by a selfless concern for the well-being of others, not for personal gain or reciprocity'. In other words, according to social psychologists, 'it is selfless behaviour with the sole motive of someone else's good, not your own personal satisfaction and sometimes at considerable personal cost'. I recall an incident where a young man tried to break up a fight to protect his friend; sadly, he lost his life when he unselfishly tried to save his friend.

When we think about Jesus, who sacrificed his life to save mankind, we can have a better understanding of what really took place at the cross of Calvary. He did no wrong; He was innocent, but because of His great love for us, He died the horrific death on the cross on our behalf. We are the ones who sinned and were found guilty and should have died, but instead, God sent His one and only Son to die for us.

Jesus' act of self-sacrifice goes beyond mere altruism; the Father paid dearly with the life of His Son, the highest price He could pay. Because of His love, He paid the price for our sins, and if that was not enough offered us eternal life. Because of His unconditional and everlasting love for us He could not allow us to die in our sins, for "where sin increased, grace increased all the more." (Romans 5:2) As you go through the day, reflect and meditate on what really happened on Calvary's cross, where the great sacrifice was paid for you.

Today's Prayer: Father, while I cannot truly comprehend the depth of your love, thank you for your great sacrifice. Amen.

July 29

I WILL GLORY IN THE CROSS

"May I never boast except in the cross of our Lord Jesus Christ, through which the world has been crucified to me, and I to the world." (Galatians 6:14)

It is AD 31 in Palestine that fateful day, the sinless one who was innocent stands accused. After His arrest in the middle of the night, He is brought in before the Sanhedrin and Caiaphas, the High Priest. It is here that the first physical trauma is inflicted. A soldier strikes Jesus across the face for remaining silent when questioned by Caiaphas. The palace guards then blind Him with a cloth and taunt Him to identify them as they pass by. They strike Him in the face and spit on Him. (Spitting on someone was the lowest form of disgrace to a person at that time.)

He was stripped of his clothing. His hands were tied to a post above His head, so that the flesh of his two shoulders and his back was stretched to the limit. He was given 40 or more lashes. He was beaten with a whip consisting of nine heavy thongs, each with small lead balls embedded with bits of glass, stone or bone attached near the ends. The heavy whip was brought down with full force again and again on the shoulders, back and legs of Jesus. With every whip, skin and flesh were torn from His body. He was finally made to walk with His heavy wooden cross to Golgotha, where He suffered an excruciatingly painful death. He did it for all mankind.

However painful this sounds you can glory in the cross. Glory in it because Jesus' death provided forgiveness for all your sins because He was willing to die in your place. Just to think that none of us has done anything to merit His grace, but He extends His grace to you even now.

Today's Prayer: Father, I will glory in the cross lest your suffering be in vain. Amen.

July 30

JESUS SAVES

"... who wants all people to be saved and come to a knowledge of the truth." (1 Timothy 2:4.)

No matter how hardened a heart is with sin, Jesus can change it. However, He will only change you if you want to be changed. His invitation to salvation extends equally to all people. The two thieves on the cross had the same opportunity to be saved; however, one chose not to accept Jesus' invitation of salvation but instead hurled insults at Him. "Aren't you the Messiah? Save yourself and us"!" However, the other criminal rebuked him. "Don't you fear God?" he said, "since you are under the same sentence? We are punished justly, for we are getting what our deeds deserve. But this man has done nothing wrong." (Luke 23:40-41)

This criminal repented and asked Jesus for forgiveness. He wanted to be saved in God's kingdom. He said, "Jesus, remember me when you come into your kingdom." Jesus answered him, "Truly I tell you today, you will be with me in paradise." (Verse 42-43) It is not our deeds that will save us, but our faith in Jesus Christ.

What happened between Christ and the two criminals should help us to understand that we are not saved by works, but by our faith in Jesus Christ. It is never too late to turn to God; however, whenever we have the opportunity, we should not put off coming to Him. He loves us and wants to save everyone who comes to Him in faith. In this chapter, Luke highlights the love and mercy of Jesus and that salvation is available to all who want to turn away from their lives of sin.

Today's Prayer: Heavenly Father, thank you for your love and mercy and your desire to save me in your kingdom. I want to be saved in your kingdom. Amen.

July 31

BETTER THAN SILVER OR GOLD

"Silver and gold, I do not have, but what I do have I give to you. In the name of Jesus Christ of Nazareth, walk." (Act 3:6)

One day, Peter and John were going to the temple to pray when they encountered the beggar at the Beautiful Gate. When he saw Peter and John, he asked for money. The Beautiful Gate was one entrance to the temple, and many went that way to enter. The beggar was strategically placed there and doubtless received a lot of money. One source states that giving money to beggars was considered praiseworthy in the Jewish religion.

You can imagine the beggar's amazement when Peter and John told him they had something better than money to give him. Quite often we ask God for what we want, however, He knows what we need and surprises us with much more. The man asked for money but Peter gave him something which he hadn't anticipated - the use of his legs. "In the name of Jesus Christ of Nazareth walk," he said and taking him by the right hand he helped him up and instantly the man's feet and ankles became strong. Can you imagine the joy he experienced of being able to walk! God gave him what he really needed, the ability to walk, after not being able to since birth.

Like the lame man, we can sometimes become contented with life as it is, and not recognise we have a greater need. The man was satisfied with begging for money to meet his daily needs. He accepted his lot in life. He was crippled and nothing could change that. However, God knows our needs. He sees the brokenness in people's lives and wants to bring restoration and hope to them, and this is what He did for the crippled man. The Bible tells us he jumped to his feet and began to walk and entered the temple walking and jumping and praising God.

Ask God for what you want, but don't be surprised when He gives you what you really need. "And my God will meet all your needs according to the riches of his glory in Christ Jesus." (Philippians 4:19)

Today's Prayer: Father, thank you for supplying all my needs. Amen.

August 1

LET NO ONE DESPISE YOUR YOUTH

"Don't let anyone look down on you because you are young." (1 Timothy 4:12)

Timothy was a young pastor, and because of his youth, the senior members of the early church could have looked down on him. In his letter to Timothy, Paul encourages him not to let his youth hinder his ministry. He should not let his youthfulness be a reason for others to undermine his authority or leadership. On the contrary, Paul tells him to set an example for the believers in his speech; his words should be kind and truthful and reflect Jesus Christ.

Are there times when your speech does not reflect Christ? As a believer, whether young or old, your speech should be seasoned with salt. "Let your conversation be always full of grace, seasoned with salt, so that you may know how to answer everyone." (Colossians 4:6) When you tell others about Christ, it is important to be always gracious in what you say. You should always be courteous and reflect Christ. Paul tells Timothy that regardless of his youthfulness, he should be a leader of integrity and good conduct. Whatever we do, we too should exemplify Christ; in other words, we should live so others can see Jesus in us. Paul encourages Timothy to maintain moral purity and an impeccable lifestyle.
If you are a young person reading Paul's instructions to Timothy, they also apply to you because there will be times when senior members may not take you seriously due to your age; however, let God take control of your life and allow yourself to be led by His Holy Spirit, and be an example to others. Make God the centre of your life and influence others for good. Don't allow your peers to draw you away from God. Be an influencer rather than be influenced by those who have not centred their life on Christ. Focus on God and do not conform to the world's standards and expectations.

Today's Prayer: Father, help me to shine like a bright light for you so others can see Jesus in me. Amen.

August 2

SHAMROCKS

'There is no one holy like the Lord; there is no one besides you, there is no Rock like our God.' (1 Samuel 2:2)

A joke is told of the preacher and the Irishman. The preacher was preaching about Jesus the Rock on St. Patrick's Day. As he preached, the man sitting in the audience kept urging and interrupting him to speak about the shamrock. (The Shamrock is the symbol of Ireland; it is used to symbolise good luck.) The preacher eventually gave in and proclaimed, Jesus Christ is the Rock, and all other rocks are sham rocks. You may smile at this; however, Jesus is the Rock of our salvation.

In the above text, Hannah, in her prayer, praises God for being her rock, firm, strong and unchanging. In our fast-paced world, it is difficult to find a strong and solid foundation that will not change. It is therefore important that we find in Jesus our security, our Rock that will always remain steadfast. In 1 Corinthians 10:4, Paul tells us that the rock is Jesus Christ, who sustained His people. "And drank the same spiritual drink: for they drank from the spiritual rock that accompanied them and that rock was Christ." He refers to the Rock Jesus Christ as the one who gave Israel their spiritual food, drink, and provisions as they travelled through the wilderness. Since Jesus is the true rock, you can be assured that during times of hardships, suffering, and discouragements, you can run to the Rock 'for the Lord is my fortress and my deliverer. My God is my rock in whom I take refuge and the horn of my salvation, my stronghold.' (Psalm 18:2) If you are feeling hopeless and helpless, if your strength has failed you, turn to the Rock; seek comfort and strength from Him, for God is a rock that cannot be moved. No one can harm you as long as you shelter under the Rock, for it is a place of safety. Jesus is the Rock, and the source of our strength. Do you want to be safe? Do you need protection? Then go to the Rock.

Today's Prayer: Father, thank you for being my Rock and strong tower. Amen.

August 3

THE RESURRECTION (1)

"He is not here; He has risen..." (Luke 24:6)

The disciples did not fully understand when Jesus told them He would rise on the third day. Even when the women told them that He had risen from the dead, they did not believe them, because their words seemed to them like nonsense. The disciples could not believe, because the event of Christ's resurrection was so extraordinary that, although Jesus had told them this would happen, they still could not accept what the women told them. Their initial reaction showed their disbelief, as they could not accept that Jesus would indeed rise again. Neither did Mary fully understand what Jesus said about being resurrected, not until she saw the empty tomb, did she understand that He was indeed risen.

As a believer, you must discover the empty tomb and that the stone has been rolled away from your heart, so you can accept that He is truly risen and is alive in your life. After you discover you must, like Mary and the other women, be filled with joy and tell others that Christ is alive, because the grave could not hold Him; He who is the resurrection and the life.

I can recall my trip to the holy land some years ago, when I visited the Garden Tomb, and a pastor, who was part of the group on that trip, spoke with such joy when he said, "I have just been to the tomb and it is empty, because I serve a risen Saviour, I do not serve a dead God!" One commentary says, "The resurrection of Jesus from the dead is the central fact of Christian history. On it the church is built; without it, there would be no Christian church today." Without the resurrection, we would have no hope. Jesus' resurrection is unique and therefore significant for Christians today, for only Christianity has a God who became flesh/human. Jesus literally died for humanity and was raised with power and was victorious over death.

Let the risen Saviour dwell in your heart today, and not let His death be in vain; because His resurrection gives us hope for the future as we look forward to the second coming of Christ.

Today's Prayer: Father, I understand more clearly how much I need you, for you are the only one who can bring hope and meaning to my life because of your resurrection. Thank you Lord, I serve a risen saviour. Amen.

August 4

THE RESURRECTION (2)

'When He said this, Jesus called in a loud voice, "Lazarus, come out!" The dead man came out, his hands and feet wrapped with strips of linen, and a cloth around his face. Jesus said to them, "Take off the grave clothes and let him go."' John 11:43 &44)

Lazarus, a friend of Jesus, had been dead for four days, and when Jesus arrived in Bethany where Lazarus had lived with his two sisters, Mary and Martha, He was met by Martha who said to Him that if He had been there her brother would not have died; however she expressed hope in the resurrection when she said, "I know he will rise again in the resurrection on the last day." (Verse 24) Jesus then affirms with these powerful words, "I am the resurrection and the life. The one who believes in me will live even though they die." (Verse 25) What a wonderful truth and Martha was actually standing in the presence of the Resurrection and the Life Giver? What a revelation of God's mighty power! He is the only one who has power over life and death, as well as the power to forgive sins, because He is the creator of life. By raising Jesus from the dead, God proved that He was indeed the Son of God; no one else could have done what He did. It also proved that He is the life-giver.

In this account, Jesus is making it clear that whoever believes in Him not only receives physical life, but more importantly, spiritual life that death cannot take away. Today, He is calling you to accept the Giver of Life, and by so doing, the hope of eternal life. It is such a wonderful assurance to those who believe in Him, for they have the certainty that they will live again, because He lives. "Because I live, you also will live." (John 14:19)

Today's Prayer: Dear God, thank you for the life I have found in you. Amen.

August 5

THE RESURRECTION (3)

"For the Lord Himself will come down from heaven, with a loud command, with the voice of the archangel, and with the trumpet call of God, and the dead in Christ will rise first. After that, we who are still alive and are left will be caught up together with them in the clouds to meet the Lord in the air. And so, we will be with the Lord forever." (1 Thessalonians 4:16)

What a momentous occasion that will be! Paul captures this wonderful phenomenon in words that should bring joy to every believer. The writer of this song, 'Oh What a Sunrise', captures the scene in such a beautiful way: 'Oh what a sunrise it's going to be, death will lose its sting, the grave it's victory, the silence will be broken, the storm clouds rolled away.' Just as Jesus rose from the dead, Paul is assuring all believers that one day all who lived and died in Christ will live again. As he comforted the Thessalonians with these words, so we should also find comfort in them and comfort each other with these words.

You might have lost loved ones or friends; however, God has left us with the promise that one day soon He will return, so let us take comfort from His words. There is no doubt that Christ rose from the dead. However, when Paul wrote his letter to the Corinthians (1 Corinthians 15: 20-32), some did not believe in the resurrection; in fact, most Greeks at that time did not believe in the resurrection of the dead. They saw the afterlife as something that happened only to the soul, which lived eternally; they did not believe that people's bodies would be resurrected after death. Paul wrote this letter to the church in Corinth to clear up this confusion, because the church at Corinth was in the heart of the Greek culture, and many believers found it difficult to believe in a bodily resurrection.

Bodily resurrection is at the centre of Christianity; the fact that Christ rose from the dead affirms the truth of the resurrection, and also the words of Jesus himself, "I am the resurrection and the life." They should comfort and reassure us as we look forward to the second coming of Christ.

Today's Prayer: Father, thank you for the assurance that because you live, I will also live again. Amen.

August 6

HEED THE WARNING SIGNS (1)

'As Jesus was sitting on the Mount of Olives, the disciples came to Him privately, "Tell us", they said, "When will this happen, what will be the signs of your coming or of the end of the age?"' (Matthew 24: 3)

Warning signs are signs that indicate potential hazards, obstacles, or conditions requiring special attention, especially traffic signs. Some signs alert you to dangers as you travel. There are warning signs on roads and railways. If you don't heed the warning signs, you might put your life at risk and also the lives of others. Warning signs are provided to keep us safe.

The Titanic is an example of what happened when the warning signs were not heeded. The Titanic received at least six warning signs of icebergs; however, the most critical warning that came from the SS Masada, detailing heavy packs of ice and large icebergs directly in the ship's path, was never passed on to the crew because the wireless operator was busy and did not see the message from the MSG, prefix that signified an urgent message from the captain. Captain Edward Smith was directly informed of at least three warnings that day (April 14 1912), including one from SS Baltic that placed icebergs within five miles of the ship's course. Despite the warnings, the Titanic maintained a high speed throughout the night.

Why did the Titanic ignore the iceberg warnings? They may have thought they could avoid danger by changing course; some say the captain was too confident in the ship's abilities. Others believe the warnings were not taken seriously; whatever the reason, the warnings were not heeded, and more than fifteen hundred people lost their lives. The ship struck an iceberg on the 15th of April 1912, resulting in the death of passengers and crew.

In Matthew chapter 24, the warning signs were given by Jesus to His disciples and to us today. Jesus said He would return to Earth one day.

The disciples wanted to know the signs of His coming. He told them to watch out that no one deceived them because many false prophets would arise to deceive many. Matthew details all the warning signs, and we are to take heed. Ignore them at your peril. Jesus left us the signs which you can read about in Matthew 24 and Luke 17:20 -32. He gave these signs because He wants us to be prepared for His coming, and He wants us all to be saved in His kingdom.

The people in Noah's day did not heed the warnings, although Noah warned them of the impending doom for 120 years. The same was true for Sodom and Gomorrah. The people did not heed the warning signs and perished. Likewise, if we do not heed the warning signs, we will perish too. The purpose of the warning signs, as told by Jesus, is to warn us to be prepared for His coming. Will you be ready?

Today's Prayer: Father, help me to heed the warning signs so I can be ready when you come. Amen.

August 7

HEED THE WARNING SIGNS (2)

"Just as it was in the days of Noah, so also will it be in the days of the Son of man." (Luke 17:26)

In warning us of what will take place before He comes, Jesus warns against false security and that we are to abandon the values and attachments of this world to be ready for His return. In essence, He is saying we should heed the warning signs.

You might have had warning signs in your life, and you need to heed them. Maybe you have been warned about your health, about your diet or lack of exercise. Your doctor may have warned you about your lifestyle, and if you don't take heed to the warnings, you might develop diabetes, for example, so the message is to heed the warning signs. There are warning signs on the road. Don't speed while driving, as you might cause injury or death. The same way we need to heed warnings in our daily lives, the same way we need to heed the warnings from God. The people in Noah's day had 120 years to get their lives in order, but they did not, and they all perished in the flood. The people of Sodom had similar warnings, yet failed to take heed, preferring rather to continue in their sinful and depraved practices.

In 2 Timothy 3:1-5 Paul tells us about the terrible times in which we are now living, and why we need to heed the warnings. We will likewise perish if we do not heed the warning signs. However, the Bible tells us about the consequences of not heeding the warning signs. Everyone has to face the judgment. "Just as people are destined to die once, and after that face the judgment." (Hebrews 9:27) The warning signs are everywhere; now is the time to get ready for the second coming of Christ; as sure as death itself, the judgment awaits everyone. If you hope for a favourable verdict, obey God's word, heed the warnings and wait in preparedness for His coming. God loves us and wants each of us to be saved in His kingdom, and that's the reason why He has given us these warning signs.

The message is "Today if you hear His voice, do not harden your heart as you did in the rebellion." (Hebrews 3:15)

Today's Prayer: Father, I realise the seriousness of not heeding the warning signs. Help me to be obedient to your word. Amen.

August 8

ARE YOU HIDING FROM GOD?

'Then the man and his wife heard the sound of the Lord God as He was walking in the garden in the cool of the day, and they hid from the Lord among the trees of the garden." (Genesis 3:8)

It is hard to believe how this beautiful, trusting relationship that God had with our first parents was so suddenly broken. God's visits to the garden must have been a daily occurrence that Adam and Eve looked forward to, but now they were hiding from their best friend, their creator. That's what sin does: it alienates us from God, and so we hide from Him. What a sight, that was, two human beings covered with fig leaves trying to hide from the all-seeing, all-knowing God. If it were not so serious, it would be almost laughable. How could they be so silly as to think they could hide from God? Isn't it amazing that people will sin against God and believe He does not see what they are doing?

In Ezekiel 8:12, those who were doing wrong said God did not see what they were doing. God showed the prophet what they were up to. "Son of man, have you seen what the elders of Israel are doing in the darkness, each at the shrine of his own idol? They say the Lord does not see us." It is so foolish to think that God does not see. In Proverbs 15:3 we read, 'The eyes of the Lord are everywhere keeping watch on the wicked and the good.' You may think God does not see, but He sees clearly both evil and good actions. David realised he could not hide from God when he asked, "Where can I go from your spirit? Where can I flee from your presence? If I make my bed in the depths, you are there." (Psalm 139:7&8)

It is sin that causes us to hide from God. Adam and Eve disobeyed Him and ate of the forbidden tree. It resulted in them hiding and being separated from their friend and creator. They hid from God when they heard him approaching. God wanted to be with them, but now, because of their sin they were afraid to come into His presence. God wants to restore His relationship with us, so don't hide from Him because He will find you wherever you are, for it is not His desire that any of us should perish in our sins. He wants to renew fellowship with us, and that's why He sacrificed His life for us.

Today's Prayer: Father, I want to remain in your presence. Amen.

August 9

CONNECTED TO THE VINE

"I am the vine, you are the branches. If you remain in me, you will bear much fruit: apart from me you can do nothing." (John 15:5)

If you observe a grapevine, you will find it is quite a prolific plant. I have one in my garden, and I am amazed when I see the number of branches that the vine supports.

What did Jesus mean when he said he is the vine and we are the branches? He is saying, He is the vine and God is the Gardener who cares for the branches so they can bear fruit. The branches are believers who obey his commands and witness to others. The verse suggests a close relationship between God and the believer. This relationship is essential for believers to bear fruit. Apart from Him, we can do nothing. We are totally dependent on Him.

Jesus, as the vine, means He is the source of all that we need in our physical and spiritual lives. The fruit that we produce, that is the fruit of the Spirit, will be seen by all. In Galatians 5:22 & 24, Paul describes the fruit as love, joy, peace, forbearance, kindness, goodness, faithfulness, and self-control. The fruits that we bear mean that we will live an exemplary life, doing what is good and honest in the sight of God. However, we can only live a godly life when we stay close to Jesus like a branch attached to the vine. If we are not connected to Christ, we cannot bear fruit. We must remain in Him when we love Him and others.

Bearing fruit means your attitude, behaviour, and character will reflect Christ. Are you bearing fruit? Are you receiving the nourishment that comes from being attached to the vine? Jesus is seeking those who want to get connected to Him today and remain connected. To remain connected, you must spend time in prayer and study of His word, and be obedient to His commands. Some people may try to be good and honest and do what is right. However, Jesus says that the only way to live a truly good life is to stay closely connected to Him, like a branch attached to the grape vine. If we become disconnected from Him, our efforts will be unfruitful. So, stay connected to the vine, bear much fruit and bring glory to God.

Today's Prayer: Father, I want to stay connected to you. Amen.

August 10

THE CALL

"Speak, for your servant is listening." (1 Samuel 3:10)

The Lord called the young boy Samuel as he ministered to the Lord, under Eli the priest. Although God had spoken audibly and directly many times to the prophets like Moses and Joshua, His word became rare during the three centuries when judges ruled Israel. The beginning of chapter 3 tells us that in those days, the word of the Lord was rare; there were not many visions. God sometimes spoke to His servants in visions. During the time of Eli, no prophets were speaking God's message to the people of Israel. Why, because Eli's sons, who should have been an example to the people, were sinful in their behaviour, and their father, the High priest, was guilty of honouring his sons above God by letting them continue in their wicked ways. He did not discipline them. Eli was just as sinful as his sons because he did not correct them.

You may wonder why God chose to give the message to young Samuel, and not Eli the priest. However, God can and will use anyone regardless of age, gender or status. Eli was much older and more experienced, and he was a priest. However, God's chain of command is based on faith, not on age or position, as one commentary states. He uses those who are obedient, committed, and faithful to His cause. Young Samuel was willing to listen to God. If you are to receive His message, you must listen to His voice. God called Samuel three times before Eli realised that it was God who had been calling him. Samuel did not yet know the voice of the Lord.

Is God calling you, and you have not recognised his voice? He has probably been steering you in a certain direction or has placed a passion in your heart that you should pursue. It could be a call to begin a ministry in your community, but you haven't recognised His voice. Samuel was willing to work for God and became one of the greatest prophets in Israel. You must also have a willing and obedient spirit, so God can work with you. He calls everyone of us to work for Him. He has a plan for your life and wants you to work for Him. He has already given you the abilities and will equip you with all you need. Do not be like the servant in the parable of the talents that Christ spoke about, who had one talent and hid it rather than use it.

God may use the most unexpected methods or persons, so be prepared to be used by Him in whatever capacity or place to work for Him. Will you answer His call today?

Today's Prayer: Heavenly Father, give me a willing and obedient spirit for the work you have called me to do. Amen.

August 11

WHEN GOD IS SILENT (1)

"To you, Lord I call; you are my Rock, do not turn a deaf ear to me..." (Psalm 22:1)

Do you sometimes feel that God does not hear you when you pray? You might have been praying for months and even years, and God has not answered, but the more you pray still you have no answer. God is still silent. He appears indifferent to your situation. When I think about Job, I can't help but think about his desperate situation. He calls to God, but He remains silent. Reading from chapter 1 to chapter 37 of the book of Job, Job speaks, and so do his friends. However, God remains silent; finally, in chapter 38, God speaks.

Now, what do you do when God is silent? It is so very human of us to become impatient because we want answers immediately. We don't always understand why God is silent. However, it is during the waiting time that our faith should be strengthened. Job's faith did not falter during the waiting period. He still trusted God, and so should you, however hard it is to wait for His answer.

I think about the woman caught in adultery. Jesus remained silent as her accusers waited for Him to respond. As the teachers of the law and the Pharisees spoke, Jesus bent down and started writing on the ground with his finger. It would have been easy to think He was being indifferent or disinterested. As for the woman, that period of silence must have caused her much anxiety as she waited. Finally, Jesus answered, and one by one, her accusers left.

David must have experienced God's silence, too. In Psalms 28:1 he prays, "To you, Lord, I call, you are my rock, do not turn a deaf ear to me, for if you remain silent, I should be like those who go down to the pit, hear my cry for mercy as I call to you for help." God does not remain silent. He answers in His own time. It is during the time of silence that God teaches us lessons of patience, faith, and trust.

Like David, you might have cried out to God in your suffering and become weary with your crying. Your throat is parched, and your eyes grow dim while waiting for God. (See Psalm 69:3) In this psalm, David is saying he cried to God until he was physically exhausted, yet he still trusted God to save him. If you are crying out and God is silent, don't give up; He will answer in His time.

Today's Prayer: Father, help me to trust you even when you are silent. Amen.

August 12

WHEN GOD IS SILENT (2)

"But when the time had fully come, God sent His Son born of a woman, born under the law." (Galatians 4:4)

When God is silent, you might be thinking that He is not listening, or He might have forgotten you, or perhaps He doesn't care. You might have even given up on prayer. You might have even taken matters into your own hands, because God is silent. In the Bible, we read about Abraham, taking matters into his own hands, because he and Sarah could not wait any longer; they could not bear the silence. After the prophet Malachi prophesied about the coming Messiah, 'this was the longest silence in Biblical history. The voice of God, seemingly, went quiet, no new prophets and no fresh revelation'. Just silence. When God seems silent, it doesn't mean He is condoning sin, nor is He indifferent to it. Instead, He is withholding deserved punishment, giving time for people to repent. His silence will not last forever. A time of punishment will surely come.
The people must have thought God had forgotten them, as there was no word from Him. However, He was still working on their behalf, for one day the Messiah would come.

When God is silent, it is easy for us to assume He has not heard us. Because we have not had an answer does not mean He is not working. We need to stop focusing on His silence and keep trusting Him like Job did. After over 400 years, God delivered His people from Egyptian bondage. One day, when the set time had fully come, God sent His son born of a woman under the law (Galatians 4:4). God had broken His silence. The long-awaited Messiah had come. For centuries, the Jews had been wondering when the Redeemer would come, and He finally came, right on time, because God's timing is perfect. There might be times when you have been praying for years and wonder why God has not responded. Don't lose hope; just keep praying until the answer comes. He will not remain silent and will answer.
Today's Prayer: Father, I know that when you are silent, you have not abandoned me. Help me to learn to wait on you. Amen.

August 13

DO NOT HARDEN YOUR HEART

"Today, if you hear His voice, do not harden your heart as you did in the rebellion during the time of testing in the wilderness." (Hebrews 3:8)

This verse refers to the Israelites who had hardened their hearts in the wilderness. After God had done so much for them, their own lack of belief and untrustworthy nature resulted in their hearts becoming hardened. Pharaoh's heart, we are told, became hardened, and he would not free the Israelites from slavery. Pharaoh had hardened his own heart by rejecting God. God sent plagues to help him repent, but he would not. (You can read the story in Exodus chapter 7-9) One commentary states, "A heart hardened is as useless as a hardened lump of clay or a hardened loaf of bread, nothing can restore it or make it useful."

Our text today clearly states that we should not harden our hearts like the children of Israel. The writer of Psalm 95 also warns us about hardening our hearts as Israel did in the wilderness. The people were so unbelieving that they did not think God could deliver them, and as a result, lost faith in Him. Those who have hardened their hearts become stubborn, become set in their ways and find it difficult to respond to the pleadings of the Lord. This is a dangerous position to find oneself in. Sadly, the hardening of the heart does not happen overnight; it is a gradual process. If God is calling you today, are you resisting Him? Do not harden your heart like Pharaoh did. He chose to disregard God's messages. Those who resist God long enough, like Pharaoh, He will "toss aside like hardened bread, useless and worthless," says one writer. The heart becomes hardened by constantly disobeying the voice of God, and by so doing, can no longer respond to His voice. Each sin committed will make the next one easier to commit. Do not allow sin to harden your heart; persistent sin will harden your heart, and it is a dangerous position to be in, because God can no longer speak to a heart hardened by sin.

Today's Prayer: Father, help me to obey you so I do not fall into sin and my heart becomes hardened. Amen.

August 14

SEARED CONSCIENCES

"Such teachings come through hypocritical liars, whose consciences have been seared with a hot iron." (1 Timothy 4:2)

What does Timothy mean by a seared conscience? The conscience is a person's sense of right and wrong. If the conscience is seared, it is literally cauterised. (Cauterisation is a medical procedure that uses heat, a cold instrument, or a chemical to burn and destroy abnormal tissue.) Every time that you deliberately do wrong, you are searing your conscience; that is, you are rendering it insensitive to guilt. The individual's conscience becomes insensitive to moral and spiritual truth because they habitually do wrong, thereby losing the ability to distinguish between right and wrong. If this continues, the person no longer feels guilty or convicted when they do wrong.

Searing of the conscience can be likened to a physical wound that has lost its nerve endings, and the patient can no longer feel pain. This is what happens to a seared conscience. The person who repeatedly does wrong no longer feels the pain of sin and will continue to do wrong. Paul, in 1 Timothy 4:2, referring to people with seared consciences was helping the Christian church to recognise this as a very serious and dangerous position to be in. False teachers with seared consciences had entered the church and had become a threat to the believers, and some believers were in danger of rejecting the truth of the Bible. In chapter 4, Timothy warned the people against such teachers who were capable of drawing them away from Christ. False teachers are still a threat to the church today, and like Timothy, we must guard against such teachings which might cause believers to dilute or reject their faith until the conscience is seared. The Bible warns us that some will abandon the faith and follow false teachings. As a believer, you should remain vigilant and stay focused on Christ and His word.

Today's Prayer: Heavenly Father, help me to do what is right at all times, and as I study your words, I will become rooted and grounded in you. Amen.

August 15

CONFESSION

'Whoever conceals their sins does not prosper, but the one who confesses and renounces them finds mercy.' (Proverbs 28:13)

It is human nature to hide our sins or overlook when we have done wrong. We often find it difficult to admit our sins. In Proverbs 28:23 Solomon is helping us to understand that concealing our sins will prevent us from prospering, and in confessing and renouncing them, God will be merciful and forgive us. If we seek forgiveness from God, confession is the first step we have to take.

David tried to cover up his sins when he committed adultery with Bathsheba. However, this only led to yet another sin as he murdered her husband, Uriah. He then married Bathsheba, thinking no one would ever know. However, when the prophet Nathan revealed his sin to him, he confessed and was repentant. (You can read his powerful confession in Psalm 51.)

In the book 'Steps to Christ', E.G. White says we are to confess our sins to God because He is the only one who can forgive them. In James 5:16, we are told to confess our sins to each other. E.G. white continues by saying, "If you have given offence to your friend or neighbour, you are to acknowledge your wrong, and it is his duty to forgive you. Once you have sought forgiveness from those who have offended you, you are then to seek forgiveness of God, because the brother you have wounded is the property of God."

If you have wronged someone or caused an offence, do not put off confessing your wrongs. God has made it possible for us to go to Him through Jesus Christ, as our mediator, to ask for forgiveness. When we confess our sins to God, we must be sorry for what we have done, and we must be repentant. Confession must be genuine, or else we'll find ourselves committing the same things over and over again. David was genuinely repentant, for he realised that confession would not have been acceptable to God without sincere repentance and reformation.

If you have unconfessed sins in your life, confess them today and ask God for forgiveness. "The humble and broken heart, subdued by genuine repentance, will appreciate something of the love of God and the cost of Calvary." (E.G. White)

Today's Prayer: Dear God, I know you are a God who is faithful and just to forgive me of my sins and cleanse me from all unrighteousness. I am sorry for sinning against you. Amen.

August 16

SALVATION

"For the Son of Man came to seek and save the lost." (Luke 19:10)

Jesus spoke these words to the tax collector, Zacchaeus. He told him he was a son of Abraham and yet was lost. Those looking on might have been shocked by Jesus' words. Firstly, they would not have accepted this dishonest tax collector as a son of Abraham, and secondly, they would not have admitted that a son of Abraham could be lost. However, Jesus was helping them to understand that one is not saved because of their good heritage or condemned by a bad heritage. He came to save everyone, because we are all lost in sin.

It is so wonderful to know that Jesus came to save all the lost, regardless of who they are: background, race, culture, or previous way of life. It is hard to get one's head around such matchless love that God would have sent His only begotten Son to a sinful world such as ours to save us. Because of sin's destructive character, Jesus Christ had to come to save mankind. Jesus did not have to come, but He gave His life for us because of His great and immeasurable love. We are reminded in John 3:16 that: "God so loved the world that He gave his one and only Son that whoever believes in Him shall not perish, but have eternal life." The entire gospel is wrapped up in this verse. It is about God's unconditional love, why He paid dearly with the life of His Son, the highest price He could ever pay. Even before man sinned, God had already established the plan of salvation, and the moment Adam and Eve sinned, the plan was already set in motion. Man was doomed to die not just physically but also spiritually, for as Paul states in Romans 6:23, "the wages of sin is death, but the gift of God is eternal life in Christ Jesus our Lord." How do you feel when you think about what God has done for you, just to think that Jesus accepted your punishment, when you are the guilty one? He paid the price for your sins and then offered you new life. Spend some time today meditating on what actually took place on the cross that day for you.

Today's Prayer: Father, thank you for salvation full and free. Amen.

August 17

WHEN WE FACE DIFFICULT SITUATIONS

"That is why, for Christ's sake, I delight in weakness, in insults, in hardships, in persecutions, in difficulties. For when I am weak, then I am strong." (2 Corinthians 12:10)

How can you delight in difficult situations and suffering? Is Paul being realistic in what he is saying? What he's saying goes against our human tendencies to throw up our arms in despair when we face challenges and difficulties. When someone insults you and treats you badly, it makes you want to retaliate, doesn't it? However, Paul knew what he was talking about; he had suffered much for the cause of God, and by trusting and depending on Him to take him through these difficult periods in his life, had learnt that through his weakness God was making him strong.

God sometimes allows us to face difficult situations in our lives because He knows that when things are going well or we think we are strong because of our abilities or resources, we can become prideful and can be tempted to think we can manage on our own. He may allow challenges to arise that we cannot handle. When we are weak, then God can fill us with His power. He does not expect us to be weak, passive, or ineffective when we face life's challenges, but we should learn to depend on Him. You may not understand why He sometimes allows hardships. Have you stopped to think that He is developing your character when you are going through challenges in your life?

Understand this, our human weakness is where God's strength is made manifest. It is through our weaknesses that God's power can be revealed in us. We must realise that we cannot depend on ourselves for strength; our strength comes from God. In this text, we find Paul saying that he delights in weakness, that is, his weaknesses were a source of pride and joy for Him, as it was through his hardships and struggles that he experienced God's power and His grace in his life. He therefore had every reason to delight in his weakness.

Will you, like Paul, delight in your weaknesses? When you do, you should be encouraged that it is only through Jesus Christ that you will find fulfilment in your life. It is God who provides the strength for you to withstand the challenges that you will have in your life.

Today's Prayer: Father, help me to remember that it is in you that I will be made strong in my weakness. Amen.

August 18

WHEN GOD DOES NOT SEEM TO MAKE SENSE (1)

'Then God said, "Take your son, your only son, whom you love – Isaac and go to the region of Moriah. Sacrifice him there as a burnt offering on a mountain that I will show you." (Genesis 22:2)

Can you imagine how Abraham felt when God gave him this command? Surely, none of this was making sense he must have thought, 'After waiting for such a long time to have my son, you're now asking me to sacrifice him?' You can be sure he never slept the night before the event. God was testing Abraham to deepen his capacity to obey Him, and by so doing, develop his character. One writer says when God tested Abraham, it was not so much a test to produce faith as it was a test to reveal faith. And what a test of one's obedience and faith!

One can imagine Abraham walking slowly up to the mountain that morning, knowing what he had to do. (You can read the story in Genesis 22.) That morning, he began one of the greatest acts of obedience to God. He travelled 50 miles to Mount Moriah, near Jerusalem, to sacrifice his own son. The one he loved. If you were Abraham, what would you have done? Sometimes God asks us to do things that don't make sense, but like Abraham we do it anyway. God didn't want to kill Isaac. Although Abraham did not know this at the time, however, he obeyed. God wanted to know whether Abraham loved Him more than he loved his long-awaited, promised son. Is God asking you to do something that seems strange to you? It is difficult to let go of the things we love; however, trust God anyhow.

This command that God gave Abraham to sacrifice his son, his only son, whom he loved, foreshadowed the sacrifice of Jesus Christ, God's only Son, who would one day become the ultimate sacrifice for mankind. The emotional impact on Abraham was great. He had waited so long for his son, and now he must kill him; however, Abraham, despite the pain in his heart and a confused mind struggling to comprehend God's command, and without hesitation, begins the painful journey to Mount Moriah. In the past, he had learnt not to question God, but to trust Him over his own misunderstandings.

Why would God make such a seemingly senseless request? What would be your thoughts if you were Abraham? Has God put your faith to the test, and if He did, how did you respond? God knows everything about us and knows how strong or how weak our faith is; however, He tests us not because He wants to know how strong or how weak our faith is, but rather to help us build our faith and trust in Him more and more each day. He wants to allow us to trust Him and have faith in Him in the good times and also in the bad times.

If you are currently going through a situation that you can't understand or make sense of, remember the story of Abraham and trust God anyhow.

Today's Prayer: Father, there are times when I can't make sense of what is happening, help me to trust anyway. Amen.

August 19

WHEN GOD DOES NOT MAKE SENSE? (2)

"Do not lay a hand on the boy," He said. "Do not do anything to him. Now I know that you fear God, because you have not withheld your son, your only son." (Genesis 22:12)

The test became more difficult when Isaac enquired about the lamb for the burnt offering. Can you imagine the pain in Abraham's heart when he knew that he would be sacrificing his only son? In faith, he replied, "God himself will provide a lamb for the burnt offering, my son". God is helping Abraham to affirm his faith in Him, strengthen his character and commitment to him. Over the years, Abraham had learnt some difficult lessons about the importance of doing what God says and obeying Him, in the things that he did not understand. It is difficult to understand what God sometimes asks us to do. Would you have offered your own child?

In asking Abraham to sacrifice his son, which appeared bizarre, God was reminding him and us that one day the Messiah would come to the Earth to save His people from their sins. His only innocent son would die for the entire human race. There is a parallel between the ram offered (verse 13), on the altar as a substitute for Isaac, and Christ being offered on the cross as a substitute for us. Christ did no wrong; He was innocent. We are the ones who have sinned, yet He was willing to die in our stead. In His love and mercy, He stopped Abraham from offering Isaac, but for our sakes did not spare His one and only Son to die for us. "He did not spare His own Son, but gave Him up for us all..." (Romans 8:32)

Abraham's willingness to give up his son showed that although he loved his son dearly, he loved God even more. Yet God loves us even more to have sent His Son to die the cruel death of the cross. It is interesting to note that the intervention of the angel the moment Abraham was about to slay his son comes at the point when God was satisfied with Abraham, that is, he had demonstrated his obedience and faith in Him.

Are you willing to sacrifice the things that are dear to you? God may not call you to sacrifice your child; however, are you willing to sacrifice your time, your resources, and leave your comfort zone and commit yourself to His service today?

Today's Prayer: Heavenly Father, no greater sacrifice was paid for my sins than the love and sacrifice of your only Son, Jesus Christ. Thank you for your unchanging and unconditional love for me. Amen.

395

August 20

WHEN GOD DOES NOT MAKE SENSE (3)

'When the Lord began to speak through Hosea, the Lord said to him, "Go marry a promiscuous woman and have children with her."' (Hosea 1:2)

As I read this account, I can almost hear Hosea thinking out loud: God, are you really asking me, your prophet, to marry a prostitute? He must have found it difficult, like I do, to believe God would ask him to do such a thing. One writer says we should view the story as an illustration and not as a historical event. Either way, God does sometimes ask us to do things that do not make sense to us. It is difficult to imagine Hosea's feelings when God told him to marry a woman who would be unfaithful to him. Despite his feelings and lack of understanding why God wanted him to do this, he trusted and obeyed God anyhow.

God, at times, asked his prophets to do extraordinary things to test their obedience. He may be asking you to do something extraordinary that doesn't make sense to you either, but do it anyway. What if he's asking you today to do something that doesn't make sense? What will you do? Will you obey him, trusting that He who knows the beginning from the end can be trusted and obeyed? God used Hosea to expose the people's sins and their own unfaithfulness to Him. They had forsaken Him and had 'married' themselves to Baal, a pagan god. They have broken their covenant with God, so He sent his messages to them through the Prophet Hosea.

It is difficult to imagine how Hosea felt when God gave him that command, like Abraham's command from God, Hosea might have been thinking that God wasn't making sense when He asked him to marry Gomer. Could it be that he may not have wanted to, but he knew better than to disobey God? Asking the prophet Hosea to marry this promiscuous woman serves as a powerful metaphor for the relationship between God and His people, Israel, who had been unfaithful to Him so many times. Hosea, the husband who marries an unfaithful woman, symbolises God, like a husband to unfaithful Israel, who had committed harlotry, by turning away from Him and worshipping other gods.

Although God had asked Hosea to do something that seemingly did not make sense, He was helping the prophet to understand the pain that He feels when His children turn their backs on Him and worship other gods. Israel had broken their covenant with Him.

God may ask you to do something extraordinary or difficult. How will you respond? Will you obey Him like Abraham and Hosea? God often required extraordinary obedience from His prophets, who went through difficult times, for example, Jeremiah, but they obeyed. Will you respond to God's command today, even if it does not make sense? He may be asking you to do something extraordinary. Will you trust Him, knowing that He who knows the beginning from the end, may have a purpose for asking you to do what doesn't make sense?

Today's Prayer: Lord, help me to be obedient to you. Amen.

August 21

IN THE DARKEST HOUR

"The Lord is good, a refuge in times of trouble. He cares for those who trust in Him." (Nahum 1:7)

What do you do in the darkest hour of your life? Can you still praise God? In the story behind the hymn, "It is Well With My Soul' which was written by Horatio Spafford in 1873 after he had experienced many tragedies in his life, we discover that his young son died of scarlet fever, he lost most of his fortune in the Great Chicago Fire, and his four daughters drowned when the ship on which they were travelling with their mother sank. After having suffered such tragedies in his life, he was still able to express his deep faith in God in the words of a hymn, 'When peace, like a river attend my soul'. Because of his faith and trust in God, he found peace in the middle of turbulence in his life.

Then there was Joseph Scriven, another songwriter who experienced tragedies in his life, too. He wrote he words of the hymn. "What a Friend We Have in Jesus." He wrote the words as a poem to comfort his mother. However, the tune for the hymn was composed by Charles Crozat Converse in 1868. Scriven had suffered a series of personal tragedies, too. His fiancée died the night before their wedding, and a subsequent fiancé died of pneumonia before they could marry.

After his fiancée died, Scriven moved to Canada. His grief was more than he could bear. Ten years later, his mother became ill, but he couldn't afford a trip across the Atlantic to Ireland, where she lived. It would also take two weeks to sail across the ocean. Instead, he wrote the poem, "What a friend we have in Jesus." In the poem, he expressed how, despite the trials that happen to us in life, Jesus is a friend who helps us carry our burdens. If you are experiencing tragedies in your life today, read the words of these two hymns and find comfort, meditate on the words of Jesus in Hebrews 13:5. "Never will I leave you, never will I forsake you." Scriven said it was a privilege to carry everything to God in prayer. He was accustomed to carrying everything to God in prayer; he had an intimate relationship with God, and for that reason, although he had suffered much heartache, his faith in God never faltered.

You might be going through your darkest hour right now, but do not forfeit your peace; just take everything to God in prayer and see the darkness roll away from your life.

Today's Prayer: Father, thank you for being with me all the time, especially in my darkest hour. Amen.

399

August 22

REJOICE IN PERSECUTION

"Blessed are those who are persecuted because of righteousness, for theirs is the kingdom of Heaven." (Matthew 5:10)

Jesus is saying here that we are to rejoice when we are persecuted for our faith. How can one be happy when persecuted? The persecution of Christians is historical, dating back to the first century of the Christian era and even to our present day. Some have even been martyred for their faith. Steven, one of the early Christian disciples, was stoned to death. (See Acts 7: 54-59) He was accused of speaking against the temple and was stoned to death. Many prophets were persecuted and killed.

The persecution of Christians today occurs mostly in Africa and Asian countries. As believers, we too can be persecuted for our faith. Some people are hostile to the Word of God and will persecute those who live for Him. However, persecution might not be a bad thing because it can strengthen one's faith in God. Think of the prophet Jeremiah or Daniel, and the early Christians who were also severely persecuted for their faith. However, persecution of the early Christians pushed them out of Jerusalem and into Samaria and Judea, where they were able to spread the gospel. This fulfilled the words of Jesus that the gospel would go to Samaria and to the uttermost parts of the world.

You may not want to experience persecution; however, like the prophets and apostles of old, God might use it to prepare you for a special ministry. The early Christians did not fear for their lives because their faith in God was strong. Their focus was on the city whose builder and maker is God. If you are being persecuted for your faith today, remember that Jesus says rejoice and be glad, because great is your reward in heaven, for in the same way they persecuted the prophets who were before you (Verse 11). The fact that you are being persecuted shows that you are being faithful to God. The future is bright for those who are being persecuted, for God will reward those who are faithful by receiving them into his eternal kingdom. Pray for those who are being persecuted for their faith today.

Someone once said persecution is a blessing no one wants. Do you pray for God to bless you with persecution? No one does. Who wants to be persecuted anyway? However, we are told in 2 Timothy 3:12, "In fact, everyone who wants to live a godly life in Jesus Christ will be persecuted." There you have it, when you go through persecution it means that God has a very special blessing for you as you suffer for your faith. We are sharing in the sufferings of Christ, what a privilege! (Philippians 1:29)

Today's Prayer: Thank you, Lord, for your assurance that those who are persecuted will one day be received into your eternal kingdom. Amen.

August 23

TURN THE OTHER CHEEK

"You have heard that it was said, "An eye for an eye, and tooth for tooth […] If a person slaps you on the right cheek, turn to them the other cheek also." (Matthew 5:38 & 39)

Here, Jesus is teaching about revenge; as humans, when we are wronged, our first response is to get even. We want the punishment to fit the crime, so how can Jesus be saying we should turn the other cheek when wronged? Instead, Jesus is saying the very opposite, that is, we should do good to those who wrong us. What He is saying goes beyond our natural, sinful nature. He asks us to love our enemies and pray for those who persecute us (Verse 43). Instead of seeking to get your own back on the person who has wronged you, Jesus wants us not to seek revenge but to show kindness and compassion.

Do you find it difficult to turn the other cheek? Look to Jesus as your example; He was ridiculed, slapped, and spat upon, but did not retaliate. When he was dying on the cross after being beaten, humiliated, and abused, rather than retaliate, he uttered words of love and forgiveness, "Father, forgive them, for they do not know what they are doing." (Luke 23:34.) Although he was suffering the most excruciating pain and horrible death at the hands of wicked men, in his love and compassion, He prayed for His enemies.

To love your enemies is not a human trait; it is of God, it is supernatural. However, only God can give us the strength to love as He does. God's purpose in asking us to turn the other cheek is an expression of mercy. In Matthew 5:7, He says, "Blessed are the merciful for they will be shown mercy." If you are finding it difficult to turn the other cheek, ask Jesus for the strength to love and forgive those who have hurt you. Instead of planning vengeance, pray for them.

Today's Prayer: Heavenly Father, you know that when I am hurt, I want to get even. Give me the strength to love and forgive. Amen.

August 24

CHOOSING WHAT IS BETTER

"But few things are needed – or indeed only one, Mary has chosen what is better, and it will not be taken away from her." (Luke 10:42)

Mary and Martha loved Jesus, who was often a guest in their home. They both loved Jesus dearly, and according to the text, at this particular visit, they were both serving Jesus in different ways. However, Martha complained that she was doing all the work in getting the meal ready for their honoured guest. Mary, on the other hand, sat at the feet of Jesus, listening to all He had to say. Martha is doing everything and needs help with the preparation of the meal. You can understand why Martha is angry with her sister. However, Martha did not realise that in her desire to serve Jesus and make Him welcome, she was actually neglecting Him. Being angry with her sister, she was expressing her unhappiness with Jesus. Was Jesus being insensitive to her need for help? "Lord, don't you care that my sister has left me to do the work by myself? Tell her to help me." (Luke 10:40)

Those were very strong words from Martha. However, look at the loving and gentle response from Jesus. "Martha, Martha," the Lord answered, "You are worried and upset about many things, but few things are needed or indeed only one. Mary has chosen what is better and it will not be taken away from her." (Verse 41 &42) Jesus was not blaming Martha for being concerned about the household chores. He was asking her to set priorities. One writer says, "Service to God can degenerate into mere busy work that is totally devoid of devotion to God." Are you so busy, like Martha, doing things for Jesus and not really spending quality time with Him? Don't let your service become self-serving. A well-presented meal is commendable, but it isn't the most important thing for your guests. You must spend time with them, too. Choosing to spend quality time with God is the best choice you can make.

Today's Prayer: Dear Father, I realise that I need to spend quality time with you. Help me, like Mary, to choose what is better. Amen.

August 25

LABELLING OTHERS

'"Nazareth! Can anything good come from there?" Nathaniel asked. "Come and see," said Philip.' (John 1:46)

Nazareth was a place despised by the Jews because a Roman army garrison was located there; the Jews hated being under Roman rule. Nathaniel came from Cana, which was not too far away from Nazareth. When he heard that Jesus was from Nazareth, he was quite surprised. However, he accepted Phillips's invitation to meet Jesus (Verse 46).

It is so easy for us to label others because of their background, where they come from, the colour of their skin, or even how they speak. To label someone is to describe the individual with a word or phrase that is often based on a stereotype or a single characteristic. Quite often, the stereotyping can be negative and sometimes harmful. Labelling someone is unfair and goes against what Christ teaches. Labels are often inaccurate, sometimes based upon misinformation and prejudice. Labelling others might prevent us from seeing their potential or value. Labelling can be harmful as it can lead to negative self-talk, which can cause you to view yourself or others negatively. For example, someone can label themselves as inferior, unwanted, or a failure, based on the label someone else places on them.

As believers, we must guard against prejudice and labelling others, especially children and young people, even in church, they can be labelled as troublemakers or not interested in knowing God. Teachers can also label children as losers. We are all one in Christ Jesus. Paul says in Galatians 3:28 & 29, "There is neither Jew nor Gentile, neither slave nor free, nor is there male and female, for we are all one in Christ Jesus. If you belong to Christ, then you are Abraham's seed." In labelling others, we risk allowing our differences to separate us from our fellow believers. We should be careful that we do not impose distinctions that Christ has removed, says one commentary. When Paul says we are all one in Christ Jesus, he is saying that no one is more privileged than or superior to another. Faith in Christ is what makes the difference and makes all believers one in Christ.

As far as Nathaniel was concerned, he had doubtless heard how bad a place Nazareth was and therefore anyone who came from such a place would be just as bad as the place, hence his surprise that Jesus was from Nazareth. Nathaniel's question showed the commonly held view of Nazareth at the time. However, his scepticism was based on his perception of the place and not Jesus. I like Philip's response to Nathaniel's question: "Come and see." One writer says, "This 'come and see' approach is presented as the best way to dispel prejudice and help people judge for themselves." Let us remember that all believers are potential heirs of the kingdom of God.

Today's Prayer: Lord, forgive me if at any time I have placed negative labels on others. I know that we are all precious in your sight. Amen.

August 26

NATHANIEL'S ENCOUNTER WITH JESUS

'"How do you know me?" Nathaniel asked.' (John 1:49)

If Nathaniel had not accepted Phillips's invitation to meet Jesus, we would most probably not be reading this story. He would have allowed his stereotype about Jesus to cause him to miss out on God's might and power to change his life. Jesus knew about Nathaniel, even before He met him. After all, He is the omniscient, all-knowing God; He knows all about us. He knows what we are really like. When Nathaniel met Jesus, he was amazed that Jesus knew and asked, "How do you know me?" (Verse 48) Jesus knew him; He knew his heart. Jesus looked beyond Nathaniel's prejudice and saw a man of unusual spirituality. When He saw him approaching, Jesus said, "Here is an Israelite in whom there is no deceit." What a wonderful commendation! Jesus saw something in Nathaniel that went far above his prejudice. He saw a heart of love and devotion to God. When he heard what Jesus said, it seemed his prejudice disappeared as he declared, "Rabbi, you are the Son of God; you are the king of Israel."

If you were to have an encounter with Jesus as Nathaniel did, how would you feel that Jesus knows all about you? He knows what you are really like. He can see past our pretences. An honest believer will feel comfortable with the thought that Jesus knows everything about him or her. However, a dishonest person would feel very uncomfortable. We cannot pretend to be who we are not because God knows the real you, and He wants you to follow Him, so that He can bring about transformation in your life. When Jesus told Nathaniel that He saw him under the fig tree, He saw into his inner self, revealing Nathaniel's sincerity and his love for Him. When Nathaniel met Jesus, his life was transformed. In his encounter with Him, there was a shift from scepticism to a profound belief that Jesus is indeed the Messiah.

Matthew Henry's commentary on Nathaniel's encounter with Jesus states, "All who desire to profit by the word of God must be aware of prejudices, or denominations of men. They should examine themselves, and they will sometimes find good where they looked for none. [...] In Nathaniel, there was no guile. His profession was not hypocritical. He was not a dissembler, nor dishonest; he was a sound character, a really upright, godly man. Christ knows what men are indeed."

If Jesus were to reveal Himself to you today, would it be in reference to your sincerity or quiet seeking for Him? Make it your desire to know Christ today, seek Him and be approved of Him. What is more precious to you, material things, or being under the 'fig tree' sitting at His feet?

Today's Prayer: Father, I know you know what I am really like. Forgive me if I have pretended to be what I am not. Amen.

August 27

NICODEMUS VISITS JESUS

'Jesus replied, "Very truly I tell you, no one can see the kingdom of God unless they are born again."' (John 3:3)

One night, Nicodemus, a Pharisee and teacher of the law, came to Jesus. He feared being seen with Jesus in full view of others, especially his peers. He came with a well-rehearsed speech, "Rabbi, we know you are a teacher who has come from God. For no man can perform the signs you are doing if God were not with him." (John 3:2) It would appear that Nicodemus wanted to examine Jesus himself to separate facts from the rumours he had heard about Jesus. Jesus did not hesitate in His reply to him, one writer says: "slicing through niceties and formalities." He said, "Very truly I tell you, no one can see the kingdom of God unless they are born again." Jesus, metaphorically speaking, 'hits the nail on the head'. "You must be born again."

What did Nicodemus know about the kingdom? As a teacher in Israel, he probably knew the Old Testament thoroughly, but did not understand what it said about the Messiah. As far as Nicodemus knew, the Messiah would come to the Jews. However, Jesus helped him to understand that the Messiah would come to the whole world and not just to the Jews, and that he could not be part of the kingdom of God unless he was personally born again. This was a completely different concept from the one Nicodemus held. Jesus was saying that being part of the kingdom was not dependent on nationality or ethnicity or status. Jesus told Nicodemus that to enter the kingdom of God, repentance and rebirth are essential requirements.

Nicodemus had difficulty understanding what Jesus meant when He said he needed to be born again. But spiritual rebirth, He told him, is what he needed. Nicodemus was spiritually blind and could not understand that one cannot enter the kingdom by living a good life, but by being spiritually reborn. How about you? Do you, like Nicodemus, know about the kingdom but have not truly understood that spiritual rebirth is necessary to enter into the kingdom of God? Do you know about God? Knowing about Him is not enough. Knowledge is not salvation. Nicodemus knew so much, but in reality, knew nothing. He hadn't learnt the most elementary truth that he had to be born again.

The church is full of Christians who know about God, but who don't really know Him. Do you know Him? Have you experienced the new birth? The message from Christ to Nicodemus should speak to your heart, that is, you cannot enter the kingdom of God without being born of the Spirit.

Today's Prayer: Father, I need to be born of your Spirit. Amen.

August 28

JESUS THE BREAD OF LIFE

'Then Jesus declared, "I am the bread of life, whoever comes to me will never hunger, and whoever believeth in me will never be thirsty." (John 6:35)

We eat bread to satisfy hunger and also, along with other foods, to sustain us physically. In John 6:1-14, we read the story of Jesus feeding the five thousand with bread and fish. Just as He fed the people, He also feeds us today. All things good come from Him. While we need physical food to live, we also need spiritual food to sustain our spiritual life. Just as Jesus is the source of our physical food, He is also the source of our spiritual life. "I am the bread of life; whoever comes to me will never go hungry, and whoever believes in me will never be thirsty." We can satisfy our spiritual hunger and sustain our spiritual life only by a relationship with Jesus, for He is the bread of life. We eat physical bread daily to sustain life. In the same way, we must invite Christ in and be committed to Him daily to be spiritually sustained. True nourishment comes only from God. Not only is He the bread of life, but also the vine, for without Him we can do nothing.

If you are experiencing spiritual emptiness in your life today, Jesus is the answer. He satisfies all our needs, a need for more than just temporary satisfaction. He says, whoever believes in Him will never hunger or thirst, suggesting an eternal satisfaction. It's not just about having our physical needs met, but also our spiritual needs, that is, a deeper and lasting satisfaction that can only be found in Christ. Your spiritual hunger can only be satisfied by a right and genuine relationship with Jesus, for He is the ultimate source of sustenance for our lives; however, you must invite Him into your life daily so that your spiritual life can be nourished and sustained.

When the five thousand were fed, their focus, doubtless, was on the physical food they had so miraculously received from Jesus; however, He pointed them to the spiritual food which He provides for all of us, as being more important than the physical food. The spiritual food is the food that leads to everlasting life. Jesus reminds the crowd that they should not labour for the food that spoils, but for the food that endures to eternal life, which Jesus Himself would give them.

There are many hungry people in our communities today who need physical food, but they also have a greater need: spiritual food. Are you meeting the spiritual needs of those in your community? They are also in need of food that will not perish.

Today's Prayer: Heavenly Father, I want to feed on the true bread which comes down from heaven. Amen.

August 29

THE NARROW AND THE WIDE – ONE WAY ONLY

"Enter through the narrow gate. For wide is the gate and broad is the road that leads to destruction, and many enter through it." (Matthew 7:13)

Jesus is telling us that the narrow gate is the one that leads to eternal life; because it is narrow, it does not mean that it is difficult to accept Christ in your life, that it is difficult to become a Christian, not so - it is about choices. When we hear the Word, we have to decide whether we want to follow Christ or not. Believing in Jesus is the only way to heaven, for 'salvation is found in no one else, for there is no other name under heaven given to mankind by which we must be saved.' (Acts 4:12)

Jesus died for our sins and is now in heaven mediating on our behalf, making us right before His Father. Living for Jesus may not be popular; however, we must live for Him because there is no other way. According to Jesus, the wide gate through which many enter leads to destruction, that is, eternal death. It is the path that is more attractive and popular, a path of selfishness and pride, a path of materialism. It is a path that makes you feel comfortable. The narrow gate, by contrast, is the path strewn with difficulties, pain, suffering, selflessness, self-denial, but hope of eternal life.

The path of destruction is wide because it does not require a commitment to serve God; it is about serving oneself. It is an easy road to follow, and sadly, many choose the easier way out. Jesus taught the people that believing in Him is the only way to heaven, because He was the only one who died for our sins, and He is the only one who can make us right before God. Travelling the narrow way may be unpopular, but it is the only true and right way. If God designated His Son as the only one through whom we can attain salvation, we must accept Him. No other religious leader came to earth to die for our sins, no other religious leader rose from the dead. Jesus Christ is the narrow way. There is no other way or name.

Which path will you choose? Which gate will you enter, the broad or the narrow? Are you ready to deny self and live in subjection to Christ? Make a conscious decision today to follow the more difficult path of righteousness, the narrow road with all its challenges, as opposed to the popular and easy road, the broad road, which will only lead to destruction.

Today's Prayer: Father, I know that the narrow road is the destination to eternal life, which I can find through faith in Jesus Christ. Keep me on the narrow road which will lead to eternal life. Amen.

August 30

WHAT IS THE PURPOSE OF YOUR LIFE?

"Heal those who are ill, raise the dead, cleanse those who have leprosy, drive out demons. Freely you have received, freely give." (Matthew 10:8)

Jesus gave His disciples this principle to guide their behaviour as they ministered to others. We should also use this principle to guide our lives. He says, "Freely you have received freely, give," because He has showered His blessings so abundantly on you, you must give generously of your means and time to those less fortunate than yourself.

There is so much poverty and suffering in our world today, homelessness, and despair. We see so many in our communities living their lives in quiet desperation. And we don't have to cross the oceans and go to foreign lands to see suffering people; they are right on our doorstep. Jesus expects us to do deeds of kindness to others, no matter how small, as long as we are motivated by love and compassion for them.

The extent of human suffering and misery around us should motivate us to help as much as we can. We must be careful that we do not get caught up in our own affairs and neglect those around us. Some Christians are criticised for not caring for those around them. It is easier to go through the motions by going to church to worship and be oblivious to the suffering around us. You might even be passing someone in need on your way to church and not stop to administer to their needs!

Matthew 10:8 should speak to us, too. Jesus was helping His disciples to understand a very important truth. He was instructing them in how they should care for those around them. They were to use their abilities and the power He had given them to "heal the sick, raise the dead, cleanse the lepers, and drive out demons." They were also to preach the Good News of salvation.

Have you ever stopped to ask yourself what your purpose is as a believer and a servant of Christ? Is it not to do what Jesus says, to reach out to others, especially the poor, disadvantaged, and marginalised in our communities? Jesus gave His disciples a principle to guide their actions as they ministered to others and also as they understood their purpose. "Freely give." God has freely bestowed His gifts on you so you can work for Him. If He is calling you today to a life of service, do not hesitate to give of your time and gifts to those who also need to hear the gospel.

Today's Prayer: Father, let me share your message of love and kindness to others. Amen.

August 31

HONOUR THE ELDERLY (1)

'There was a prophetess, Anna, the daughter of Penuel of the tribe of Asha. She was very old. She had lived with her husband, seven years after her marriage and then was a widow until she was 84. She never left the temple, but worshipped night and day. Fasting and praying.' (Luke 2:36 & 37)

In our Western society today, the elderly are sometimes marginalised and not cared for as well as they should be. In other societies, the elderly are respected and well cared for. It is so good to read these verses and see Luke showing us that the elderly are important, as he gives Anna and Simeon a mention in his book. Luke seemed to have had an interest in the elderly and shows us that they have a role in God's work. Anna is an amazing woman. In fact, she was a prophetess. She was widowed at an early age, and rather than spend her time as a lonely widow, Luke tells us that she spent all her time in the temple, worshipping, praying and fasting. He presents Anna as one who was committed, of unwavering faith and devotion to God.

She lived her life for God and prayed that one day she would see the promised Messiah before she died. He granted her request, and you can imagine the day when Mary and Joseph brought the baby Jesus to the temple to be blessed. With divine eyesight, she recognised the Christ child, and gave thanks to God, and spoke about the child to all who were looking forward to the redemption of Jerusalem (Luke 2:38). What joy she must have felt in her heart as she looked upon the Christ child. What great honour and privilege!

One commentary says that her life demonstrated that faithfulness is worth waiting for. She is presented as a model of a woman who feared God and was willing to patiently wait on Him. She demonstrates the value of waiting on God, even if it takes a long time. What else can we learn from this elderly, devout woman? The importance of praying and fasting is highlighted, showing her commitment and consistency. If we expect God to answer our prayers, we must also spend time in earnest prayer. She also bore witness that the child was indeed the promised Messiah. She did not keep this revelation to herself, but immediately began to tell everyone in Jerusalem about the Christ child who would bring redemption to His people. Anna had spiritual discernment and was able to recognise the Christ child as His parents brought Him to the temple to be dedicated to God.

Each one has a part to play in God's work. Do not think that you are too old to work for Him, and do not allow anyone to look down on you because of your age. Model the lives of those who, like Anna, remained faithful to God, those who have been exemplary in prayer and devotion to Him.

Today's Prayer: Father, let my life be an exemplary one to those around me and, like Anna, remain steadfast, committed and faithful. Amen.

September 1

HONOUR THE ELDERLY (2)

'Now there was a man in Jerusalem called Simeon, who was righteous and devout. He was waiting for the consolation of Israel, and the Holy Spirit was on him.' (Luke 2:25)

Here again, we find Luke giving a place in the gospel to the elderly Simeon, who is described as righteous and devout. God gave him a special revelation, telling him he would not die until he saw the Messiah. What an honour for this elderly man. We do not know how many times Simeon went to the temple; however, you can imagine him going to the temple daily, looking for the promised Messiah. Like Abraham and Sarah, he might have been waiting a long time. Who knows, his daily visits to the temple might have attracted the attention of many as he was a permanent fixture there.

The Bible calls attention to Simeon because of his patience. Eventually, it was his faith and patience that led him to hold onto the object of His faith, Jesus Christ Himself; such unwavering faith in God's promise should encourage us to hold on to God's promises too.

Simeon was unique in that it was said that the Holy Spirit was upon him, and for this reason, he was confident that he would not see death until he beheld the Christ child, and he did. Simeon expected the Lord Jesus to come at any moment, and the older he grew, the more confident he became that the Saviour's birth was near. Are you living in expectation of his soon coming too? Every year as we grow older means we are nearer to the second coming of Jesus.

Mary and Joseph brought the Christ child to the temple to be consecrated to God, only to be met by this elderly gentleman, who took the child in his arms and praised God, saying, "Sovereign God, as you have promised, you may dismiss your servant in peace. For my eyes have seen your salvation, which you have prepared in the sight of all nations: a light for revelation to the Gentiles, and the glory of Israel." (Luke 2:29-32)

What a great honour for an elderly gentleman who had waited many years for the fulfilment of God's promise.

Mary and Joseph must have been amazed to hear the testimony of Simeon as he spoke prophetic words about their son. He told them that he recognised the Christ child as the long-awaited Messiah. Although Simeon and Anna were very old, they had not lost their hope or their faith. Led by the Holy Spirit, they were among the first to bear witness to Jesus. If you have been praying and waiting a long time, like Simeon and Anna, continue to be hopeful.

Today's Prayer: Father, help me to remain faithful to you. Amen.

September 2

I HAVE FOUGHT A GOOD FIGHT

"I have fought a good fight, I have finished the race, I have kept the faith. Now there is in store for me a crown of righteousness, which the Lord, the righteous Judge, will award me on that day, not only to me, but also all who have longed for His appearing." (2 Timothy 4:7 & 8)

As Paul neared the end of his life, he could confidently say that he had faithfully finished the work God had given him to do. He was able to face death calmly, knowing that his reward was sure as he looked forward to meeting Christ. Are you eagerly looking forward to His coming? One day, can you confidently say you have fought a good fight? When my father was diagnosed with a terminal illness at the age of 87 years, he confidently told my siblings and me that he knew God was calling him home because he had, like Paul, faithfully finished the work God had called him to do. He was confident that his reward was awaiting him, so he told us we were to bury him in his pyjamas because he was just going to sleep. This was such an encouragement. Paul also encouraged Timothy with the words found in (2 Timothy 4:7 & 8.) Although Paul did not receive earthly accolades and rewards, he knew and was confident that he would be rewarded in heaven.

As Paul neared the end of his life, he could confidently say that he had been faithful in the work God had called him to do. He faced death calmly because he knew he would be rewarded by Jesus. He was satisfied that he had 'kept the faith', meaning that he had remained loyal and steadfast, especially after having been persecuted and having faced opposition many times as he preached the gospel. If you are facing sickness, discouragements, persecution, or death, be encouraged by the words of Paul to Timothy. Be sure that if you remain faithful, there will be a crown of life waiting for you, and not just for you, but for all who look forward to His appearing.

Today's Prayer: Lord, help me to remain faithful so I can spend eternity with you. Amen.

September 3

THE ROYAL WEDDING

'Jesus spoke to them in a parable, saying, "The kingdom of heaven is like a king who prepared a wedding banquet for his son [...] He sent his servants to those who had been invited to the banquet to tell them to come, but they refused to come." (Matthew 22:1-3)

Can you imagine receiving an invitation to Buckingham Palace to attend a wedding? I am sure you'd be so thrilled that you would be telling everyone about your invitation to the palace. In this parable told by Jesus, the king invited his guests three times, and each time his invitation was rejected. (Read the entire story in Matthew 22: 1 to 14.) In the culture at that time, two invitations were expected when banquets were held. The first invitation asked guests to attend; the second announced that the banquet was ready.

God has invited us to the heavenly banquet. Will you accept His invitation today? He wants us to sit around at the banqueting table with all the saints of all the ages. Do not refuse His invitation. In the parable, the refusal of the guests represents the rejection of Christ and His message by the Jewish people. Because of the rejection of Christ, the invitation was extended to the Gentiles. Israel should have taken the message to the Gentiles, but failed to do so. The invitation is extended to all; the Bible says, 'whosoever will, may come'. As we see what is happening in our world today, all the signs of the coming of Christ are fast fulfilling; we cannot afford to reject God's invitation. The parable is also a warning to those who reject God's invitation.

The Jewish leaders and the people of Israel (who are represented as the first guests) rejected God's invitation to the heavenly banquet when they killed His prophets and also killed Jesus, His only Son, who had come to save them. God had chosen them to take the gospel to the Gentiles, but they did not. God wants every one of us to be at His banquet; that is why He sends invitation after invitation. However, we are the ones who will choose whether we accept His invitation or not. Have you accepted His invitation?

Today's Prayer: Lord, thank you for your invitation to the royal banquet. I accept your invitation without delay. Amen.

September 4

ARE YOU WEARING WEDDING CLOTHES?

"But when the king came in to see the guests, he noticed a man there who was not wearing wedding clothes." (Matthew 22:11)

Once invited to the wedding, it was customary for guests to be given wedding outfits to wear to the banquet. To refuse to wear the wedding clothes would be an insult to the host. In this parable, Jesus speaks about the guest who was not wearing wedding clothes. Of course, he was not allowed to attend the banquet. The guest's refusal to wear the wedding clothes symbolises those who accept the invitation to God's kingdom but reject His provision of salvation.

The wedding clothes are symbolic of Christ's righteousness that is needed to enter the kingdom. He provides clothes of righteousness for everyone who accepts Him. However, each one has the choice to either wear the wedding clothes or not. The wedding clothes are the righteousness of Christ. You can put on wedding clothes, which also signifies a right relationship with God when we put our trust in Him.

Refusing to wear the wedding clothes would cause the host to assume the guest was rude and arrogant, or that he did not want to participate in the celebrations. The wedding clothes symbolise the righteousness that each person needs to wear before entering heaven. Each of God's faithful servants will be clothed in His righteousness. Christ Himself has provided wedding clothes for us; however, each one must choose to put their wedding clothes on before they can enter heaven. Christ's invitation is an open one that extends to all.

Are you looking forward to wearing your wedding clothes? God is waiting to clothe you with garments of salvation and array you in a robe of righteousness (Isaiah 61:10). We have all been invited to the marriage supper of the Lamb. "Let us rejoice and be glad and give Him glory! For the wedding of the Lamb has come, and His bride has made herself ready. Fine linen, bright and clean, was given her to wear." (Revelation

19:7) Fine linen stands for the righteous acts of God's holy people. Not even Earth's costliest garment can be compared to the royal garments we will be given. Because "this robe, woven in the loom of heaven, has in it not one thread of human devising." (E.G. White)

You have already been invited to the wedding. Are you looking forward to putting on new clothes, the righteousness of God? For without the wedding garment, no one can enter heaven or partake of the marriage supper of the Lamb.

Today's Prayer: Heavenly Father, thank you for my invitation to the banquet. Help me to remain faithful until you return. Amen.

September 5

THE DAMASCUS ROAD EXPERIENCE

"Saul, Saul, why do you persecute me?" (Acts 9:4)

Saul, who became known as Paul, while travelling to Damascus to persecute the Christians, experienced a dramatic encounter with God, which changed his life forever. He was confronted by Christ himself. Saul who was zealous for his Jewish beliefs, saw the Christians as a threat and began a persecution campaign against anyone who believed in Jesus, anyone who belonged to the 'Way'.

In Acts 4, we find him on his way to Damascus to persecute the Christians there when he was challenged by the risen Christ himself with a question, "Saul, so why do you persecute me"?" His response was "Who are you, Lord?" Saul knew that he had now come face-to-face with Christ himself. In 1 Corinthians 9:1, 15: 8 and Galatians 1:15 & 16, he refers to his changed life in Christ. He speaks about his conversion and how God was guiding his ministry.

Paul's encounter with Christ was a complete reversal of his mission, and demonstrated that God is capable of changing a murderer like Saul. You may not have such a dramatic encounter with God, but He wants to transform your life. God had a plan for Saul. He wanted him to take the gospel to the Gentiles. God also has a plan for your life. Experience shows that God can include even those whom we deemed to be beyond redemption. If you have not yet responded to God's call, do so today, for He wants to transform your life. We must not limit God; He can do the impossible.

Today's Prayer: Heavenly Father, help me to surrender my life to you, so I can be used by you to minister to others.

September 6

DO NOT CONFORM TO THE WORLD

"Do not conform to the pattern of this world, but be transformed by the renewing of your mind." (Romans 12:2)

Paul warns the believers not to conform to the pattern of the world, a world that is hostile, corrupting, and selfish. As a Christian, you must understand that and decide that a large portion of the world's behaviour is unacceptable. You should not conform to the world's standards. One writer says, "Many Christians wisely decide that a large portion of the world's behaviour is off limits for them." The Christian should refuse to conform to this world, and "their refusal to conform must even go deeper than just behaviour and customs – it must be firmly planted in values rooted in our mind."

We must be careful to allow the Holy Spirit to transform our lives. Some believers can avoid conforming to the world, yet it is possible to be proud, selfish and covetous. It is only when the Holy Spirit renews our minds that we can be truly transformed. God calls us to be in the world, but not of the world (John 17:11-17). J.B. Phillips' translation of Romans 12:2 reads: "Don't let the world around you squeeze you into its own mould, but let God remould your minds from within, so that you may prove in practice that the plan of God for you is good, meets all His demands and moves towards the goal of true maturity."

Paul, in his letter to the Romans, tells them to abandon the patterns and desires of the world, such as materialism, pleasure and all the things that distract from serving God. The message is just as relevant to us living in the twenty-first century as it was then. This world has become even more evil; there are so many voices vying for our attention. Paul is calling believers to be different from the culture around them. We cannot afford to be 'squeezed' into the world's mould. Rather than conforming, Paul is asking believers to be transformed, not outwardly, but inwardly, by the mind, a deep inner change. This transformation can only take place when we align our minds with that of Christ's. We are to have the same mind-set as Jesus Christ, as we are guided by His word. However, we can only live a transformed life when we allow the Holy Spirit to change us. He is the one who guides our thoughts and behaviours.

Be not conformed to this world. "To be conformed to this world is to act as other men do, heathens who do not know God: in opposition to this, the Apostle exhorts his readers to undergo that total change which will bring them more into accordance with the will of God." (Elliot's Commentary) Are you willing to let the Holy Spirit transform you? God wants you to stand out in the world as you stand for Him.

Today's Prayer: Father, you know how easy it is to conform to the pattern of this world. Let me align my mind with yours so I can live a transformed life. Amen.

September 7

GUARDING YOUR MIND

"Finally, brothers and sisters, whatever is true, whatever is noble, whatever is right, whatever is pure, whatever is lovely, whatever is admirable – if anything is excellent or praiseworthy – think on such things." (Philippians 4:8)

There is a definite relationship between thought behaviour and the state of the mind. What we put into our minds determines our words and behaviour. Each of us has the capacity to control our thoughts and therefore direct our actions. We decide whether we want to do right or wrong. The thoughts that we feed into our subconscious minds will ultimately determine how we behave. In Romans 4:8, Paul is saying just that, and that we should program our minds with thoughts that are true, noble, right, pure, lovely, admirable, excellent, and praiseworthy.

Living in this age of technology, we have to be more careful than ever before. There are so many unwholesome things on the Internet that can absorb our thoughts and our minds. Stop and examine what you are allowing into your mind, what you are allowing your mind to dwell on. What are you putting in your mind as you passively watch television? What movies are you watching? What books or magazines are you reading? What about the video games you play or the conversations you have with friends?

One Christian writer says that Christians should "guard the avenues of the soul," meaning the five senses, to prevent Satan from corrupting the mind. This involves choosing to fill your mind with pure thoughts. As Paul says, in Philippians 4:8, you are to replace the harmful things with wholesome material rather than spend time on things that keep you away from God's word; spend time in prayer and study of His word. Pray and ask God to help you to focus your mind on what is good, noble, admirable, and pure. 'Above all else, guard your heart, for everything you do flows from it.' (Proverbs 4:23)

What we put into our minds determines what comes out in what we say and do. Do you have problems with thinking impure thoughts? If you do, stop and reflect on what your mind is feeding on. The movies, programmes on television, and reading materials, for example, may be causing the problem. Start cleaning up your mind by replacing harmful input with wholesome material. Spend time praying and studying God's word.

Today's Prayer: Father, help me to guard well the avenues of my mind. Amen.

September 8

HOW TO GUARD THE MIND (2)

'Above all else, guard your heart, for everything flows from it.' (Proverbs 4:23)

One commentary says, "Our feelings of love and desire dictate to a great extent how we live because we always find time to do what we enjoy. Solomon tells us to guard our hearts or our minds, above all else; that is, our focus should be on the things that will lead us to God rather than lead us away from him."

How can we guard our minds? One writer says, "This involves choosing to fill the mind with pure heavenly influences and resisting temptations from worldly and impure sources through prayer, vigilance and controlling what is consumed through our senses". Our hearts, which relate to our feelings of love and desire, will dictate to a great extent how we live, because we will always find time to do what we enjoy. Solomon says we are to guard our hearts above all else, ensuring we concentrate on those desires that will keep us on the right path.

We can guard our minds by being vigilant. Paul reminds us in Ephesians 6:12 that our struggle is not against flesh and blood but against the powers of this world. We must concentrate on the things that will not distract us from the right path, but we must also put boundaries on our desires. Keep your eyes fixed on Jesus, don't get side-tracked. Don't take any detours. Have your eyes fixed on Jesus, upon the prize of the high calling in Christ Jesus.

To guard your mind, pray continually. In 1 Thessalonians, Paul says, "Pray without ceasing." By praying, you will gain the strength to resist the temptation to sin. Focus on God. In Colossians 3:2, we are admonished to set our hearts on things above. This means we are to make heaven's priorities ours and focus on them daily. We should concentrate on the eternal rather than the temporal things, that is, earthly things. Root out evil. One writer says root out every "pernicious weed from the garden of your heart." Study God's word and meditate on it. Do not just read the Bible like another storybook; spend quality time studying it diligently. We must build our lives on the word of God and build His word into our lives. By doing so, we will guard our minds against the distractions of the world. Seek Christ; He is never far away from us. However, He wants us to seek Him, for those who do will find Him. Do not underestimate the battle going on for your mind; the evil one seeks to control our minds.

"If the heart is not well guarded, out of it will proceed murders, adulteries, prostitution, false witness, and blasphemies. These are the things that defile a man. By God's grace, we need to control the avenues of the soul so that our hearts may be full of the heavenly influence, then out of it will proceed only those things that are for the honour and glory of God."

Today's Prayer: Lord, examine my heart and what is not good, please remove it. Amen.

September 9

THE BLOOD HAS NOT LOST ITS POWER.

"The blood will be a sign for you on the houses where you are, and when I see the blood, I will pass over you. No destructive plague will touch you when I strike Egypt." (Exodus 12:13)

The Israelites had been enslaved for over 400 years in Egypt; however, at last, deliverance had come. The Egyptians had suffered as a result of the plagues caused by the hardness of Pharaoh's heart. But, on this particular night, they were instructed to eat the Passover feast and prepare to leave Egypt that same night. However, the final plague would fall on Egypt, the slaying of the firstborn. The Israelites were instructed by God through Moses to take some blood from a lamb with no defect, and put the blood on the doorpost of their homes, and when the destroying angel sees the blood, God said, "I will pass over you. No destructive plague will touch you when I strike Egypt."

The blood was a visible sign of God's protection. It also signified readiness. Also importantly, it showed God's power to deliver His people. God made provision for His people to be delivered from bondage if they put the blood on their doorposts. The blood to this day has not lost its significance, for God provided His only son, the Lamb of God, who spilt His blood on Calvary's cross to save us from eternal death.

The blood has not lost its power for Jesus still saves; however, He will only save us if the blood is on the doorposts of our hearts. The blood served as God's divine sign to pass over the homes of the Hebrews, and they would not be destroyed with the Egyptians. To this day, the blood is still the symbol of God's saving grace. It is the blood of Jesus, the Lamb of God, that provides atonement for our sins. Applying the blood to the doorposts of their homes, the Hebrews were exercising faith and obedience that God would deliver them. We are also called to have faith in God and receive His salvation.

The Hebrews were also asked to eat the Passover supper before leaving Egypt. They were to eat it hastily, while wearing their travelling clothes, although they were not yet free, they were to prepare themselves, and they were also demonstrating faith in God by their actions. The Passover, like the blood on the doorpost, was to be a constant reminder of God's deliverance and His promises, and His power to save. One writer says, "Just as the blood on the doorposts of the Israelites in Egypt was a physical sign of their faith in God's Word, so a heart that has been sprinkled with the shed blood of Christ by faith in His sacrificial death on the cross, is the spiritual sign that we have passed from death to life- from slavery to freedom that is in Christ Jesus."

Is the blood on the doorpost of your heart?

Today's Prayer: Father, thank you for your blood that brings deliverance from sin. Amen.

September 10

THE GRATEFUL LEPER

'One of them, when he saw he was healed, came back, praising God in a loud voice.' (Luke 17:15)

Jesus healed ten lepers; however, only one returned to thank Him. When he returned, Jesus asked, "Were not all ten cleansed? Where are the other nine? Has no one returned to give praise to God except this foreigner?" (Luke 17:17 & 18) Leprosy was a highly contagious disease, and people with leprosy were required to isolate themselves from others and had to announce their presence if they had to go near anyone. It is interesting to note that Jesus sent the lepers to the priest before they were healed. Usually, if a leper was healed of the disease, by law, he would have to see the priest who would pronounce the leper clean, so he could be welcomed back into society.

The ten lepers responded in faith, and Jesus healed them as they made their way to the priest. Therein lies a lesson for us. Do you trust God enough to act on what He says, even before you see the evidence at work, the kind of faith the writer of Hebrews describes, as faith being "confidence in what we hope for and assurance about what we do not see?" (Hebrews 11:1). Only one leper returned to thank Jesus. Are we sometimes like the nine ungrateful lepers? Is it possible that God has granted you gifts to use for His glory, and you have not accepted them in gratitude, but behave as if the gifts came from you?

Interestingly, Jesus remarked that the grateful leper was a foreigner, a Samaritan, a race despised by the Jews because they were a mixed-race people. Jesus' comment is significant because it shows that God extends his grace to everyone. His grace is not limited by race, ethnicity, or social divisions, or prejudices. It is said that true faith and gratitude are expressed through action and worship, and this narrative shows that the despised leper, a Samaritan, showed not just gratitude but faith in Jesus Christ.

The action of the leper also shows that gratitude is not a passive response but an active one. Gratitude is demonstrated through actions and worship, not just by the things we say. The leper, seeing that he was healed, went back to thank Jesus, even before he had gone to the priest, illustrating his depth of gratitude. Have you ever been kind to someone and they did not even bother to say thanks? Are you grateful to God for what He does for you, or do you take him for granted like the nine lepers? The attitude of the nine highlights the sin of ingratitude. You might not have considered ingratitude as a sin, but it is. Paul reminds us in 1 Thessalonians 5:16-18 that we should "rejoice always, pray continually, give thanks in all circumstances." The key point in the text is that we should give thanks in all circumstances. Thankfulness should be a way of life for believers, one writer says, "flowing naturally from our hearts and mouths." We have so many reasons to be thankful to God; it is in Him that we have life, and also hope of life everlasting.

Today's Prayer: Lord, if I have failed to give you thanks, please forgive my ingratitude. Amen.

September 11

DO NOT LOSE YOUR FOCUS

"Therefore, we do not lose heart. Though outwardly we are wasting away, yet inwardly we are being renewed day by day." (2 Corinthians 4:16)

It is easy to lose heart and quit when things are not going right. We all have at some point in our lives faced challenges at work, at church and even in our relationships that will cause us to think about quitting. Some have given up because the burdens were too heavy to bear.

Paul went through many trials and persecutions. He knew what it meant to even face death. He says, "three times I was beaten with rods. Once I was pelted with stones, three times I was shipwrecked. I spent a night and a day in the open sea [...], in danger from bandits [...] in danger from believers [...], I have known hunger and thirst." (2 Corinthians 25:25) He went through all of this and more yet did not give up. Paul was willing to suffer for the cause of Christ.

Would you have given up if you were Paul? Rather than give up when he faced persecution and physical harm, Paul focused on the inner strength that came from the Holy Spirit dwelling in him. He told the Ephesian believers he would pray "that out of His glorious riches that God would strengthen them with power through God's Spirit in their inner being." (Ephesians 3:16) It was the Holy Spirit that gave him the inner strength to endure hardships and not give up. In today's chosen text, he encouraged the Corinthians not to lose heart and not to give up, but to allow the Holy Spirit to renew them inwardly every day.

There might be times when you feel you cannot go on any longer; however, Paul is saying, don't lose your focus. Your focus should be on the inner strength God has given you to cope with life's challenges. Don't let others wear you down, don't let frustration, fatigue, pain or criticisms cause you to lose your focus and quit. Keep your focus on Christ and be strengthened inwardly. One writer says, "Renew your commitment to serving Christ, do not forsake your eternal reward because of the intensity of today's pain. Your very weakness allows the resurrection power of Christ to strengthen you moment by moment." Don't quit, but focus on the inward instead of the outward.

Today's Prayer: Father, when I feel like quitting, give me the inner strength that I need to remain focused on you. Amen.

September 12

THEY FAILED TO FIND JESUS IN THE SCRIPTURES

"You study the Scriptures diligently because you think that in them you have eternal life. These are the very Scriptures that testify about me, yet you refuse to come to me to have life." (John 5:39 & 40)

If you read the Bible from Genesis to Revelation, you will find Jesus. He is on almost every page of Scripture. Some people read the Bible to appear scholarly. Consider the religious readers in the time of Christ; they knew the Scriptures inside and out. As I recall, in Jesus' encounter with the rich young ruler, he told Jesus that he had kept all the commandments - he knew the Scriptures. (You can read the story in Matthew 19:16-22.) The religious leaders and teachers of the law knew the Scriptures but failed to apply its teachings to their lives. They knew what the scriptures taught, but they failed to see Jesus, the Messiah to whom the Scriptures pointed.

As you study the Bible, stop and meditate on each passage and consider how it applies to you. What is it telling you about Jesus and His message to save you? John is telling us that the Jewish leaders, although they had studied the Scriptures diligently, missed the central purpose: the Scriptures testified to Jesus on every page, because He is the subject of the very Scriptures they read. Their search of the Scripture was misguided. They knew all the rules and regulations, but were so entrenched in their own religious system that they missed the Saviour and the opportunity to change their lives. Have you become so involved in your 'religion', going through the motions, appearing busy doing God's work and yet miss the Christ of the Bible? The religious leaders in the time of Jesus did just that. You must be careful that your study of the Bible is not a superficial one, but a genuine desire to meet with Jesus and learn from Him. The core message today is that it is in the Scriptures you will find Jesus; they are meant to point to Him, the truth and the way.

Today's Prayer: Father, help me to seek you, because those who diligently search the scriptures will find you. Amen.

September 13

HERE'S HOW TO IMPROVE BRAIN HEALTH

"Oh, how I love your law! I meditate on it all day long." (Psalm 119:97)

Do you know that praying continually and meditating on Scripture can improve your health? I have a friend who suffered severe memory loss due to a brain condition that affected her memory. Her memory became so poor that she could not even remember her children's names. However, being a woman of prayer, and as she communed with God, He revealed to her that she should memorise Scripture if she wanted to improve her memory. She told me it took her one year to learn Genesis 1:1, "In the beginning God created the heavens and the earth," that was how bad her memory was! If you should meet her today, she is always praising God and quoting the Scriptures, book, chapter and verse of the Bible. She knows for sure that it is by learning Scripture which has enabled the return of her memory.

Research shows that there are centres in the brain that respond positively to prior reading and meditating on Scriptures, also worship, and hymn singing. Neuroscientist Andrew Newberg believes that doing all these things and practising your faith is the most powerful way to maintain a healthy brain. Our attention, rational thinking, and decision-making processes take place in the frontal lobe of the brain, and it is this part of the brain that responds to prayer and meditating on God's Word. Research shows that the mental training involved in memorising Scripture has a positive impact on the brain; it creates and reinforces neural connections, which helps the brain to become more efficient at learning and remembering new information. In another study on ageing adults, it was discovered that there was a potential link between reading the Quran and better cognitive function, suggesting that religious engagement could help delay cognitive decline. Little wonder that the psalmist praised God by saying, "I praise you because I am fearfully and wonderfully made; your works are wonderful." (Psalm 139:14)

In Joshua 1:8, God directs Joshua to meditate on His Word. "Keep this book of the Law always on your lips; meditate on it day and night." (Joshua 1:8) David also knew what it meant to meditate on God's Word, too. In fact, he appears to have taken pleasure in doing so. "Oh, how I love your law. I meditate on it all day long."

If you want to improve your brain health, spend time in prayer and meditating on Scripture.

Today's Prayer: Father, let your word abide richly in me. Thank you for the power of your word to improve my health. Amen.

September 14

YOUR BUSINESS OR HIS BUSINESS?

"Why were you searching for me?" He asked. "Didn't you know I had to be in my Father's house?" (Luke2:49)

Luke records the story of when Jesus' parents lost Him. It was customary for families to go to Jerusalem yearly for the Festival of Passover. When Jesus was twelve years old, He and His family went to the festival as was the custom. After the festival was over, while His parents were returning home, unknown to them, the boy Jesus stayed behind in Jerusalem. (Luke 2:41-43) After travelling for a day, they realised that He was not with them, so they returned to Jerusalem and eventually found Him in the temple in discussion with the religious leaders.

The temple courts in Jerusalem were famous as places of learning, especially during Passover time. At the time of Passover, many of the greatest rabbis and teachers would gather to teach, discuss, and have intellectual debates. It was among those learned men that Joseph and Mary found Jesus, discussing and asking questions well beyond His years. The rabbis were astounded by the depth of Jesus' wisdom, knowledge, and profound understanding of the Scriptures. It must have been quite a scene, listening to this twelve-year-old discussing with the intellectuals in the temple. His understanding and the answers He gave amazed everyone who heard Him. Even as a child, He had begun to demonstrate His divine nature.

Luke tells us in chapter two, verse 48-49, that when His parents found Him, they were astonished to see Him in discussion with the great rabbis. His mother scolded Him, saying, "Son, why have you treated us like this?" He responded by saying, "Do you not know that I am about my Father's business?" In essence, Jesus at that point revealed His identity and His mission as the Messiah in His reply to His mother, "Didn't you know I had to be in my Father's house?" (Verse 49) He was explaining that He was about his divine calling – His Father's business. You may be wondering how Mary and Joseph lost Jesus; were they bad parents? Luke is not suggesting this; however, one writer says, "Luke was setting the stage for Jesus to state clearly His own understanding that He has a special relationship with God. God is Jesus' parent (not Joseph), and Jesus is to be about God's interests, that is, must serve God's purpose."

It would appear that Jesus' parents did not fully understand what He meant by being about His Father's house or His Father's business. He was making the distinction between His earthly and heavenly Father and declaring His allegiance to God, and at the same time, honouring His earthly parents. Mary and Joseph knew He was the Son of God, but they may not have fully understood His mission.

How about you, are you going about your business or God's business? You, too, have been called to a mission. Before Jesus went back to heaven, He gave us the commission found in Matthew 28:19-20, "Therefore, go and make disciples of all nations, baptising them in the name of the Father, and of the Son and of the Holy Spirit and teaching them to obey everything I have commanded you. And surely, I am with you always, to the very end of the age." Are you faithfully fulfilling your God-given mission?

Today's Prayer: Father, help me to be about your business and not my own. Amen.

September 15

STEPPING DOWN

"He must become greater; I must become less." (John 3:30)

Jesus had now arrived on the scene of action. John the Baptist, who had preached the message to prepare the way for the Saviour, recognised that the time had come for him to step down. Jesus must now take His place. John's willingness to become less shows profound humility. He was ready to step down and was happy to become number two. John was a popular figure as he preached about the coming Messiah. The crowds flocked to hear him. He knew the time would come when Jesus would come to begin His earthly ministry, and he would have to step aside. John was willing to deny himself to let Jesus begin His work. He understood his role was to herald the announcement of the one who was greater than himself and was therefore willing to step aside.

Are you willing to step aside for others? You might have been serving as a leader in your church for a number of years, and it is now time for you to step aside so someone else can take your place. Are you happy like John to become number two? Some leaders do not find it easy to step aside because of pride and wanting to focus on their achievements in ministry, rather than on what God has allowed them to achieve. Be careful not to emphasise your achievements, for when you do, you are not showing humility. You must realise that Christ and only He should be elevated. John made it very clear by showing his willingness to step down when Jesus began His mission.

God requires those who are humble, not those who are self-seeking, those who seek to be popular. He seeks those who are humble, where self decreases, and Christ is lifted up and becomes prominent in their ministry. John the Baptist knew his role well, to be Christ's forerunner, and rejoiced that Jesus' fame was increasing even as his own was decreasing. If you are feeling unhappy that someone else has been asked to carry out your role, learn lessons from John, rather than focus on yourself, which will stunt your spiritual growth, focus on God's word, spend much time in prayer, and you will soon find that your selfish desires will disappear and you will be more accommodating of others.

Becoming less should be your mantra as you seek to serve God and not yourself. If you are a spiritual leader, you should be spiritually mature to move away from self-centeredness to a Christ-centred life. Are you willing to humble yourself and step aside for others? Consider your motives and allow Jesus to take centre stage in your life.

Today's Payer: Father, humble me so I can become your servant. Amen.

September 16

LIVING A SUCCESSFUL LIFE

'Open my eyes that I may see wonderful things in your law.' (Psalm 119:18)

Nearly everyone wants to succeed in life, in whatever they do. After being a teacher for over twenty- five years, I have been privileged to enjoy the success of my students with them. Those who attained success were those who worked hard and were committed to learning. Just as success in the world of academia is dependent on the student's hard work and desire to succeed, success for the believer is much more than studying the work of educators and academics. In this verse, David is telling us that true success is to be found in the study of God's word. In his prayer, he asked God for spiritual insight, "Open my eyes that I may see wonderful things in your law." Spiritual understanding is a gift from God. David recognised that to be successful, he would have to accept God's gifts to him. He understood that his intellect was not sufficient and that he needed to depend on the Holy Spirit for spiritual insight. It is the Holy Spirit who teaches us and leads us into all truth.

In this psalm, David prayed for understanding because he realised that if he depended on his knowledge and understanding, he would fail to understand God's word. Mankind is limited by sin, and it seems as if sin has cast a veil of darkness over intellectual ability to discern God's word. It is for this reason that one needs the Holy Spirit to reveal His word to enable understanding. Each one needs to pray this prayer, "Open my eyes." David understood that his physical eyesight would not be enough; he was asking for perception; that is, going beyond what his physical eyes could see.

If you are going to be truly successful in life and experience spiritual growth, you will need to study God's word. Like the psalmist, don't depend on your human intellect but ask for a deeper and more profound spiritual discernment to understand spiritual truths that can only be found in God's word. In requesting that his eyes be opened, David realised that he needed the Holy Spirit to open his eyes for his mind to be enlightened with God's truth.

Will you pray this prayer today if you wish to succeed and experience spiritual insight and growth in your life? Pray to God like David and ask to have your eyes opened to see wondrous things (spiritual truths), truths about God's wisdom, might and power, and His character. Jesus Christ was successful in His ministry while on earth, especially when He was tempted by Satan, because He knew God's Word.

Today's Prayer: Father, please remove spiritual blindness so I can understand your truths and live a successful life. Amen.

September 17

LOST AND FOUND (1)

"I tell you in the same way there will be rejoicing in heaven over one sinner who repents than over ninety-nine righteous people who do not need to repent." (Luke 15:7)

Do you know that they know how to party in heaven? Luke tells us that there is rejoicing in heaven over one sinner who repents. I have witnessed many baptisms and have observed the joy of those who have given their hearts to God - the same joy that I experienced when I was baptised. However, your joy or my joy is nothing compared to the joy in heaven when one sinner repents.

There is rejoicing in heaven, for each one of us is of worth and value to God, for it is not His desire that any of us should perish, but that everyone should repent from their sins. (See 2 Peter 3:9) One Christian writer says: "The value of a soul, who can estimate it? Would you know it's worth, go to Gethsemane and then watch with Christ through those hours of anguish, when He sweat, as it were, great drops of blood. Look upon the Saviour uplifted on the cross. It was at Calvary where he laid down his life for mankind." "Greater love has no one than this: to lay down one's life for one's friends." (John 15:13) If you were the only sinner on earth, He would have died for you.

Do you know that at every baptism, God and all of heaven rejoice with immense joy when a person who never knew Him, or has strayed away from Him, returns. It is said that 'heaven erupts with joy at the news of one person's genuine repentance, which signifies a change of heart and a turning toward God.' It is also reassuring to know that God actively seeks out those who are lost in sin. In the parable of the lost sheep, the shepherd leaves the ninety-nine and goes out to find the one lost sheep. It seems foolish for the shepherd to leave the ninety-nine sheep to go in search of just one sheep, but that one sheep was just as valuable to the shepherd as the ninety-nine. When the sheep was found, the Bible tells us that the shepherd called all his friends and neighbours to rejoice with him because he had found the one lost sheep. (Luke 15:6) In the same way, each one is of worth to God, and He will seek and save those who are lost. (See Luke 19:10)

If you have not yet given your life to Christ, do not delay. Not only will you experience joy, but there will be rejoicing in heaven when one sinner repents. God is inviting you now to come to Him, for He will be throwing a big party in heaven for you.

Today's Prayer: Dear Father, thank you for saving me when I was lost. Amen.

September 18

LOST AND FOUND (2)

"Rejoice with me: I have found my lost coin. In the same way, I tell you, there is rejoicing in the presence of the angels of God over one sinner who repents." (Luke 15: 9 &10)

Jesus told the parable of the lost sheep and the lost coin in Luke chapter 15. To understand the parable of the lost coin, we must first familiarise ourselves with the Palestinian culture of the day. Apparently, Palestinian women received ten silver coins as a gift on their wedding day. Apart from the monetary value, these coins held sentimental value like that of a wedding ring; therefore, losing a coin would be very distressing for the owner. You can understand why the woman searched so diligently until she found it.

Just as the woman rejoiced when she found the coin, so the angels rejoice when a sinner repents and turns to God. Each of us is precious in the sight of God, and it grieves Him when we walk away from Him and become lost. Equally, He rejoices when His lost children are found and return to Him. One writer says, "perhaps we would have more joy in our churches if we shared Jesus' love and concern for the lost, diligently seeking them and rejoicing when they come back to the Saviour."

Jesus spoke this parable and the others found in Luke chapter 15 after the Pharisees criticised Him for welcoming sinners and eating with them (Luke 15:2). Why were they so bothered by what Jesus did? The religious leaders were always careful to avoid certain people whom they deemed to be unclean, for example, lepers. Based on the Old Testament Law on cleanliness, they justified their behaviour, although they went well beyond the law in their avoidance of certain people. They completely misunderstood, and this is why Jesus told them the parable. They took things too far by avoiding individuals whom they saw as sinners. Jesus explained to them that He had come to offer salvation to all, because we are all sinners.

The woman diligently searched everywhere for the coin until she found it. The coin was of great value to her and, for that reason, she would not give up looking for it. This illustrates God's love for His people, and because of His desire to save us in His kingdom will search for those who are lost in sin. Unlike the religious leaders who believed that God found joy in the destruction of the sinner, Jesus, in relating this parable, helped them to understand that it was His mission to save sinners and not to condemn them. In Ezekiel 18:23, we are reminded that God does not take pleasure in the death of the wicked. He says, "Do I take pleasure in the death of the wicked...? Rather, am I not pleased when they return from their ways and live?

Jesus wants you to join in the celebrations. He is seeking you and will restore and give you a new start if you are willing to accept Him.

Today's Prayer: Lord, I too was lost, but you found me. Thank you for still seeking those who are lost. Amen.

September 19

GOD'S ARM IS NOT SHORT

'Surely the arm of the Lord is not too short to save, nor His ear too dull to hear." (Isaiah 59:1)

Sin is offensive to God, and when we sin against Him, it destroys our relationship with Him and separates us from Him. However, according to the prophet Isaiah, God's power to save us, despite our sins, is not limited. He is the only one who can save us, and his ability to hear our cries for help is not impaired. During Isaiah's time, the people had rebelled against God and had become separated from Him. He wanted to restore the relationship they had with Him. God was saying to the people that if they repented of their sins, He would restore them. He alone had the power to do so. In Joel 2:25, He shows His desire to restore His people if they repented. "I will repay you for the years the locusts have eaten." His power is not diminished, and He is willing to listen to those who call upon Him.

Have you walked away from the Lord and feel there is no way back? You might be saying 'I have done so many bad things, wasted so much time, I have made such a mess of my life, surely, He won't have me back'. Not so, God is letting you know that He has the power to save you. All you need to do is confess your sins, ask for forgiveness and repent. It is sin that builds a barrier and separates one from Him. It is Satan, the deceiver and liar, who makes you think that your case is a hopeless one and that God has abandoned you. During Isaiah's day, God's people wondered why it seemed like God was not hearing their cries for help; they wondered if He had no more power to deliver them. Clearly, the problem was not with God - because of their sins, they had become separated from Him.

One commentary says, "Because God is holy, He cannot ignore, excuse or tolerate sin as though it didn't matter. Sin cuts people off from Him, forming a wall to isolate God from the people He loves." If we continue to sin, it forces God to turn away from us. In Isaiah 1:15, we read God's scathing rebuke of His people, "When you spread out your hands in prayer, I hide my eyes from you; when you offer many prayers, I am not listening." Because of their sinful condition, the people felt that God had forsaken them or had lost His power to save; however, Isaiah reminds them that God's arm is not too short to save, nor His ear too dull to hear. This must have been good news to the people, and should be good news to you, too if you are thinking you are too sinful for God to save you.

God is waiting for you to come to Him and ask forgiveness. In the parable of the Prodigal son, after wasting his substance and living a riotous life, he finally returned home to his father, who welcomed him home with open arms. The father symbolises God, who will take you back and restore you to your rightful place, as a valuable and loved member of the family of God. He is waiting to restore you, so return to Him. Jesus says, "All those the Father gives me will come to me, and whoever comes to me I will never drive away." (John 6:37)
What are you waiting for?

Today's Prayer: Father, please forgive me and restore me to my rightful place. Amen.

September 20

WHICH VOICE?

"Whether you turn to the right or to the left, your ears will hear a voice behind you saying, "This is the way, walk in it." (Isaiah 30:21)

Today, many voices are vying for your attention, telling you which way to go and what to do. Which voice will you listen to? In order to go the right way, you should recognise the right voice. You must be able to distinguish the right voice. Throughout generations, God has been calling His people, and they know His voice. "My sheep listen to my voice." (John 10:27). It is God's voice that will guide you.

To hear and know His voice, you must have a relationship with Him, so you can recognise His voice. To enable you to distinguish His voice from any other, you must have direct communication with Him through prayer and study of His word. It is His voice that will guide and instruct you. It is His voice you will hear guiding you through the chaos and confusion of this sinful world. Whether you turn to the right or to the left, your ears will hear a voice behind you saying, "This is the way, walk in it." When the people, during the time of Isaiah, left God's path, He had to correct them and bring them back. He will do the same for His people today. However, when we hear His voice of correction, we must respond and be willing to follow where He leads.

Does it not fill you with hope and assurance and comfort to know that as you try to navigate the many directions in life, you do not have to worry about getting lost? Just listen and you will hear His voice. It calls for spiritual discernment and spiritual attentiveness to hear God's voice, so learn to listen. Isaiah is not just saying that God will guide you personally; He is also helping us to understand that when God instructs you, when He says, "You will hear a voice", it is suggesting a close relationship with Him. As you relate to Him, the more likely you will recognise His voice. You will be more sensitive to His voice amidst all the other voices competing for your attention. Which voice will you listen to today?

Today's Prayer: Father, please give me spiritual discernment to distinguish your voice amidst all other voices. Amen.

September 21

FILTHY RAGS RIGHTEOUSNESS

"All of us have become like one who is unclean and all our righteous acts are like filthy rags..." (Isaiah 64:6)

No matter how good we think we are, God is not impressed with us at all. All of us have become like one who is unclean, and 'all our righteous acts are like filthy rags'. When you read Isaiah chapter 1, you get a sense of how low Israel had descended into sin. They worshipped other gods and disobeyed the God of heaven. Their situation became so bad that God, in very scathing terms, said He would hide His eyes from them. Even their best efforts were infected with the virus of sin. In their present state, it seemed there was no hope; their only hope was to turn back to God and ask for forgiveness.

God is not saying that He will reject you if you sin against Him, but we cannot come to Him demanding acceptance based on our good conduct. He says, 'Your righteousness is but filthy rags' compared to His infinite righteousness. If you are truly repentant, God will forgive you so you can make a new start. After He had pointed out the sins of Israel and Judah, in Isaiah chapter 1, God invited them to come to Him. "Come now, let us settle the matter," says the Lord. "Though your sins are like scarlet, they shall be as white as snow; though they are as crimson, they shall be like wool." (Isaiah 1:18) (Scarlet and crimson were the colours of a deep permanent dye, and its deep stain was virtually impossible to remove from clothing). The stain of sin appears to be equally permanent and only God can remove it from our lives. We don't have to go through life permanently soiled with sin, for God is waiting to forgive us; if we are willing and obedient, He will forgive and remove our most indelible stains.

The message of Isaiah chapter 1 is primarily for the unrepentant person and not for the follower of God. While this might be so, how do we come to terms with the one who professes to be a child of God but behaves in a manner inconsistent with God's standards and His love? This is evidence that none of us is perfect and that our righteousness is indeed like filthy rags in the sight of God. Our best deeds are marred with sin and are not acceptable to a Holy God. It is only by His grace that we are saved.

Today's Prayer: Lord, you are the only one who is righteous. Cleanse me from all unrighteousness. Amen.

September 22

YOU ARE GOD'S TEMPLE

"Do you not know that your bodies are temples of the Holy Spirit, who is in you, whom you have received from God? You are not your own; you were bought with a price. Therefore, honour God with your bodies." (1 Corinthians 6:19-20)

What does Paul mean? When he says your body belongs to God? He is referring to the body as God's temple. It therefore means that although we think our bodies belong to us and think we can do what we like with them, our bodies belong to God. When we become followers of Christ, the Holy Spirit takes up residence in our lives; therefore, we no longer own our bodies. For this reason, you will not abuse or violate your body in any way; you will live a pure and holy life, because the Holy Spirit now dwells in your body, His temple. Paul tells us we have been bought with a price. Sin had enslaved us, but Christ's death on the cross has freed us from sin and also binds us to serve God. Because we have been bought with a price, the blood of Jesus Christ, our bodies do not belong to us, so we should honour Him with our bodies and bring glory to Him.

During the time of Israel in the wilderness, as they journeyed to the promised land, they would stop on the journey, set up the tabernacle or temple, and then the various tribes would pitch their tents around it. The tabernacle, which contained the most holy place, would be where the presence of God would dwell. God desired to have His people close to Him, and by dwelling in us, He can be close to us, too. In Old Testament times, the temple was the central place of worship for the Jews; it was a most sacred place which was dedicated to the worship of God. Like the temple of old, so are our physical bodies, which, when we accept Christ in our lives, become a dwelling place for the Holy Spirit to dwell, and represent God to the world. You are a living temple where the Spirit of God has taken up residence.

If you have truly accepted Christ in your life, then honour Him with your body; use it for His purpose and not your own. Treasure it, do not dishonour it in any way at all; it is to be treasured because no greater honour has been bestowed upon you than to have the Holy Spirit dwelling in you. Meditate on the words of Paul in this text, worship God and give glory to Him as you dedicate yourself to His service.

Today's Prayer: Lord Jesus, come and dwell in me today. Amen.

September 23

YOU ARE NEVER ALONE

"Do not be afraid or terrified because of them, for the Lord your God goes with you. He will never leave you or forsake you." (Deuteronomy 31:6)

Do you sometimes feel alone and lonely? 'Loneliness is an unpleasant emotional response to perceived or actual isolation'. Loneliness is also described as 'social pain, a psychological mechanism that motivates individuals to seek social connections. It is often associated with a perceived lack of connection and intimacy'. You might be living on your own with no one to talk with, you might be widowed, and all your friends have died. Your children might have left home and rarely visit. There can be a number of reasons why you are on your own and feeling lonely. Loneliness can affect anyone. It can have serious mental and physical consequences. Social isolation and loneliness, it is said, can lead to a higher risk of high blood pressure, heart disease, obesity, anxiety, depression, memory issues, and even death.

According to the 'BBC Loneliness Experiment', 40% of people within the age group 16 to 24 admit to feeling lonely, while the percentage of people above age 75 is about 27%. Your friends and family may forsake you, but God says He will never leave you or forsake you. God promises never to leave you. In the history of Israel, we find Him constantly reassuring them of His presence. When Joshua succeeded Moses as leader, God reminded him, as he did Moses, that He would not forsake him.

In this text, we find Moses reassuring the Israelites that they should be strong and courageous and not be terrified because God would be with them and would never leave them. He was to be a constant presence in their lives. Although these words were spoken generations ago, the promise remains the same for God's people. You don't have to feel lonely or alone, for God says He will always be with you. If you are feeling lonely today, stop focusing on your loneliness and start focusing on God, trust

Him, and remain in His presence. He is the friend who will be with you through thick and thin. He loves you so much that He cannot bear to leave you alone. What a beautiful thought!

Today's Prayer: Father, thank you for not leaving me alone. Amen.

September 24

GOD WILL DELIVER YOU (1)

"For if you remain silent at this time, relief and deliverance for the Jews will arise from another place, but you and your father's family will perish. And who knows but that you have come to your royal position for such a time as this." (Esther 4:14)

The Jews in Persia had been a minority since their deportation from Judah. They lived in a world that was hostile to them. When Esther became queen, she and the Jews found themselves threatened and doomed to die. However, most remarkably, we see God's divine guidance, protection, care, and deliverance from those who sought to exterminate them. Although outnumbered by their enemies, Mordecai and Esther courageously took on their enemies, and God delivered them. Likewise, if you have found yourself in a life-threatening situation, God will deliver you, too. Watch what God will do for you. It could be that, like Esther, it is His will for you to go through what you're going through now. Perhaps He has prepared you to act in 'such a time as this'. If you call on God and trust in Him, He will deliver you.

When the three Hebrew boys were thrown into the fiery furnace, God delivered them. When you serve and trust God, all you have to do is call on Him in the time of trouble, and He will deliver you (Psalm 50:15). Because of their faith in God, the three Hebrew boys were able to boldly proclaim to the King that the God they serve would deliver them. "The God we serve is able to deliver us from it, and He will deliver us from Your Majesty's hand." (Daniel 3:17) What a mighty deliverance that was! When the pagan king Nebuchadnezzar witnessed God's deliverance, He ended up praising the very God whom He had defied. "Praise be to the God of Shadrach, Meshach and Abednego, who sent His angel and rescued His servants!"

Those three faithful servants of God brought honour and glory to Him that day in Babylon. When you trust God and remain faithful to Him, He can deliver you from any situation if He chooses. The three Hebrew boys told the king that even if God chose not to deliver them from the fire, they would remain faithful to Him. We should be faithful to Him no matter what happens. You must trust God and remain faithful regardless of the consequences. One writer says, "If God always rescued those who were true to Him, Christians would need no faith. Their religion would be a great insurance policy, and there would be lines of selfish people ready to sign up."

Are you prepared to remain faithful to God even if He chooses not to deliver you out of your current situation? Remain faithful to Him, for your eternal reward is worth more than any suffering you may have to endure.

Today's Prayer: Thank you, Lord, for delivering me from my troubles. Amen.

September 25

GOD WILL DELIVER YOU (2)

"...If God is for us, who can be against us?" (Romans 8:31)

Daniel had been taken captive and deported to Babylon by Nebuchadnezzar in 605 BC. He served the government there for about seventy years during the reigns of Nebuchadnezzar, Belshazzar, Darius and Cyrus. Daniel, this great statesman, had achieved much by being faithful to God. He became Darius's most trusted advisor; however, his privileged position angered other government officials, who plotted to kill him by convincing the king to outlaw prayer for thirty days, and that no one else should be worshipped but the King. Despite this law, Daniel continued to pray to the God of heaven and, as a result of his obedience to God, was condemned to die in a den of lions. However, God was faithful to Daniel and delivered him from death. Isaiah tells us that "No weapon forged against you will prevail, and you will refute every tongue that accuses you." (Isaiah 54:17)

God delivered Daniel, and He will deliver you, too. When he was thrown into the lion's den, God intervened and saved him from the hungry lions by shutting their mouths. God has so many ways of delivering His people, even shutting lions' mouths! Paul tells us, "If God is for us, who can be against us?" (Romans 8:31). Like the three Hebrew boys, Daniel remained faithful to God and was spared death. If you trust God and remain faithful to Him, He will deliver you from any situation.

Take Jeremiah, who suffered greatly for the cause of God. He was poor and underwent severe deprivation to deliver God's message to the people. He was thrown into prison and into a cistern, but God delivered Him. Despite persecutions and opposition and attempts on his life, Jeremiah courageously and faithfully remained true to God. When God called him, He promised him that He would deliver him. "Do not be afraid of them, for I am with you and will rescue you," declares the Lord. (Jeremiah 1:8). Although God promised Jeremiah that He would look after him and deliver him from trouble, He did not 'insulate' him from imprisonment, ridicule, and opposition.

If you are facing a difficult time right now, learn from Daniel and Jeremiah, just trust God and remember that He will deliver you. He will step in on time all the time. Read His promise to you in Psalm 34:7. 'The angel of the Lord encamps around those who fear Him, and He delivers them.'

Today's Prayer: Lord, help me to remain faithful to you no matter what I am going through. Amen.

September 26

ARE YOU PREPARED TO LOOK FOOLISH?

"But God chose the foolish things of the world to shame the wise: God chose the weak things of the world to shame the strong." (1 Corinthians 1:27)

Are you prepared to look foolish? No one wants to look foolish in the eyes of others. However, in 1 Corinthians 1:27, Paul says that God chose the foolish things of the world to shame the wise. In verse 25, we are told that 'the foolishness of God is wiser than human wisdom and the weakness of God is stronger than human strength.' One commentary says, "The message of Christ's death for sins sounds foolish to those who don't believe." The gospel of Christ is so simple that many people won't accept it. They think that accepting would make them look foolish. What Paul is really saying is that no amount of human intellect, learning, or knowledge can replace or bypass Christ's work on the cross. If that were the case, Christ would only be attainable to intellectuals, the gifted, and well-educated.

I recently read about a politician who claimed they no longer believed in God. "I am not an atheist, I am agnostic. I describe myself as a cultural Christian." Does any of that make sense? Here is someone who is supposedly educated and well learned, but sadly is totally confused and rather foolish. Paul is right when he says, "for the foolishness of God is wiser than human wisdom." The politician might say their thinking is rational. Thinking rationally allows you to use your mind to question and draw conclusions. It allows you to weigh up the evidence and hopefully make the right choices. However, Paul is saying that if you do not believe the gospel, that Christ died to save you from your sins, then, as simple as that sounds, it is foolishness to the one who does not believe. On the contrary, those who believe that Jesus died to save them will be deemed foolish in the eyes of those who do not believe. The truth is, the foolish ones are the wisest of all because they have accepted Christ as their Saviour.

Are you prepared to look foolish for Christ? God has chosen those who believe and have accepted Him, the weak and foolish ones, as defined by human terms, to come to Him through Christ Jesus. According to Matthew Henry, "God did not choose philosophers, nor orators, nor statesmen, nor men of wealth and power, and interest in the world, to publish the gospel of grace and peace [...] Often, a humble Christian, though poor as to this world, has more knowledge of the gospel than those who made the letter of Scripture the study of their lives..." Give God thanks that He has chosen you, even though you might be considered foolish to the world; you are wise in the eyes of God.

Today's Prayer: Father, although the world deems me foolish, thank you for putting the wise of this world to shame. Open their eyes so they can become wise in you. Amen.

September 27

LONGING FOR HEAVEN

"What no eye has seen, what no ear has heard, and what no human mind has conceived – the things God has prepared for those who love Him." (1 Corinthians 2:9)

Have you ever tried to imagine what heaven is like? People often speak of streets of gold and saints playing on their harps! If you try to imagine heaven based on what we have here on earth, it will fall short of what it will be like. That is the very reason Paul makes the above statement: "What no eye has seen, what no ear has heard, and what no human mind has conceived – the things that God has prepared for those who love Him." He is saying that we cannot imagine what God has in store for us, both in this life and eternity. If we try to imagine heaven based on what we have here on earth, it just won't match up, for the Bible tells us that God will create new heavens and a new earth (Revelation 21:1).

Can you imagine a city laid out like a square, as long as it is wide, with walls of Jasper; a city of pure gold, whose foundation is decorated with every kind of precious stone? The first foundation is made of Jasper, the second Sapphire, the third Agate, the fourth Emerald, the fifth Onyx, the sixth Ruby, the seventh Chrysolite, the eighth Beryl, the ninth Topaz, the tenth Turquoise, the eleventh Jacinth and the twelfth Amethyst. There are twelve gates, being twelve pearls; each gate is made of a single pearl. The great street of the Holy city is made of pure gold, as pure as transparent glass (Revelation 21:16-20). According to John, to whom God gave this vision of heaven, he said that the city does not need the sun or the moon to shine on it, for the glory of God gives it light, and the Lamb is its lamp (Revelation 21:23).

What is even more beautiful about heaven, and this should make us rejoice, the city will be completely without sin and evil, and God himself will be there! Are you longing for heaven? Are you longing to be with God the Father, God the Son and God the Holy Spirit? God is longing for His children to come home so we can spend the ceaseless ages of eternity with Him. This old, sinful earth holds nothing for us but pain and suffering. How often do you talk about heaven? Are the things of earth more attractive to you? "This world is not my home, I am just passing through, my treasures are laid up somewhere beyond the blue," says one songwriter. Our citizenship is in heaven, not here on earth, and Jesus is our passport into heaven. "But our citizenship is in heaven. And we eagerly await a Saviour from there, the Lord Jesus Christ, who by the power that enables Him to bring everything under His control will transform our lowly bodies so that they will be like His glorious body." (Philippians 3:20 & 21)

As believers, we ought to "promote heaven's interests on earth and lead lives worthy of heavenly citizenship. Too many Christians have failed to transfer their citizenship to heaven. They seek earthly pleasures and treasures instead of heavenly ones," says one writer. Paul reminded the Philippians that they were citizens of heaven. Are you promoting heaven's interests? Are you a citizen of heaven?

Today's prayer: Father, I want to live with you in heaven forever. Amen.

September 28

OBEDIENCE (1)

"To obey is better than sacrifice and to heed is better than the fat of rams." (1 Samuel 15:23)

According to the dictionary definition, the word obedience means dutiful, submissive compliance. For the believer, it means surrendering to God. Sacrifice, on the other hand, is an act of giving up something valued for the sake of something else regarded as more important or worthy. In 1 Samuel 15:22, the prophet urges King Saul to consider his reasons for making the sacrifice rather than the sacrifice itself. Saul convinced himself that he had obeyed God when he made a sacrifice. However, his motives were selfish and wrong in the sight of God.

Obedience is important to God as it is an expression of your love for Him. The Bible is filled with accounts of the consequences of Israel's sins because of their disobedience and their refusal to do what God told them to do. Like Israel, throughout the ages, many kinds of sacrifices have been used as a method of expression of devotion to God; therefore, it was not unusual for King Saul to offer sacrifices; however, he did it in defiance of God's commands. We are told in the Bible that "to do what is right and just is more acceptable to the Lord than sacrifice." One writer says, "Our good deeds and offerings are not bribes to make God overlook our character faults. We cannot exchange good behaviour in one area for bad behaviour in another."

Any sacrifice made to God should demonstrate a relationship with Him, and the one who makes the sacrifice, an expression of love and obedience to God. Obeying God brings blessings, whereas disobedience results in consequences. This is evident when we see throughout the Scriptures what happened to Israel as a result of their disobedience. When they left Egypt, the journey should have taken them three days or so to the Promised Land, but because of disobedience and sin, it took them forty years. Only two of the original people who left Egypt entered the Promised Land. What about King Saul? He became both rebellious and arrogant, and was finally rejected by God and had his kingdom taken away from him.

God does not force us to obey Him; however, if we love Him, we will obey His commandments. Going through religious acts, rituals, and ceremonies without real love for God is empty and useless; it is like Saul's sacrifice, selfish and sinful. Jesus says, "If you love me, keep my commandments." (John 14:15) Remember that even your most wonderful and elaborate acts of 'worship' are meaningless to God if you are not obedient to His commands.

Today's Prayer: Father, help me to do what is obedient and acceptable to you. Amen.

September 29

OBEDIENCE (2)

"For just as through the disobedience of the one man the many were made sinners, so also through the obedience of the one man many will be made righteous." (Romans 5:19)

I remember the boy next door. He was always getting into trouble because he did what he wanted to do and seldom obeyed his parents. One day, he asked if he could go swimming, but his parents said he wasn't allowed to go unless he was accompanied by an adult. However, when they were not looking, he quietly left the house and went to the beach; sadly, he did not return home. He apparently got into difficulties in the water and lost his life.

Disobedience is a sin against God. Adam and Eve, our first parents, ate of the forbidden fruit and suffered the consequences; they were expelled from their Garden home. Sin is never without its consequences. Their son Cain disobeyed God and offered the sacrifice that he wanted to, even though God had clearly instructed him what sacrifice he should give. This resulted in him murdering his brother Abel. As a result of his disobedience, Cain was cursed and forced to become a wanderer.

Moses, that great leader of God's people, disobeyed Him when he struck the rock to provide water to the children of Israel instead of speaking to it as God had commanded. This resulted in Him not being allowed to lead the Israelites into the Promised Land. These are all examples of people who disobeyed God and suffered the consequences. When individuals disobey God, their actions can hurt others, and they can also lead to personal downfall, or even death, as we saw in the case of my neighbour's son. From a spiritual perspective, disobedience can be seen as a failure to trust in God, which means that the individual is saying they know best, they are better off without God's guidance.

Jesus says, "If you love me, keep my commands." (John 14:15) He is saying that there is a direct link between love and obedience. In other words, when we obey God's commands, we are telling those around us that we love and trust Him. Jesus is saying that if we genuinely love Him, we will want to please Him, and keeping His commandments is an act of worship. Because of the disobedience of Adam and Eve, we are all sinners; however, our key text is full of hope, for through the obedience of one man, Jesus Christ Himself, we are made righteous. It is because of man's disobedience that Jesus suffered and died on the cross.

Do not continue in disobedience and violate God's principles, but live a life of obedience to His will. If you love Him, obey His commands.

Today's Prayer: Dear God, help me to learn to obey your commands. Forgive me for my disobedience. Amen.

September 30

ENEMY TERRITORY

'The great dragon was hurled down – that ancient snake called the devil, or Satan, who leads the whole world astray. He was hurled to the earth, and his angels with him.' (Revelation 12:9)

It is hard to imagine how sin happened in a perfect place such as heaven. We are told in Ezekiel 28:17 that Lucifer's heart became proud on account of his beauty, and he wanted to be like God. He said in his heart, "I will ascend to the heavens: I will raise my throne above the stars of God [...] I will make myself like the Most High." (Isaiah 14:13-14) "Then war broke out in heaven. Michael and his angels fought against the dragon, and the dragon and his angels fought back. But he was not strong enough, and they lost their place in heaven. The great dragon was hurled down [...] to the earth and his angels with him." (Revelation 12:7-9)

CS Lewis, in his book 'Mere Christianity', says, "Thus this universe is at war, a civil war, a rebellion, and we are living in a part of the universe occupied by the Dark Power that is rebelling against good. Enemy territory – that is what this world is." God never intended it to be so when He created the world, for all He had made was very good. However, when Adam and Eve disobeyed Him, the whole Earth became contaminated by sin. Lucifer, after rebelling against God in heaven, was cast out, and a relentless war continued between good and evil. And as a result, the Earth became enemy territory, and we are living on this Earth in the midst of this war.

God knew that man would sin and would need a Saviour, and before the foundation of the world, the plan of salvation was put in place. "But when the set time had fully come, God sent His son born of a woman, born under the law to redeem those under the law that we might receive adoption as sons." (Galatians 4:4-5) Jesus, the son of God, came to Earth on a rescue mission to save mankind. "For God so loved the world that He gave His one and only Son that whoever believes in Him shall not perish but have eternal life". (John 3:16)

The evil one has made war against God's people, which is being intensified as we near the coming of Jesus Christ. However, as the battle escalates, Peter warns us to: "be alert and sober of mind. Your enemy, the devil, prowls around like a roaring lion looking for someone to devour." (1 Peter 5:8) If you do not want to be engulfed by the devil and his angels, you must be rooted, and firmly rooted, in Jesus Christ. Keep your eyes on Him at the times when you are especially vulnerable to Satan's attacks. James says, "Resist the devil and he will flee from you." (1 Peter 5:8) Although Christ and Satan are still at war, Satan was defeated when Christ died and rose again. However, we will have to remain in combat until Jesus comes, for Satan is even now trying to win you over to his evil course. Christ tells us to put on the whole armour of God, so that you can take your stand against the devil's schemes (Ephesians 6:10-11).

Today's prayer: Father, I know I am living in enemy territory; because you are in control, I have nothing to fear. Amen.

October 1

WHAT ABOUT HIM?

'When Peter saw him, he asked, "Lord, what about Him?"' (John 21:21)

Peter asked Jesus how John would die. Jesus replied that Peter should not concern himself with that. If He wanted John to remain alive until His return, He asked Peter, "What is it to you? You must follow me." Jesus had predicted that Peter would die by crucifixion, and despite what would happen to Peter in the future, Jesus told him to follow Him. This was the context of the question about John.

We sometimes tend to compare ourselves with others and might even think another person is more gifted or a better Christian than us. However, it is a human tendency to compare oneself to others. You should not compare yourself with others; they might disappoint you, for no one is perfect. Jesus is the only perfect one and the only one we should emulate. When we compare ourselves to others, we should be careful, as this can lead to covetousness, jealousy, bitterness, and discontentment. These are all sinful desires that we should avoid.

That was why Jesus told Peter to follow Him, which is a reminder for all of us to focus on what God has called us to do, rather than comparing or being preoccupied with what others are doing. He has given us talents according to our abilities to do the work He has called us to do. When Jesus told Peter to follow Him, He was redirecting Peter's focus from John and back to Peter's assignment. It is easy to follow the crowd; however, the majority is rarely right, so it's not wise to follow the crowd. Follow Christ instead. When you follow those who you believe to be better Christians than yourself, they will sometimes, by their un-Christian-like behaviour, cause you to stumble and fall. However, when you follow Jesus, you will not stumble. He is the Light and the Way, and as you follow Him, He will illuminate your path, so you can see clearly. Even the disciples could not follow each other, because they all had their flaws. Peter himself, in his unconverted state, denied Christ three times.

Thomas doubted the resurrected Christ. David, a man after God's own heart, fell into sin.

Don't concern yourself with what others are doing, or try to rationalise your own devotion to Jesus or question God's justice, just take your eyes off others, look to Jesus and follow Him.

Today's Prayer: Dear Father, I don't want to compare myself with others. Help me to learn to look to you and follow you. Amen.

October 2

ARE YOU SURPRISED AT TRIALS?

"I have told you these things so that in me you may have peace. In this world you will have trouble. But take heart! I have overcome the world." (John 16:33)

The Christian life is not an easy road. I remember my mother singing the song 'No, no it's not an easy road we are travelling to heaven'. It is naïve to believe that the Christian life is easy. Jesus tells us that we should expect difficulties; we should not think it's going to be easy all the time. We should therefore anticipate suffering along the way. Jesus told His disciples that in this world, they would have trouble, but that they should take heart because He had overcome the world. Jesus knew that it would not be easy for His followers. Therefore, as Christians, we should expect opposition from an unbelieving and sometimes hostile world. Although we will experience trials, we have the assurance from Jesus that as our relationship with Him grows, we can expect peace and comfort.

Peter says it quite succinctly, "Dear friends, do not be surprised at the fiery ordeal that has come upon you to test you, as though something strange were happening to you. But rejoice in as much as you participate in the sufferings of Christ, so that you may be overjoyed when his glory is revealed." (1 Peter 4:12 &13) Peter is encouraging you not to view your suffering as something strange; you should see it as an opportunity to share in the sufferings of Jesus Christ. However difficult this might be for you, you should count it all joy as you look beyond your present suffering to the prospect of future glory and living with Jesus eternally.

Jesus wants believers to understand that suffering is inevitable, but we are to take courage, and the good news is that He will be with us; He will never abandon us. Jesus has already won the victory.

Today's Prayer: Father, I look beyond the trials and suffering to the glories that await me. Amen.

October 3

GOOD STEWARDS

"...Well done, good and faithful servant! You have been faithful with a few things; I will put you in charge of many things. Come and share your master's happiness." (Matthew 25:21)

God has given everyone talents, gifts, and abilities to bring glory to Him. This parable that Jesus told about the talents is telling us that the talents, resources, our abilities, and even our time have been loaned to us. He expects us to invest them wisely until He returns.

Do you have talents or abilities that you have been given? It is not about how much you have, because God has given you your talents and resources according to your ability to handle them. It is not so much about what you have; it is about how well you use it. The talents He has given you and how you use them will determine your level of responsibility and faithfulness to Him. Can God trust you to use them wisely? The servant with the one talent we are told hid his talent. He was thinking only of himself. He hoped he would play it safe and protect himself from his hard master, but he was judged for his self-centredness, says one writer.

Are you like the servant who was given the one talent, making excuses instead of using it wisely? We must not make excuses to avoid doing what God has asked us to do. It is human of us to make excuses, Moses did, so did Jeremiah, yet they were willing to obey God. You should be willing and obedient to do the work God has called you to do. If He is truly your Lord and Master, you should be willing to work for Him using the talents He has entrusted to you. Our time, abilities, and money do not belong to us, for God is the giver of all good gifts. When we do not use what He has given to us, or abuse them, it means we are selfish and rebellious and deserve to be punished like that servant in the parable.

This parable describes our attitude towards the return of Christ. Are you diligently preparing for His coming by investing your time and ability to serve Him? Those who do so will be rewarded when Jesus comes. However, those who squander their time and talents and have no heart for the work will be punished. It is God who has given you your talents, gifts and abilities so use them wisely and bring glory to Him.

Today's Prayer: Thank you, Lord, for the talents you have given me. Help me to use them wisely and bring glory to you. Amen.

October 4

DO NOT JUDGE

"Do not judge, or you will be judged." (Matthew 7:1)

In this text, Jesus is telling us to consider our own motives and behaviour instead of judging others. By judging others, we become hypocritical, which is what Jesus is saying. We are seeing the fault of others, and by tearing them down, we are trying to build ourselves up. The faults that we see in others are often the ones we ourselves have. Our bad habits are what we want to change in others. It is easy to see what is wrong with others and not with ourselves.

Recently, I found myself judging someone who sat next to me on the train. He was a young man covered all over with tattoos. All kinds of thoughts went through my mind about him, and in general about people who tattoos themselves. As these thoughts occupied my mind, suddenly, as if another voice within me, said, 'Speak with him', and so we began a conversation. He told me much about himself, and as I listened, I could not help but feel ashamed for judging him. He was a young man who was honest, caring, and possessed good values. He was someone who wanted the best for his children and was working hard to support them, financially, emotionally, and to instil good values in them.

In Matthew 7:1 &2, Jesus says, "Do not judge, or you too will be judged. For the same way as you judge others, you will be judged, and with what measure you use, it will be measured to you." Jesus is quite clear in what He is saying. He is telling us to consider our own motives and behaviour instead of judging others. Quite often, you will find that the behaviours we don't like in others are the very behaviours we possess. One writer says, "Our bad habits and behaviour patterns are the very ones we most want to change in others." Jesus is warning us against this kind of behaviour.

When you judge others, you are being hypocritical and self-righteous. You are actually saying they have faults, and you have none. However,

Jesus is saying that when you judge others, you are failing to recognise your own sins and imperfections. None of us is perfect; on the contrary, all of us have sinned and come short of God's glory. "All have sinned and fall short of God's glory." (Romans 3:23) Therefore, we should avoid condemning and judging the motives of others. You must recognise that you are a sinner; you have flaws and imperfections too, so how dare you judge others? In fact, how dare any of us judge? God is the ultimate judge, and He will judge us according to our deeds.

Today's Prayer: Father, forgive me for judging others. Amen.

October 5

DID YOU MISS THE ANSWER?

"Before they call, I will answer; while they are still speaking, I will hear." (Isaiah 65:24)

Have you ever been praying for God to intervene in your life? Did it seem that He was taking a long time to answer your prayer, or do you think He didn't even bother to answer? Could it be that He answered and you were not even aware that He had?

God always hears and answers our prayers. In today's text, Isaiah says, "Before they call, I will answer, while they are still speaking, I will hear." Picture this, you are on your knees praying and even before you utter one word, God has already answered your prayer! How did you manage to miss the answer?

I am reminded of the story in Acts 12 about Peter's miraculous escape from prison. Herod Agrippa the First persecuted the early Christians to please the Jewish leaders who opposed him, hoping that they would solidify his position. He had James, the brother of John, put to death, and then he proceeded to imprison Peter. Whilst in prison, Peter was miraculously rescued by an angel. A group of believers had been praying for his release. However, when Peter knocked on the door of the house where they were praying for him, they had trouble believing that he was released. Amazingly, they were having a prayer meeting for his release, yet when Peter showed up, they did not believe. The Bible says, they were astonished to see him standing there and even thought it was his angel! Their prayers were answered, but when the answer arrived at the door, they didn't believe it!

Are there times when God has answered your prayers, the answer arrived, but you missed it? Is it because you were so focused on the problem that you missed the answer? Or your faith might have faltered the very moment when it should have remained firm? As a believer, you must really believe that God does answer prayers. When you pray, you must have faith to believe He will answer your prayer, not in your time, but in His time. You must exercise faith and trust in Him so that when the answer comes, you won't be astonished but be thankful. So, if you are waiting for an answer to your prayers, stop focusing on the problem that is looming like a mountain in your life; instead, focus on the mountain mover.

Today's Prayer: Lord, help me to focus on you so I don't miss your answers. Amen.

October 6

A THORN IN THE FLESH

"...Therefore, to keep me from becoming conceited, I was given a thorn in my flesh, a messenger of Satan to torment me." (2 Corinthians 12:7)

We do not know what Paul's thorn in the flesh was because he does not say. Some have speculated that it might have been a problem with his eyes. However, we don't really know for sure. According to Paul, he prayed three times for God to remove this problem that was seemingly causing him some concern. However, God refused to. It could have been that this impediment, whether physical or spiritual, might have been affecting his ministry, but God chose not to remove it. Paul states that the thorn was given specifically to prevent him from becoming conceited and prideful. This should remind us that God can sometimes use challenges to humble us. It is sad sometimes to see some who call themselves spiritual leaders who are conceited and proud. Clearly, this kind of attitude has no place in God's work.

Having a thorn in the flesh, no doubt, was a constant reminder to Paul of his dependence on God's grace and power in his life. When he asked God to remove the thorn, He responded by saying His grace was sufficient for Paul. After which, Paul accepted and was able to boast in his infirmities, so that God's power would rest on him.

Are you being challenged like Paul and have asked God to take away an impediment from your life, and He hasn't? It could be that you have had a diagnosis from the doctor that you had not expected to hear. It could be that the prognosis is not good, you have prayed for healing, and God has not healed you. Your response to Him in this situation is crucial. Paul prayed three times for healing, but God chose not to heal him. It could be that God is saying to you, as he did to Paul, that His grace is sufficient for you. If you have prayed for physical healing, can it be that God wants to heal you spiritually instead? God, in His wisdom, heals some of their physical ailments to bring glory to Himself and for others to accept Him and His might and power in changing their lives. You might not understand why sometimes God chooses not to heal, or why some are healed and not others. However, He is God and He knows what is best for you according to the plan He has for your life.

It is sometimes difficult to understand or accept God's answers; however, we must learn to accept the things we cannot change or understand. Paul accepted God's response to his request and continued in the ministry to which God had called him. God used him in a mighty way to take the gospel to the world at that time, and fulfilled his mission to the Gentiles. By not healing you physically, God is building your trust and faith in Him, the moment you accept the answer to your prayer. You must also accept that your spiritual condition is also important to Him, and He will heal you spiritually because He wants you to have a place in His kingdom. Go ahead today and boast of your infirmities and let God unleash His power in you.

Today's Prayer: Father, I accept whatever answer you give me, for you know best. Amen.

October 7

HYPROCRISY

"In the same way, on the outside you appear to people as righteous, but on the inside, you are full of hypocrisy and wickedness." (Matthew 23:28)

Hypocrisy is defined as 'the practice of feigning to be what one is not or to believe what one does not'. In the Biblical sense, it is often described as wearing a 'spiritual mask' or being a 'play actor' where individuals pretend to be righteous for the approval of others. Hypocrisy is often linked to pride, where one desires to be praised by others, and not recognising that you are a sinner like everyone else.

Jesus condemned hypocrisy, which was so evident in the Pharisees. They were prideful to the point of seeking the best for themselves, and this is illustrated in the following texts; everything they do is done for people to see. "They make their phylacteries (that is, their little leather boxes, containing Scripture verses) wide and the tassels on their garments long." The phylacteries had become more important for the status they gave than the truth they contained. "They love the place of honour at banquets and the most important seats in the synagogues. They love to be greeted with respect in the marketplaces and to be called Rabbi by others." (Matthew 23:5)

Jesus warned the people against the religious leaders of His day because they did not practise what they taught. He was scathing of them and, describing them, said, they "tie up heavy cumbersome loads and put them on other people's shoulders, but they themselves are not willing to lift a finger to move them." (Matthew 23:4) Jesus said their behaviour was hypocritical; they knew the Scriptures but did not live by them. Jesus condemned their hypocritical behaviour, and still does today. Jesus hates hypocrisy and condemned the Pharisees and religious leaders of His day. Outwardly, they gave the impression they were holy and righteous, but inwardly, they were full of hypocrisy and wickedness. Living for Christ is not about showing how righteous and how good you are on the outside; your goodness should come from within.

Today's Prayer: Father, help me to practise what I preach. Amen.

487

October 8

MOULDED AND MADE

"Yet you, Lord, are our Father. We are the clay, you are the potter; we are the work of your hand." (Isaiah 64:8)

Have you ever watched a potter at work on the wheel? It is truly fascinating to watch as an ordinary and seemingly useless piece of clay is moulded, shaped and transformed into a beautiful object. To watch those skilful hands fashioning that clay into something worthwhile is truly amazing. Pottery is the process of using clay and other ceramic materials to form vessels. God is like the Potter; He can mould us and make us into who He likes us to become. The prophet Isaiah likens God to the Potter, "Yet you, Lord, are our father. We are the clay you are the Potter. We are all the work of your hand." (Isaiah 64:8) This is such beautiful imagery of God as our Creator and the moulder of our lives. Can you imagine God like the Potter, shaping us as only He can, the all-powerful God who has called us to be His sons and daughters?

Just as the useless clay is dependent on the Potter to create something beautiful, so God wants to show you that, even if you are broken and living a life of desperation, He can make you whole again, He can transform you and make your life beautiful and meaningful. We are the clay, says Isaiah, meaning we are totally dependent on God for our existence and growth. However, God can only mould and shape you if you are willing to let Him. This calls for humility and submission on your part. Whoever comes to God must be willing to be moulded by Him; He will never force or even coerce you to submit to Him.

The moulding, refining process and shaping of your life, by the Master Potter, might be painful at times; however, you must sometimes go through trials and tribulations so that He can transform you. No one knows better than Job about the painful process of transformation and refining. He says, "But he knows the way I take when He has tested me; I shall come forth as gold." (Job 23:10) Therefore, when you go through the refining process, the potter is ensuring that you will emerge flawless without imperfections to become someone beautiful in His eyes. You must remember that you will have challenges in your life, for the refining process is not going to be easy, but if you are to be perfect in Christ, you must go through this process. Are you willing to be moulded and transformed by Jesus, the Master Potter?

Today's prayer: Father, I want to be moulded and shaped by you. Amen.

October 9

GIVE THANKS AND PRAISE

"I will extol the Lord at all times; His praise will always be on my lips." (Psalm 34:1)

To praise God is to express admiration for who He is. It is to give honour, glory and thanks for who He is and what He has done for you. In Psalm 34, David says that praising God is what he would always do. In Psalm 107, he says, "Give thanks to the Lord, for He is good, His love endures forever." You should have every reason to praise, give thanks, and glorify God for He has brought you through difficult times and He has blessed you with immeasurable blessings.

Have you experienced storms in your life when you felt that you would go under by the waves of despair, disappointment, and hopelessness? Can you recall when you cried out to God, and He rescued you? "The righteous cry out, and the Lord hears them; He delivers them from all their troubles. The Lord is close to the broken-hearted and saves those who are crushed in spirit." (Psalm 34:17 &18)

He was with you when you suffered pain, loss, sorrow, and failure, so you have every reason to praise Him and give thanks because when you were down and out, He was your comfort, your source of power and courage. In the song 'Give Thanks with a Grateful Heart,' the writer says, "Give thanks because He's given you Jesus Christ, His Son!" What more could God have done? Give thanks. When you look back today, look back in gratitude for what God has done for you, and give praise.

God promises great blessings to His people; however, many of these blessings require your active participation, and you must do your part in trusting Him. Continue to give thanks, and may His praise be always on your lips.

Today's Prayer: Father, your praise will always be on my lips. Amen.

October 10

ONLY GOD'S KINGDOM WILL LAST

"But after you shall arise another kingdom inferior to yours." (Daniel 2:39)

When Nebuchadnezzar ruled Babylon from 605 to 539 BC, he thought his kingdom would last forever, but he was wrong. One night, he had a dream that would shatter that belief, for in 539 BC, Babylon fell to the Medes & Persians. They also thought that their kingdom would last forever, but Medo-Persia too fell to Greece, and Greece to Rome.

History shows us that the kingdoms of this world will not last forever. Just as surely as Babylon, Medo-Persia, Greece and Rome fell; by the same token, the kingdoms of our present world will not last. In the interpretation of Nebuchadnezzar's dream, Daniel said, he saw a rock cut out of a mountain, but not by human hands – a rock that broke the iron, bronze, the clay, the silver, and the gold to pieces, and it filled the whole earth (Daniel 2:45). This symbolises the return of Jesus Christ and the setting up of His everlasting kingdom.

Despite man's best efforts to establish a kingdom that will last forever, the Bible tells us that this will never happen. However, various countries are trying to unite to achieve a New World Order; they will fail just like the kingdoms that have been before them. Organisations such as the United Nations, European Union, NATO and others are striving for unity to create this New World Order; this too will fail, for the only kingdom that will last is the kingdom of God. The Bible tells us that "In the time of those kings, the God of heaven will set up a kingdom that will never be destroyed, nor will it be left to another people..." (Daniel 2:44).

You should never doubt this prophecy; history confirms that all of the great kingdoms of the world have fallen, and they did not last forever. It is therefore certain that Jesus will return as He says, and set up His kingdom that will last forever. History has proven the accuracy of the prophecy, and there is no reason to doubt that the final events will take place as predicted.

God's kingdom will never be destroyed. If you are feeling fearful about world events that are currently happening, and upset by threats of war and the prosperity of evil leaders, remember that it is God who decides the future of this world and the outcome of history; therefore, you have nothing to fear. God's kingdom is indestructible, and those who serve Him are members of His kingdom and are secure in Him.

Today's Prayer: Father, as I look forward to your soon coming kingdom, let me tell others so that they, too, can have a place in your kingdom. Amen.

October 11

THE BIBLE – GOD'S WORD (1)

"...But prophets, though human, spoke from God as they were carried along by the Holy Spirit." (2 Peter 2:21)

The Bible is not an ordinary book. However, some claim it is just a fairy tale, a myth. Others say it was written by man; therefore, it cannot be true. The chances are that those who make these claims have perhaps never read it. I once heard a preacher describe it by using the following acronym: Basic, Instruction, Before Leaving Earth (B.I.B.L.E). It is much more than that, for it is the inspired word of God. The above text by Peter is a strong statement on the inspiration of the Bible.

The Bible is a book of science. If you want to learn biology, read your bible. Take a look at the book of Genesis, and you will notice that God created plant life in an orderly way. First, He created light, (Genesis 1:3) then water (verse 6), then soil (verse 9). And then He created plant life in that order. Plants need sunlight, water and minerals in order to grow and make their own nutrients and energy. If plants do not get sunlight and water, they will die.

Years ago, doctors and scientists did not understand the importance of blood in the body, and up until one hundred and twenty years ago, if you were ill, you would be 'bled' as a medical treatment, because it was believed that to restore balance to the body's 'humours,' which were thought to be the fundamental fluids regulating one's health, the patient would be 'bled'. In the book of Leviticus, we learn that blood is the source of life – if you lose it, you'll lose your life (Leviticus 17:11). It was Willian Harvey who discovered that blood circulation is the key factor in physical life, thus confirming what the Bible revealed many centuries ago.

Have you ever thought you could learn about astronomy in the Bible? In Genesis 1:14, we are told, "Let there be lights in the vault of the sky to separate the day from the night, and let them serve as signs to mark sacred times, and days and years." Astronomers will tell you that it takes a year for the Earth to travel around the Sun; it takes roughly three hundred and sixty-five days or one year for the Earth to complete its orbit around the Sun. Long before astronomers discovered that the 'lights' of the Sun and Moon were what determined the year's length, Moses already knew, of course, he was inspired to write this in the book of Genesis. Astronomers will tell you that the seasons are caused by the changing position of the Earth in relation to the Sun. They can tell you exactly from the Earth's motion around the Sun when one season ends and the other begins.

The Bible and science show the powerful depiction of the transcendence and Omnipresence of God. The Bible is indeed the inspired word of God, written by holy men who were directed by the Spirit of God. Read it for yourself and you will find that it is true.

Today's Prayer: Father, thank you for revealing yourself in nature and through Scripture. Amen.

October 12

THE BIBLE GOD'S WORD (2)

'For the word of God is alive and active, sharper than any double-edged sword. It penetrates even to dividing soul and spirit, joint and marrow; it judges the thoughts and attitudes of the heart.' (Hebrews 4:12)

The writer of Hebrews is saying that the 'word of God' is not simply a collection of words from God, a vehicle for communicating ideas; it is much more than that - it is a living, life-changing word of God. One commentary describes it as "more than a book to be studied. It's a compilation of sacred writings God gave us to know and love Him better." A.W. Tozer describes it as "God's present speaking voice – that which makes the written word all-powerful and as relevant today as it was to first-century believers." Yet still many do not believe it.

The Bible speaks for itself, and there is every reason to believe it is true. You can learn about every subject you can think of. I have heard of individuals who, because of poverty and lack of opportunities, educated themselves by reading and studying Scriptures. If you want to learn about history, science, health or any other topic, you can learn it by studying the Bible. During the time of Christopher Columbus, it was believed that the Earth was flat; however, the Bible tells us that it is round. "He sits enthroned above the circle of the Earth..." (Isaiah 40:22). The word circle suggests that the Earth is round and not flat.

The book of Genesis explains the origin of the sexes. Almost all forms of complex life have both male and female – humans, horses, dogs, monkeys, birds, fish, etc. Males need females to reproduce; the species cannot carry on life without the other. The Bible tells us quite clearly that in the beginning, "God created mankind in His own image, in the image of God He created them; male and female He created them. (Genesis 1:27). "Haven't you read," He replied, "that at the beginning the Creator made them male and female." (Matthew 19:4)

Long before medical science discovered the importance of quarantine of people with infectious diseases, the Bible instigated it. "As long as they have the disease, they remain unclean. They must live outside the camp." (Leviticus 13:46) You will remember that we were all quarantined during the COVID 19 pandemic.

In Psalm 19:6, we are reminded of God's creative power. We are surrounded by wonderful displays of God's work; the heavens give us clear and irrefutable evidence of His existence, His power, love and care for His created beings. Critics scoffed at this verse, claiming that it taught that the Sun revolves around the Earth. At that time, scientists thought that the Sun was stationary. However, we now know that the Sun moves through space at approximately 600,000 miles per hour. It travels through the heavens and has a 'circuit', (orbit) just as the Bible says. "The circuit is so large that it would take approximately 200 million years to complete." (R. Comfort) Surely, God's word is true. Search the Bible for yourself and discover its truth.

Today's Prayer: Father, thank you for your word. Your word is true. Amen.

October 13

INTEGRITY

'Whoever walks in integrity walks securely, but whoever takes crooked paths will be found out.' (Proverbs 19:9)

As a child of God, you must be a person of integrity, which means that you must be honest, have strong moral principles and live by them.

As a Christian, your life should exemplify Christ in all that you say and do. You will demonstrate integrity by behaving and living according to your faith and beliefs. There is no room for pretence or any behaviour that is contrary to your beliefs. You cannot say you love God and don't love others. In 1 John 4:20, Jesus makes it very clear that you cannot say you love God and hate your brother. "Whoever claims to love God yet hates a brother or sister is a liar." One writer says, "It is easy to love God when that love does not cost us anything more than weekly attendance at religious services. But the real test of love for God is how we treat the people right in front of us, our family members and fellow believers."

As a Christian, you show integrity by being loving, truthful, honest, and acting with a strong moral compass. However, integrity for a Christian is a life that has been lived in accordance with God's will, a life that shows you have a relationship with Christ. Your behaviour will be consistent as you strive to live in a way that pleases God and brings glory to Him. As a follower of Christ, you must be careful to uphold the truth of the Bible. If you are a leader in God's church, it becomes even more important that you emulate Christ and be a person of integrity. You are in a position of leadership, and your behaviour will impact and influence others. Take King Saul, for example; he was not a man of integrity. He demonstrated a lack of it through disobedience, pride and jealousy, and this became his downfall.

Stories from the lives of Daniel and Job highlight the importance of integrity, even in the face of adversity. Integrity, one writer says, "It's not just a moral choice, but a spiritual requirement that provides all aspects of a believer's existence. You should live your life to reflect God's truth, fidelity and love." You may criticise Saul or even feel sorry for him; however, examine yourself. Are there times when you have behaved badly and caused others to stumble? You might even have more in common with Saul than you care to admit. His failures should come as a warning to us; disobedience, pride and jealousy can bring you down.

In Philippians 4: 8, Paul describes the qualities of a person of integrity. "Finally, brothers and sisters, whatever is true, whatever is noble, whatever is right, whatever is pure, whatever is lovely, whatever is admirable, if anything is excellent or praiseworthy, think about such things." To be a person of integrity, Paul is saying you should programme your mind with what is good. Pray and ask God to help you focus your mind on those things that will define you as a person of integrity and a child of God.

Today's Prayer: Father, help me to focus my mind on what is good and pleasing to you. Amen.

October 14

RIGHT ON TIME

'But when the set time had fully come, God sent His Son, born of a woman, born under the law.' (Galatians 4:4)

The prophets had, for centuries, prophesied that one day Jesus Christ, the saviour of the world, would come to earth to save mankind from their sins. In AD 1 (approximately), a baby was born in a manger in Bethlehem just as the prophets had predicted. He came right on time. In this verse, we are told that "when the set time had fully come, God sent His Son to earth to die for our sins. For centuries, the Jews had been wondering when their Messiah would come – He came right on time, because God's timing is perfect.

In the above text, we read that 'when the time had fully come, God sent His Son, born of a woman, born under the law. From the time the plan of salvation came into being, God appointed a time when Jesus would enter our sinful world to redeem mankind. There could be no question about the timing; Jesus came on time, for God's timing is precise. The arrival of Jesus on planet Earth was not random or ad hoc; His coming did not happen by chance; it had been divinely ordained.

Are you good at timekeeping? I remember my grandmother's cousin, who was never late for anything in her life. If she had an appointment, she would always be on time, even getting there before the person with whom she had the appointment! Going to church was the same; she would be there before the church doors were opened. She ensured that she was never late for anything. As believers, we have been asked to be ready and wait for the second coming of Christ. He has not told us when He will come. However, God has appointed a time, and although we do not know when He will return, we must be ready.

Just as Christ's first coming was on time, in the same way, His second coming will be on time. We do not know when He will return, "But about that day or hour no one knows, not even the angels in heaven, nor the

Son, but only the Father." (Matthew 24:36) Jesus has given us the opportunity to be ready when He comes back a second and final time to earth. We can be assured that He will return, right on time. "For, in just a little while He who is coming will come and will not delay." (Hebrews 10:37)

Will you be ready when He comes back a final time to earth?

Today's Prayer: Father, I do not know when you will come, but I know for sure that you will come. Help me to be prepared to meet you. Amen

October 15

SHARING THE GOSPEL

"Therefore, go and make disciples of all nations..." (Mathew 28:19)

I remember the first time I went to the High Street to share Christ with others. It was a daunting moment, being ridiculed and mocked is not a pleasant experience. However, when Jesus told his disciples to go, they were under His authority, and so are we, and we should not be afraid. Where are we to go? It could be on the high street, next door, or to another town or country, or anywhere He wants you to go. However, this Great Commission has been given to all of us; it is a command from Jesus Himself, and it is not an option.

This verse is the final instruction Jesus gave to His disciples before He went back to heaven. Here, He outlines the mission for His followers, they were to make disciples of all nations, and baptise them in the name of the Father, Son and the Holy Spirit. Jesus helped His followers to understand that the gospel should be taken to the entire world and not just the Jews alone; it is for every people, culture and ethnicity and background. The command involves more than just conversion; the disciples were also required to teach believers to obey God's commands.

You might not be able to preach like Paul, or sing like an angel, but you can tell someone that Jesus died for them and He is coming back a second time. You might be saying, like Moses, that you cannot speak, or like Jeremiah, that you are too young. However, you have nothing to fear, for God always equips those who are willing to work for Him. He is the one who will put words in your mouth and tell you what to say. If you feel afraid, be reassured that He is always with you. When Elijah thought that He was the only one who had not bowed to Baal, God told him that He had reserved seven thousand in Israel who had not bowed down to Baal.

Have you accepted the call to go and make disciples? You must be willing like Isaiah, who, when he heard the question, "Whom shall I send, and who will go for us"? he replied, "Here am I. Send me!" God can only use those who love Him and are willing. As believers, you should see each person you meet as a potential for heaven. It was Bill Bright, a great soul winner, who said, "Assume that whenever you are alone with another person for more than a few moments, you are there by divine appointment to explain [...] the love and forgiveness he or she can know through faith in Christ Jesus." How many times have you missed these divine appointments? And later express regret for not having told the person you met about the love of God. Make it your goal today to tell someone about the Good News of salvation.

Today's Prayer: Heavenly Father, you have called me to be a disciple and to disciple others. Help me not to fail you. Amen.

October 16

THEY GOT IT ALL WRONG

"Indeed, to them you are nothing more than one who sings love songs with a beautiful voice and plays an instrument well, for they hear words but do not put them into practice." (Ezekiel 33:32)

Ezekiel, the prophet of God, encountered stubbornness and disobedience from God's people as they resisted his messages. They refused to act upon Ezekiel's messages because he challenged them; he challenged them to turn from their evil ways. Despite their obvious disobedience and rejection of God, Ezekiel continued to preach as the Holy Spirit directed him. He predicted the siege of Jerusalem and God's punishment if they did not repent of their sinful ways. He told them that God offered them hope and restoration if they would only turn to Him. Instead, they mocked the prophet and preferred to continue in their wicked and sinful ways. Are you being mocked and ridiculed for preaching God's word? Don't give up, but continue to speak for Christ like Ezekiel did.

In the above text, we find the people listening to Ezekiel, but not really listening to what he was saying or giving their hearts to the Lord. The text tells us that they were listening just to be entertained. "Indeed, to them, you are nothing more than one who sings love songs with a beautiful voice and plays an instrument well." (Verse 32) It's hard to imagine, but they had no interest in Ezekiel's message from the Lord, let alone putting His words into practice. You might be saying that people don't behave like that today. However, can it be that there are people who attend church just to be entertained? They enjoy the music, the singing and the fellowship, but they don't take the message seriously. They don't seek to be challenged or to serve in God's church.

Stop and think for a moment, have your church services been reduced to a level of entertainment? One cannot help but notice the Contemporary Christian Music that has crept in and has replaced the hymns that are testimonies in themselves that speak of God's goodness, might and power in the lives of those who have experienced Him. Your church worship service should impact your life to glorify God. As you listen to God's words, you should be motivated to praise Him for who He is. "God is Spirit, and His worshippers must worship in the Spirit and in truth." (John 4:24)

The people in Ezekiel's time got it all wrong; worship is not about entertainment. Be careful you don't get it wrong like Israel of old.

Today's Prayer: Father, let me not forget that I am called to worship and serve you and not to be entertained. Amen.

October 17

YOU WILL BE HELD ACCOUNTABLE

"Son of man, I have made you a watchman for the people of Israel; so, hear the word I speak and give them warning from me." (Ezekiel 33:7)

A watchman's job is a very responsible one; he guards and protects, and alerts others to potential dangers. In ancient times, watchmen were stationed on walls and towers where they had a good view of the land, to enable them to warn of impending danger. Today, they are referred to as security guards; however, their role remains the same, monitoring premises and ensuring the safety and security of properties.

In Ezekiel 33:7, we read where God tells the prophet that he has been assigned as a watchman for the people of Israel. It was his responsibility to warn the people of any impending danger. Israel continued to disobey and sin against God and, therefore, needed to be warned of God's judgment that would be meted out to them if they did not repent of their sins. While it is the watchman's responsibility to warn the people, they too are equally responsible for heeding the warnings. This verse also shows that the people were accountable for their own actions. This verse also shows that if the watchman fails to warn the people, he will be held accountable; however, if he warns them and they refuse to turn from their wicked ways, the watchman will not be held accountable, and the people will be accountable for their sins. This imagery of a watchman is relevant to us as believers today. We are God's messengers who have been appointed to tell others about Christ and of His soon coming. We have been commissioned to "preach the gospel to the whole world as a testimony to all nations, and then the end will come." (Matthew 24:14)
Are you telling others about Christ? Are you warning them of the impending danger? God is telling you to sound the alarm. God says, He "takes no pleasure in the death of the wicked." (Verse 11) Commit today to be the watchman God has called you to be.

Today's Prayer: Father, let me be the watchman sounding the alarm. Amen.

October 18

FROM WEAKNESS TO STRENGTH

"Pardon me, my Lord," Gideon replied, "but how can I save Israel? My clan is the weakest in Manasseh, and I am the least in my family." (Judges 6:15)

The Midianites were always in conflict with Israel. They were an oppressive people, and Israel was no match for them. Midian so impoverished the Israelites that they cried out to the Lord for help. (Verse 6) Israel had disobeyed God and had therefore brought calamity on itself. They cried out to God, and He heard their cries by sending an angel to one of their own men, Gideon. When the angel appeared to Gideon, he addressed him as a 'mighty warrior' and said that God was with him. The angel informed him that he had been called to deliver Israel from the hand of the Midianites. Gideon asked how he could save Israel, seeing as his clan was the weakest in Manasseh, and he was the least in his family (verse 15). Although the angel assured him that God would be with him and strengthen him, he still made excuses.

Are we sometimes like Gideon, focusing on our weaknesses and our limitations? Do you make excuses rather than work with God and allow Him to accomplish His purpose in you? One can identify with Gideon; how could he fight against the warlike Midianites? He had every reason to be afraid. However, he was overlooking perhaps the most important thing the angel said: "Go in the strength you have and save Israel out of Midian's hand. Am I not sending you?" Here God is promising him that He would be with him; however, focusing on his limitations prevented Gideon from seeing how God could work through him.

Like Gideon, each of us is called to serve God. He knows our weaknesses and our limitations, yet He sees potential in all of us, and if we are willing to work with Him, He will accomplish great things in us. Although God promises to give us the strength and the resources we need, if you are making excuses, stop and do what God wants you to do. Once Gideon stopped focusing on his weaknesses, he was able to successfully accomplish the task God gave him.

Today's Prayer: Father, help me not to make excuses but to allow you to supply all my needs to accomplish the task you have given me. Amen.

October 19

ARE YOU PACKED AND READY TO GO? (1)

"So, you also must be ready, because the Son of Man will come at an hour when you do not expect Him." (Matthew 24:44)

This text urges believers to live with a sense of urgency and preparedness. What does it mean to live in a state of preparedness? Recently, my sister and I planned a year in advance to visit her brother and his family in Canada. If you have travelled, you can appreciate the need to be prepared, ensuring you have your travel documents and all you need for your journey. As the date of the departure nears, you check and double-check that your suitcase is packed and you are ready to go.

When Jesus spoke these words, it was a command to help us to be ready; that is, we are to actively prepare for His coming. My sister and I actively packed and prepared for our journey. How can we actively get ready for our heavenly journey? First of all, we are required to live a sinless life. However, only by the grace of God can this be accomplished. Part of this active preparation process means we must live a life of faith, prayer, and service; a life that brings glory to God. Jesus, in Matthew 28:19 & 20, says that when we have accepted Him, we are duty-bound to make disciples of others. He says we should go into all the world and make disciples of others as we share the gospel with them, and in so doing, they too will become disciples and disciple others.

Being prepared means living in this present world with all its challenges and looking forward with anticipation for the world to come. It is about living your life according to God's will and being faithful to Him. Because we do not know the exact time when Jesus will come, as believers, we are being urged to be in a state of constant vigilance, a life of faithfulness and obedience to God. We should also remain spiritually alert.
Are you packed and ready to go? Will you be as confident as Paul and say that you have been faithful, and a crown of life is awaiting you?

Today's Prayer: Lord, I want to be ready when you come. Amen.

October 20

ARE YOU PACKED AND READY TO GO? (2)

"Five of them were wise, and five were foolish." (Matthew 25:2)

This parable is yet another reminder in Scripture about the importance of being prepared and remaining in a state of preparedness. There were ten virgins, five were wise and five were foolish. They were all ready and waiting for the bridegroom to arrive. They were packed and ready to go. They all had lamps and oil. However, no matter how packed and well prepared you might be, remember this is earth and not heaven, things can go wrong when you least expect, and that is why you have to be vigilant. You can face a number of challenges and distractions, and if you are not careful, you can easily lose focus. The five foolish virgins seemingly became distracted, lost focus, and forgot to pack sufficient oil.

To give context to this parable, it is about a wedding. In the Middle East at that time, on the wedding day, the bridegroom went to the bride's house for the ceremony. After the ceremony, the bride and groom and a great procession would then go to the groom's house for a feast, often lasting for a week. The ten virgins/bridesmaids were waiting to join the procession, hoping to participate in the wedding banquet. However, the groom was delayed, and after staying awake for some time, when he hadn't arrived, they all fell asleep. When he arrived, five of them had run out of oil, and by the time they purchased extra oil, it was too late for them to join the feast.

You must remain prepared. In the process of being prepared, you will need to get rid of worldly baggage that will cause you to lose focus. The parable clarifies what it means to be ready for the return of Jesus and how we should live until He comes. Are you packed and ready to go? Jesus says He will come like a thief in the night. "So, you must also be ready, because the Son of Man will come at an hour when you do not expect Him." (Matthew 24:44)

Today's Prayer: Heavenly Father, thank you for the promise of your soon return. I want to remain prepared until you come. Amen.

October 21

GIVE US WATER TO DRINK

'So, they quarrelled with Moses and said, "Give us water to drink."' (Exodus 17:2)

In Exodus chapter 15, we find the children of Israel in the wilderness complaining that they had no water. They had travelled for three days without water. However, arriving at Marah, they found water, but to their utter disappointment, they could not drink it for it was bitter. Although they complained and grumbled, God miraculously made the water palatable for them to drink. He asked Moses to throw a piece of wood into the water, and it became fit for drinking. Later, when they arrived in Elim, there were twelve springs and seventy palm trees, and they had more than enough water to drink. Despite their murmurings, God always provided for them.

Are you like Israel, always grumbling and complaining when things are not going your way, and forgetting what God has done for you in the past? When you begin to complain and think negatively, it means you are ungrateful and not exercising faith and trust in God. How can you forget the way God has led and provided for your needs?

In Exodus chapter 17, we find the children of Israel grumbling and complaining to Moses, yet again. They have no water. Instead of trusting God and remembering the miracle at Marah, again they started complaining about their problem instead of praying. Has God provided a way out of your situation? You are now facing a dilemma, and all you can do is complain and ask where God is. Have you forgotten what He has done for you in the past?

At the time, you prayed and God heard your prayer. Some problems can be solved only by prayer. Make every effort to pray rather than complain. God hates complaining; it is a sign of ingratitude. Complaining raises your stress levels, whereas prayer creates an atmosphere of calm;

it quietens our thoughts and emotions and prepares us to listen to the voice of God.

Because God hates complaining, stop murmuring and grumbling and forgetting how He has led you in the past. Make a determined effort to trust Him, spend time in prayer and give thanks. Reflect on His faithfulness to you.

Today's Prayer: Father, forgive me for complaining and forgetting how you have led me in the past. Amen.

October 22

WHO ARE YOU TRUSTING?

'Do not put your trust in princes, in human beings who cannot see.' (Psalm 146:3)

In Psalm 146:3, we are advised against placing our trust in humans or human things. Even those whom you look up to and admire can fail you. Therefore, God is the only one you should trust because your help comes from Him.

How often do we hear people say they don't trust anyone anymore? They are finished with people, for you can't trust anyone. Their ability to trust is completely broken. These comments are from people who have been hurt because someone had betrayed their trust. The psalmist makes it very clear in verse three that we should avoid placing our ultimate trust and faith in human beings, including human rulers or leaders. Being human, they have their limitations, and might not be people of high moral and Christian standards. Therefore, God is the only one we should trust. God is infallible, whereas humans are fallible.

In Proverbs 3:5, Solomon, the wisest man who ever lived, says, 'Trust in the Lord with all your heart and lean not on your own understanding'. In other words, we are to rely on God's guidance and His wisdom. It is foolish to rely on our limited understanding, but rather we are to put our faith and trust in the all-wise and all-knowing God. Our understanding and wisdom are limited, and therefore we cannot rely on our own opinions, ideas or judgements. We are bound to make mistakes because we are human beings.

You would save yourself pain and anguish if you trust and depend on no one else but God. Even those closest to you can sometimes fail you. Trusting God takes faith and understanding that He is the ultimate source of wisdom. He will never betray you. The psalmist portrays powerful and influential people ('princes') as inadequate saviours, making false promises they cannot deliver. We see this kind of behaviour in governments and other world leaders who cannot be trusted because of the false promises that they make.

In the spiritual sense, the psalmist is saying that human leaders, not even your minister, can offer true help or salvation. God is the only one who can save; therefore, He is the only one who can be trusted. Barnes' commentary on the verse states: "Rely on God rather than on man, however exalted he may be. There is a work of protection and salvation which no man, however exalted he may be, can perform for you; a work which God alone, who is the Maker of all things, and who never dies, can accomplish." So trust Him today.

Today's Prayer: Father, help me to trust in you at all times. Amen.

October 23

INGRATITUDE

"Give thanks in all circumstances; for this is God's will for you in Christ Jesus." (1 Thessalonians 5:18)

A dictionary definition of ingratitude is forgetfulness of, or a lack of appreciation for, kindness or especially a gift received. One writer says, "Ingratitude is a rejection of God. It is rejection of Him as Creator and Ruler of all things. It is rejection of God as the giver of life, the giver of every blessing, whether expected or unexpected."

My sister told me of the time when she gave a beggar on the street a sandwich. She asked him if he was hungry, so she bought him a sandwich, which he took; however, he still stretched out his hand asking for money. She left him with the sandwich and no sooner had she left than she noticed he threw the sandwich in the bin. Talk about ingratitude! What about Joseph and the butler? After interpreting his dream, he asks him to remember him to Pharaoh, hoping that he would be released from prison. The butler was finally released from prison, no doubt promising Joseph that he would speak to the king on his behalf. However, time passed, and Joseph remained in prison, forgotten by the butler. How could he have forgotten such kindness?

The cupbearer's ingratitude highlights the way that, as humans, we can sometimes forget the kindness that has been shown to us by others. (You can read the account in Genesis 40.) If you have experienced ingratitude, you may understand how disappointed Joseph must have felt. Ingratitude hurts others as it conveys a message of lack of appreciation, and disrespect. The person who shows ingratitude may not even be aware of the hurt they have caused the other person.

The same can be said of the times you have disappointed God when you have forgotten to thank Him. How often has He answered your prayers and brought you out of impossible situations? How often has He provided food when you had nothing to eat? How often has He provided clothes for you to wear when you had none? Did you remember to thank Him? "In some religious traditions, ingratitude is considered a sin and a rejection of a higher power, indicating pride and a failure to acknowledge divine grace." In Psalm 136:1, we are reminded to give thanks to God because He is good. He is the giver of all good gifts.

Some of us might have experienced ingratitude and know how it feels when you have gone out of your way to show kindness to others, only to be disrespected. Think about Jesus when He left heaven and came to the sinful earth to die for mankind, and was rejected by the very people He came to save! Ingratitude is indeed a sin.

Today's Prayer: Father, forgive me if I have not shown gratitude for what you have done in my life. Amen.

October 24

CONTENTMENT

"But godliness with contentment is great gain […] But if we have food and clothing, we will be content with that." (1 Timothy 6: & 8)

Have you ever met someone who complains about everything? No matter how much they have, they are not content. In these verses, the apostle Paul is highlighting the fact that godliness, when it is combined with contentment, brings much. He explains that as humans we are born with nothing, and when we die, we cannot take anything with us, not our wealth, or possessions. Since this is the case, we should be content with what we have and give thanks instead of complaining, whether you have a little or much. You have much to gain by living your life in contentment. One writer states that the gain is not a financial one, but a spiritual one, "a priceless spiritual benefit that material possessions cannot offer."

To be content does not mean you never want anything. It is not wrong to want something; however, if you become preoccupied with wanting, there is the risk of becoming greedy and covetous. The text states that 'godliness with contentment is great gain', suggesting that true gain is not to be found in the material and perishable things of this world. As believers, we should be content with the basic needs of food, clothing and shelter; however, true gain comes from our relationship with Christ. Society does not want you to be content. If you are not careful, advertisers will often get you to buy their products because they make you feel you need them when you don't. They make you feel discontented with what you have. They are focused on material things and wealth. God wants us to be content, for it is a spiritual discipline that we can only find in Him. Generally speaking, contentment does not come naturally because we always want more. However, as a child of God, you should find contentment in knowing and serving God.

In Philippians 4:11, Paul says, "…I have learnt to be content whatever the circumstances." As he surrendered his whole life to God, he learnt how to be satisfied with what he had because he knew God would always provide for all his needs. Contentment in Christ is a learned virtue, cultivated through faith and the understanding that God's provision and Christ's presence are more than enough.

Are you content in any circumstances you face? Paul knew how to be content because he knew he had to draw on Christ's power and strength. If you are to be content, then you will need to do the same, learn to detach yourself from the pressures of society and focus on what is eternal.

Today's Prayer: Father, let me not focus on the non-essentials in my life but on eternal things. Amen.

October 25

MAKING MEMORIES

'But Mary treasured up all these things and pondered them in her heart.' (Luke 2:19)

What memories are you making for your children? What treasures will you store up in your heart? In Luke 2:19, we are told, 'Mary treasured up all these things and pondered them in her heart'. Mary had been visited by an angel, who announced that she would give birth to the Son of God. Not only did she hear what was said, but she internalised the information, stored it in her memory, and reflected on it. As parents, what memories will your children have of you? What memories are you making for them? Will they be memories of parents who loved and attended to all their needs? Will they be able to recall the fun times you had together as you engaged them in social pursuits and educational activities, as you built loving relationships with them?

However, more importantly, what memories will they have of Jesus? As parents, God expects you to emulate Him in such a way that whatever you do, your life will reflect and bring glory to Him and leave lasting memories in your children's minds. One Christian writer says, "Fellow parents, let's have our homes so full of the word of God that our children can't help but see and hear it wherever they go and whatever they do. The bottom line is we are to make God real to our kids." In making memories, you need to impress upon the minds of your children all that God has done for you. He wants you to be careful not to forget. That is why in Deuteronomy 6:12, God instructed Moses to tell the children of Israel to make lasting memories on their children's minds, to tell them what God had done for them. Impress them on your children, talk about them when you sit at home, and when you walk along the road, when you lie down and when you get up. Tie them as symbols on your hands and bind them on your foreheads. God did not want the nation of Israel to forget Him or what He had done for them.

God wants us to build memories for our children because He doesn't want them to forget Him. When He parted the waters of the river Jordan, for the people, He directed Joshua to build a memorial from twelve stones drawn from the river. He wanted His people not to forget that He was the one who had guided and protected them since they left Egypt.

I can recall the happy times in my family and have fond memories of my godly parents, who would tell us of God's love. I can still remember worship times when mother played the piano or the organ, while father played the violin, and all the children sang as father tapped his feet to the beat.

What memories are you making for your children?

Today's Prayer: Dear God, help me to store up your words like treasures in my heart. Amen.

October 26

HAVE YOU MESSED UP?

"But I have prayed for you, Simon, that your faith may not fail, and when you have turned back, strengthen your brothers." (Luke 22:32)

When you have made a mistake in your life, people don't forget or, in some instances, won't forgive you. Therefore, you can go through life bearing the scars. You might even feel unloved and devalued.

Take Peter, if ever there was someone who was always putting the proverbial foot in it and getting into trouble, it was he. When he denied Jesus, this was the most devastating thing he had ever done. This time, he really messed up! You will recall that it was the same Peter who had promised Jesus that he was ready to go with Him to prison and even to death. I am sure He meant every word; however, Jesus pointed out to him that Satan wanted to crush him like grains of wheat, but Jesus assured him that even though his faith would falter, He would restore him. "But I have prayed for you, Simon, that your faith may not fail." (Luke 22:32) Isn't that beautiful, to have Jesus pray for you!

When Peter denied Jesus three times, and seeing the look of love and compassion on Jesus' face, he realised what he had done, went outside and wept bitterly. However, Jesus did not give up on him; not once did he remind him of his past. He looked beyond his mistakes and saw Peter's potential. In the same way, God will look beyond your faults and mistakes. Do not let anyone make you feel as if you have no hope because of the mistakes you have made. When Peter repented, God used him in a mighty way. When we next meet Peter in Acts chapter 2, he is filled with the Holy Spirit, speaking in different languages, and three thousand people accepted Jesus Christ when he preached on the day of Pentecost. Jesus forgave Peter of his mistakes, restored him and filled him with His Spirit. He'll do the same for you, too.

Today's Prayer: Lord, I pray that you will forgive me for the mistakes I have made in my life. Amen.

October 27

YOU ARE SPECIAL TO HIM

'I praise you because I am fearfully and wonderfully made; your works are wonderful.' (Psalm 139:14)

Do you realise how special you are to God? He made you in His image. 'So, God created man in His own image, in the image of God He created them, male and female He created them.' (Genesis 1:27). Doesn't it make you feel special to know that God values you? You are beautiful and unique, and He loves you with immeasurable love. You are special in His eyes, and although marred by sin, each one of us reflects God's glory in some way or another.

You are unique; David, in Psalm 139:13 says, "For you created my inmost being, you knit me together in my mother's womb. I praise you because I am fearfully and wonderfully made; your works are wonderful…" God gave you your distinctive looks, brown eyes or blue eyes. He made you special, for when He did, His character was formed in you. "Indeed, the very hairs of your head are numbered. Don't be afraid; you are worth more than many sparrows." (Luke 12:7) Your true value is God's estimate of your worth, not the estimate that others place upon you. Other people will evaluate and categorise you according to how you look, how you perform, and your achievements. But God loves and cares for us, we are special to Him, He has no favourites, we all belong to Him. You should not base your self-concept on what others think of you. You have been chosen by God to be His very own. Peter expresses our royal lineage when he says: "But you are a chosen people, a royal priesthood, a holy nation, God's special possession…" Just to think that you have been chosen by God should fill you with an immense sense of joy and belonging. Your value does not come from your parents or your friends; your value comes from being a child of God. One writer says, "You have worth because of what God does, not because of what you do."

Today's Prayer: Father, thank you for being my father and that I am special to you. Amen.

October 28

NO COMPROMISE (1)

"Do not love the world or anything in the world. If anyone loves the world, love for the Father is not in him." (1 John 2:15)

John cautions us against loving the world or the things of the world. He is helping us to understand that both are not compatible. You cannot compromise your faith and your Christian values when you choose to accept worldly values too. As a believer, you might be faced with pressures to conform or compromise your principles; you must resist the temptation to conform, realising there will be consequences.

Daniel and his friends did not compromise their standards. They were far away from home, but refused to eat the King's food. Although Daniel and his friends found themselves in a heathen land, a culture that did not honour God, they still obeyed God and did not compromise their standards. It is obedience to God that will enable you not to conform. You must have faith and trust in God and an unwavering, determined resolve to stand for Him even in situations where your life may be threatened. However, you cannot make the decision not to conform the moment you face temptation; you must think through your convictions and what God expects of you well before the temptation comes. Daniel had done this because we are told, "But Daniel resolved not to defile himself with the royal food and wine." He was devoted to his principles and was committed to a course of action.

You cannot afford to compromise your standards. If you do, you will be letting God down, you will be denying Him. Daniel and his friends, though tempted with the King's delicacies, made the decision long before then that they would remain faithful to God. Make the decision today not to compromise your standards and stand for God like Daniel and his friends did.

Today's Prayer: Father, help me to remain faithful to you and not compromise my standards. Amen.

October 29

HOW NOT TO COMPROMISE (2)

"If anyone, then, knows the good they ought to do and doesn't do it is sin to them." (James 4:17)

Have you ever thought that when you compromise your standards, you might be sinning against God? As you go through life, there will be times when you will be tempted to compromise your faith and your standards. For example, your employer might ask you to work on the Sabbath (Saturday). You know that God says we should keep the Sabbath holy and not work or do anything secular on His holy day. However, you might say, 'I'll work because it's only this once'. You would have compromised your faith and would have sinned against God, because you broke His commandment. In the commandments, God instructs us to remember to keep the Sabbath day holy. When the three Hebrew boys were asked to bow down and worship Nebuchadnezzar's golden image, they refused because they would not compromise their faith or disobey God's command not to have any other gods before Him.

How do you not compromise? You must first decide not to compromise before the situation arises. The Bible tells us that Daniel 'resolved not to defile himself with the royal food and wine.' (Daniel 1:8) This means that he was devoted to principle and was committed not to compromise. When he made up his mind not to compromise by defiling himself, he was being true to a lifelong determination to do what was right and not to give in to pressures around him. We, too, are being pressured to compromise our standards, but like Daniel choose to obey God rather than succumb to the pressure to compromise.

You must stand firm in your faith, don't compromise, and consider your integrity. When we read about Joseph, we learn that, like Daniel, he had resolved in his heart not to compromise. In Genesis 39:9, when he was tempted by his master's wife, he resisted her temptation by saying it would be a sin against God to compromise his faith and his integrity. We must realise that when we compromise, we are sinning against God and bringing His name into disrepute. Remember that you are a child of the King, and certain behaviours are unacceptable. "A character formed according to the divine likeness is the only treasure that we can take from this world to the next." (E.G. White) Why blot your character by compromising your faith? Strength of character consists of two things – power of will and power of self-control." (E.G. White)

If you are tempted to compromise your standards, remember to call upon God, for He will help you to resist the temptation to compromise. "Submit yourselves, then, to God. Resist the devil and he will flee from you. Come near to God and He will come near to you." (James 4:7 & 8) How can you draw near to God? Yield to His authority and will, commit your life to Him and His control, and be willing to follow Him. Don't allow Satan to entice and tempt you. The Bible tells us that when we are tempted, God will make a way of escape for us. You should consider the consequences of compromising your values and remain faithful to God in your beliefs.

Today's Prayer: Father, help me not to compromise my standards. Amen.

October 30

GOD IS HOLY (1)

"Do not come any closer," God said, "take off your sandals for the place where you are standing is holy ground." (Exodus 3:5)

Moses saw a burning bush, and went to investigate why it was burning and not consumed. As he drew closer to God to look at the bush, God commanded Moses to take off his sandals. This was an act of reverence, for he was now in the presence of a holy God; even the very ground that Moses stood on was holy due to the presence of God.

Moses hid his face because he was afraid to look at God. He recognised God's holy presence. Moses, like anyone else, was curious and wanted to check what was happening to the bush. However, he did not realise that he was in the presence of God, but when he did, his response was one of humility and awe and submission to a higher authority. Moses became aware of his unworthiness to stand before a holy God and was afraid to look at Him. One commentary states that the act of removing sandals is symbolic. It shows reverence and submission before the divine; it shows humility, readiness to obey and submit oneself to God's will, and enter His service. It also signifies separation from the world. Because God was present, even the ground where Moses stood became holy.

You must learn from Moses' encounter with God that when we come into His presence, we should approach Him in reverence and humility. To approach Him in an irresponsible, shallow and whimsical manner is to show a lack of respect and a lack of sincerity, especially if we are at worship. When you come into His presence to worship, how do you approach Him? Do you come casually, or do you come recognising that you are entering into the presence of Almighty God, Creator of the universe, King of Kings and Lord of Lords? The writer of the book of Hebrews tells us in chapter 12:29 that 'our God is a consuming fire'. The writer is saying that we should approach God with reverence and awe because of His holiness. Because He is holy, He is worthy of awe and reverence when we come into His presence. When the prophet Isaiah came into His presence, He experienced the holiness of God as the seraphim proclaimed His holiness. "Holy, holy, holy is the Lord Almighty: the whole earth is full of His glory." (Isaiah 6:3)

Learn from Moses and Isaiah's encounter with God that when we come into His presence, we should approach Him in reverence and humility. To do otherwise is to show disrespect and a lack of sincerity. Worship does not begin when you go to church; it begins in your heart. Therefore, when you come into His presence, your attitude should be one of awe and reverence.

Today's Prayer: Father, may I feel your holy presence in my heart when I come to worship you. May I worship in awe and reverence. Amen.

October 31

GOD IS HOLY (2)

'The commander of the Lord's army replied, "Take off your sandals, for the place where you are standing is holy ground." (Joshua 5:15)

Joshua, Moses' successor, is given the same direction as Moses when he comes into the presence of a Holy God; to take off his shoes for the ground, by the manifestation of God's presence, is made holy. We, too, must approach God in reverence and humility. If you were ever to meet an earthly monarch, you would be required to show respect, bowing or curtsying. There are set rules of etiquette and protocol that you must adhere to as you enter the royal's presence.

Joshua is commanded to remove his sandals as a sign of respect because he was standing on holy ground, a pivotal moment when he encounters the divine being. Although Joshua was the leader of the Israelites, he was now in the presence of a divine being and must subordinate himself in total obedience to this heavenly presence. Joshua does not hesitate at the command to remove his sandals, and does so immediately, demonstrating his willingness to submit to the divine authority, says one writer.

Do you recognise God's presence in your life? He is a holy God, and like Joshua and Moses, as you come into His presence, you should also show respect and reverence. John, in a vision, caught a glimpse of the heavenly beings' response when they came into God's presence: "You are worthy, our Lord and God, to receive glory and honour and power, for you created all things and by your will they were created and have their being." (Revelation 4:11) When you worship God, are you aware of His presence? Do you approach Him in reverence? One preacher said, "Irreverence is a sign that you are not aware of God's presence." When you understand God's holiness, you should be inspired to be holy, that is, to live a life that reflects His character. Peter reminds us to be holy, "Be holy, because I am holy." (1 Peter 1:16) "I am the Lord your God;

consecrate yourselves and be holy because I am holy..." (Leviticus 11:44) God wants His people to be holy (set apart, different, peculiar, unique) just as He is holy.

Today's Prayer: Father, I desire to be holy as you are holy. Amen

November 1

HE COULDN'T HAVE DONE MORE.

'For God so loved the world that He gave His one and only Son, that whoever believes in Him shall not perish but have eternal life.' (John 3:16)

Whenever I think about what Jesus Christ did for humanity, I can scarcely take it in. It is difficult to comprehend how He could have left the splendour of heaven and willingly given His life for us. He died in our stead, accepted our punishment, and paid with His life for our sins. It is hard to believe that anyone could have done such a thing; well, He was not just anyone, He is Jesus! Peter explains it thus: "You see, at just the right time, when we were powerless, Christ died for the ungodly. Very rarely will anyone die for a righteous person, though for a good person, someone might possibly dare to die. But God demonstrates His love for us in this: while we were still sinners, Christ died for us." (Romans 5:6-8)

According to one writer, the cross was "the central focus of God's plan of salvation and a profound expression of His love". The cross reveals the depth of God's love for humanity, as it demonstrates the consequences of sin and provides the means for overcoming sin's power. It is further stated that the cross is "the focal point of all truths, and understanding it is crucial for comprehending the character of God and the plan of salvation". However, the cross was a place of pain, suffering, decision, but more importantly, a place of victory, because it represents the defeat of Satan.

Christ's death on the cross was horrific. Before being nailed to the cross, He was beaten with a whip consisting of nine leather thongs, each with small balls, embedded with bits of glass, stone or bone attached near the ends. The heavy whip was brought down with full force again and again on the shoulders, back and legs of Jesus. With every whip, the skin and flesh were torn from His body. This is what Jesus went through and more for us. His suffering was intense, yet He didn't have to do it; He was innocent, but died in your stead.

Jesus could not have done more. What are you doing for Jesus? If you have not yet accepted Him in your life, accept Him now. If He is knocking at your heart's door, let Him in.

Today's Prayer: Father, I know these words are feeble, but my human vocabulary fails me when I think of your great sacrifice of love for me. Thank you for dying in my stead. Amen

November 2

GOD USES WHOM YOU LEAST EXPECT

'But the woman had taken the two men and hidden them...' (Joshua 2:4)

God sometimes uses the most unlikely persons to carry out His work. Joshua, who had succeeded Moses, sent spies to look out the land of Jericho because he had planned to invade it. However, it was a highly fortified city. Joshua needed as much information as possible to enable Israel to plan strategically. In Joshua 2:2, we are told that the spies entered the house of Rahab, a prostitute. You might be wondering why the spies went to a prostitute's home and stayed there. It would have been a good place because no one would have suspected them, and it was also a good place to gather information and have no questions asked in return. Rahab's house was in an ideal position as it was built into the city wall, thereby allowing for easy escape from the city.

God must have directed the spies to Rahab's house, despite her lifestyle. God knew her heart and used her to be part of Israel's victory over Jericho. When the king of Jericho heard that spies had entered the city, he sent a message to Rahab to bring the men out; however, she lied and said she didn't know where they had come from and had left, but she didn't know where they had gone. You may ask why would God use a prostitute and a liar at that, to deliver the people of Jericho into the hands of His people? God works in ways we do not understand.

Rahab's story is one of faith and trust in God. Although living in a pagan society, she must have heard about Israel's God and was ready to put her life on the line to save His people. She demonstrated faith in what she heard. The all-knowing God can use the most unlikely persons to make an impact, and Rahab certainly did! (You can read the story in Joshua chapter 2.) Because of God's love and mercy, she is not only highlighted in the hall of faith (see Hebrews 11), but she is also included in the lineage of Jesus Christ Himself. Be encouraged by this story; if God used Rahab, He can use you too, despite your past or current situation, to accomplish much. God used her to advance His kingdom, and He will do the same for you.

Today's Prayer: Father, use me to fulfil your purpose. Amen.

November 3

GOD THE CREATOR

'In the beginning God created the heavens and the earth.' (Genesis 1:1)

Some scientists and evolutionists would have us believe that God had nothing to do with creation. However, our key text for today challenges their belief that the universe evolved in some bizarre way. Some are constantly trying to reduce God's creation to merely scientific terms. They don't believe that there is a God anyway. Is it any wonder that the psalmist says, 'The fool says in his heart, there is no God. They are corrupt, their deeds are vile; there is no one who does good.' (Psalm 14:1 & 2) In the Bible, those who say there is no God, despite the evidence that God exists, are deemed foolish or else wicked. Their unbelief shows they are defiant and utterly foolish, and disobedient because they refuse to live by God's truth.

Scientists have even tried to find out how the Earth was created; in fact, it is still the subject of debate to this day. Some say the universe appeared after a sudden explosion, others say it slowly evolved over billions of years, but God started the process. Such debates are futile. You will find that almost every scientist has their own opinion about how the universe came about. You and I will never know all the answers about how God created the Earth, but Genesis 1:1 tells us that He did, and by faith we accept that He did. The fact that God created the heavens and the Earth is difficult for some to accept because finite human minds cannot comprehend the infinite mind of God. He is Almighty and all-powerful; therefore, we cannot limit the infinite God by our finite understanding. We should humbly accept that He is the Creator.

'Can you fathom the mysteries of God? Can you probe the limits of the Almighty? They are higher than the heavens above – what can you do? They are deeper than the depth below – what can you know?' (Job 11:7-8) To deny the existence of God and His creative power is foolish, especially when we look at the world in which we live, which He has created. Nature displays His creative power. 'The heavens declare the glory of God: the skies proclaim the work of His hands.' (Psalm 19:1 &2) God declares that He is the creator of all things. In Job 38:1, He asks Job, "Where were you when I laid the earth's foundation? Can you bind the chains of the Pleiades? Can you loosen Orion's belt? Can you bring forth the constellations in their seasons?" (Job 38:31 & 32) In so many more places in the Bible, you will find evidence that God is the creator. "Through Him all things were made; without Him nothing was made that has been made." (John 1:3)

Do you need any more evidence? It is God who has created all things. One commentary says, "To say that the universe 'just happened' or 'evolved' requires more faith than to believe that God is behind these amazing statistics. God truly did create a wonderful universe." As you study God's word, remember that He chose to create the universe and all that is in it, including us, because of His love. He created the world as an expression of His love.

Today's Prayer: Father, I may not know all the answers, but I accept in faith that you are the creator. Amen.

November 4

JESUS IS PRAYING FOR YOU

"But I have prayed for you, Simon, that your faith may not fail..." (Luke 22:32)

I have read this text so many times and not really given much thought to it. However, recently, I read it again, and was completely overwhelmed when it suddenly dawned on me that not only did Jesus pray for Peter, but that He prays for you and me. Satan wanted to destroy Simon Peter and the other disciples, but Jesus told Peter that He would pray for him that his faith would not fail him. Jesus tells him that He has prayed for him specifically. Jesus knew that Peter would deny Him, but in praying for him, Jesus displayed such love for Peter. This text also serves as a reminder that Jesus loves us and prays for us, too.

As I meditated on the words of Christ to Peter, the very thought of Jesus praying for me filled me with such joy. Just like how a parent prays for his or her child, in the same way, Jesus loves us so much that He prays for us. The Bible says, "Therefore He is able to save completely those who come to God through Him, because He always lives to intercede for them." (Hebrews 7:25) You can be assured that Jesus is with God our heavenly Father interceding on our behalf. As our High Priest, He is the mediator between us and God. He is our advocate pleading on our behalf. It is such a wonderful thought to know that Jesus is praying for us and that we are being kept by His power and intercessory prayer even in the difficult times in our lives, and especially when we are weak and feeling vulnerable. This verse helps us to understand the importance of prayer in our lives. If Christ prays, we should also pray not just for ourselves, but for others.

Christ prayed for the other disciples too, but particularly for Peter, because he was in the greatest danger (Satan wanted to sift him as wheat). Because Jesus prayed for Peter and restored him, he was changed; no longer do we see the impulsive, self-confident Peter, but one who is converted. He was able to strengthen the other disciples once he was restored.

When you are going through tough times, when it seems your world is caving in, remember that Jesus is praying for you. What a comforting thought! Peter's faith failed him when he denied Christ three times; however, he repented and was restored. Jesus will restore you, too.

Today's Prayer: Father, thank you for praying for me. Amen.

November 5

WHAT IS IN YOUR HAND?

'Then the Lord said to him, "What is in your hand?"' (Exodus 4:2)

After fleeing from Egypt, Moses became a shepherd in the land of Midian. When God called him, he was reluctant and fearful, making excuses; however, God made him understand that He would be with him and equip him to do what he had been called to do. God does not call us without equipping us. We just have to trust Him and go where He leads us. He will give you the courage, confidence and the resources you will need.

When God asked Moses what he had in his hand, He was helping him to understand that He is almighty and all-powerful and that He can use ordinary things for extraordinary purposes. Moses' simple shepherd's rod was nothing special, yet God was able to use it to teach Moses an important lesson. Moses could never have imagined that his staff, which was an ordinary one and nothing special, could wield such power in the hand of the Master Shepherd. What do you have in your hand? What talents has God gifted you? It could be your beautiful singing voice, or your ability to communicate well, your social skills, or your ability to lead. Whatever skills you have, they were given to you by God to be used to bring others to Him and to give glory to Him.

Joni Eareckson Tada is a quadriplegic, author, and a Christian speaker who ministers to people with disabilities. At seventeen, a diving accident left her paralysed from the shoulders down; however, she has not allowed her disability to stand in her way. She has committed her life to the service of God. Do you sometimes doubt your abilities or feel unqualified to do what God has called you to do? You might be feeling that you don't have the experience or training. Jeremiah thought he was too young and inexperienced to be God's spokesman, but God promised to be with him and take care of him.

Use what is in your hand. Do not let fear or your lack of confidence hinder you. What do you have in your hand? What talents has God given you? Whatever you have in your hand has been given to you by God to equip you for service. Do not be like the servant in the parable who hid the talent he had instead of putting it to good use. What do you have in your hand? God will use what you have if you let Him.

Today's Prayer: Father, thank you for the gifts you have given me. Please help me to use them for your glory. Amen.

November 6

LET'S SETTLE THE MATTER

"Yet I will remember the covenant that I made with you in the days of your youth, and I will establish an everlasting covenant with you." (Ezekiel 16:60)

The people of Judah, despite warnings from God through the prophet Ezekiel, continued to sin against Him. Judah had fallen so far in sin that God described them as an 'adulterous wife'. After all He had done for His people; it is painful to read God's description of them. "I bathed you with water and washed the blood from you and put ointment on you [...] adorned you with jewellery [...] your clothes were of fine linen, costly fabric..." God loved and cared for His people, only to have them turn away from Him. Although the people had broken their promises and did not deserve anything but punishment, God did not break His promises with them. If they turned back to Him, He would forgive them again and renew His covenant with them.

The nation of Israel had grown to maturity and had become famous, but the people of Judah had forgotten who had bestowed so much on them. Their apostasy was great. In fact, they had become more corrupt than the surrounding pagan nations. One commentary states that the conduct of the Jews was so disgusting that even those who worshipped other gods, including their great enemy, the Philistines, would have been ashamed to behave that way. The Jews outdid them in doing evil. This must have pained the heart of God. Have you walked away from the Lord and forgotten Him? Remember, He has not broken His covenant with you. You are the one, however, no matter how far you have gone in sin, God is waiting with arms open outstretched to forgive and restore you. He still wants to establish His everlasting covenant with you. Let Him into your life today before it is too late. No one is beyond God's reach. He wants to save you, and He will not break His promise to you.

Today's Prayer: Lord, I am sorry for the sins I have committed. I want you to establish your covenant with me. Amen.

November 7

ARE YOU WILLING TO CHANGE?

"Can an Ethiopian change his skin or a leopard its spots? Neither can you do good who are accustomed to doing evil." (Jeremiah 13:23)

I once overheard someone saying 'that's how I am'. Here is someone whose behaviour was less than acceptable. However, what was really being said was, you just have to accept me as I am - I am not willing to change. We are all imperfect beings because of sin, but Jesus, because of His love for us and His sacrificial death on the cross, offers us the opportunity to change. However, before change can happen, you must have the desire and a willingness to change. Quite often, we can see the faults in others and pray for them to change. It could very well be that you are the one who needs to change. However, as humans, we are all resistant to change, but if you are to experience growth in your life, you must be willing to change.

In Jeremiah 13:23, the question is being asked: 'can an Ethiopian change his skin or a leopard its spots? Neither can you do good who are accustomed to doing evil'. God's people had gone so far away from Him because of their sins that not even the threat of captivity could motivate them to repent and change from their sinful ways. They had become so accustomed to doing evil that they had lost their ability to change, or even recognise that they needed to change. If you recognise that you need to make some changes in your life, God is warning you through His word to ask forgiveness and repent before it is too late to change. If you continue to indulge in sinful behaviours, after a while, you will become desensitised to wrongdoing until it doesn't feel wrong anymore, and you no longer fear the consequences.

Are you willing to change? Pray and ask God for the strength to do so. When David realised, he had sinned, he prayed, "Search me, God and know my heart; test me, and know my anxious thoughts, see if there is any offensive way in me and lead me in the way everlasting." (Psalm 139:23 & 24)

David asked God to search his heart for sin and point it out to him so he could change. You must do the same and be willing to change. God is waiting to change you right now.

Today's Prayer: Dear Father, please bring about the changes that need to take place in my life. Amen.

November 8

BE COURAGEOUS

"Be on your guard; stand firm in faith; be courageous; be strong." (1 Corinthians 16:13)

Someone once said, "Courage is not the absence of fear, but the willingness to act in faith despite fear." There are times in your life when you are fearful, when you cannot move forward; there are times when you don't have the strength or the courage to face life's challenges. There comes a time when you need strength outside of yourself. When Queen Esther was faced with the greatest challenge in her life, she exercised courage. It was a matter of life and death. Faced with death, Esther and Mordecai set aside their own fears and took action. Esther decided to risk her life to save her people. She risked her life by asking the king to save the Jews.

In today's society, it is sometimes difficult to see this kind of boldness; most are concerned about saving themselves, 'look out for number one' some will say, demonstrating their selfish outlook on life. However, Esther's attitude stands in bold contrast to this: "I will go to the king, even though it is against the law, and if I perish, I perish." Here is someone who is truly altruistic, that is, having concern for the well-being of others, a rare quality found in humans! Take a moment to read the story of Esther and reflect upon her courage. Would you, if faced with a similar situation, act with such boldness? Would you have the same commitment to do what is right, despite the circumstances, or would you try to save yourself? To be bold in the face of danger means that you must exercise faith and trust in God. Mordecai and Esther trusted God, and the Jews were delivered.

Queen Esther's boldness was rooted in faith, not recklessness; it wasn't just a sudden act of courage, it was a deliberate action on her part. She realised that she and her people would be killed if she did not take action. It was out of selflessness that she acted, which, no doubt, involved planning, seeking counsel, and encouragement from her cousin

Mordecai. Although God is not mentioned in the book of Esther, we know that God led her and Mordecai to do what they did to save His people. This story is a reminder that when faced with challenges or facing immense fear and uncertainty that as long as we trust God, we can exercise courage even in desperate situations.

If you are feeling fearful and overwhelmed by situations in your life, be courageous. God says, "When you pass through the waters, I will be with you, and when you pass through the rivers, they will not sweep over you. When you walk through the fire, you will not be burned. The flames will not set you ablaze for I am the Lord your God, the holy one of Israel, your Saviour." (Isaiah 43:2 &3) Go forward today and act in faith. Be courageous and strong.

Today's Prayer: Heavenly Father, please give me the courage to fight life's battles. Amen.

November 9

DEEP CLEAN YOUR MIND

'Above all else, guard your heart, for everything you do flows from it.'
(Proverbs 4:23)

It is customary at springtime to spring clean your house, which gives it a thorough clean. However, there might be other times when you might do a deep cleaning, which is a process to remove dust, bacteria and grime. It means sanitising to prevent the spread of bacteria and diseases. During COVID-19, most households were careful to keep their homes clean and sanitised. It is important that we keep our surroundings clean, for bacteria can be harmful to the body. Therefore, we need to keep our bodies clean and also be careful how we handle food.

Have you ever thought of deep cleaning your heart or your mind? Over time, you will find, just as in your home, you can have a build-up of dust and grime; similarly, all kinds of toxins can build up in your heart, toxic thoughts, such as bitterness, anger, hatred, jealousy, guilt and covetousness can build up in your mind and cause damage. If you don't deep clean regularly, permanent damage can occur, and before you know it, you become a very sick person, physically and spiritually. For this very reason, you are admonished by Solomon to 'guard your heart, for everything you do flows from it'. Whatever your mind dwells on, that is what you will become. If your heart needs deep cleaning, you cannot unclog it yourself. You cannot deep-clean your mind because you have no power to do so; only God can, but you must be willing to cooperate in this cleaning-up process.

Do you have problems with impure and negative thoughts? Stop and examine what you're putting into your mind through the Internet, music, books, television, movies, and video games. These things will clog up your mind, and they will drown out God's voice in you. Therefore, to deep clean your mind, first fill it with good thoughts, is what Solomon is saying in our key verse. In Philippians 4:8, Paul tells us how to let God deep-clean our minds: "Whatever is true, whatever is noble, whatever is right, whatever is pure, whatever is lovely, whatever is admirable – if anything is excellent or praiseworthy – think about such things."

What we put in our minds determines what comes out in our words and actions, so let God deep-clean your mind today so that your actions will tell others that the Holy Spirit has taken up residence in your heart.

Today's Prayer: Father, please create in me a clean and pure heart. Amen.

November 10

ARE YOU READY TO SUFFER FOR JESUS? (1)

"I have told you these things, so that in me you may have peace. In this world, you will have trouble. But take heart! I have overcome the world." (John 16:33

In John 16:33, Jesus warned His disciples that they would suffer like He did. As you read about the life of God's prophets and His apostles, you will discover the sufferings they went through for the sake of Christ. Paul, for example, gives us an insight into some of his sufferings. He had been in prison, flogged severely, and exposed to death again and again, "five times I received from the Jews forty lashes minus one, three times I was beaten with rocks, once I was pelted with stones, three times I was shipwrecked. I spent a night and a day in the open sea. I have been constantly on the move. I have been in danger from bandits, in danger of my fellow Jews, in danger from Gentiles, in danger in the city, in danger in the country, in danger at sea, in danger from false believers."

It couldn't have gotten any worse for Paul. When he listed his trials, he had been angry with the false teachers who had deceived some of the Corinthian believers. He therefore had to re-establish his credibility and his authority as God's servant by listing the trials he had endured in his service for God. These were just some of the trials he endured for the sake of Christ because of his love and dedication, and commitment to the cause of God. He was willing to suffer and would have even given his life for the sake of the gospel.

Are you willing to suffer for Christ? What would you have done if you were Paul? He did not give up but kept going, knowing that the crown of life was awaiting him in glory. He advises you not to lose heart, "Though outwardly we are wasting away, yet inwardly we are being renewed day by day." (2 Corinthians 4:16) Paul knew that it is easy to lose heart under such circumstances. There are times when you are ready to quit, but like Paul, do not quit, but focus on the inner strength that comes from the Holy Spirit as you surrender your life to Him. Are you ready to suffer for

Christ? Paul says, "In fact, anyone who wants to live a godly life in Christ Jesus will be persecuted." (2 Timothy 3:12)

Today's Prayer: Father, help me to stand firm even though I am suffering for your cause. Amen.

November 11

ARE YOU READY TO SUFFER FOR CHRIST? (2)

"Consider it pure joy, my brothers and sisters, whenever you face trials of many kinds, because you know that the testing of your faith produces perseverance." (James 1:2 & 3)

When you read what James is saying in this text, to consider it pure joy as you go through trials and suffering whenever you face trials, you might be asking yourself, how is this possible? James himself experienced trials in his life, but he does not say *if* you face trials, he says *whenever* you face trials, he assumes that as a child of God, you will face trials. However, more importantly, we should not go around feeling sorry for ourselves, but to learn from trials and build up our faith in God. He's asking you to turn your trials and hardships into times of learning. He says consider it pure joy, as you are learning to trust God in these trying times. In other words, be positive; he's not saying to walk around with a smile on your face when you are in pain or pretend to be happy, but to have a positive outlook. I recently visited a friend who was suffering from a terminal illness, and it was so much joy to be with her as she prayed to God, and expressed her faith in Him. This is what James is speaking about: turning those tough times over to Jesus and trusting in His promise that He will always be with you, and that your suffering will not last forever. The prophet states 'when you pass through the rivers, they will not sweep over you; when you walk through the fire, you will not be burned. The flames will not set you ablaze.' (Isaiah 43:2) What a wonderful promise God has given to us.

You might be going through rivers of challenges, difficulties, and disappointments, and suffering right now. However, James is advising you to use your sufferings as stepping stones to make you grow stronger in God. If you approach your trials with a negative mind-set, or if you go in your own strength, you are more than likely to fail. So, accept God's promise today that He will be with you. Suffering is inevitable for the believer; there is no getting away from it. It is a reality because we are living in a world broken by sin. Suffering is not always a direct punishment for one's sin, as some think. We just have to take a look at Job and realise that his suffering was not a result of any sin he had committed. James' advice is that you should see your suffering as stepping stones to make you grow stronger in God.

Today's Prayer: Father, please give me strength for each trial or suffering that I experience. Amen.

November 12

ARE YOU READY TO SUFFER FOR CHRIST? (3)

'Then Paul answered, "Why are you weeping and breaking my heart? I am ready not only to be bound, but also to die in Jerusalem for the name of the Lord Jesus."' (Acts 21:13)

Paul knew he would be imprisoned on arriving in Jerusalem; although his friends pleaded with him not to go, he insisted on going because he was convinced that was what God wanted him to do. He was fearless because he knew that God was with him. I am sure he did not necessarily wish to suffer pain. However, he knew that he had to be obedient to God.

Are you prepared to suffer for Christ? We, like Paul, are aware of what awaits us, but are we willing to suffer for our Lord? It is through trials and tribulations that we must enter into the kingdom. John writes, "These are they who have come out of great tribulations, they have washed their robes and made them white in the blood of the Lamb." (Revelation 7:14) Are you ready to suffer hardships and suffering for God? Your desire to please God should motivate you to serve Him despite the pain. You must accept all that comes with doing God's work. Are you ready to count it all joy to suffer for Christ? James says, "Consider it pure joy, my brothers and sisters, whenever you face trials of many kinds, because you know the testing of your faith produces perseverance." (James 1:23) You will have trials and, strangely enough, you can profit from them if you turn hardships into times of learning. However difficult it is to be joyful during trials, we must remember that Jesus says that in the world you will suffer persecution, but we must be cheerful, for He has overcome the world.

If you're going through persecution, trials, and suffering today, know this: God is refining and preparing you for the glory that one day will be revealed to you. Read again what Paul says, "I consider that our present sufferings are not worth comparing with the glory that will be revealed in us." (Romans 8:18) This should give you hope, for Paul is saying that your present suffering cannot be compared to the future glory that will be revealed when Christ comes. He helps us to understand that suffering is real, but it is temporary. The future glory is so wonderful that it makes the current suffering we are going through as nothing by comparison.

Today's Prayer: Father, help me to glory in my sufferings as I look forward to an eternal, glorious future with you. Amen.

November 13

GOD SENT AN ANGEL

'The angel of the Lord encamps around those who fear Him, and He delivers them.' (Psalm 34:7)

My cousins had been tired after a long journey from church. They had gone to church with their father, who was the local preacher, and they were now on their way home. It was a long way from the church, and they had to climb many hills before reaching home. When they were about to climb the steepest hill of their journey, my nine-year-old cousin said to his father, "I wish someone would come along and offer us a lift. I'm so tired." No sooner had he said the words than a car came by and gave them a lift. When they eventually alighted from the car and turned around to wave goodbye, the car simply vanished into thin air. Their father, in a state of shock, said, "Boys, that was an angel." God had sent an angel to take them home. The Bible tells us that the angel of the Lord encamps around those who fear Him, and He delivers them, and He certainly did that for my cousins that day.

God will send an angel in situations when you least expect. Take Lot, for example, he had been living in Sodom, a most wicked city, when God sent His angel to get him out of the city before its destruction. What about Daniel in the lions' den? The Bible says that God sent His angel to shut the lions' mouths so they could not harm him (Daniel 6:22). What about the three Hebrew boys when they were cast into the fiery furnace? God sent his angel to rescue them.

You might find yourself in dangerous and difficult situations; be assured that God will send His angel to your assistance. He will send His angels to deliver you when you think that all hope is gone. It could be that He has sent His angels when you weren't even aware, to deliver you. The Bible describes them as ministering spirits. However, they are always there to protect and guide you. Isn't it reassuring to know that God loves and cares for you so much that He will send His angels to help you? It should fill you with confidence that your angel's protection is constant and vigilant as you are being kept from danger. Give God thanks for His constant, present and watchful protection over you.

Today's Prayer: Father, thank you for sending your angels to protect me. Amen.

November 14

WHAT IF IT WERE YOUR LAST DAY ON EARTH?

"...I tell you, now is the time of God's favour, now is the day of salvation." (2 Corinthians 6:2)

If today were your last day on earth, what would you do? Would you make wrongs right with family and friends? Would you put on your best clothes and go out and have a good time? Would you cook your favourite meal and feast with family and friends? If it were your last day, would you be nervous or afraid? It would be interesting to know what you would do if it were your last day on earth.

In Genesis 18: 20 & 21, the Bible tells us that it was the last night for Sodom and Gomorrah. Life was lived in the fast lane; it was all about entertainment, music, partying, fun, materialism, violence and crime, and immorality and depravity. God had sent warnings to Sodom, but the people continued in their wickedness. On the last night before the destruction of the city, God sent His angels to give the final warning, but the people did not respond. That was their last night on earth, and everyone except Lot and his two daughters perished.

It was the last night in Egypt, and Pharaoh had witnessed nine terrible plagues; the tenth was about to happen. That night was the last night for the Egyptians; the firstborn of every family perished. It was also the last night for the Hebrew slaves, but they obeyed God and were finally freed from Egyptian bondage. Pharaoh was convinced of the truth, but chose to be stubborn. The Bible says, "Now is the time of God's favour, now is the day of salvation." (2 Corinthians 6:2) The Hebrews were saved from the plagues because they obeyed God's commands; their last night in Egypt was a night to remember; it was a night of rejoicing, because they were finally free.

If today were your last day on earth, would you be prepared, or die like the people in Sodom? Jesus is coming back soon, and He wants us to be ready to meet Him. Now is the time to prepare. He has given us warning signs. "Even so, when you see these things happening, you know that the kingdom of God is near." (Luke 21:31) Spend some time reflecting on this question and ask God to help you to live in a state of readiness. Jesus wants us to spend eternity with Him. He is getting heaven ready for us. "My Father's house has many rooms, if it were not so, would I have told you that I am going to prepare a place for you?" (John 14:2)

Today's Prayer: Father, help me to be prepared for you when you come. Amen.

November 15

FREEDOM

"So, if the Son sets you free, you will be free indeed." (John 8:36)

The Hebrews were enslaved in Egypt for over 400 years, and it wasn't easy for them. The Egyptians made life almost impossible for them. The book of Exodus details a period of the enslavement of the Hebrews by the Egyptians. It describes their oppression by Pharaoh and the suffering of the Israelites. They spent over 400 years in captivity, where they were subjected to hard labour and oppression. God said He saw the suffering of His people and set them free. Throughout history, we see that people, even to this day, have been, and are still being, enslaved.

The enslavement of Africans was horrendous, especially the transatlantic slave trade, where millions of people from Africa were transported to the Americas. This was an evil and brutal system driven by the Europeans' demand for labour. Africans were subjected, like the Hebrews, to this brutal system from the 15th to the 16th century. The African slaves were treated inhumanely by their white masters. Like the Hebrews of old, the Africans cried out to God, and He heard and delivered them.

What does it really mean to be free? One definition states, 'To be free generally means to be independent and not subject to external control or constraint. It can encompass a range of meanings from political freedom and personal autonomy to freedom from obligations or negative emotions. It is the right to speak and act without restriction, interference or fear...'

Given the above definition, you would probably say that you are free. However, are you really free? No one is really free because we are all enslaved by sin. The Bible says, "For all have sinned and fall short of the glory of God." (Romans 3:23) All sin, whether big or small, and this makes us sinners, and all sin cuts us off from God. Sin leads to death because it disqualifies us from living with God. However, we can be free from sin: "But God demonstrates His love for us in this: while we were still sinners, Christ died for us." (Romans 5:8) This is an amazing statement of freedom for the sinner. For while we were still sinners, God, because of His great love for us, sent His Son to die for us. This means we have all been liberated from sin.

Although Jesus has died for our sins, we must be actively involved in the freedom His death offers us. We can access it when we recognise that we are sinners in need of forgiveness and repent from our sins. If we are to be truly free, we must be willing to submit to God, and when we do, we are no longer enslaved by sin. If you want to be set free from sin today, repent, turn away from your sinful life, ask for forgiveness and turn to God. However, this is an ongoing process, a daily dying to sin. If you are to gain freedom from sin, you must also recognise that true freedom in Christ gives you the ability to choose to obey God, and not continue in sin.

Today's Prayer: Father, thank you for setting me free from sin. Amen.

November 16

WHAT VOICES ARE YOU LISTENING TO?

'I will listen to what the Lord says; He promises peace to His people, His faithful servants - but let them not turn to folly.' (Psalm 85:8)

On waking up this morning, I heard the birds in the garden singing their beautiful songs of praise to their creator. As I listened, I reflected on the question that came into my mind. What voices are you listening to? Living in a world such as ours, where many voices are calling for our attention, what voices are you listening to? Are you listening to the voices of peace and love, or are you listening to the voices of dissent, fear, and doubt? The voices you listen to can influence how you feel and behave. When the young Samuel heard the voice of God, he acted on what God told him. He was able to hear the voice of God amid the voices of disregard and contempt in his environment.

Today, we are exposed to so many voices, yet God is still speaking to us. Sometimes we may think that He no longer speaks as He did in the time of the prophets and the apostles. However, God is not limited to one particular manner of speaking; He speaks in so many different ways. In Exodus 19:18, He speaks dramatically. We are told 'Mount Sinai was covered with smoke, because the Lord descended on it in fire...' The imagery of fire and smoke communicates that His presence is both 'purifying and consuming'. In 1 Kings 19:12, we find God speaking to Elijah in a 'still small voice'.

What voices are you listening to? What kind of voices are you being drawn to? Try listening to the voice of God. He often speaks through His word, so spend time studying His word and praying for guidance. Sometimes He speaks by making an impression on your mind; the more you study His word, the more you will hear His voice more clearly above the noise and the chaos of the world. He speaks through nature. Stop and listen, and you will hear His voice in so many places. To hear His voice, you must be still, pay attention, and you will hear His voice. It takes time and stillness to tune into His voice amid the distractions of this world. Spend more time in prayer and study of His word, and you will hear His voice. He promises you peace as you listen.

Today's Prayer: Father, let me hear your voice today in the stillness of the moment. Amen.

November 17

LOVE EACH OTHER

"My command is this: Love one another as I have loved you." (John 15:12)

In John 15: 9-12 Jesus makes it clear about His relationship with the Father and us. "As the Father has loved me, so have I loved you." (Verse 9) Just as His Father's love is constant, so must our love be. How can we remain in His love? It is by keeping His commands. Not only are we to love Him, but we should also love our neighbours. In Leviticus 19:18, we are told to love our neighbours as we love ourselves.

Do you find it hard to love someone who is not lovable? If we are truthful, some people are not very easy to love; however, God wants us to love them. He has even told us to love our enemies. What does it really mean to love someone? In today's society, the word love means different things to different people. You can love your husband or your wife, your children, your dog, your car or your mobile phone. But you don't love your husband or your wife the same way you love your car. The TV and tabloid kind of love, where you fall in and out of love at the drop of a hat, is not the kind of love Jesus is speaking about. He is speaking of real, genuine love for God, the love that makes you love others.

The Biblical word agape (God's love) is an unconditional commitment to love that is rooted in an unchanging decision. It always gives, and doesn't change whether the love is returned or not. In 1 Corinthians 13:5, we are told that love is not self-seeking and it does not dishonour others. What does it mean to love someone? It means we are to love each other as Jesus loves us. He just cannot help loving us; it is His nature. The Bible tells us that God is love.

So, how about those people you find difficult to love? Jesus says we are to love them, too. You might say, you have tried, but you just can't love them. The command is to love them. If you are struggling with loving someone, go to Jesus and ask Him to put love in your heart for that person. Pray for the person; it could be that they are unlovable because of how they behave. You might even pray and ask God to change them. I wonder if it might be that you should pray that prayer for yourself, too, that is, ask God to change you. Jesus wants us to love others as He loves us. He loves us so much that He gave His life for us. Now that's love! And that's how we should love. You may not have to die for someone, but there are other ways to practice sacrificial love, giving, listening and encouraging.

Remember God's command, "Love each other as I have loved you."

Today's Prayer: Father, please give me the strength to love, especially those who are unlovable. Amen.

November 18

SO, YOU ARE CALLED TO LEAD?

"Do nothing out of selfish ambition or vain conceit, rather in humility value others above yourself, not looking to your own interests but each of you to the interest of others." (Philippians 2:3 & 4)

Leadership appears glamorous at times, but it is often lonely, thankless, and filled with pressures to conform. As a leader, you will face opposition and criticism; however, you must deal with them in a Christ-like manner. Rather than ask God to remove those who are causing the problem, pray and ask God for strength and wisdom, and pray for those who 'despitefully use you', as Jesus says. When you pray for those who despitefully use you, you show tremendous determination and character to remain steadfast in your responsibility. Praying for wisdom and strength will allow God to bless you abundantly, and you will find yourself growing spiritually and maturing in Christ. As a leader, you will need to spend much time in prayer and study of God's word.

If you have been called to lead, emulate godly leaders. Nehemiah comes to mind. He had little power, but he had great influence. He was a man of God; he was a man of character, persistence and prayer, a man filled with the Spirit of God. Although he was just an ordinary man, he found himself in a unique position. He was secure and successful as a cupbearer to the Persian king Artaxerxes. Nehemiah was a brilliant organiser and motivator. (You can read about him in the book named after him.) Before he undertook any assignments, he always took the matter to God in prayer until he received the answer.

In our key text today, Paul is reminding the believers that selfish ambition can ruin a church, but genuine humility can build it. Being humble means having a true perspective of ourselves; however, it does not mean we should put ourselves down - we should recognise our worth in Christ Jesus. Selfishness has no place in God's work; therefore, leaders are called to be selfless, to be servants. As a leader, you should treat others with respect and common courtesy. In Philippians 2:5-8, we are told that Jesus, "who being in very nature God [...] made himself nothing by taking the very nature of a servant." This is the kind of leadership you are called to: servant leadership.

Now that you have been called to leadership, spend time with the Master Teacher, Jesus, for He is the source of all wisdom. Pray for the Holy Spirit's guidance as you lead in whatever capacity God has called you to lead.

Today's Prayer: Lord, give me courage and unwavering faith as I faithfully serve you. Amen.

November 19

DISLOYALYTY

'The people all responded together, "We will do everything the Lord has said..."' (Exodus 19:8)

In Genesis chapters 15 & 17, God made a covenant with Abraham, promising to make his descendants as numerous as the stars of heaven and as the sand on the seashore. They were to become a great nation. In chapter nineteen, God restates His agreement with the children of Israel. He promises to bless and care for them. They, in turn, promised to obey all His commands. "We will do everything the Lord has said." They were so sure that they would keep their part of the covenant. Have you committed to God? How well are you keeping it?

After promising God faithfully to keep His covenant, and learning that they were to become His 'special treasure', you can be sure they were happy to serve Him. "Now if you obey me fully and keep my covenant, then out of all nations you will be my treasured possession." You can imagine how special that made them feel, and so they enthusiastically agreed to what God had said. However, that promise was short-lived, for very soon after, they sadly broke their promise. Their best intentions were short-lived. We are told that under the leadership of Aaron, the High Priest, he built a golden calf for the people to worship. And worship they did! The Bible tells us, "So the next day the people rose up early and sacrificed burnt offerings and presented fellowship offerings. Afterwards they sat down to eat and drink and got up to indulge in revelry." (Exodus 32:6) It is hard to believe that Aaron would have done such a thing, made a golden calf for the people to worship. Even though the people had seen the invisible God in action, after all, He was the one who took them out of Egypt by His mighty hand - they still wanted the familiar gods they could see and shape into what they desired.

Could it be that the people felt that they could have kept their part of the covenant; however, they did not realise that they were incapable of doing so in their own strength. It is so very human to think we can manage without God's help. It was St. Paul who said, "So if you think you are standing firm, be careful that you don't fall." (1Corinthians 10:12) One Christian writer says that, "God cannot save those who believe they are strong [...] God does not ask His children to do great things, but to surrender their lives to Him so that He may do great things through them."

Israel was disloyal to God after He had done so much for them. Are you being disloyal to God by creating your own gods? How much like Israel are we? One commentary says, "Our great temptation is still to shape God to our liking, to make Him convenient to obey or ignore." God desires that we keep all His commandments and remain loyal to Him. Once you have committed to serve Him, He will give you the strength to keep His promises. He says, "...my strength is sufficient for you, for my power is made perfect in weakness." (2 Corinthians 12:9) You should have courage and hope that God will keep His part of the covenant if you remain obedient and loyal to Him.

Today's Prayer: Father, help me to remain loyal to you. Amen.

November 20

WHEN YOU DON'T KNOW WHAT TO DO, LOOK TO JESUS

'Our God, will you not judge them, for we have no power to face this vast army that is attacking us? We do not know what to do, but our eyes are on you.' (2 Chronicles 20:12)

What do you do when your world has caved in and you have no one to turn to, or nowhere to go? Sometimes situations can occur in life that cause us to become so overwhelmed that we don't know what to do. This was the situation when King Jehoshaphat and the people of Judah were surrounded by enemies who were bent on attacking them. Judah was outnumbered by their enemies, who were now set to invade their land. The people had no might or power to defeat their enemies. However, the Bible tells us that the king, along with the people, 'Came together to seek help from the Lord; indeed, they came from every town in Judah to seek Him.' (2 Chronicles 20:4) As a believer, this is what you do: look to Jesus. He is the only one who can deliver you. However, you must look to Him in faith, knowing that He can do what seems impossible to you. Nothing is too hard for Him.

When the nation was faced with disaster, the king knew exactly what to do; he called the people to get serious with God, that is, to put away their sins and spend time praying and fasting, and asked God for forgiveness. When you are faced with life's challenges, you must spend time in prayer; it might also call for fasting. You must also admit that you have no power in yourself to take you out of your situation and that you are totally dependent on God. King Jehoshaphat expresses total dependence on God when he says, "We do not know what to do, but our eyes are upon you." He committed the situation to God, acknowledging that only God could save them. If you are going through a challenging time in your life and you cannot see a way out, look to Jesus and admit your helplessness and allow Him to take charge of your situation.

Since you cannot see a way out, look to Jesus with faith and hope, stop relying on your strength and God will see you through. Jehoshaphat and the people of Judah did just that, and God fought for them, because the battle was not theirs; it was His.

Today's Prayer: Lord, help me to focus on your power rather than my own. Amen.

November 21

BLESSED ARE THE PURE IN HEART

"Blessed are the pure in heart, for they shall see God." (Matthew 5:8)

What does it mean to have a pure heart? To have a pure heart does not mean you do not have any sin; it refers to those who are morally clean, sincere, and whose life focuses on God; they have a commitment and devotion to God. The Holy Spirit dwells in their heart because they have been transformed by Him. One commentary says that this beatitude 'emphasises the internal spiritual condition of a person's heart over external rituals.'

This is such a beautiful promise that the person who has a pure heart will see God. Would you like to see God? This is the desire of true believers. When Jesus spoke this beatitude, He was aware that some of His hearers, the Pharisees, for example, were more concerned with ceremonial cleanliness than the inward purity that He spoke about. Ceremonial cleanliness, which was included in the health laws in the Old Testament, was important; however, Jesus wasn't saying they were not. His emphasis was on the inward state of the individual. We are reminded that 'People look at the outward appearance, but the Lord looks at the heart' (1 Samuel: 16:7).

The promise that the pure in heart will see God is not a physical sight (however, one day we will behold Him). Jesus was referring not to physical eyesight, but the ability to perceive Him clearly as a result of our faith and trust in Him, experiencing His presence in our lives, and having an intimate relationship with Him. Jesus refers to a heart that is completely devoted to Him; someone who spends time in prayer and study of His word.

Do you want to see Jesus? Right now, you are not able to see Him fully because of sin. St Paul in 1 Corinthians 13:12 says, "For now we see only a reflection as in a mirror, then we shall see face to face. Now I know in part; then I shall know fully, even as I am fully known." When Paul speaks about knowing Him fully, He was referring to the time when we will see Christ face to face. The songwriter captures this truth in the hymn: 'Face to face with Christ my Saviour, face to face, what will it be when with rapture I behold Him, Jesus Christ who died for me [...] But a blessed day is coming when His glory shall be seen.'

Why not make it your goal to see Jesus face-to-face?

Today's Prayer: Father, I want to see you face-to-face in your kingdom. Amen

November 22

BLESSED ARE THE MERCIFUL

"Blessed are the merciful, for they will be shown mercy." (Matthew 5:7)

In Matthew 18:21-32, Jesus tells the parable of the unforgiving debtor who owes the king a huge sum of money; however, he is unable to pay his debt. The king shows mercy and wipes out his debt. The same servant encounters a fellow servant who owes him a small amount of money and insists that he repays him; in fact, he demands immediate payment and has him thrown into jail because he is unable to pay his debt. When the king hears about the unmerciful behaviour of the servant, he is furious and has the servant imprisoned; he also has to repay the debt. This servant was shown mercy by the king, yet he refused mercy to his fellow servant. Because of his behaviour, the first servant to whom mercy was granted lost everything. He did not appreciate the mercy shown to him. In this beatitude, Jesus states clearly that those who are merciful will be shown mercy.

Shakespeare in 'The Merchant of Venice' says, "The quality of mercy is not strained; It droppeth as the gentle rain from heaven upon the place beneath. It is twice blest: It blesseth him that gives and him that takes." Jesus says, blessed or happy is the one who shows mercy. Mercy begets mercy; if you show mercy to others, God will also show mercy to you. When you show mercy, it shows that your heart has been transformed by the Holy Spirit because of the mercy you have received from God, and this motivates you to act with compassion, forgiveness, and mercy to others.

Are you showing mercy to others? As a believer, showing mercy should be a natural outpouring from a heart that has been truly submitted to God. Mercy is very much intertwined with forgiveness. When the king showed mercy to the servant, it also meant he had forgiven him. This is precisely what Jesus meant when he said, "Forgive us our debts as we also have forgiven our debtors." (Matthew 6:12)

Today's Prayer: Father, as you have shown me mercy, let me also show mercy to others. Amen.

November 23

ARE YOU HUNGRY AND THIRSTY?

"Blessed are those who hunger and thirst for righteousness, for they will be filled." (Matthew 5:6)

Have you ever felt really hungry and thirsty? Perhaps not, living in an affluent society such as ours, it is unlikely that you will truly understand what it means to be really hungry and thirsty. Of course, you might say that homeless people living on the streets may tell you that they have experienced real hunger and thirst. However, Jesus is not speaking about physical hunger or thirst. Commentaries on this text refer to 'both a deep personal desire to live in accordance with God's will and an urgent longing for justice and goodness in the world.'

When you feel hungry and thirsty, you desire and look forward to when you will receive food and drink, and then you are satisfied. Do you long to be filled spiritually with God's word? Seek Jesus, and you will be filled. In John 6:35, Jesus says: "I am the bread of life, whoever comes to me will never go hungry, and whoever believes in me will never thirst." When you eat bread, you eat to satisfy your physical hunger and to sustain your physical life. However, your spiritual hunger can only be satisfied by a right relationship with Jesus Christ; that's why He calls Himself the bread of life.

In the same way, you need physical bread daily to sustain you physically; you need to sustain your spiritual life by inviting Jesus daily into your life. In John chapter 4, we read about the Samaritan woman, who, on encountering Jesus, asked for water so she would not thirst any longer. Jesus told her that: "Everyone who drinks this water will be thirsty again, but whoever drinks the water I give will never thirst. Indeed, the water I give them will become in them a spring of water welling up to eternal life."

You wouldn't think of depriving your body of water and food when you are hungry and thirsty, would you? However, are you depriving yourself of spiritual food and water - Jesus Christ, the water and bread of life?

Today's Prayer: Dear Father, like the woman at the well, give me water so I won't get thirsty. Give me food that I hunger no more. Amen.

November 24

TWO BROTHERS, TWO DIFFERENT PATHS

'The Lord looked with favour on Abel and his offering, but on Cain and his offering, He did not look with favour. So, Cain was very angry and his face was downcast.' (Genesis 4:4 & 5)

God had told both Cain and Abel what offering was acceptable to Him. "Abel brought an offering – fat portions from some of the firstborn of his flock. The Lord looked with favour on Abel and his offering, but on Cain and his offering, He did not look with favour." Cain brought some fruit as an offering, clearly defying God. Cain's intent was evil. In Proverbs 21:27, we are told, 'The sacrifice of the wicked is detestable – how much more so when brought with evil intent!' God evaluates both our motives and the quality of what we offer Him.

Both brothers had the same instructions from God, yet chose different paths leading to terrible consequences. In Genesis 4:8 we are told that while they were in the field, Cain attacked his brother Abel and killed him. What a tragedy! Just because one chose to go their own way rather than the path God had chosen for them. When Cain did what he did, God gave him the chance to repent; however, he refused. God said to him, "Sin is crouching at your door; it desires to have you, but you must rule over it." Cain chose to go his own way, rather than repent and go God's way. His behaviour is a startling example to us today of what happens when we choose to go our own way.

Like Cain, we are all victims of sin, and it is crouching at our doors even now. Like Cain, we will become victims of sin if we refuse to accept Christ into our lives. The sins that beset us, like Cain's jealousy of his brother and his anger against God, will cause us to walk away from God and choose our own path. God wants us to choose the right path, the path that leads to eternal life. In Matthew 7:13 & 14, Jesus says, "Enter through the narrow gate. For wide is the gate and broad is the road that leads to destruction, and many enter through it. But small is the gate and narrow the road that leads to life and only a few find it." Cain chose the broad road, which led to his destruction. Which path will you choose today? Which road will you travel on? It was John Oxenham who wrote: "To every man there openeth a way. And the high soul climbs the highway and the low soul gropes the low, and in between on the misty flats, the rest drift to and from. But to every man there openeth a high way and a low. And every man decideth the way his soul shall go."

You must decide which way you wish to go. Which one will you take the broad one or the narrow one?

Today's Prayer: Father, help me to take the path you have directed me to take. Amen.

November 25

THE RICH FOOL

"You fool! This very night, your life will be demanded from you; then who will get what you have prepared for yourself?" (Luke 12:20)

Jesus tells the parable of the rich fool, which serves as a warning against greed, and that it is futile to amass wealth and that life is uncertain. The rich man had an abundant harvest, and rather than share what he had with others, he decided to tear down his existing barns and build larger ones to store his crops. He would then be able to 'take life easy, eat, drink and be merry,' he thought to himself.

In this parable told by Jesus, the rich man died before he could begin to enjoy his riches. The parable highlights that possessions are fleeting and that life is not defined by riches, but more importantly, by our relationship with God. However, it is wise to prepare for retirement and to live a good life, but preparing for life after death is crucial; neglecting to do this is foolish. If you accumulate wealth only to enrich yourself, with no concern for helping those in need, you stand like a pauper before God on the day of judgment. What are you doing with the money you have? Are you saving it up to buy the things you want rather than what you need? Are you using it to help the poor and disadvantaged in society? Are you spending your money on the latest phone or the newest car? Are you spending money on things that will not last? In this parable, Jesus challenges us to think beyond earthly ambitions and goals and to use what He has given us for His kingdom.

Do you want to be really rich? The only wealth that counts is to obey God, exercise faith in Him and serve others. In Micah 6:8, we are told, "He has shown you, O mortal man, what is good and what does the Lord require of you? To act justly, and to love mercy, and to walk humbly with your God." You might have tried all kinds of ways to please God; however, in this text, God has made His requirements clear. Do what is just and right, love mercy, and walk humbly with Him. Do you want to be rich in heavenly goods? If you do, God wants you to be a 'living sacrifice', not just doing religious deeds but living rightly.

Today's Prayer: Father, I recognise the brevity of life. Please help me to be a faithful steward as I serve you and those around me. Amen.

November 26

APPOINTMENT OF THE TWELVE

'He appointed twelve that they might be with Him and that He might send them out to preach.' (Mark 3:14)

Mark records Jesus appointing twelve apostles, not just to be His companions, but His understudies; they would be with Him to learn from Him and to be sent out to preach and have the authority to cast out demons. Jesus would prepare them to take over and carry on the work when He returned to heaven. Jesus wanted them to change the world and could have done it Himself, but He chose ordinary people and entrusted them with the important task of taking the gospel to the world. He told them they would "receive power when the Holy Spirit came upon them to be His witnesses in Jerusalem, and in all Judea and Samaria, and to the ends of the earth." (Acts 1:8) The twelve apostles changed the world as God had intended.

God has also called you to active ministry. The verse highlights the importance of fellowship with Christ in order to be able to undertake ministry. The twelve spent time in the presence of Jesus, learning from Him. If you are to carry out His work, you must also spend time in His presence. Jesus chose the twelve that they might be with Him, showing us that having a relationship with God is crucial in carrying out His work. It is also about fellowship with Him and continuous training, which will equip us for ministry. The apostles were called to be messengers of the good news. Sharing the good news is the central and most important part of being called to minister to others. When Jesus chose the twelve, it was a crucial and major turning point in His ministry, as this constituted a divine appointment for them to continue His work after His earthly ministry would end.

As you read the gospels, you will notice the relationship Jesus had with His disciples, and which relationship serves as a model for believers today who have been called to continue the mission of Christ. The relationship is a model for discipleship, showing how important it is to teach and mentor others in discipleship making. The appointment of the twelve was an act of formal commissioning, that is, a transfer of authority from Jesus to them. They were chosen to become God's representatives on earth. They were given authority to cast out demons, a sign of the power of Jesus in their lives.

When you accept Jesus Christ in your life you are also being commissioned to His service. You have been anointed to "proclaim good news to the poor. He has sent you to bind up the broken-hearted to proclaim freedom for the captives and release from darkness for the prisoners, to proclaim the year of the Lord's favour the day of vengeance of our God, to comfort all who mourn, and to provide for those who grieve in Zion - to bestow on them a crown of beauty instead of ashes, the oil of joy instead of mourning, and a garment of praise instead of a spirit of despair." (Isaiah 61:1-3) Are you ready to spread the gospel?

Today's Prayer: Father, make me the kind of disciple you would like me to be. Amen.

November 27

WHEN JESUS BECAME ANGRY

'So, he made a whip of cords, drove all from the temple courts, both sheep and cattle. He scattered the coins of the money-changers and overturned their tables.' (John 2:15)

There is a song entitled 'Gentle Jesus Meek and Mild' that I used to sing as a child. So, what has happened here to the gentle and mild Jesus? God's temple was being misused by the people who had turned it into a marketplace. They had forgotten or didn't care that God's house is a place of worship and not a place for buying and selling and making a profit. Jesus was angry at those who had desecrated the house of worship by exploiting those who had come to worship.

Jesus was angry because the people had obviously used the temple to perform their evil acts, and He saw it as an insult to God. Jesus was 'consumed with righteous anger against such flagrant disrespect of God,' says one writer. God hates sin, and Jesus was showing us that He will not tolerate it in any shape or form. Jesus was indeed gentle in nature; however, He was capable of dealing with sin. This incident reflected how sinful God's people had become; they no longer respected the house of God. Jesus took swift and decisive action; the people had to learn that God would not tolerate sin. Jesus was angry because the religious leaders who should have been guiding the people were themselves guilty of disregarding God's commands.

Do you feel anger over sin when you hear someone blaspheming God's name or bringing His church into disrepute? Or have you become complacent, and so politically correct that you are failing to call sin by its right name? One Christian writer says, 'The greatest want of the world is the want of men, men who will not be bought or sold men who, in there in most souls, are true, and honest, men who do not fear to call sin by its right name, men, whose conscience is true as the needle to the pole, men who will stand for the right though the heavens fall.'

Are you ready to call sin by its right name? Are you ready to defend God's word, even if it is the preacher who is not fulfilling His commands? Your attitude toward church is wrong if you see it just as a place for personal contacts and fellowship, or a business advantage, and not a place to worship God.

Today's Prayer: Father, help me to act against injustice and things that are clearly not right, and not condone sin. Amen.

November 28

JESUS AND THE ORDINARY PEOPLE

'...And the common people head Him gladly.' (Mark 12:37) (KJV)

Someone once said, 'God must love the poor (or the common people), because He made so many of them.' During the time of Christ, as we read the gospels, we find the ordinary people flocking to Him. They were the ones who listened to Him as He told them the good news of the gospel. On the contrary, we find the religious leaders were the ones who were criticising Him or else ignored Him, looked down on Him with contempt, and plotted to kill Him. The ordinary people received Him gladly; this was in contrast to the hostility that the religious leaders showed Jesus.

The ordinary people thrilled over the messages they heard from Jesus. Quite unlike the religious leaders, they recognised by His words and actions that He was the long-awaited Messiah. The religious leaders were looking for a king who would deliver them from Roman bondage and, therefore, could not accept the lowly and humble Christ whom the ordinary people had come to love and accept. The acceptance of Jesus by the ordinary people highlights the divide between them and the religious leaders, who, because of their pride and status, were resistant to Jesus and His message. They could not accept that the Messiah would be far more than just a descendant of David, but also God Himself in human form.

After Jesus' resurrection, you would have thought that the religious leaders would have been finally convinced that He was indeed the Messiah; however, that was not the case, but the ordinary people believed all the more that He was truly the Son of God. The common people's delight suggests that they had come to realise that Jesus was more than just another king or prophet, but that He was the eternal divine King that David himself had anticipated.

Have you accepted Jesus as your Lord and Saviour? You are of worth and value to Him regardless of your position or status in life. Paul told the Corinthian believers, "Brothers, think of what you were when you were called, not many of you were wise by human standards; not many were influential; not many were of noble birth." (1 Corinthians 1:26) Make the decision today to follow Him or to recommit yourself to Him, and help spread the message of His soon return.

Today's Prayer: Thank you, Father, for using ordinary people to spread the gospel throughout the world. Amen.

November 29

THE WRESTLER

'So, Jacob was left alone, and a man wrestled with him till daybreak.' (Genesis 32:24)

You can read the entire story in Genesis 32 when Jacob wrestles with the angel. Jacob thought he was wrestling at first with a mere human being; however, as it turns out, this was not the case. Jacob mustered all his strength and would not stop, and wrestled all night. The Bible tells us that when 'the man saw that he could not overpower him, he touched the socket of Jacob's hip so that his hip was wrenched as he wrestled with the man.'

What can we learn from Jacob's experience? The wrestling with Jacob was God's way of showing him that relying on his own strength and power is futile. Like Jacob, we are all dependent on God. We can do nothing without Him. The act of weakening Jacob's hip is a lesson showing us that we are weak and helpless and therefore dependent on God for all our needs. By dislocating his hip, Jacob was left weakened and dependent. Jacob's encounter with the heavenly being brought about a much-needed transformation that was needed in Jacob's life. He was forced to stop struggling and fighting his way through life, and forced to acknowledge a power that is greater than any of us. As a result of his transformed heart, God chose to give Jacob a new name. No longer would he be called Jacob, but Israel.

You might be struggling in the night with doubts of many kinds. Spend time reflecting on Jacob's encounter with God. His struggle took place at night, which continued to daybreak. This can be seen as a symbol of hope that the long night of weeping and struggles that you might be going through at the moment will end in joy.

The psalm states: 'Weeping may stay for the night, but rejoicing comes in the morning.' (Psalm 30:5). God can meet you in the darkest moments of your life and bring hope and transformation to your life. Those dark moments in your life can be transformed by God to give you a new start. After his wrestling match, Jacob, no doubt, limped for the rest of his life, a lasting memory that he struggled with God and with humans and overcame; however, more importantly, he saw God face to face.

Today's Prayer: Father, I am looking forward to the day when I shall see you face to face. Amen.

November 30

GOD CHOOSES STRANGE WAYS TO GET OUR ATTENTION

'There, the angel appeared to him in flames of fire from within a bush. Moses saw that though the bush was on fire, it did not burn up.' (Genesis 3:2)

God sometimes uses some very strange ways to get our attention. Take Moses, for example, as he was out looking after his sheep, he saw this strange phenomenon and went to investigate why there was a fire, and the bush was not consumed. Little did he know that God was in the fire and that this would be the beginning of a major change in his life. As he drew closer to the bush, he heard God calling him from the bush. God told Moses to take off his sandals because he was standing on holy ground. It was here that God gave Moses the assignment to bring His people out of Egyptian bondage. Moses' encounter with God tells us that when we come into His presence to worship, we must approach Him in reverence and awe.

What about a talking donkey? The false prophet Balaam was stopped on his journey to curse God's people, when, after having struck his donkey, it spoke! The animal could see an angel with a drawn sword, but Balaam could not see. He was so blinded by greed for the wealth that the king offered him that he could not see that God was stopping him. Though we may know what God's plans are for us, we can become blinded by the desire to acquire wealth, possessions, status or prestige. Try to avoid Balaam's mistake by looking past the material things of this world. The donkey saved Balaam's life but made him look foolish in the process, so Balaam lashed out at the donkey. Do you sometimes lash out at blameless people who get in your way because you are embarrassed or your pride is hurt? Do not allow such matters to cause you to hurt others. (Read the story in Genesis 22.)

God has also used a fish once to draw attention by having Jonah swallowed by one. This story is a profound illustration of God's mercy and grace. God had asked Jonah to warn the people of Nineveh that if they did not repent from their sins, they would suffer the consequences. Jonah hated the people and did not want God to save them, so God provided a fish to swallow him. Like Jonah, God might be calling you for a special assignment, and like Jonah, he might be calling you to do something that you do not want to do. You might even find yourself wanting to run away. However, it is better to obey God than try to run away from Him. Sometimes, in spite of our unwillingness and defiance, God in His mercy will give us a second chance.

A bright light and a voice from heaven were ways by which God was able to get Saul's (later Paul's) attention. He was abruptly stopped by God as he was on his way to persecute His people. On the Damascus Road, Saul was confronted by the risen Christ and brought face to face with the truth of the gospel. Sometimes God will bring us to accept the gospel in spectacular and dramatic ways because He wants to save us.

Today's Prayer: Father, when I reflect on the many times you have tried to get my attention, I realise that it is because you want to save me for your kingdom. Amen

December 1

MOTHERS DON'T STOP PRAYING FOR YOUR CHILDREN

'...Pour out your heart like water in the presence of the Lord. Lift up your hands to Him for the lives of your children.' (Lamentations 2:!9)

I have met many mothers who have been praying for their children for many years. Recently, I met one who told me that she has been praying for her child for fourteen years. The key text today is a call to urgent, desperate prayer during times of crisis, encouraging the people of God in Jeremiah's time to pray because of their sins. They had turned their backs on God. Similarly, a lot of mothers are crying and praying for their children who have walked away from God. We live in a sinful and dangerous world, and when our children walk away from God, they are at the mercy of the evil one. This is the very reason why we need to pray for them.

"When you pray for your child," says Stormie Omartian, "do it as if you are interceding for his or her life [...] God has a perfect plan for your children's lives; Satan has a plan for them, too. Satan plans to destroy them, and he will try to use any means possible to do so: drugs, sex, alcohol, rebellion, accidents, disease. He will always try to make a case against our children so he can have access to their lives. If we are armed with Scriptures, however, he will have to contend with the Word of God."

If you have been praying for your children and they still haven't returned to the Lord, just keep praying, for He is a God who answers prayers, and for that reason, we should keep praying, pray without ceasing. I once read a story of a mother who, one night, had an urge to pray for her daughter. Unknown to her at the time, her daughter was in real danger. As she was walking home alone that same night, she heard footsteps behind her and before she knew it, someone came from behind, pulled her scarf and was about to strangle her when he quite suddenly dropped her scarf and ran away. It happened at the very moment when the Holy Spirit urged her mother to pray.

Mothers, do not give up, keep praying for your children, for God wants to save them in His kingdom.

Today's Prayer: Father, I lift up my children to You and ask that You place a hedge of protection around them. Amen.

December 2

WOMEN IN THE ANCESTRY OF CHRIST

"...And so, He condemned sin in the flesh, in order that the righteous requirement of the law might be fully met in us, who do not live according to the flesh, but according to the Spirit." (Romans 8:3 & 4)

It is sometimes hard to believe that some of the women in the Bible are part of Christ's ancestry, but in the genealogy of Jesus, they are listed. Tamar, for example, who was the daughter-in-law of Judah, pretended to be a prostitute and deceived Judah by giving him a son. (Genesis 38:13-30) You will find that she is mentioned in the ancestry of Christ in Mathew 1:5. It is hard to understand; however, God in His mercy can change a bad situation into something good. There was also Rahab the prostitute, who helped the spies when they came to view the land of Jericho. The story can be found in (Joshua 6: 22-25). Because of her faith and kind acts to God's people, she is also mentioned in the hall of faith in Hebrews 11:31. She showed that she had faith in God. Faith helps us to turn around and do what is right, regardless of our past or the disapproval of others. Bathsheba is yet another woman mentioned in Christ's ancestry. She became King David's wife after he committed adultery with her, and had her husband killed when he discovered she was pregnant.

Ruth, unlike all the others, was of impeccable character; she was a virtuous woman; however, she was a Moabite, who should not have married an Israelite, as this was forbidden (See Deuteronomy 23:3). However, God had a plan and works in ways we cannot understand. These stories illustrate God's sovereign grace, the universal scope of salvation, and that His redemption cuts across race, ethnicity or culture. They also show God's redemptive grace and the inclusion of those who are marginalised in society. Tamar's inclusion in the ancestry of Christ is also very significant because it demonstrates that God can work through painful and morally complex situations, using the actions of less-than-perfect, and flawed, sinful individuals to fulfil His plan. These stories of God's redemptive work should give us hope.

Today's Prayer: Thank you, Lord, for your grace and mercy. Amen.

December 3

WOULD YOU DO THIS FOR YOUR FRIEND?

'Since they could not get him to Jesus because of the crowd, they made an opening in the roof above Jesus and, after digging through it lowered the mat the paralysed man was lying on.' (Mark 2:4)

This is such an amazing story. Can you imagine making a hole in someone's roof so your friend can be healed by Jesus? Well, this is precisely what these friends did for their paralysed friend. Imagine Jesus is in this crowded room speaking, when suddenly bits of the ceiling begin to fall in the room. This is a remarkable story of faith born out of sheer desperation for a loved one. Commentaries on this story emphasise not just the physical struggle of these four friends, but it represent breaking through barriers to reach the healing power of Jesus. The verse demonstrates the love the friends had for each other and their faith in the healing power of Jesus. The verse also shows that faith is central to receiving God's help. Bringing their friend to Jesus meant that the paralytic would be in a position to receive Christ's forgiveness. The action of the friends also demonstrates their love and commitment to their friend. Theirs was a faith that refused to be limited by obstacles or barriers like a large crowd.

Are you prepared like those friends to break barriers so that others can learn about Christ? Are you prepared to go against societal, religious and physical limitations to reach out to Christ and bring others with you to receive His saving grace? Can it be that, as believers, we can be so preoccupied with our own relationships and agendas and not notice those who are on the outside trying to get in? In Matthew Henry's commentary on this story, he says, "It was this man's misery that he needed to be so carried, and shows the suffering state of human life; it was kind of those who so carried him, and teaches the compassion that should be in men, toward their fellow-creatures in distress."

Today's Prayer: Father, help me not to be so preoccupied with my own agenda that I fail to bring others into your presence. Amen.

December 4

SHOWING HOSPITABILITY (1)

'Let a little water be brought, and then you may wash your feet and rest under this tree.' (Genesis 18: 4)

To be hospitable means to be welcoming and friendly towards guests. Abraham, like most people living in the Middle East at that time, was eager to show hospitality to these two visitors. In Abraham's day, a person's reputation was largely connected to their hospitality - the sharing of home and food. Even strangers were to be treated as highly as honoured guests. Meeting another's need for food and shelter was and still is one of the most immediate and practical ways to obey God. The writer of Hebrews goes as far as to say that when we are hospitable, we might sometimes even be entertaining angels unawares (Hebrew 13:2).

This verse is reminding us about the importance of showing kindness and generosity to others, even those who are strangers. In Abraham's culture, washing someone's feet was not only a sign of politeness and respect but also of hospitality. It is an act of servanthood and purification. It is an act that prefigures when Jesus would one day wash His disciples' feet both as a sign of humility and the cleansing of sin. When Jesus washed his disciples' feet, it was to be a lesson for them in humility and servanthood.

God expects us to treat each other with kindness and respect, and so we should be hospitable to everyone. Who are the people around you that you need to welcome and bring into your community so that they can experience God's love? There are so many in our communities who are disadvantaged and marginalised who need to experience God's love for them. You are God's hands and feet and should reach out in love to the vulnerable in your community. How often do you stop to speak to someone who is sleeping rough on the street? Are you showing hospitality only to those who are like you, or are you open to people who are different? Are you being selective? True hospitality is about embracing everyone regardless of their culture, race, ethnicity, or status.

Remember, hospitality is not just a kind gesture to a few people; rather, it is a command from God that we should love one another as He loves us.

Why not think of ways that you can show hospitality to others and make a difference in someone's life today?

Today's Prayer: Father, help me to be intentional in looking for ways to extend hospitality to those who are marginalised in society. Amen.

December 5

SHOWING HOSPITALITY (2)

"Anyone who welcomes you, welcomes me, and anyone who welcomes me, welcomes the one who sent me." (Matthew 10:40)

Making others feel loved is a hallmark of discipleship. Welcoming new members was important in the early church, and it is just as important today. Social customs may change, but God's word doesn't. In the above text, Jesus says anyone who welcomes you welcomes Him. As a follower of Christ, you are duty-bound to make people feel a part of the household of faith (Galatians 6:10). Establishing friendship within churches can easily become religious cliques where we smile and speak to newcomers, but spend our time with a select group of people we already know. Most of us are satisfied with our existing circle of friends; however, we should be looking for ways to include others.

People attend church hoping for love and acceptance, and if they don't find it within a month or two, they will leave. As believers, we should keep our eyes open for newcomers, especially those who appear uncomfortable, shy and out of place. Because believers sometimes do not show hospitality, some people will have a negative experience of the church and will not wish to return. However, we should reach out to others so no one feels isolated or 'out on a limb'. Church should be a place where our believers' love for people who are hurting is evident from the minute they walk in the door.

Showing hospitality means that you will go out of your way to actively welcome others, especially strangers. Show them unconditional love, show kindness and tell them how glad you are that they have chosen to worship with you. To show kindness to others reflects the teachings of Christ, when you actively serve them by meeting their needs and making them feel loved and cared for. As a believer, when you show hospitality to others, it is a way of displaying and preaching the gospel. It is not what we say, but what we do to show people that we truly care. It was

Stephen Covey who said, "What you do has far greater impact than what you say."

Peter says, "Offer hospitality to one another without grumbling." (1 Peter 4:9). One writer says, "Hospitality is an opportunity to prove that God is better than anything an unshared, more comfortable home can ever afford." Jesus says in Mathew 24:`40, "Truly, I tell you, whatever you did for one of the least of these brothers and sisters of mine, you did it for me." Show hospitality to others for God expects you to. "But when you give a banquet, invite the poor, the crippled, the lame, the blind, and you will be blessed." (Luke 14:13 &14)

Today's Prayer: Father, I know that you have commanded us to be hospitable. Help me to practise hospitality as I interact with others. Amen.

December 6

GOD IS NOT IMPRESSED

'All of us have become like one who is unclean, and all our righteous acts are like filthy rags; we all shrivel up like a leaf and like the wind our sins are swept away.' (Isaiah 64:6)

No matter how righteous we think we are God is not impressed with us: 'our righteous acts are like filthy rags'. Israel had sunk so low in idolatry and disobedience that their situation had become so bad that God was not impressed with them. Their best efforts were infected with sin. However, God would not reject His people if they came to Him in faith and humility and repented of their sins.

In Isaiah chapter 1, the people were trying to please God; however, He wanted none of it. He was disgusted with their behaviour. "From the sole of your foot to the top of your head, there is no soundness – only wounds and bruises and open sores." (Verse 11) God was not impressed with the behaviour of His people in Isaiah's day, nor is He impressed with our behaviour today. He is calling us to examine ourselves, to see if we are really serving Him. In 2 Corinthians 5:2, Paul urges us to give ourselves a spiritual check-up. We should look for a growing awareness of Christ's presence and power in our lives. Only then will we know if we are true Christians or merely impostors. If you are not actively seeking to grow closer to God, you are drawing further away from Him.

Today ask God to help you to draw close to Him. He says those who draw close to Him He will draw close to them (James 4:8).

Today's Prayer: Father, I know my righteous acts are like filthy rags. I want to draw close to you. Thank you for drawing close to me. Amen.

December 7

JEALOUSY

'For where you have envy and selfish ambition, there you will find disorder and every evil practice.' (James 3:16)

Jealousy is a negative and destructive emotion. It is often rooted in insecurity, fear, and a sense of inadequacy; it often stems from envy. In Genesis 4:3-8, we read the story of Cain and Abel. Cain became jealous of his brother Abel because God favoured Abel's offering over his own, which led to Cain murdering Abel.

There are other examples of jealousy in the Scriptures that show us the consequences of this very destructive emotion. Rachael was jealous of her sister Leah, leading to a rivalry for the affection of their husband, Jacob (Genesis 30:1). Joseph's brothers were jealous of the favour their father Jacob showed him, which was symbolised by his 'coat of many colours'. Their jealousy led to Joseph nearly being killed and later being sold into slavery. However, in this case, God used this situation to bring reconciliation to this very dysfunctional family.

King Saul became jealous of David after he was successful in defeating the Philistine giant Goliath. King Saul was so consumed with jealousy that he threatened and attempted to kill him; jealousy eventually led to Saul's downfall.

In all these stories, we learn about the consequences of jealousy. God hates it. If we are truthful, we have probably at some time experienced jealousy. If you have this problem, you should pray and ask God to help you overcome this tendency. You will recall that Aaron and his sister Miriam had this problem too and spoke against their brother Moses, God's leader, "Has the Lord spoken through Moses?" they asked. "Hasn't He also spoken through us?" God heard and He was displeased with them. God struck Miriam down with leprosy. This is how God hates sin. So, if you are struggling with jealousy, acknowledge your sin to God, confess and ask for forgiveness. Remember that you will not be able to overcome in your own strength; you must ask Him to give you the strength to overcome. Very often, jealousy begins when you start comparing yourself with others. You will need to stop doing that, be grateful for the blessings God has bestowed upon you; this will help you to fight against resentment. God is ready to forgive you and restore you, so seek His help.

Today's Prayer: Father, I know how destructive the sin of jealousy is. If I have jealousy in my heart, please remove it so I will not sin against you and others. Amen.

December 8

THE FOUR SOILS

"Whoever, has ears, let them hear." (Matthew 13:9)

Jesus told many parables while He was here on earth. This parable is about the four soils, which explain how people receive God's message. The farmer scatters the seeds on different types of soil. It is a parable that should encourage 'spiritual farmers', that is, those who teach, preach, and seek to lead others to Christ. The farmer sowed good seeds, but not all the seeds sprouted, and even the plants that grew had varying yields. This is telling us that we should not be discouraged if we do not always get results; you must continue to tell others about Christ.

In the parable, some seeds fell along the path and were snatched by the birds. Some fell on rocky places where there was not much soil, the seeds sprang up quickly because the soil was shallow, but were later scorched by the sun and withered because they had no root. The seeds that fell among thorns grew up and were choked by the thorns. Still other seeds fell on good soil.

Jesus was not hiding the truth when He spoke to the people in parables; rather, He was compelling His listeners to discover the truth, while at the same time concealing it from those who were too lazy or too stubborn to see it. For those who are honestly seeking, the truth will become clear. The parable is helping us to understand that as we witness for Christ, we will meet all kinds of people who will respond in different ways to the gospel; however, we should not become discouraged. Some will listen, others won't. You might be mocked and ridiculed, but you should continue because some want to hear. Human ears may hear many sounds, but there is a deeper kind of listening that will result in spiritual understanding.

In the parables that Jesus spoke, those who were receptive to spiritual truth understood what He was saying; to those who were not receptive, the stories were meaningless. As you witness for Christ, you must understand that not everyone will accept the message. One writer says, "A man's reception of God's word is determined by the condition of his heart." It is only God who can change the heart; however, we must continue to do our part by scattering the seed of His word. The Sower represents God, the seed represents the word of God, and the soil represents the heart of the person who hears the word. Do not worry about how you will be received; just continue to spread God's word because some are waiting to hear.

Today's Prayer: Father, help me not to become discouraged if I do not see results, let me continue to spread the gospel. Amen.

December 9

NO NEED TO PATCH UP YOUR OLD HEART

"I will give you a new heart and put a new spirit in you. I will remove your heart of stone and give you a heart of flesh." Ezekiel 36:26)

When we accept Christ in our lives, He has to replace our rebellious, hard heart of stone with a new, responsive heart. It is only when our hearts are transformed by God that we will be able to obey His commands.

During the time of Ezekiel, the children of Israel had forgotten God, and their hearts became hard and calloused. However, God said if the people would turn from their wicked ways, He would come to their aid. We cannot expect God's mercy until we allow Him to remove our stony hearts in exchange for a new one. Your Physician, Jesus Christ, is also the surgeon who will operate on you and do the exchange. Is your heart right with God? Do you need a new heart?

Medicine has progressed dramatically, whereby heart diseases that were not curable years ago are now curable. You can also be given a new heart. However, God promises to not only give us a new heart but also put His Spirit in us so we can serve Him. If we are to enter the kingdom of God, He has to get rid of envy, hatred, jealousy, malice, murder, and all the sins that are causing our hearts to become hard and diseased. No human surgeon can transform a heart that is 'deceitful above all things and beyond cure' (Jeremiah 17:9).

God makes it clear why we sin; it is a matter of the heart. Our hearts are inclined to sin from the moment we are born. David says: "Surely, I was sinful at birth, sinful from the time my mother conceived me." (Psalm 51:5) It is easy to fall into the routine of forgetting and forsaking God; we see it with Israel, who were always forsaking God and going after other gods. However, God promised to restore Israel, not physically, but spiritually, and He will do the same for you. If you have wandered away from God and, as a result, your heart has become hardened by sin, return to Him. No matter how impure and sinful your life night be right now, God offers you a fresh start. You can have your sins washed away and receive a new heart and have His Spirit within you. There is no need to patch up the old heart when you can have a new one.

Today's Prayer: Father, create in me a new heart, and renew a right spirit within me. Amen.

December 10

GOD IS WITH US

'The virgin will conceive and give birth to a son, and they will call Him Immanuel (which means God with us).' Matthew 1:23

Whenever I read this verse and reflect upon the incarnation, I can scarcely take it in. The fact that Jesus, the Son of God, left heaven and all its glories to come to sinful earth to die for me, overwhelms me. He would fulfil the prophecy of Isaiah the prophet, for He would be Immanuel (God is with us). (Isaiah 7:14) Jesus was God in the flesh; thus, God was literally among us, and with us. Through the Holy Spirit, Christ is present today in the life of every believer.

Have you really thought about what it means, Immanuel, with us? It means that He is always with us, in our joys and our sorrows. When tragedy strikes, He is with us. He says, "Never will I leave, never will I forsake you." (Hebrews 13:5) Immanuel, God with us. You may be going through some storms in your life right now, but He is in the storm with you. As you go through your storm, you can become so focused on it that you cannot feel His presence with you. But rest assured, He is in it with you, because He is Immanuel. We are reminded by the prophet Isaiah that "When you pass through the waters, I will be with you. When you walk through the fire, you will not be burned; the flames will not set you ablaze. For I am the Lord your God, the Holy one of Israel, your Saviour." What more assurance do you need?

As you go through the rivers of difficulty in your life, the evil one wants to take you under; he wants you to drown, and if you start swimming in your own strength, you are bound to go under, you are likely to drown. Remember, Immanuel is with you, so cry out to Him and He will protect you and give you the strength to battle the waves of despair and hopelessness that engulf you. No matter what you are going through in your life, remember, Immanuel, God with us.

Today's Prayer: Father, I invite you into my life to be with me. Amen.

December 11

UNREST IN BETHLEHEM

'For to us a child is born, to us a son is given, and the government will be on His shoulders.' (Isaiah 9:6)

When the Duchess of Sussex gave birth to Prince Archie, I remember going into my local Marks and Spencer shop when a woman who I had never met before came up to me and said, "It's a boy!" For a brief moment, I thought she must have mistaken me for someone else, then it dawned on me that she was referring to the birth of the prince. Isn't it amazing that not only our country knew about the birth of this royal baby, but the entire world! What a contrast to when Jesus, the Prince of Peace, King of Kings, entered planet Earth. There was no fanfare; all was still and calm, no one in Bethlehem knew that the long-awaited Messiah had arrived, except for the shepherds who were watching their flocks that night, and the animals in the stable, and of course the wise men. He wasn't born in the local hospital (if they had any in that time), not even in a home, but in a stable, surrounded by animals.

In the fullness of time, in a time of great darkness, God promised to send a light that would shine on everyone living in the shadow of death. This light was a person who would be both 'Wonderful Counsellor' (all-loving) and 'Mighty God' (all-powerful). This is a message of hope, even to this day, that was fulfilled in the birth of Jesus Christ and the establishment of His eternal kingdom. He came to deliver all people from their slavery to sin. From the time of His birth, His life was threatened. From a worldly perspective, He had no protection and security that our royal family and their children have; He had much more than that. The Holy Spirit was with Him. He was protected by the mighty hand of God, His Father. When it became public knowledge that the baby Jesus had been born in Bethlehem, it caused no end of unrest, to the point where Herod felt threatened and insecure and sought to destroy the infant Jesus. Throughout His time here on earth, He lived in constant threat to His life and was rejected by the very people He had come to save. The birth of

Christ was Satan's biggest nightmare, and that is why He sought to destroy Him.

What does Jesus' birth mean to you? The event of His birth should be your foundational belief that He came to save you from your sins. Does it bring you hope and joy that He is your Saviour, Redeemer, and soon coming King? His birth was the beginning of God's plan to redeem His children who are lost in sin. The prophets prophesied that He would be our Saviour who would take away the sins of the world. His birth is associated with peace. He would bring peace, both earthly and eternal, with God through His sacrifice on the cross. His birth gives us hope of eternal life with Him.

Spend some time each day in meditation on what Christ's birth really means to you, and as you contemplate His love for you; remember that everything that He did, He did it for you. None of what He did was for Himself, and He didn't have to do what He did, but He did it all for you.

Today's prayer: Father, thank you for what you have done for me, which is truly beyond my comprehension. Amen.

December 12

IT IS FINISHED

"It is finished." (John 19:30)

The word finished means the same as paid in full. Jesus paid with His life. He came to pay the full penalty of our sins. With His death, the complex sacrificial system which we read about in the Old Testament ended, because Jesus took all our sins upon Himself and became the ultimate sacrifice. This means that we can approach God freely because of what Jesus did for us on the cross. Those who believe in Jesus' death and resurrection can live eternally in heaven and escape the penalty that comes from sin.

When Jesus said 'It is finished' His mission was accomplished. As He hung on the cross, the whole world was wrapped in gloom, but He rose again, as He said He would. He had completed His earthly work and was ready to return home to His Father. His mission to save humanity was now completed triumphantly.

What do these words mean to you? Jesus' words 'it is finished' should bring hope to you and every believer. We can now find rest from trying to earn our own salvation through our own efforts, for Jesus paid it all at Calvary. We have the assurance of salvation through faith in Jesus Christ and live a victorious life in Him. However, these words should also remind you that God's word is true, for at the death of Christ, all the prophecies that foretold of His coming and ultimate death were fulfilled, giving us confidence in His word.

Are you preparing for the next phase? By dying on the cross and shedding His blood for us, He provided forgiveness of sin. However, when Jesus said it was finished, it marked the end of His mission to earth and the beginning of His role as intercessor in heaven for us. "Therefore, he is able to save completely those who come to God through him, because he always lives to intercede for them." (Hebrews 7:25). No one can add to what Jesus did to save us, and as He continues His mediatorial work in heaven for us, He is giving us every opportunity to live above sin as we await His soon coming. Are you preparing for His return?

Today's Prayer: Father, thank you for your great sacrifice of love. It is my desire to be saved in your kingdom. Amen.

December 13

THE DANGER OF CRITICISM

'Brothers and sisters, do not slander one another. Anyone who speaks against a brother or sister or judges them speaks against the law and judges it.' (James 4:11)

Have you ever met someone who has nothing good to say about anyone? They are always criticising and saying negative things about others. In today's key text, James is saying do not speak evil against one another. There is only one lawgiver and judge who can save and destroy. Criticism is not always destructive; it can be positive. Destructive criticism includes personal attacks, insults, and generalisations that can be hurtful, whereas constructive criticism would involve someone providing helpful feedback on your work, assignment, or project. However, in this text James is referring to destructive criticism.

There is a famous quote that says, 'To avoid criticism, say nothing, do nothing, be nothing,' which suggests criticism is an unavoidable part of life. Why do people criticise? It is said that overly critical individuals may project their own insecurities or fears onto others, such as criticising a life choice they are too afraid to make themselves. Criticism can also arise from one's childhood experiences, where parents will constantly criticise their child, which can lead to self-talk and project it onto others as a coping mechanism. When a child is constantly being told he is no good and will not amount to much, this will cause him or her to lack confidence. Teachers can also be destructive in criticising students. A teacher told Thomas Edison that he was "too stupid to learn anything." Despite these harsh words, Edison went on to become one of history's most prolific inventors, with thousands of failed attempts before successfully inventing the commercially viable light bulb. Oprah Winfrey, after working as an evening reporter, was fired for being too emotionally invested in her stories. She went on despite criticism to create one of the most successful and influential talk shows in television history.

James is speaking to believers about the dangers of criticising each other. How often do you hear believers criticising others, the pastor, the members, nothing is ever right? They will even criticise the governance of the church. You must be careful not to fall into this trap. St Paul says: "Do not let any unwholesome talk come out of your mouths, but only what is helpful for building others up according to their needs, that it may benefit those who listen." (Ephesians 4:29) Do you know that when you criticise and speak badly about others that you can grieve the Holy Spirit? Paul warns us against unwholesome language, bitterness, improper use of anger, brawling, slander and bad attitudes towards others. Instead of behaving that way, we should be tolerant of each other, show love and forgive as God has forgiven us. Are you pleasing or grieving God because of your attitudes? Do you always criticise others? Ask God to forgive you and transform you so you can see only the good in others?

Today's Prayer: Father, forgive me for the times I have criticised others. Amen.

December 14

CONFIDENCE

'I can do all things through him who gives me strength.' (Philippians 4:13)

How confident are you? To be confident means you have a feeling or a belief in yourself and your abilities, but not in an arrogant way, but a realistic and secure sense of capability. As a believer, you do not rely on yourself, but realise that you can do nothing of any worth by yourself. Instead, your confidence is in God, for He alone can give you the strength to accomplish your goals and your tasks.

Quite often, I have seen believers who are reluctant or refuse to accept any role in the church. They doubt their ability or feel intimidated by others they perceive as being more capable than themselves. However, the text is saying that, through faith, one can be confident and persevere through difficult situations. God promises strength to persevere through hardships. The apostle Paul, while imprisoned, was helping the Philippians to rely on God for their strength. Often, we lack confidence because we fail to acknowledge that it is only through God's strength that we can gain the strength to overcome whatever is holding us back. True confidence is to be found in God; it is not based on your self-assurance but on having faith in God's power and presence in your life. With God on your side, you will have a better source of courage than self-confidence.

As a believer, your confidence should come from the assurance that God is the giver of all your needs, and if you find yourself lacking confidence, go to Him in prayer. He says if we lack anything, we should ask; we don't receive, because we do not ask. So, if you are lacking in confidence, go to Him in prayer, for confidence is rooted in Him. If you feel intimidated, go to Him in prayer; ask Him to remove your fears. Jeremiah, the prophet, when called by God, made excuses, saying He was too young, and he didn't know how to speak; he lacked confidence. However, God assured him that he did not need to be afraid, for He would be with him. Once

Jeremiah trusted that God would be with him, he became a mouthpiece for Him and became one of the most successful prophets Israel had. What about Moses? He also lacked confidence, and when called by God, like Jeremiah made excuses. He became a mighty leader, one of the greatest leaders in Israel.

You might be making excuses, too, and telling God you are not capable. Will you allow Him to use you today like He did Jeremiah, Moses and others? He has called you for a mission; why should it suffer because you have failed to answer His call, because of fear? If you are lacking in self-confidence today and struggling with new challenges, because you think you are inadequate, remember God has promised He will be with you. If God has given you a job to do, do it. He will provide all you need to do it.

Today's Prayer: Lord, help me to rely on you to remove my fears so I can have confidence to do the work you have called me to do. Amen.

December 15

ARE YOU PERFECT?

"Be perfect therefore, as your heavenly Father is perfect." (Matthew 5:48)

Surely not, Father! Are you forgetting that I am only human? You Yourself have said You are the only one who is perfect. How then can You expect me to be perfect? You know that, because I am a sinner, no matter how hard I try, I can never be perfect. According to one Christian writer's comment on today's key text, he says, "Jesus not only issues the command for perfection, but he sets up God as the standard for that perfection." "Walk before me, and be thou perfect," God commanded Abraham in Genesis 17:1. "The only thing one can conclude from the Bible is that perfection must be possible, or its writers would not have urged it upon believers. Thus, the issue is not whether perfection is possible, but what the Bible writers mean by perfection."

What does perfection mean to you? Do you see it as a state when you are completely free from sin? In verses 44 – 48, it would seem that Jesus is speaking about how the believer should live. It appears to be more about how we relate to each other, suggesting therefore that perfection will be seen in the way we treat others and how we respond to them. This also includes our enemies. Jesus tells us to love our enemies and those who despitefully use us. If we fail to do this, we are not showing perfection in our relationship with others.

We cannot achieve perfection in our own strength. One writer says, "We will never be perfect enough to satisfy the sin debt against us. And we don't have to be! Christ gave himself for our sins as one sacrifice for all time and then sat down in the highest place of honour at God's right hand." It appears then that perfection can be understood to be spiritually mature in our behaviours and relationships with others. Love your enemies, pray for those who persecute you, and let God handle justice rather than seek revenge. Perfection, then, is about spiritual wholeness, which encompasses God's commands to love. "A new commandment I give you: love one another. As I have loved you, so you must love one another." (John 13:34) What Christ is saying is that our Christ-like love will show we are His disciples, a mark of perfection. Such love will not only bring believers to a saving knowledge of Christ, but it will also benefit the believer to remain strong and united in a world that is hostile to followers of Jesus.

Are you perfect? What do people see in you? Do they see backbiting, gossiping, jealousy, covetousness, and division in your church? Or do they see one who is gentle, humble, and meek?

Today's prayer: Lord, I understand that perfection emanates from you. I look forward to the time when I will be made perfect in you. Amen.

December 16

TAKEN UP, BUT I WILL BE BACK (1)

'After He said this, He was taken up before their eyes, and a cloud hid Him from their sight.' (Acts 1:9)

By now, Jesus had been resurrected, and after spending forty days with His disciples, He returned to heaven. You can only imagine their sadness when Jesus finally returned to heaven. His mission was completed, and the fledgling church must continue its work under the leadership of the disciples whom He had trained for three years. Although sad at His parting, Jesus assured them that they would not be alone; He would send the Comforter, the Holy Spirit. He said: "But truly, I tell you, it is good that I am going away. Unless I go away, the Advocate will not come to you; but if I go, I will send him to you." (John 16:7). Unless Jesus did what He came to do, there would be no gospel. If He did not die, He could not remove our sins; He could not rise again and defeat death. If He did not go back to the Father, the Holy Spirit would not come. Christ's presence on earth was limited to one place at a time because He came in human form. His leaving meant He could be present to the whole world through the Holy Spirit.

As the disciples witnessed Jesus being taken up into heaven from them, as He ascended, they could still feel the assurance of His protecting care, and remember the words that He told them that He had to go. He had finished his work, but the Holy Spirit would come in His stead, and as He slowly, but surely, was taken up into heaven, He told them, "Lo, I am with you always, even unto the end of the world." It was important for the disciples to see Jesus taken up into heaven if they had any doubt about his divinity, that He was God and that His home was in heaven. All their doubts would have vanished after witnessing this momentous and dramatic event. What a spectacular sight that must have been for the disciples, even though they were saddened at His leaving, they were privileged to be part of this event.

As they were gazing up into heaven, there appeared two angels in white, bringing comfort to them, telling them that one day, Jesus would return. "Men of Galilee," they said, "why do you stand here looking up into the sky? This same Jesus, who has been taken from you into heaven, will come back in the same way you have seen him go into heaven." (Verse 11) He would return visibly and bodily, in the same way that He went up.

Are you longing to see Him return? No one knows when; however, we should be ready for His sudden return, not by standing around looking into the sky, but by sharing the gospel with others so that they, too, can be ready when He comes to share in His great blessings.

Today's Prayer: Lord Jesus, I await your coming with great anticipation. Help me to be ready. Amen.

December 17

TAKEN UP, BUT I WILL BE BACK (2)

"This same Jesus, who is taken up from you into heaven, will come back in the same way you have seen him go into heaven." (Acts 1:11)

Jesus promised that He would return; however, "the day or hour, no one knows, not even the angels in heaven, nor the Son, but only the Father." (Mark 13:32) When Jesus spoke these words, He did not know the time of His return; He was affirming His humanity. Of course, God the Father knows the time, and Jesus and the Father are one. When Jesus became man, He voluntarily gave up His unlimited use of His divine attributes. The emphasis of this verse is not on Jesus' lack of knowledge, but rather on the fact that no one knows. It is God the Father's secret to be revealed when He wills. No one can predict by Scripture or science the exact date of His return. Jesus is teaching that preparation, not calculation, is needed.

Mark, the apostle, tells us how we should live while we are preparing for the second coming of Jesus. "Therefore, keep watch because you do not know when the owner of the house will come back – whether in the evening, or at midnight, or when the cock crows, or at dawn. If he comes suddenly, do not let him find you sleeping. What I say to you, I say to everyone: "Watch!" (Mark 13:35-37).

Are you watching and waiting for the Master's return? "Therefore, keep watch, because you do not know on what day your Lord will come, so you also must be ready because the Son of Man will come at an hour when you do not expect Him." (Matthew 24:42 & 44) In telling us that He will return, Jesus' purpose is not to stimulate predictions, speculations, and calculations, as some have done, but to warn us to be prepared. He has also given us signs indicating that He will return. "The sun will be darkened. And the moon will not give its light, the stars will fall from the sky, and the heavenly bodies will be shaken." (Matthew 24:29) These and other signs can be found in this chapter.

The return of Jesus is to judge and rule over the Earth. We should be ready for His sudden return and not become distracted by what is happening around us. One can easily become desensitised to what is happening in the world today. However, Jesus tells us that we must be ready. Keep watching and waiting.

Today's Prayer: Father, I know that your return is soon. I want to be ready when you return. Amen.

December 18

WHAT WILL HIS COMING BE LIKE?

"Look, He is coming with the clouds, and every eye will see Him, even those who pierced Him: and all peoples on earth will mourn because of Him." (Revelation 1:7)

The second coming of Christ will be a glorious event for His faithful followers. However, for those who have failed to accept Him, it will be a terrifying time. In Revelation 6:15-16, we are told, 'Then the kings of the earth, the princes, the generals, the rich, the mighty, and everyone else, both slave and free, hid in caves and among the rocks of the mountains. They called to the mountains and the rocks, "fall on us, and hide us from the face of him, who sits on the throne, and from the wrath of the Lamb! For the great Day of the wrath has come, and who can withstand?'

At the sight of God, sitting on the throne, all human beings, great and small, will be terrified, calling for the mountains to fall on them, so that they will not have to face the judgment of the Lamb. John's vivid picture is not intended to frighten believers. For them, the Lamb is a gentle Saviour. But those kings, princes and generals and other powerful people who previously showed no fear of God and arrogantly flaunted their unbelief, and even persecuted God's people, will find that they were wrong, and in that day, they will have to face God's wrath.

While we are waiting for Christ's return, we are duty-bound to spread the gospel. "And this gospel of the kingdom will be preached in the whole world, as a testimony to all nations, and then the end will come." (Matthew 24:14). Jesus said before His return, the gospel of the kingdom (the message of salvation) must be preached throughout the world. No one who has heard will have an excuse.

We are told in 1 Thessalonians 4:16 'For the Lord himself shall come down from heaven, with a loud command, with the voice of the archangel, and with the trumpet call of God, and the dead in Christ will rise first. After that, we who are still alive and are left will be caught up together with them in the clouds to meet the Lord in the air. And so, we will be with the Lord forever. Therefore, encourage one another with these words.'

Are you looking forward to that momentous day when our Saviour will take us home? Watch and be ready.

Today's Prayer: Father, I am looking forward to spending eternity with you. Amen.

December 19

DOES THE WAIT SEEM LONG?

'They will say, "Where is this 'coming' He promised? Ever since our ancestors died, everything goes on as it has since the beginning of creation."' (2 Peter 3:4)

Peter is telling us that in the last days we will hear scoffers claiming that Jesus is never coming back, but Peter makes it clear in verse five that this is not the case. We know from the Scriptures that Jesus says He will return, but we do not know when because He hasn't told us. As believers, we must be careful that we do not become complacent. It is dangerous to be spiritually complacent; we cannot afford to dismiss the divine promises due to a lack of visible, immediate fulfilment as we focus on the present world. By denying the return of Christ, scoffers are dismissing the coming judgment for sin, which, in turn, eliminates the need for accountability. This frees them to live according to their own desires.

For the believer, the second coming is the 'Blessed Hope'. In the hope that one day 'God will wipe away every tear from our eyes, there shall be no more death, nor sorrow, nor crying. There shall be no more pain for the former things have passed away.' (Revelation, 21:4) Although the wait may seem long to us, we know that God has an appointed time when He will return; His timing is not our timing. In Hebrews 10:37 we read, "In just a little while, He who is coming will come and will not delay." In verse 35, Paul tells us not to throw away our confidence, for it will be richly rewarded. As believers, we are confident that Christ will come, for we live in hope and anticipation based on our faith, "while we wait for the blessed hope – the appearing of the glory of our great God and Saviour Jesus Christ." (Titus 2:13) "We live by faith, not by sight." (2 Corinthians 5:7). It is our faith and trust in God's word that should sustain us. From a human perspective, it does appear that it is a long wait; we are limited by time, but God is not. We must therefore continue to wait in expectation of His coming.

The children of Israel waited over four hundred years to be delivered from Egyptian slavery. Now that's a long time from our human perspective, but God delivered them as He said He would. Abraham and Sarah waited a long time for their promised son; they waited past childbearing years, but the promise was fulfilled. In the same way, the promise of Christ's return will happen. Do not cast away your confidence, for He that will come, will come.

Today's Prayer: Lord, help me not to lose confidence or lose my hope. Amen.

December 20

ARE YOU HEAVEN BOUND OR EARTH BOUND?

"Do not store up for yourselves treasures on Earth, where moths and vermin destroy, and where thieves break in and steal. But store up for yourselves, treasures in heaven, where moths and vermin do not destroy. For where your treasure is, there your heart will be also." (Matthew 6: 19-20)

Jesus made it clear that having the wrong treasure leads to our hearts being in the wrong place. One writer says that the things that you treasure most are the things that will control you. It could be your wealth, your house, your car, or any material possessions that have become your god. Material things are temporary; therefore, we should not set our hearts on them. I can recall a stock market crash some years ago, where many lost their wealth. Some even took their own lives because they had lost everything. Do not store up treasures on earth Jesus warned. The rich fool in the parable tore down his barns and built bigger ones to store His excess grains, but died that same night; He did not live to enjoy his wealth. Therein lies the danger of storing up treasures on Earth. Try not to fall into the materialistic trap, where you spend all your time and energy storing up treasures, only to die and leave it all behind you.

Do not spend your time collecting and storing up earthly treasures; rather, seek God's kingdom. "But seek first His kingdom and His righteousness, and all these things will be given to you as well." (Matthew 6:33). This means putting God first in your life. What is really important to you: money, people, status, your education, or the latest gadgets? These cannot give you eternal life. You must actively choose to make God first place in your life.

Today's Prayer: Father, my desire is to make you first place in my life. Amen.

December 21

ARE YOU SPIRITUALLY HEALTHY? (1)

"Dear friend, I pray that you may enjoy good health and that all may go well with you, just as you are progressing spiritually." (3 John:2)

Quite often in health lectures, we hear about physical, mental and sometimes emotional health, but rarely about spiritual health. God is concerned about all aspects of your health. He is concerned about our body and soul. We are both physical and spiritual beings. How do you become a spiritually healthy individual? You must first have a connection with God and also a personal relationship with Him, thereby creating a balance between the physical, psychological and social aspects of human life. One writer says spiritual wellness acknowledges our search for a deeper meaning in life. When we are spiritually healthy, we feel more connected not only to a higher power but to those around us. Spiritual health is about allowing Christ to dwell in us. In John 15:5 & 6, Jesus explains what it means to be spiritually healthy. He says, "I am the vine; you are the branches. If you remain in me, and I in you, you will bear much fruit; apart from me, you can do nothing."

If you are receiving the nourishment and life offered by Christ, the vine, then and only then can you claim to be spiritually healthy. If you want to enjoy spiritual health, make Jesus Christ the centre of your life. The spiritually healthy person has committed himself or herself completely to the will of God and asks continually for the Holy Spirit's guidance in their life. You will experience an abundant life in Christ and will be filled with all the fullness of God.

The spiritually healthy person rejoices that she or he has been saved through faith: 'For it is by grace that you have been saved through faith – and this is not from yourselves, it is the gift of God.' (Ephesians 2:8). Although the spiritually healthy person will face temptations and setbacks, he or she will remain healthy as long as they fix their eyes on Jesus.

How is your spiritual health? Can you say you are progressing well spiritually? The Laodicean situation described in Revelation 3:14-21 describes a state of spiritual sickness. Jesus Christ was their only hope. If you are feeling a little under the weather spiritually today, seek Jesus, the greatest Physician this world has ever known.

Today's Prayer: Father, I need to be made spiritually healthy. Amen.

December 22

ARE YOU SPIRITUALLY HEALTHY? (2)

"Here I am! I stand at the door and knock. If anyone hears my voice and opens the door, I will come in and eat with that person, and they with me." (Revelation 3:20)

The spiritual condition in Laodicea is described by Christ as lukewarm, neither hot nor cold. The believers did not take a stand for anything, says one commentary. Indifference had led to idleness. There is nothing more disgusting than a half-hearted nominal Christian who is self-sufficient; in other words, a Christian who is spiritually sick. Laodicea was so spiritually sick that God describes it as being neither hot nor cold: "I wish you were either one or the other. So, because you are lukewarm – neither hot nor cold – I am about to spit you out of my mouth. You say I am rich, I have acquired wealth and do not need a thing, but you do not realise you're wretched, pitiful, poor, blind, and naked."

It would seem that there was no hope for Laodicea; however, God, in His mercy and grace, offers a panacea of hope. If you are spiritually sick, He also offers hope; it is not His desire that anyone should perish but that all should come to repentance. He counsels Laodicea to "Buy from me gold refined in the fire, so that you can become rich; and white robes to wear, so that you can cover your shameful nakedness; and eye salve to put on your eyes, so that you can see. Those whom I love, I rebuke and discipline. So, be earnest and repent." (Revelation 3:18 &19)

If you find yourself not spending time in prayer and not studying His word, can it be that you are becoming spiritually unwell? If that is the case, Jesus can restore your relationship with Him. Go to Him in prayer, ask forgiveness and repent of your sins.

Today's Prayer: Father, thank you for your saving grace. Amen.

December 23

DAILY BREAD

"Give us today our daily bread." (Matthew 6:11)

My sister's four-year-old granddaughter called down from upstairs to her father, "Daddy, please have my breakfast ready when I get down." This might cause you to smile; however, it is such a wonderful thought to know that our heavenly Father provides for all our needs, even more than our earthly father. You are dependent on Him for everything. It is He who provides you with strength, the ability and skills to work. Even when you have nothing, He still provides. He is God who owns the world and all that is within it. He says, the cattle on a thousand hills are His (Psalm 50:10). He is more than able to take care of all your daily needs.

This four-year-old was sure when she arrived downstairs that breakfast would be waiting for her; in the same way we can be sure that God will supply all our daily needs. When you pray to Him, 'Give us today our daily bread', you are acknowledging that He is the one who provides and sustains you. You must trust that He will supply you with your needs and not your wants. He knows what you need and what is best for you. It is easy to think that because you work to obtain money to care for all your needs, you are the one who is the provider.

In Exodus chapter 16, we find the Israelite community grumbling against Moses (and effectively God) for not providing food for them. He rains down manna and quails, and they find they have more than enough to eat. However, while God provides for all your physical needs, He is also concerned about your spiritual needs. In John 6:48-57, Jesus compares himself to manna, for He is the only one who can provide for your physical and spiritual needs. He says, "I am the Living Bread that came down from heaven. Whoever eats this bread will live forever." To eat living bread means that you are to accept Jesus Christ into your life and become united with Him.

If today you are worried about not having food, or any other needs, you can be assured that God will provide your daily bread. However, unlike Israel, who sought to be satisfied with physical food only, do not crave only physical food, but spiritual food which has eternal value. As you come to God each morning, remember that not only will He provide for your physical needs in abundance, He'll also provide for all your spiritual needs.

Today's Prayer: Lord, I accept that you are indeed my provider. I hunger to eat of this Living Bread so I can live eternally with you. Amen.

December 24

STOP COMPLAINING

'And do not grumble, as some did - and were killed by the destroying angel.' (1 Corinthians 10:10)

My mother and a group she often sang with would sometimes sing a song that I referred to as 'the grumbling' song. It begins like this, 'In county town or city, some people can be found who spend their lives grumbling at everything around. O yes, they always grumble, no matter what we say, for these are chronic grumblers and they grumble night and day'. The last stanza of the song says, 'If you don't quit your grumbling and stop it now and here, you'll never get to heaven, no grumblers enter there. Repent and be converted, be saved from all your sins. You know that grumbling Christians find it hard to win a crown'.

Are you a grumbling/complaining Christian? In 1 Corinthians 10:10, Paul is warning the Corinthian believers not to grumble. When you grumble, you might lose your focus on God and fail to notice what He is doing for you. One writer says, 'We start to grumble when our attention shifts from what we have to what we don't have'. The Israelite community spent most of their time complaining; they complained about not having food, and told Moses they would rather go back into slavery because he had brought them out of Egypt to die. They complained and grumbled so much that they seemingly lost sight of what God had done for them and continued to do for them. God had set them free from bondage, established them as a nation and provided a new land for them.

How about you? Do you spend your time grumbling and complaining? Are you grateful for what God has done and is doing in you now? Are you grateful for the things He has provided for you, or are you always thinking about what you would like to have?

When some Israelites grumbled against Moses and Aaron, God struck them down, for He hates complaining, so don't allow your unfulfilled desires to cause you to forget what He has done for you. Give thanks and praise instead. We are reminded in 1Thessalonians 5:8 to 'Give thanks in all circumstances, for this is God's will for you in Christ Jesus'. So rather than grumble and complain, give thanks.

Today's Prayer: Father, forgive me for complaining; help me to be always thankful. Amen.

December 25

BEARING FALSE WITNESS

'You shall not give false testimony against your neighbour.' (Exodus 20:16)

If you went to court and lied, you would be giving false testimony. In this command, God is telling us we should be honest in whatever we do. Giving false testimony includes telling a half-truth, omitting something from a story, exaggeration, or a white lie. God hates lying. 'The Lord detests lying lips, but delights in people who are trustworthy' (Proverbs 12:22). God warns us against telling lies or giving false testimony.

In Acts 5:1-11, we read about Ananias and Sapphira, who, during the early church period, sinned by lying. They had sold a piece of property and promised to give all of the money to the church. During the time of the early church, believers shared their possessions to support the church. They all shared what they had, and God blessed the church. However, after having sold the land, the couple secretly held back some of the money for themselves, after having promised to give all of it to the church. Peter, guided by the Holy Spirit, detects their deception and confronts the couple separately. They both lied, saying that they gave the full amount for which the land was sold. Peter said to them, "How could you conspire to test the Spirit of the Lord?" (Acts 5:9) In other words, how could they have lied? Swift judgment overtook them, and they both died in the presence of Peter and the believers.

God's judgment on the couple produced shock and fear among the believers, making them realise how seriously God regards sin in the church. The sin Ananias and Sapphira committed was not stinginess or holding back part of the money – it was their choice whether or not to sell the land and how much to give. Their sin was lying to God and the believers by claiming they had given the whole amount, while holding back some for themselves and attempting to make themselves appear more generous than they really were. Some might say that God acted harshly; however, this is not the case. God hates sin, and He had to deal with it there and then. God had to show the believers that dishonesty, greed, and covetousness are destructive because they prevent the Holy Spirit from working effectively. All lying is bad, but when we lie to deceive God and His people about our relationship with Him, we destroy our testimony for Christ.

This incident is an example of the ongoing battle between the forces of good and evil and how Satan will try to deceive and cause problems in the church and lead believers to sin. We must obey God's commands and not lie or bear false witness. He is a loving God and wants us to obey Him.

Today's Prayer: Father, help me to live my life with integrity and honesty and not fall into sin. Amen.

December 26

ARE YOU BUILDING WALLS AROUND YOU?

"I was a stranger and you did not invite me in, I needed clothes and you did not clothe me, I was ill and in prison and you did not look after me." (Matthew 25:43)

The first Great Wall of China, 4,000 miles long, was built by Shi Huangdi, the first emperor of China (259 -210 BC). The wall was built primarily as a defensive fortification to protect the Chinese Empire from nomadic invaders. The wall also played a role in border control and preserving Chinese culture from outside influences.

Have you erected a wall around yourself to protect yourself from the corrupting influence of the sinful world in which you live? Are you afraid of being contaminated by the sins of society? Has your wall become a defensive fortification that prevents you from hearing the cries of the poor and needy in society? Has your wall become impenetrable so you can no longer hear or respond to the cries of those disadvantaged and marginalised living on the fringes of society? Did Jesus not say we should go out, leave our fortified walls of selfishness, pride, and lack of compassion and reach those who need our care, love and attention? In Isaiah 61:1 & 2, Jesus says that He came to "proclaim good news to the poor, bind up the broken-hearted, to proclaim freedom for captives and release from darkness for the prisoners [...] and to comfort all who mourn." That is what He expects us to do, to reach out in love and compassion to the vulnerable in society.

Jesus says, "Truly I tell you, whatever you did not do for one of the least of these, you did not do for me." (Matthew 25:45) On the contrary, He says, "Whatever you did for one of the least of these brothers and sisters of mine, you did it for me." (Matthew 25:40) God is waiting for you to emerge from your walled fortress of selfishness, piety, and lack of empathy for those who are suffering to do the work He has called you to do: to feed the hungry, clothe the naked, visit the sick and those in prison. Then and only then will you hear, "Well done, good and faithful servant!" Make it your goal today to reach out to someone less fortunate than yourself.

Today's Prayer: Dear God, place in my heart a love for a dying world, may I be motivated by your Spirit to do good. Amen.

December 27

BAPTISM - DIVINE APPROVAL

'But as Jesus was coming out of the water, He saw heaven being torn open and the Spirit descending on Him like a dove. And a voice came from heaven: "You are my Son, whom I love; with you I am pleased." Mark 1:10 & 11)

Jesus had just been baptised by John the Baptist when the Holy Spirit and God the Father gave their divine approval. However, much more than that, we can know for sure that there are three persons of the Godhead: God the Father, God the Son, and God the Holy Spirit; they were all present at the baptism, showing their divine approval. The dove and the voice from heaven were signs that Jesus was indeed the Messiah. Mark is showing us that at Jesus' baptism, His divine identity and mission were being affirmed before He began His ministry of teaching, healing, and eventual sacrifice on the cross.

Jesus was sinless, so why did John baptise Him? In fact, John was initially reluctant to do so because He knew that Jesus was the sinless one and did not need to be baptised. Jesus did not need forgiveness, but was baptised for the following reasons: (1) To begin His earthly ministry to bring salvation to the world. (2) To show support for John's ministry. (John had preached about the coming Messiah to the people; his was a message of repentance). (3) To identify with our humanness and sin. (4) To give us an example to follow.

Baptism is a crucial rite in the life of believers as it signifies a declaration that you have left your life of sin behind and have been born again in Christ Jesus and want to follow His leading. Baptism is a sign that our sins are washed away. St. Paul reminds us that Jesus did not need to be baptised but that He was baptised for our sakes, 'God made Him who had no sin to be sin for us, so that in Him we might become the righteousness of God.' (2 Corinthians 5:21) When we accept Jesus, we make an exchange - our sin for His righteousness. This is what we are saying when we are baptised. Just think that God offers to trade His righteousness for our sin – something of immeasurable worth for something completely worthless; how grateful we should be for His everlasting love and kindness to us.

If you are already baptised or intend to be baptised, count it all joy because you have received divine approval from God the Father, God the Son, and God the Holy Spirit. And as you arise from the water of baptism, He says, "This is my beloved child, in whom I am well pleased."

Today's Prayer: Father, thank you for what you have done for me. Amen

December 28

TEMPTATION

'Then Jesus was led by the Spirit into the wilderness to be tempted by the devil.' (Matthew 4:1)

It is foolhardy to believe that everything will go well for you after your baptism; this is not the case. The devil will be hot on your heels because he is not happy that you have given your life to Christ. Matthew records what happened after Jesus was baptised. In chapter 4, he tells us that after Jesus had been in the wilderness fasting for forty days, the tempter came to Jesus when He was hungry from fasting, tempting Him to tell the stones to become bread. Jesus wasn't tempted inside the temple or at His baptism but in the wilderness, where He was tired, hungry, and alone, and therefore most vulnerable.

Satan often tempts us when we are vulnerable, especially when we are under physical and emotional stress, for example, when we are tired, lonely and upset or angry, or at our weakest point. He will even tempt you through your strengths; that is, when you are being successful and doing well and achieving your goals, it is during these times that you can become prideful if you are not careful. The Bible tells us that pride comes before a fall, and Satan will cause you to fall.

Just as Jesus was tempted, so will you be. Temptation is not a sin; it is yielding to temptation that results in sin. James says, 'But each person is tempted when they are dragged away by their own evil desire and enticed.' (James 1:14) You might be saying that you have given your life to Christ, so why am I being tempted? Paul says, "No temptation has overtaken you except what is common to mankind. And God is faithful; He will not let you be tempted beyond what you can bear. But when you are tempted, He will also provide a way out so that you can endure it." (1 Corinthians 10:13)

Living in a world of sin, Paul is saying that as believers we will be tempted; it happens to everyone, so if you are being tempted, do not think you are being singled out. However, the good news is that you do not have to fall into sin, for God has made a way of escape for you.

Today's Prayer: Father, deliver me from evil. Amen.

December 29

HOW TO OVERCOME TEMPTATION

'Because He himself suffered when He was tempted, He is able to help those who are being tempted.' (Hebrews 2:18)

This verse should fill you with hope, knowing that Jesus suffered pain and faced temptation should help you when you are tempted to do wrong. To know that Jesus understands when you are being tempted should be reassuring. He understands your struggles because, as a human being when here on earth, He was severely tempted and overcame. We can therefore trust Him to help us overcome when we are tempted. Paul says, 'He will also provide a way out so that you can endure it.' (1 Corinthians 10:13) 'Because He himself suffered when He was tempted, He is able to help those who are being tempted.' (Hebrews 2:18)

How do you overcome temptation? When Jesus was tempted, He was at His weakest point, being in human flesh, He was hungry and tired. One writer says, "Jesus had given up the unlimited, independent use of His divine power in order to experience humanity fully; He wouldn't use His power to change the stones into bread." Jesus, in His human form, was able to resist temptation because He knew and obeyed the Scripture. For every temptation from the devil, Jesus countered with the words, "It is written." Jesus overcame temptation because He prioritised spiritual obedience over immediate gratification, power and worldly glory. You must also prioritise obedience to God over temptation to sin against God; do not give in to the tempter. Decide what is important - your physical or your spiritual needs. Jesus constantly and consistently relied on the Scripture and was victorious. He was able to overcome temptation because He was full of the Spirit. His ultimate victory happened because of His obedience and His faithfulness to His Father.

Jesus has set the example for us to follow, so when tempted to sin, call upon Him. The devil will offer you the whole world and its pleasures. He will entice you with power and materialism, that's what He offered

638

Christ; Jesus overcame, and so can you. If you find yourself craving for the things of this world, pray to God for strength, repeat Scripture, "It is written." "Worship the Lord your God, and serve Him only." James tells us to: "Submit yourselves, then, to God. Resist the devil, and he will flee from you." (James 4:7)

Today's Prayer: Father, help me to draw near to you when tempted. Amen.

December 30

BE CAREFUL WHO YOU BELIEVE

"Listen, Hananiah! The Lord has not sent you, yet you have persuaded this nation to trust in lies." (Jeremiah 28:15)

In this chapter of Jeremiah, we read about the prophet Hananiah, a false prophet, who prophesied what the people wanted to hear. They preferred to believe a lie rather than the truth. Jeremiah, God's true prophet, had prophesied what would happen to the nation of Israel several times, and all his prophesies came true, because they were from God. Jeremiah's messages were not all palatable to the people, and how he must have agonised to deliver these messages. He is often referred to as the 'weeping' prophet. However, no matter how difficult the message was, he faithfully delivered the truth to God's people. Unfortunately, the people refused to respond to God's warning to them, but rather than believe the truth, they believed the lie of Hananiah, the false prophet. Hananiah spoke lies, but his deceitful words brought false hope and comfort to the people.

Jeremiah spoke the truth and was unpopular; Hananiah, by contrast, prophesied falsehood, and the people believed him. This is no different to what we are witnessing in our world today. Today's postmodern generation does not see truth as absolute; rather, truth is based on feelings, that is, if it feels good, then it must be true. The people in Jeremiah's day were saying the same thing because what Hananiah said made them feel good, so they would rather believe a lie than the truth. The confrontation between Jeremiah and Hananiah represents the struggle between truth and deceit. Hananiah represents the temptation of easy answers and false hope, while Jeremiah represents the difficult but necessary truth that people must face. One source states that the attitude of Hananiah and the people is "a powerful reminder of the importance of discerning true prophets from false ones, the significance of trust and faith, the accountability of those who claim to speak for God, and the symbolism of truth and deception."

You should be careful who you believe. One of the signs of Christ's coming, found in Matthew 24: 11, is that many false prophets will appear and deceive many. There were false prophets in Jesus' day, and we have them today. Jesus warns us not to listen to them.

How will you know what is truth from what is falsehood? It is only as you study God's word and are guided by the Holy Spirit that you will know the truth.

Today's prayer: Father, help me to study your word and be guided by your Holy Spirit so that I will not be deceived. Amen.

December 31

YES, I AM COMING SOON

He who testifies to these things says, "Yes, I am coming soon." (Revelation 22. 20)

Today marks the end of the year. As you reflect on the 364 days spent with Jesus every morning, I hope that you can look back in gratitude for the way in which He has led you. If you are honest, you will admit that you have not always got it right. We have all made mistakes along the way. In fact, we are not proud of what we have thought, said, or done. However, thank God He forgives sin. As we approach the final hours of this year, we can say that we are one year closer to the coming of our Lord and Saviour Jesus Christ. This should fill us with joy.

In John 14:3, Jesus says: "I will come back and take you to be with me that you also may be with me; that you also may be where I am." Jesus' words suggest that the way to eternal life, though unseen, is secure. He has given us this promise, so we can rest assured that what He says, He will do. "God is not a human, that He should lie." (Numbers 23:19) "Heaven and earth will pass away, but my words will never pass away." (Matthew 24:35) For believers everywhere, we can trust Him and can feel secure in His promise. However, the sceptics and the naysayers will deny this fact and say, "Where is this 'coming' He promised? Ever since our ancestors died, everything goes on as it has since the beginning of creation." (2 Peter 3:3) This should not surprise us. Peter says, "Above all, you must understand that in the last days scoffers will come, scoffing and following their own evil desires." (2 Peter 3:1) Regardless of what anyone says, you must hold firmly to your faith and trust in Jesus.

The fact that Jesus has not yet returned to earth; does not mean that He will not return. In our key verse, the King James version states, "...Surely I come quickly." The word 'surely' implies, without a doubt, a firm belief. Christ has not delayed His coming as some say. He hasn't come because He wants to allow everyone to accept Him and be saved in His kingdom. In Ezekiel 18:32 God says, "For I take no pleasure in the death of anyone...Repent and live." As we approach the new year, remember the sure promise of Jesus, "I am coming soon." We do not know how soon is soon, but we must be ready and live our lives with reference to this fact.

Today's Prayer: Father, I know you are coming back soon. Help me to live in a state of readiness. Amen.

www.ingramcontent.com/pod-product-compliance
Lightning Source LLC
Chambersburg PA
CBHW011718220426
43663CB00019B/2924